Golf Course Development and Real Estate

Desmond Muirhead
and
Guy L. Rando

 the Urban Land Institute

About ULI– the Urban Land Institute

ULI–the Urban Land Institute is a non-profit education and research institute that is supported and directed by its members. Its mission is to provide responsible leadership in the use of land to enhance the total environment.

ULI sponsors educational programs and forums to encourage an open international exchange of ideas and sharing of experience; initiates research that anticipates emerging land use trends and issues and proposes creative solutions based on this research; provides advisory services; and publishes a wide variety of materials to disseminate information on land use and development.

Established in 1936, the Institute today has some 13,000 members and associates from 46 countries representing the entire spectrum of the land use and development disciplines. They include developers, builders, property owners, investors, architects, public officials, planners, real estate brokers, appraisers, attorneys, engineers, financiers, academics, students, and librarians. ULI members contribute to higher standards of land use by sharing their knowledge and experience. The Institute has long been recognized as one of the country's most respected and widely quoted sources of objective information on urban planning, growth, and development.

Richard M. Rosan
Executive Vice President

This book is dedicated to my children, Marco, Tony, and Gaetano, with special thanks to my colleague Desmond Muirhead for his trust and support.—G.L.R.

Project Staff

Senior Vice President, Research, Education, and Publications
Rachelle L. Levitt

Vice President/Publisher Project Director
Frank H. Spink, Jr.

Managing Editor
Nancy H. Stewart

Manuscript Editor
Barbara M. Fishel/Editech
Monkton, Maryland

Art Director
Betsy VanBuskirk

Artist
Melinda Appel
Electronic Publishing Solutions
Annapolis, Maryland

Production Manager
Diann Stanley-Austin

Word Processing
Joanne Nanez
Maria-Rose Cain

Recommended bibliographic listing:
Desmond Muirhead and Guy L. Rando. *Golf Course Development and Real Estate*. Washington, D.C.: ULI–the Urban Land Institute, 1994.

ULI Catalog Number: G09

International Standard Book Number: 0-87420-762-2

Library of Congress Catalog Card Number: 94-60767

Cover: The Woods #11. *Photo:* Guy L. Rando & Associates Inc.

About the Authors

Desmond Muirhead, one of the world's leading golf course architects, was educated in engineering at Cambridge University in England and received formal training in architecture, urban planning, art, and agronomy. He has written five books, lectured at universities from the East-West Center in Honolulu to MIT near Boston, and designed golf courses in partnership with Gene Sarazen, Jack Nicklaus, Arnold Palmer, and Nick Faldo.

Muirhead designed two golf course communities in the eastern and western United States that have set the standard for this genre: Mission Hills in Palm Springs, California, and Boca West in Boca Raton, Florida. The golf course at Muirfield Village that Muirhead designed with Jack Nicklaus is on most lists of the top 10 golf courses in this country. His most recent courses, Aberdeen, Stone Harbor, and Wakagi, introduced the idea of themes and signature holes with symbols.

In the late 1960s, Muirhead established an office, Desmond Muirhead, Inc. (DMI), that incorporates the various disciplines necessary to plan and design a golf course community and is capable of undertaking the entire process, including planning, architecture, and golf course design. Currently the company is designing projects in Europe and Asia.

Guy L. Rando, founding principal of Guy L. Rando & Associates Inc., has been responsible for the master planning and design of over 700,000 acres of golf course and planned communities, resorts, recreation projects, and institutional projects throughout the United States and abroad. With Rees L. Jones, he coauthored ULI's *Golf Course Developments* in 1974, which became the standard reference for the development of golf-oriented real estate. He served on the review committee for ULI's *Developing with Recreational Amenities* (1986) and is currently working on a how-to book about designing golf courses.

Rando was awarded the 1991 Ralph Hudson Environmental Fellowship in support of his research, Golf Courses as Ecologic Sanctuaries™. He has received awards for excellence in design from the American Society of Landscape Architects, International Design, Take Pride In America, and many others. Rando is the inventor of Point-to-Point Golf™ and a popular lecturer and teacher of golf course architecture. He has taught and lectured in universities across the United States, South America, Europe, Japan, and China, and is a frequent guest speaker for professional conferences.

Rando is a golf course architect, land planner, ecologist, and licensed landscape architect, having earned bachelor's degrees from Syracuse University and State University of New York and a master's degree in landscape architecture from Harvard University in 1961. He also undertook postgraduate studies in architecture at Columbia University. One of his first assignments was with Whittlesey and Conklin as a member of the design team that master planned the 7,500-acre new town of Reston, Virginia. He then went to Europe as a Fulbright Scholar to study urban and open space land use systems and sculpting of the landscape. In the early 1960s, he established his full-service, multidisciplinary firm in Reston, Virginia, to service an international clientele of private and public developers. He has collaborated closely with the world's premier golf course architect, Robert Trent Jones, Sr., on projects throughout the United States and Europe.

Contributing Authors

Golf course architect **William W. (Bill) Amick** fell in love with golf as a teenager. After preparation at two universities and apprenticeships with two golf course architects, he opened his own design office in Daytona Beach, Florida, in 1959. Amick has designed all types of courses, from courses used for professional tours to a number of shorter par-3 and pitch-and-putt courses. He is a registered landscape architect and a past president of the American Society of Golf Course Architects.

Jane Baxter is president of Country Club Designs, Knickers, Inc., which offers services in architectural and interior design, layout and specifications, renderings, complete prepurchase budgeting for controlled purchasing, and installation. A graduate of the New York School of Design, Baxter has over 22 years of experience in the design of clubhouses, resorts, and recreational facilities. She has been involved in award-winning clubhouse projects worldwide, is frequently called upon as a consultant, and was recently named to "Who's Who in American Executives" and "Who's Who in Interior Design International."

Tim Casey is a registered architect in California, Florida, and Nevada with 22 years of experience in the planning and design of residential communities. His notable designs include work at the golf course communities of Mission Hills and Desert Island in Palm Springs, California, at Jupiter Bay in Florida, the golf club-house at New St. Andrews golf course in Japan, the sports center and lodge at Century Country Club in Rayong, Thailand, and golf course townhouses at Kooralbyn resort community in Queensland, Australia.

Casey has a master's degree in architecture from the University of California–Berkeley and a Bachelor of Architecture degree from the University of Washington, where he graduated with honors.

Christopher Degenhardt received a Bachelor of Science degree from Wye College at the University of London, a diploma in landscape architecture design from the University of Newcastle upon Tyne, England, and a Master of Landscape Architecture at SUNY–Syracuse. He is a council member of ULI, a Fellow of the American Society of Landscape Architects, a director of the Building Research Board of the National Academy of Sciences, and a member of the Design Review Board for the University of California–Berkeley. Degenhardt has been involved with the management of major projects for EDAW in the United States and around the world.

Richard J. Diedrich is an architect and president of Diedrich Architects and Associates, Inc., in Atlanta, Georgia. For more than a decade, he has programmed, planned, and designed over 30 golf clubhouses, including Grand Cypress in Lake Buena Vista, Florida, Country Club of the South in Atlanta, and Admirals Cove in Jupiter, Florida. Eleven projects by Diedrich have received Awards for Excellence in Design from the American Institute of Architects and the Southeast Builders Conference.

Diedrich received his Master of Architecture degree from the University of Illinois and a diploma in architecture from the Ecole d'Art Americaines in Fontainbleau, France. He has taught at the University of Illinois and the University of Wisconsin, and has made presentations on programming and designing clubhouses at numerous conferences on golf course development.

Alice O'Neal Dye began working on her golf game in 1950 with her husband, Pete, in Indianapolis. Over the years, she has won amateur titles in Indiana and Florida, five Women's Western Senior Championships, and two USGA Women's Senior Amateur Championships. In 1959, the Dyes formed a company and began designing and building small courses around central Indiana. It was an extremely low-budget operation in the beginning; for one project, the stand of bent grass propagated in their front yard was transported to the course in the trunk of their Oldsmobile.

Dye considers her most valuable contribution to golf architecture the attention she has devoted to planning and placing tees and hazards for women golfers. In 1982, she became the first woman member of the American Society of Golf Course Architects.

Perry O. Dye founded Dye Designs, Inc., a full-service golf development corporation offering golf course design, construction, maintenance, management, and irrigation services, now under the direction of his eldest son, Perry. Dye-designed golf courses are known as masterpieces and are often built on the most difficult terrain. A hallmark of courses by Dye Designs is the use of railroad ties, telephone poles, or planking to shore up greens, bunkers, and banks of water hazards. The company's strategies focus on playability, offering formidable opposition for accomplished players as well as accommodations for those less skilled.

Robert Muir Graves has been designing golf courses since 1959 as a licensed landscape architect and site planner. The scope of his golf projects spans the tropics at sea level to coniferous forests at elevations over 9,000 feet above sea level. Some of the notable courses include Port Ludlow and Canterwood in Washington state, and Sea Ranch, La Purisima, and Big Canyon in California. Graves is a long-time member and past president of the American Society of Golf Course Architects.

Michael J. Hurdzan is one of North America's most active and respected golf course architects, well known in the golf industry as a leading authority on environmental issues, construction, golf course safety, and turf maintenance. His innovations in the use of specialized grasses and ornamental plants have set new standards for golf course design and reduction of maintenance expenses. Hurdzan has a Ph.D. in environmental plant physiology and an M.Sc. in turfgrass physiology from the University of Vermont, and a bachelor's degree from Ohio State University. He is a member of the American Society of Golf Course Architects, the American Society of Landscape Architects, the National Golf Foundation, the U.S. Golf Association, and the Golf Collector's Society. He has written approximately 100 articles on golf course design or maintenance.

Robert Trent Jones II was president of the American Society of Golf Course Architects in 1989–90 and has written several articles about planning golf course communities. He is presently a member of ULI's Recreational Development Council. Jones is an outstanding amateur golfer and has competed in many international events. In 1991, he was inducted into the California Golf Hall of Fame.

Jack Kidwell, together with Mike Hurdzan, has been responsible for the design of many golf courses in central Ohio, including Hickory Hills, Oakhurst, Thornapple, Bolton Airport, Indian Springs, Eagle Sticks, Wilson Road, and Blacklick Woods.

Gene P. Krekorian is senior vice president for Economics Research Associates in Los Angeles. With 20 years of experience in consulting, Krekorian evaluates market support for municipal, daily-fee, and private country clubs; analyzes financial performance and golf course valuation; and assesses the potential for conversion of equity clubs and public/private joint ventures. He has authored a number of articles on the subject of golf course economics, including "The Changing Economics of Golf" and "Golf's Real Estate Value," both published by ULI. He earned his bachelor's degree in mathematics and economics from Pomona College and a master's degree in business economics from the UCLA Graduate School of Management.

Legg Mason Realty Group (LMRG) is the real estate consulting subsidiary of Legg Mason, Inc. It evaluates the feasibility of public and private golf courses and golf course communities, and, along with Legg Mason's investment banking and public finance divisions, provides debt and equity financing for golf course projects. LMRG also assists in the acquisition and disposition of golf facilities. LMRG specializes in evaluating the market support and financial feasibility for proposed golf course projects. It has become known for its market feasibility studies of public golf course master plans. **Robert T. Kleinpaste,** president, **Jerry L. Doctrow,** vice president, and **David K. Wells,** associate, all contributed to this book.

Daniel R. Levitan is senior vice president and principal of The Greenman Group, responsible for the research and conceptualization of the firm's real estate development and marketing strategies for properties throughout the United States, Canada, and the Caribbean. A noted speaker, lecturer, and author in the shelter industry, he is a charter member of the Institute of Residential Marketing, a housing marketing specialist, a senior designated member of the National Association of Real Estate Appraisers, and a member of the International Real Estate Institute.

Meda Ling, a certified landscape architect, is senior associate and golf course architect with Guy L. Rando & Associates Inc. She received her bachelor's degree in landscape architecture from the University of Virginia and was a lead researcher and writer for this book. She developed the methodology for Golf Courses as Ecologic Sanctuaries™ in close collaboration with Guy Rando.

J. Richard McElyea is executive vice president at Economics Research Associates in San Francisco. He earned a bachelor's degree in economics at Stanford University, where he was captain of the golf team and the Pacific Coast Conference Champion, and a master's degree in business administration at the Stanford Graduate School of Business.

McElyea is a past trustee of ULI and a member of its Recreational Development Council. He has written several articles on golf, including "The Changing Economics of Golf," published by ULI. With a strong background in golf course economics, McElyea provides consulting services for market analysis, financial feasibility, valuation, and strategic planning of golf courses and clubhouses.

John Williams McGrath is a graduate of Amherst College and Yale Law School. With a background as executive vice president at Sea Pines Plantation Company on Hilton Head Island, director of resort land development, a principal and partner in course design with Arnold Palmer and Frank Duane, a real estate investment officer of the Ford Foundation, vice president for development for Associated Inns and Restaurant Company of America, senior vice president for development for VMS Realty Partners, and an independent consultant to major resort land developers, McGrath has lectured and written extensively on the subject of resort/recreational land development, management, and operations. He is a longtime active member of ULI.

Patrick Shane Mulligan is an independent consultant with over 20 years of experience in planning, approvals, design, construction, maintenance, marketing, and operation of resort/recreational land developments. He lectures and writes on these subjects, with a special interest in the safety of golf courses. Mulligan's extensive professional background includes stints as a construction superintendent, senior golf course design associate with Frank Duane, Arnold Palmer, and John Williams McGrath, independent golf course designer, and consultant to major resort land developers. Mulligan is a principal in Irish Golf Limited, a European planning, design, construction, maintenance, and management firm.

Douglas Nickels is the senior golf course architect for Desmond Muirhead, Inc. Specializing in golf course construction, he has a wide range of experience in landscape architecture, engineering, planning, and golf course architecture and construction. Before joining DMI, he spent seven years with the Robert Trent Jones II Group working on such projects as the Lansdowne Conference Resort in Virginia, the Dragon Valley resort in Korea, and Poppy Hills golf course at Pebble Beach, California. Nickels received a Master of Landscape Architecture from the University of Michigan.

Nicklaus Design has become over the past three decades the world's largest golf course design firm, with services in design, construction management, agronomy, maintenance, and marketing.

In 1993, Nicklaus opened his 100th course at Las Campanas in Santa Fe, New Mexico. Ten Nicklaus designs have been ranked in *Golf Digest*'s "Top 100 in America" and four in *Golf Magazine*'s "Greatest Courses in the World." More than 150 professional golf tournaments have been staged around the world at Nicklaus-designed courses over the past 20 years.

With golf course designs on five continents, Jack Nicklaus has developed courses in numerous terrains and climates, including mountains, deserts, volcanic islands, and coastal marshlands. Each course represents Nicklaus's commitment to preserving the natural setting of the courses he designs.

Joe O'Brien is senior developer for Marriott Golf, the largest resort operator in the industry, where he is responsible for marketing and developing golf management contracts for quality public facilities and selected private clubs. Before joining Marriott Golf, O'Brien served 17 years with the PGA of America as director of education, manager of member services, and senior director of strategic planning. O'Brien received a bachelor's degree in business marketing from the University of Illinois and an M.B.A. from De Paul University; he is on the board of the Florida Golf Council.

Palmer Course Design Company is a worldwide golf course planning and design organization that has been involved in some 140 golf course projects in 28 states and 20 countries.

With the expertise of Arnold Palmer and his partner Ed Seay, the Palmer-Seay touch has left its mark on courses located throughout the world. Seay, who is a past president of the American Society of Golf Course Architects, designed many well-known courses before joining Palmer in 1971. The most prominent of these is Sawgrass in Ponte Vedra Beach, Florida, which was the site of the Tournament Players Championship from 1977 through 1981, as well as some 100 other courses and residential developments in the United States.

Rick Pariani is a landscape architect with experience in planning, designing, and implementing mixed-use, commercial, retail, office, residential, resort, and recreational projects. A partner with The SWA Group, he began working on golf-oriented residential and resort projects over 10 years ago in Boca Raton, Florida. Pariani has prepared master plans for Arvida Country Club and Weston Hills Country Club, and plans for the renovation and expansion of the Boca Raton Resort and Club. More recently, he designed and implemented a $15 million tropical landscape for the Toyo Country Club in Chia-yi, Taiwan. He is currently working on the Lily Country Club in Taiwan and a

4,500-acre new town at the base of Mt. Rainier in Washington.

Pariani received a Bachelor of Landscape Architecture degree with honors from the University of Georgia and studied art abroad at Cortona, Italy.

Michael L. Ramsey is a principal and one of the founding members in Architectural Design Group, Inc., heading the firm's North Carolina office. A registered architect, Ramsey holds a Bachelor of Science degree from Davidson College in North Carolina and a Bachelor of Architecture degree from the University of Tennessee, where he graduated with highest honors.

Craig A.W. Roberts is a designer with 20 years of experience as an architect. His experience includes work in Canada, France, Germany, Mexico, Florida, the Caribbean, and the Far East. Educated at Witwatersrand Teknikon in Johannesburg, South Africa, his work has been published in *Architectural Rendering Techniques* by Mike Lin, *Architectural Drawing Options for Design* by Paul Laseau, and *Art in America*.

Larry Rodgers graduated from Michigan State University's turfgrass management program. In 1980, he went to Denver, where he worked for an irrigation equipment distributor and later a company manufacturing prefabricated pump stations. He started his own design/consulting firm in 1987. Since then, Rodgers has designed over 175 golf course irrigation systems all over the world, including some in Dallas, Las Vegas, Flagstaff, Kansas City, and Nashville.

John J. Rossi serves as senior adviser to PGA Golf Services, Inc., a subsidiary of the PGA of America that provides consulting services in golf course development, financing, and operations. His expertise lies in the areas of golf course development and operations, real estate portfolio analysis, and market and financial feasibility analysis. Rossi received a Master of City and Regional Planning degree from the University of California and a Bachelor of Architecture degree from the University of Notre Dame.

W. Wade Setliff is president of Architectural Design Group, Inc., a full-service architectural firm whose practice includes resorts and leisure facilities. Setliff received his Bachelor of Architecture degree from the University of Florida and is a member of the American Institute of Architects, the AIA Committee on Architecture for Justice, and the AIA Committee on the National Trust for Historic Preservation. Setliff has been a lecturer, a visiting critic, and a contributing author.

Michael P. Sim is an attorney with Hillier & Wanless, P.A., in West Palm Beach, Florida. He has extensive experience in designing and preparing club membership programs for recreational amenities, representing developers in connection with a broad variety of real estate transactions, and representing lenders in all types of real estate and commercial loans. He has written several articles about private clubs, golf courses, and related topics that have been published in *Thirty Days* and *Current Developments*, and has lectured on subjects involving golf courses and club membership programs.

Sim graduated with high honors from the University of Florida College of Law, where he was an editor of the law review. His undergraduate degree was in marketing from the College of Business Administration at the University of South Florida.

Walter R. Stewart is currently the senior planner for DMI. Educated and licensed as an architect, his work over the past 20 years includes a wide range of projects involving architecture, urban design and redevelopment, land planning, and recreation (golf courses, ski resorts, and waterfront projects). Stewart's work ranges from the design of residential and commercial projects to golf course communities to new towns.

Darrell Wilson is a design manager for Dye Designs, Inc., and a licensed civil engineer providing technical coordination and review for Dye's golf course projects. Wilson works closely with Perry Dye and has been responsible for design preparation of projects in the United States and in many other countries throughout the world.

John Wong, managing principal of The SWA Group's Sausalito office, is a landscape architect with design experience on both the East and West Coasts. He has directed design for several commercial and office complexes in Los Angeles and other locations in California, and in Seoul, Korea. Wong is currently working on the design for the Akebien Membership Resort Hotel and a master plan for Nasu Highland Resort in Nasu, Japan, and the Towa Green Golf Club and West Golf Courses in Hiroshima, Japan.

Wong received a bachelor's degree with honors from the University of California–Berkeley and a master's degree from the Harvard Graduate School of Design. He received the Rome Prize from the American Academy in Rome and served as a Visiting Critic in Landscape Architecture at the Harvard Graduate School of Design and at the University of California–Berkeley.

Acknowledgments

This work is a result of the efforts of many. We gratefully acknowledge the contributions of information, knowledge, and support from our friends and professional colleagues, among them:

Frank Spink, ULI vice president/publisher, whose vision and guidance made this work possible;

Barbara Fishel, the editor who helped us find the right words, organizing and fixing our sentences to make them mean what we wanted to say;

Betsy VanBuskirk, ULI art director, who composed our words and illustrations into a work of art itself;

Meda Ling of Guy L. Rando & Associates, chief researcher/writer and wearer of many hats, for her creative input, firm direction, remarkable dedication, dogged determination, and good humor through thousands of pages of manuscripts, rewrites, more rewrites, and yet more rewrites;

David Barley, president, Desmond Muirhead of Florida, Inc., and Golf Worldwide, for his unflagging coordination efforts on behalf of Desmond Muirhead during the manuscript review and editing process;

Craig Roberts, Tim Casey, Douglas Nickles, and *Walter Stewart* of Desmond Muirhead, Inc., for their creative input, expertise, and advice;

Ella of Desmond Muirhead, Inc., who bridged our bicoastal offices with warmth and efficiency;

Richard McElyea and *Gene Krekorian* of Economics Research Associates, for their inspiration and substantial contribution to our understanding and knowledge about golf and real estate value, the economics of golf course development, and alternative development ventures;

Richard Norton and the National Golf Foundation for many volumes of information about golf, countless hours of reviews, and a steady stream of much needed advice;

Charles E. Fraser of Fraser Group, Inc., for his concise information on developing golf-oriented real estate;

Michael P. Sim of Hillier & Wanless, P.A., for his contributions of knowledge and legal advice about the operation and management structures of golf courses and golf-oriented communities;

John Rossi of PGA of America, for his insights and guidance on the management and marketing of golf;

Joe O'Brien and Marriott Golf for supplying philosophical insight and nuts-and-bolts information about managing and marketing golf and golf-oriented resorts;

Dan Levitan of The Greenman Group, for enlightening us about marketing golf-oriented real estate;

Jerry L. Doctrow, David Wells, and *Robert Kleinpaste* of the Legg Mason Realty Group, for sharing their experience and knowledge about golf and real estate;

Larry Rodgers of Rodgers Design Group, for his first-hand knowledge and precise input about irrigation systems;

Richard J. Diedrich of Diedrich Architects & Associates and *W. Wade Setliff* and *Michael L. Ramsey* of Architectural Design Group, for their contributions on golf clubhouses and to beauty in the built environment;

Sam Butz and *Jack Wilbern* of the Butz • Wilbern Partnership, for their architectural insights, honest critiques, and willingness to brainstorm problems with us;

Jane Baxter of Country Club Designs, Knickers, Inc., for her insights on interior design;

Perry O. Dye, Darrell Wilson, and *Kenny May* of Dye Designs International, for their insights about the use of timber ties in the design of golf course features;

Alice O'Neal Dye, for her eloquent enlightenment on women golfers and golf course design;

Peter T. Dye of Thompson Dyke & Associates for sharing his knowledge of land planning, urban planning, and landscape architecture, and for sharing two articles from *Chicagoland Golf;*

Nicklaus Design, for sharing knowledge and experience in golf course construction and safety;

Palmer Course Design, for contributions on golf academies;

William W. Amick, for sharing his insight and experience as a golf course architect about executive, par-3, and compact courses;

Patrick Shane Mulligan and *John Williams McGrath,* for their insights on golf safety;

Dr. Michael Hurdzan, for his insightful viewpoints and technical expertise on golf safety and reclamation of sanitary landfills for golf courses;

Brian Terry, for his insights on dissolving ownership of a golf course;

Christopher Degenhardt of EDAW, for sharing both his knowledge and time as a contributor of information on golf resorts and as a reviewer of more than a few manuscript drafts;

Rick Pariani and *John Wong* of The SWA Group, for their information and experience on golf-oriented resorts;

Robert Muir Graves, Ltd., golf course architects, for information on cost estimating and their insights on fitting golf courses to the topography;

Robert Trent Jones II, for sharing experiences about Poppy Hills golf course;

Ray Johnston of Potomac Valley Properties, for his developer's and educator's viewpoint about The Woods resort;

Wayne Hurd of LBJ Improvement Corporation and the staff of Horseshoe Bay for sharing their experiences and for their warm Texas hospitality;

Tim Skogens of Marriott's Desert Springs resort and *Tony Austin* of Marriott's Orlando World Center, for information about their resorts;

Ronald Dodson of the New York Audubon Society, for his review and support of our efforts;

Craig Tufts and *Roy Geiger* of the National Wildlife Federation, for their contributions to our understanding of the environment and fellow creatures of Earth;

The review committee—*Thompson A. Dyke* and *Peter T. Dyke* of Thompson Dyke & Associates, *Philip S. Stukin* of Lowe Enterprises Realty Services, *Christopher Degenhardt* of EDAW, and *Walter A. Koelbel* of Koelbel and Company—for their guidance, suggestions, words of wisdom, and encouragement;

Nicholas Park, for his assistance and graphic talent;

Susann Gerstein, for her editorial patience, fresh viewpoints, constant support, and encouragement;

Keenan Hardy, for logistical and moral support, too many late hours at the keyboard, the best coffee on this planet, and provision of sustenance and negative ions for body and soul through the most difficult hours of this undertaking;

Cheryll Chew and *John Frye,* for their reminders to keep priorities in check, to read, to learn, and to savor life and real butter on fresh homemade bread;

Earl Leister, for his valued advice and insights on golf from the viewpoint of a truly dedicated golfer;

Paul Lyons of TransAtlantic Venture Associates, for his challenging questions and insightful encouragement; and

The Landscape Architecture Foundation/CLASS Fund and *1991 Ralph Hudson Environmental Fellowship,* for their grant support of Golf Courses as Ecologic Sanctuaries™.

Contents

Golf Course Development and Real Estate

CHAPTER ONE

The Development Process

O ptimism, enthusiasm, passion, joy. These emotions ignite creativity, fire desire, and drive the will to build. Financing provides the essential fuel to convert imagination, ideas, and the will to succeed into manicured turf, pristine lakes, attractive buildings, and places for people to live, work, and play. During the boom years of real estate development, lenders and investors more willingly undertook the risk associated

Shinyo #3.

with innovation and creative alternatives in real estate, such as golf-oriented real estate developments. But the days of readily available financing for real estate development are gone, and, while hope springs eternal that economic conditions will improve, finding financial support for golf-oriented real estate development is very difficult, although improving. Projects borne on pure optimism and on trial and error cannot even hope to find a source of financing, as lenders and investors are very conservative about taking on risk during tight economic times. The allowable margin for error is virtually nonexistent. Instead, lenders and investors look for solid evidence of feasibility and plans that minimize risk and maximize return. ULI member Walter Koelbel has a word of warning for developers: "Before you get too far along in the initial stages of the development process for a golf-oriented real estate project, get some sort of commitment or preconditioned commitment of financing before spending a lot of time, effort, and money, only to find out that development money is terribly difficult to come by."

The Eight-Stage Model of Development

This methodical approach to a very complex process is based on objective analysis and reasoned decision making. At first glance, it might seem to be technical, dry, and devoid of the emotional spark so critical to real estate development. In actuality, it frees the creative spirit and fuels the drive, for it is far easier to be innovative and enthusiastic when risk has been minimized. And risk *must* be minimized to gain support from lenders and investors. A methodical approach allows the concentration of creative energy to focus on the task of solving specific problems, as the creative process is significantly compromised when left to cast about aimlessly without a clear objective. A methodical approach provides a defined structure for anticipating prob-

The Eight-Stage Model of Real Estate Development, Adapted for Golf-Oriented Real Estate Development

STAGE	REAL ESTATE DEVELOPMENT	GOLF-ORIENTED REAL ESTATE DEVELOPMENT
1 INCEPTION OF AN IDEA Not Feasible Feasible ⟶	Developer with knowledge of the market looks for needs to fill, sees possibilities, has several ideas, does quick general feasibility tests (legal, physical, financial).	Developer does quick feasibility tests (legal, physical, financial) for both golf course and golf-oriented real estate development.
2 REFINEMENT OF THE IDEA Not Feasible Feasible ⟶	Developer finds a specific site for the idea; looks for physical feasibility; talks with prospective tenants, lenders, partners, design professionals; settles on a tentative design; might option land if idea looks good.	Developer assembles a team with skills in golf-oriented real estate development, including land planner/landscape architect, golf course architects, ecologists, and others. Design team prepares alternative studies.
3 FEASIBILITY Not Feasible Feasible ⟶	Developer commissions formal market study to estimate market absorption and capture rates, commissions feasibility study comparing estimated value of project to cost, processes plans through government agencies.	Developer commissions formal market studies to estimate depth of golf market and real estate market, environmental management plan as required, financial feasibility analysis for golf course and real estate. Takes plans through approval process.
4 CONTRACT NEGOTIATION Cannot reach binding contracts Can reach binding contracts ⟶	Developer decides on final design based on what market study says users want and will pay for. Contracts are negotiated. Developer gets loan commitment in writing, decides on general contractor, decides on general rent requirements, gathers permits from local government.	Developer decides on final design for golf course development. Contracts are negotiated, commitments made, and permits, including special permits for golf courses, gathered.
5 FORMAL COMMITMENT	Contracts are signed. Often contingent on each other, they include joint venture agreements, construction loan agreements, permanent loan commitments, construction contracts, options to purchase land, agreements to purchase insurance, and prelease agreements.	Additional documents related to golf course development are signed.
6 CONSTRUCTION	Developer switches to formal accounting system, seeking to keep all costs within budget. Developer approves any changes suggested by marketing staff, resolves construction disputes, signs checks, keeps work on schedule, brings in operating people as needed.	Construction of golf course must be coordinated with construction of real estate. Specialists in construction of golf courses and golf operations and maintenance people are brought in as needed.
7 COMPLETION and FORMAL OPENING	Developer brings in full-time operating people, increases advertising. Occupancy approved by government agency, utilities connected, tenants/users move in. Construction loan is ended, permanent loan closed.	Full-time golf operations people are put on board. Advertising is coordinated with real estate marketing program. Memberships (for private clubs) are sold. Golf course is put into play.
8 ASSET AND PROPERTY MANAGEMENT	Owners oversee property management, including re-leasing, remodeling, remarketing, and reconfiguring the asset to extend its economic life and to enhance its economic life and performance.	Owners of golf course oversee the management and maintenance of the course.

Source: Adapted from Mike E. Miles et al., *Real Estate Development Principles and Process* (Washington, D.C.: ULI–the Urban Land Institute, 1991), p. 5.

Water, golf, and real estate at Horseshoe Bay Resort and Conference Club.

lems, clearly defining problems, and assessing solutions based on rational, quantifiable criteria.

The eight-stage model of the development process is such an approach.[1] It provides a foundation on which to build a methodical approach for manipulating information to solve complex problems associated with golf-oriented real estate development.

The real estate development process is by no means a neat, straight-line progression, particularly during the earlier stages when many ideas are being explored, analyzed for feasibility, and almost constantly adjusted and readjusted. The developer must think ahead to remaining steps of the process and might have to reposition a project many times during its course. Decision making and renegotiation between the developer and other participants on the development team are almost never continuous.

Real estate development has a long life expectancy, and developers must be willing to—and capable of—anticipating and responding to changes. Careful planning and design during the earlier stages of development can significantly decrease the need to renovate a project to keep it in step with the competition and with evolving markets.

Real estate development is a complex, interdisciplinary process. Every aspect of creating a built environment, including (but not only) politi-

cal, economic, physical, legal, and sociological, must be considered in the development process. Thus, a team approach is strongly recommended for real estate projects. One primary role of the real estate developer is that of team leader, manager of the interactions between disciplines. Golf-oriented real estate development adds another level of complexity to the process, as a number of intricate interactions occur when real estate development and golf courses are brought together and the addition of a golf course increases risk. Golf-

oriented development requires greater attention and care to each aspect of the process and to their interactions. The selection of the development team can make or break a project.

The Development Team

Developers come from varied backgrounds, and each brings his or her own expertise to a development venture. Unless the developer is unusually well versed and experienced in all the aspects and disciplines of golf-oriented real estate development, the services of many experts, consultants, and professionals are required to supplement the developer's expertise. Generally, developers hire the expertise they lack, either putting the experts on the payroll or contracting with outside consultants. In some cases, developers seek joint venture partners to provide needed expertise without a direct outlay of cash.

A typical development team includes the developer, the design team, the project administration team, economic and market analysts, the finance team, contractors, the sales and marketing team, and the property management team. Public regulatory agencies and consumers should also be considered integral parts of the development team. When

Jack Nicklaus and team in action on a project site.

4

a golf-oriented real estate development is contemplated, the golf course architect and specialists in the architecture of clubhouses become necessary additions to the design team. Specialists in construction of golf courses, management and operations of the course and clubhouse, and even golf-oriented sales and marketing also become necessary parts of the development team. With the advent of increasingly stringent and complex environmental protection regulations, ecologists, environmental specialists, engineering specialists, and attorneys all play an increasingly important role in the development team for a golf course.

Roles of Team Members

The developer's single most important function is leadership. As the team leader, the developer must put together the development team, direct their work, and keep them motivated, on schedule, and within budget. With few exceptions, the developer is the primary decision maker—and the primary risk bearer.

The design team must work as a tightly coordinated unit itself and as part of the overall development team. Every member of the development team has potentially critical input for the project's design, and the design team must be responsive to that input. Because most golf-oriented real estate development involves relatively high risk, it is crucial to bring in the design team as early as possible in the process.

The design team does far more than simply translate ideas to paper with the preparation of plans and construction documents. The design team is a well of creativity. Often, it can see opportunity in what might appear to be a negative situation to the untrained eye. Beyond its essential role in creative design, however, it plays a critical role in assisting the developer and minimizing political, economic, and market risk. The design team provides critical data and analyses to assist the developer in assessing the feasibility of alternative sites and development ideas, it often

Who's Who on the Development Team

The Developer
The developer is the leader and manager of the development team, the primary decision maker, and lead promoter/negotiator for the project. The developer employs or contracts with the members of the design team.

The Design Team
Land planner, landscape architect, ecologist, architect, engineers, golf course architect, and other design professionals and special consultants who help the developer analyze and shape ideas into a project. The design team receives input from other members of the development team, which might be used to guide the preparation of alternative concept plans. The design team prepares construction drawings, specifications, and other construction documents and supervises construction and administration until the project is completed. But the design team does far more than simply translating the developer's vision to a physical form. It serves a critical role in minimizing political, economic, and market risks.

Project Administration
Attorneys, accountants, economic and market analysts, project manager, construction manager, and other administrative assistance

Project Financing
Joint venture partners, investors, construction lenders, permanent lenders, mortgage brokers, surety companies, appraisers

Contractors
General contractor, subcontractors, and others involved in construction of the project

Sales and Marketing
Brokers, public relations and advertising agencies, graphic artists, appraisers

Property Management and Operations
Property managers, the golf pro, the golf course superintendent, and others involved in managing the course

Public Sector
Regulating government agencies, public policy makers, community leaders, concerned citizens and neighbors, the targeted market, and owners and tenants

Consumers and Users
Homebuyers, purchasers of property, tenants, concessionaires, the community, and others to whom the developer sells or leases the development's assets. During the earlier stages of the development process, the developer anticipates consumers' needs and expectations through market studies. In some cases, the real estate broker or developer's sales representative acts as a liaison to communicate a user's specific needs to the developer and design team.

Source: Guy L. Rando & Associates Inc.

acts as a negotiator and public relations liaison with the public sector, it plays a significant role in balancing the project's construction costs with the cost of long-term asset management, and it provides construction supervision, monitoring, and administrative services. The development

process should allow the design team ample opportunity to exercise creative problem solving and expand upon the developer's ideas.

The following paragraphs describe the roles of various professionals involved in the development process.[2] Each development project will require the expertise of most, if not all, of these consultants, depending on the project's specific requirements. Many professionals have expertise in several disciplines or provide multidisciplinary services through a single firm. For example, architects, landscape architects, and golf course architects might be skilled in land planning or knowledgeable market analysts or have people on staff who provide these services.

Developer/Owner

The developer might be the owner of the project or might be a contracted representative for the owner of the property. With few exceptions, the developer is the primary risk bearer, decision maker, manager, and promoter of the development project.

Land Planner

This individual or firm is charged with preparing site plans (including site analysis, alternative concept plans, master plans, and construction documents) for the development based on input from the entire development team. Often, the landscape architect is the land planner. The land planner is often the designated leader of the design team. The land planner allocates proposed land uses for the project to maximize the site's potential and determines the most efficient layout for adjacent uses, densities, and infrastructure. For a golf-oriented real estate development, the land planner works closely with the golf course architect and other consultants to determine the best location for the golf course to realize the objectives for the development. The land planner examines how the property can be developed to meet requirements for zoning, subdivisions or planned unit developments, the environment, and regulatory agencies. The land planner should provide the developer with several alternative schemes that expand on the developer's program along with an analysis of the advantages and disadvantages of each scheme.

Landscape Architect

The landscape architect is very closely allied to the land planner and might be the same person or work under the same roof. The landscape architect is concerned with the location, arrangement, and relationships of elements of the development (buildings, infrastructure, and plants, for example) on the land. The landscape architect is usually charged with analyzing the physical attributes of a project site to determine its suitability for the proposed land uses. The landscape architect might employ or contract with an ecologist to provide additional expertise when the site contains sensitive conditions. If the project requires, the landscape architect prepares an environmental management plan to preserve, protect, and/or enhance the plant and animal life on the site. The landscape architect determines what plants are required to meet regulatory requirements and to establish the project's image for enhanced marketability. And the landscape architect prepares detailed specifications and construction documents for all landscape elements.

Golf Course Architect

The golf course architect is responsible for the layout and design of the golf course and its related features. As a design professional, the golf course architect also is responsible for managing construction of the golf course. In a golf-oriented real estate development, the golf course architect must work closely with the land planner and other consultants to ensure the best relationship between the golf course and objectives for the real estate.

Ecologists and Environmental Consultants

In addition to the studies undertaken by the landscape architect to determine the suitability and/or sensitivity of a site for the proposed land uses, the special knowledge and skills of an ecologist or other environmental consultants could be required if the proposed project has the potential to adversely affect the surrounding community. The kind of environmental analysis to be performed is dictated by local, state, and federal laws. An environmental impact statement (EIS) identifies potential impacts of the proposed project, as dictated by the National Environmental Policy Act of 1969. An environmental impact report (EIR) is based on local and state legislation and could be ordered when a proposed project poses a substantial danger to the environment. EIRs are usually required in environmentally sensitive communities, and many communities regard the presence of floodplains, wetlands, endangered or sensitive habitats, flora, or fauna, sensitive geologic conditions, and hazardous materials or contaminated soils as a condition warranting an EIR. An environmental analysis determines the effect that a proposed project might have on the surrounding environment's air and water quality, soils, noise, sunlight and shade, and traffic. The ecologist might assist the team to identify sensitive flora and fauna, delineate sensitive habitats like wetlands (land surveyors are vital for accurately mapping or delineating wetlands), and provide critical input for an environmental management plan that would preserve and enhance plants and wildlife on a site. Such materials are often submitted with plans during the public approval process. The developer must be a skilled diplomat in working with the public, particularly communities that are sensitive about environmental issues. To help the developer, the environmental consultant should be well respected, technically qualified, and impartial so that the report remains credible, even if the issue becomes politicized.

Architect

The architect is a critical member of the team, with responsibility for the public health, safety, and welfare. The design of a building makes a statement about the development project. The architect's experience with regulatory requirements and physical constraints on development is essential in guiding the efforts of the team. The developer might want to retain an architect specializing in golf clubhouses in addition to the architect for the overall project to design the clubhouse and other golf-related structures, such as the golf car storage building, pump house, maintenance building, and golf shelters.

Engineers

Engineers—civil, structural, mechanical, electrical, traffic, and others—provide the technical expertise to ensure that a design can accommodate required physical systems. A civil engineer, for example, designs major utility systems and other infrastructure, such as roads, fire protection, and stormwater management systems, to make the land plan work. Other engineers design the structural integrity of buildings, or design plumbing, HVAC (heating, ventilation, and air conditioning), and electrical systems. Some projects might require engineering specialists in wastewater treatment systems, soils, or hydrology. Traffic engineers, increasingly vital members of the design team, determine the present traffic volume and project the effect of the new development on the existing or proposed street system. Traffic engineers design improvements needed to serve the proposed development. The testimony of the traffic engineer regarding the impacts of traffic is a necessary part of the approval process for most projects.

Land Surveyor

The land surveyor provides accurate maps of a property's physical and legal characteristics. Typically, developers use two types of surveys: a boundary survey delineating the boundaries of the property, with rights-of-way, easements, dedications, and other legal requirements affecting ownership; and a site survey showing topography, existing roads, utilities, structures, vegetation, bodies of water, and other information about the site the design team must consider. During the early stages of planning, site maps can be based on aerial surveys, but as more detailed and accurate maps are required—delineation of a wetland or location of a sensitive habitat, for example—ground surveys by the landscape architect, ecologist or environmental consultant, or other specialists might be required.

Archeologist

Significant archeological finds can derail a project indefinitely, and the developer usually hires an archeologist to satisfy state or local regulatory requirements. The archeologist's thorough analysis of the property determines whether it contains any important historical artifacts. If it does, the archeologist advises how best to preserve the relevant portion of the site and helps determine whether it can be successfully integrated into the overall design of the project.

Interior Designer/Space Planner

The interior designer/space planner advises the architect and land planner about square footage requirements and the location and relationship of interior spaces. The interior designer also plays a critical role in specifying the finishes and decor of the sales office, sales models, the clubhouse, and other interior spaces, consistent with the market and long-term objectives for asset management.

Attorneys and Accountants

As a member of the design team, the attorney is involved with the normal legal problems pertaining to annexation, zoning, financing, buying and selling, leasing, contracting and subcontracting, and procedures. The attorney solves legal questions that arise as the project goes through the approval process and is often involved in hammering out annexation agreements between the development and the municipality to obtain sewer and water connections or secure water rights, which are so important for a golf course. The attorney sometimes acts as the developer's liaison with public regulatory agencies, although the developer's direct involvement tends to establish greater credibility, particularly with concerned citizens and neighbors.

Throughout the entire process, beginning with preliminary planning, accountants provide the team with regular financial reports comparing costs to date and the approved budget. They are the project's watchdogs, preventing cost overruns that can cause a project to fail to meet economic projections.

Cost Estimator

The cost estimator, often closely associated with the architect, land planner, landscape architect, engineer, and/or golf course architect, provides data used to calculate a proposed project's feasibility; the developer might use it to guide certain decisions about design. The cost estimates become more detailed and more accurate with each stage of the development process.

Market Consultants

Reliable and accurate market and economic studies aid decision making and reduce risk throughout development. The market consultant assesses a proposed project's chances of success, objectively analyzing its feasibility in terms of current and projected market conditions. Beyond technical proficiency, a good market consultant is aware of and understands subtle influences that could affect the market, such as the local political situation and competitive projects.

Real Estate Consultants, Brokers, And Leasing Agents

A developer might use the services of one or several real estate consultants to help locate property for development. In some cases, the real estate consultant conducts feasibility studies to determine the demand for a proposed project, particularly for a golf course. The real estate consultant might assist the developer in marketing the real estate products to be sold or leased, providing important insights on conditions of the local market, market demand, expectations, and trends that can guide the design team's efforts, such as identifying special needs like extra electrical or HVAC capacity.

Appraiser

The appraiser's key role is to estimate the value of property, using standard methodologies. The appraiser's contributions inform reviewing public agencies and neighborhood property owners how the new development will affect the value of existing properties. The appraiser might also as-

Golf-oriented housing at Tuscawilla West #9 in Charles Town, West Virginia.

sist the team during the earlier stages of development by providing comparative analyses of potential project sites and the potential value of alternative development plans. The appraiser's input about property values also helps the developer in securing financing for the project and in arriving at the market value of the real estate products.

Construction Manager or Project Manager

The construction manager represents the owner and keeps development concepts in line with the budget.

User/Consumer

The final user is the consumer of the finished product. Throughout development, the developer and the design team create a product that they hope will meet the needs of the final user. As such, the final user is part of the design team. In some cases, the user might contract for space before construction begins, interacting with the design team, usually through the developer's marketing agent, to ensure that the final product accommodates specific needs.

Regulatory Agencies and the Public Sector

Local, regional, state, and national regulations on development abound, ranging from environmental and consumer protection to oversight of financial intermediaries, mortgage in-

struments, and lending practices. Theoretically, public regulation of the development process should result in protection of the public's interest and well-designed projects that serve the community's needs. In reality, conflicting rules and regulations and the costs of compliance often stifle creative solutions to complex problems.

The public sector should be regarded as an integral part of the design team early in the development process. Site plans for a proposed development usually must go through public approval to secure required permits before development can begin. In many jurisdictions, a special use permit must be obtained for golf courses. Because design professionals—architects, engineers, and landscape architects—are charged with responsibility for the public health, welfare, and safety, they often have established a working relationship with representatives of local regulatory agencies and can be invaluable to the developer.

Property Manager/Golf Pro/Golf Course Superintendent

As the development process enters the final stages, the developer must hire building maintenance and janitorial services, a grounds maintenance service, and a property man-

ager. Ongoing management includes remarketing or re-leasing space, which might include renovations to suit current or new users. The involvement of the property manager and golf course superintendent can provide valuable insight about the long-term management of the asset.

Selecting Team Members

Developers usually have their own criteria and methods for selecting professional consultants, among them experience, expertise, scope of services offered, and reputation. Rosters of professional consultants are usually available from the associated professional organizations, such as the American Institute of Architects, the American Society of Landscape Architects, the American Society of Golf Course Architects, and the National Golf Foundation.

Many design professions have responsibilities for ensuring the public health, safety, and welfare; therefore, states could require certain design professionals, particularly architects, engineers, surveyors, and landscape architects, to be certified or licensed. While requirements for certification and licensure vary from state to state, key design professionals generally must be licensed or certified in the state where the project is located. State licensure of the design professionals who have primary responsibilities for a project is usually *mandatory* when the public sector is the developer or an equity partner in the project. Rosters of certified or licensed professionals are usually available from state or local government agencies. Local municipalities might also maintain rosters of specialized consultants, such as ecologists, environmentalists, naturalists, soils or environmental engineers, appraisers, archeologists, contractors and subcontractors, and others who are knowledgeable about local conditions.

An essential consideration in selecting the design team for a golf-oriented real estate development is the specific expertise of the land planner in such development. The landscape architect, architect, or engineer might offer land planning services, and large, multidisciplinary planning and design firms might offer some or all of these services. Landscape architects commonly take the lead in land planning, because their training includes the combination of technical and creative skills required to solve land planning problems. The golf course architect might also be an expert in land planning or have someone on staff with that expertise, and many golf course architects have a background in landscape architecture. However the design team is structured, the land planner/landscape architect must coordinate work with the golf course architect and other consultants. The entire development process requires the developer, land planner, golf course architect, and other consultants to resolve complex issues of integrating golf course and real estate development. Because the process is a team effort, just as much consideration should be given to the compatibility of personalities and design philosophies of individuals with the developer as to all other criteria for qualification.

The benefits of hiring a well-known golf course architect are often debated. While the obvious benefits are established reputation and high-profile market appeal that can provide a competitive edge for the project, many well-qualified, creative golf course architects without a recognized name can offer equally professional services at much lower or competitive fees. Beyond qualifications and affordable design fees, the main criterion in selecting the golf course architect should be compatibility of the golf course architect's

personality and design philosophy with the developer and the users. The golf course architect's design philosophy regarding the costs of construction and long-term asset management must be compatible with the developer's budget, and experience and established reputation are not necessarily synonymous with cost-effectiveness. The developer might be able to write off the cost of a name golf course architect as a marketing cost, but it is difficult to make a profit if the cost of building and maintaining the asset far outstrips its marketing benefits.

Getting Started

The eight-stage real estate development model provides a technique for manipulating and processing vast amounts of information in making a built environment. But therein lies its limitations. It is a technique. It does not provide the basis for ideas or the inspiration to embark on a creative endeavor or to seek innovative solutions to a problem. Creativity and the desire to create are necessary ingredients in real estate development, but they are not given to a standard technique or methodology. Real estate development always begins with the inception of an idea—the first spark of the imagination in the mind of an individual, whether from intuition or methodical study.

Once the idea is born, the eight-stage development model is a useful means of processing and manipulating complex information to manage risk, determine the feasibility of the idea, guide the development of the

idea, gain support for and market the idea, and ensure the successful implementation of the idea. The following chapters explore the details of this model and the basic knowledge essential to golf-oriented real estate development. While none of this information guarantees a good idea to begin with or a successful project in the end, it does provide the basis needed to make the most of an idea. "The best ideas result in products that serve the user well and add value to the community—something that most often distinguishes good development from bad."[3]

Notes

1. Many excellent texts have been published on the topic of real estate development (see, e.g., Richard B. Peiser with Dean Schwanke, *Professional Real Estate Development: The Guide to the Business* (Washington, D.C.: ULI–the Urban Land Institute, 1992); and Arvind Bhambri et al., *Strategies and Structure of Real Estate Development Firms* (Washington, D.C.: ULI–the Urban Land Institute, 1991)). Of the many theories and methodologies available, some are specific to certain types of real estate, such as commercial/office parks, shopping centers, or industrial parks. This book uses a basic methodology that can be adapted to golf-oriented real estate development. See Mike E. Miles et al., *Real Estate Development Principles and Process* (Washington, D.C.: ULI–the Urban Land Institute, 1991).

2. Adapted from Peter T. Dyke, "Course Planning and Design Requires Team Effort," *Chicagoland Golf*, June 1991, pp. 16–18.

3. Miles et al., *Real Estate Development*, p. 151.

The Economics of Golf and Real Estate

Golf courses can be developed as stand-alone business ventures or as an integral part of a real estate development. Developers of golf courses include public agencies, private enterprises, and joint ventures between the public and private sectors. Both public agencies and private enterprises have recognized the potential of golf courses to increase the value of an asset, and real estate developers have learned to capitalize on the

Wakagi #17.

© PAUL BARTON

potential of a golf course through the creation of golf-oriented real estate development. A developer might have several economic motivations for integrating golf with real estate:

- To increase land values throughout the development or community, resulting in a higher-profile product;
- To accelerate absorption of real estate;
- To create an asset that can be sold or retained as a revenue producer;
- To preserve open space as a means of increasing or maintaining the allowable development density of the site.

Golf historically has generated value for real estate. During the 1980s, the rapidly growing interest in golf boosted the market for high-priced, golf-oriented residential property, but a much more cautious and reasoned approach became necessary in the 1990s as a number of factors affected the economics of both real estate development and golf course development. Among the lessons developers learned is the importance of coordinating every step of the process to ensure the best relationship between the golf course and the real estate elements of a project. Combining golf and real estate results in direct physical, economic, and political consequences. Including a golf course in a real estate development as an afterthought or a quick-fix solution to use otherwise unbuildable land or to increase marketability is rarely physically, economically, or politically successful. Golf courses have the potential to be a financial asset— or a costly problem—for a real estate development. The key between success and failure, asset and problem, lies in knowledgeable, diligent, and coordinated planning and objective, rational decision making during the entire development process.

A large number of private golf courses and an increasing number of public courses have been developed as part of real estate developments. The desire to live on or near a golf course is not confined to golfers, for many non-golfers associate golf-front real estate with a desirable lifestyle. Many people enjoy living next to a golf course because their lawns merge visually with

Housing overlooking the golf course at Horseshoe Bay Resort and Conference Club.

COURTESY: HORSESHOE BAY RESORT AND CONFERENCE CLUB

150 or more acres of lush green grass, giving them the sense of living on a large estate, especially if the golf course can appear to merge into the house through the windows. Living by a golf course is akin to extending the bit of land defined by the property boundaries of one's own house.

The majority of golf-oriented real estate developments are associated with residential or resort real estate developments. While some commercial, office, industrial, or institutional developments are oriented around a golf course, they are usually associated with very large mixed-use community developments, major land reclamation projects, or broad-based community economic development projects, possibly because the economic benefits of a golf course are generally more direct and readily apparent in a residential or resort development than other types of real estate. The economic benefits of golf course frontage for a commercial, office, industrial, or institutional development are usually not as direct in terms of increased marketability or competitiveness with similar projects, increased lease revenues, or an increased market base for golf. Substantially less risk is involved in making improvements like dining terraces, exercise trails, landscaping, and ponds. If, however, a golf course is considered for a nonresidential or nonresort development, then operation of the golf course must be self-sustaining and

possibly an independent business operation, particularly in a highly competitive or overbuilt market.

A golf course does, however, offer a creative solution to land use problems; it could create greenbelt buffers around industrial parks, reclaim landfills and other "spoiled" landscapes, or protect sensitive wildlife habitats in land zoned for commercial, office, or industrial development. Thus far, however, this potential remains largely untapped.

Although studies have shown a growing demand for golf courses and golf-oriented real estate development, the demand is not evenly distributed. Participation in golf shows marked regional patterns across the United States, and a strong relationship exists between demographics (age, income, education, occupation, regional location) and participation in golf. The availability of financing for golf courses and golf-oriented development tends to follow economic trends: construction of golf courses and golf-oriented real estate boomed in the 1980s, but it has become more difficult to find financing for golf-oriented real estate development in the tight economy of the 1990s.

The development of a golf course or golf-oriented real estate involves many risks and millions of dollars. Many factors beyond a developer's control can waylay the success of a golf-oriented real estate project. Although objective analysis of cost factors, market demand, and long-range costs and benefits, and market and economic studies have become standard and necessary tools in the development process, the developer must keep in mind that even the best market analysts and the most detailed studies can only, at best, *anticipate* future events. Information can change rapidly. It might be inaccurate, incomplete, unavailable, or overabundant. To control costs and risks during the development process, the developer should have clearly stated objectives and a strategy for achieving each objective. In the long run, the developer and the development team must have the flexibility, willingness, and capability to adapt to unanticipated change. (Appendix A summarizes general information about the development process, which can be applied to golf-oriented real estate development.)

Market and economic studies to gauge a project's feasibility can serve dual purposes: as a decision-making tool for the developer and as a tool to gain support from financial partners, lenders, and the public sector. In any case, they are essential for risk control. For most golf-oriented real estate projects, lenders and the public sector might require the use of objective outside consultants for formal market and economic studies. A rigorous study of the market early in the development process is essential, particularly if the developer is unfamiliar or inexperienced with golf-oriented real estate development.

The identification of a problem to be solved stimulates creative problem solving. In real estate development, the problem can manifest itself in a number of ways. Perhaps a golf enthusiast owns a large parcel of land and dreams of building a house with his own golf course, a hotel corporation is looking for a site to develop a resort in a market known to have a strong demand for golf, or a foreign investment company is looking for a site where it can develop a golf-oriented real estate project. Each case involves a distinctive set of problems to be solved. Whatever the problem and whoever the players, however, it is ul-

timately the developer who generates the ideas to solve the problem, develops the solutions, takes the risk, bears the costs, and judges the value or potential of an idea in terms of fit with the market. The development team, particularly the design team, is the creative backbone for the developer. Many of the most notable and livable real estate developments, with or without golf, were the result of the creative energies of highly talented, bold designers who brought shape and substance to the developer's initial ideas.

Geographic, socioeconomic, and behavioral factors are particularly important in golf-oriented real estate projects, as the target market often has a distinctive lifestyle, prefers a certain location, and has a certain amount of purchasing power.

When the idea involves golf-oriented real estate, the quick pro forma usually involves a three-step calculation:
1. Calculate estimated value to cost of the golf course itself to determine estimated golf proceeds.
2. Calculate the estimated added value that the golf course will provide and compare it to the cost of the real estate development.
3. Combine net proceeds from the golf course with net proceeds from the real estate development to determine total proceeds from development.

Traditionally, developers relied on sales of real estate as the principal means for recovering the cost of the golf course. The added value that golf brings to a real estate development is thus considered in the quick pro forma by estimating the potential real estate premium.

In some cases, the developer might want to complete a comparative analysis between a real estate development with a golf course and a real estate development without a golf course to determine whether the net proceeds from the golf course plus added real estate value resulting from the golf course are significant enough to justify further consideration of the golf-oriented development. In this case, the developer also calculates value to cost of the real estate development without the golf course and compares it to the evaluation of total proceeds

from development of the golf-oriented real estate development.

These quick pro forma calculations require some general information on costs and values for golf and golf-oriented real estate. At this stage, cost and value data come primarily from the developer's attained knowledge and experience with the market, but data could also be available from golf research organizations like the National Golf Foundation, private market research firms, or trade publications.

Golf development costs vary widely, depending on a number of variables like the physical characteristics of the site and the desired quality of the product. In 1993, development costs for an 18-hole regulation golf course ranged from $2 million to over $8 million, excluding the cost of land. The cost of constructing a clubhouse, which also varies according to the size and quality of the facility, must be added to that figure. Generally, the developer can anticipate costs of $150 to $200 per square foot for construction of the clubhouse, and the clubhouse can range from 3,500 square feet for a public course to over 50,000 square feet for a private country club. Other capital costs, such as construction of maintenance and storage facilities, engineering and design fees, general and administrative expenses, and maintenance during grow-in, can add 40 percent or more to the basic construction budget for a golf course and clubhouse.

Development costs for a golf course also vary depending on the type of golf operation anticipated. These and some other alternatives for operation of a golf course are more fully described, with an analysis of their advantages and disadvantages, in Chapter 5. The potential value of a golf course and its potential operating income are directly related to the structure of the facility's business operation. A number of alternatives for ownership and operation of a golf course in a golf-oriented real estate development are possible, and determining the operational structure for the golf course is one of the first decisions to be made before feasibility can be assessed. The standard operational structures are public, private, and semiprivate.

The value of a golf course, like any other income-producing property, is based on anticipated benefits derived from its operation and reversion.[1] The most common basis for measuring the future benefits of a proposed business investment is projected net operating income (NOI), which represents the actual or anticipated funds remaining after all operating expenses are deducted from the effective gross revenue and before mortgage debt service and book depreciation are deducted. The principles and methodology of financial analysis are discussed under "Financial Analysis of the Golf Course," later in this chapter. For public golf courses, the primary source of revenue is fees charged for use of the golf course (daily greens fees); additional sources of revenue come from rental fees for golf cars, fees for the driving range and lessons, sales in the pro shop, and food and beverage operations. Thus, net proceeds for a public course are derived from the NOI added to the value of the golf course. For private golf courses, the primary source of revenue is the sale of memberships; additional revenue comes from services for members, and fees for guests and transfer of memberships. Thus, the net proceeds for a private course are derived from the net cash flow from sales of memberships plus NOI and the value of the golf course.

For public golf operations, a break-even matrix for greens fees provides a quick tool to analyze the investment that is justified by the number of rounds and amount of greens fees. Although greens fees for public golf courses are often based on the market and set at a rate that is competitive with comparable courses in the area, this matrix provides an alternative means of estimating annual rounds necessary to break even (that is, the point at which revenues cover operating expenses and the amortized cost of capital improvements) at different development costs. If, for example, the estimated average fee for 50,000 rounds is $29, the developer can afford to spend $8 million on the golf course.[2] These break-even fees are based on

Types of Operational Structures

Type of Operation/Ownership	Description
Public/Municipal Ownership or Private Ownership	Course is open to the general public for use upon payment of a daily greens fee and other user fees. Ownership and operation can be controlled by a public agency, such as a parks department (a municipal course), or a private business (a daily fee course).
Private Club	Use of the course is restricted to members and their guests upon purchase of a membership and/or payment of membership dues. Private clubs entail various membership structures: • *Equity memberships*, in which memberships are sold. Ownership, fiscal responsibilities, and operational control of the facilities are transferred from the developer/owner to the membership when all memberships are sold or at some other predetermined time. • *Nonequity memberships*, in which members, upon payment of membership fees and/or membership dues, are entitled to use the facilities for a specified period. Developer/owner retains ownership, fiscal responsibilities, and operational control.
Semiprivate Club	A combination of private and public operational structures, in which both membership and daily-fee play are permitted to attain the best economic performance for the facility.

Source: Michael P. Sim, Esq./Hillier & Wanless, P.A.

Golf Course Development Costs by Operational Type
(Millions of 1993 Dollars)[1]

	Range	Private Country Club	Tournament-Quality Resort	Daily-Fee Public Course
Golf Course Construction (18 holes)	$2.0 to $8.0	$4.0	$4.0	$3.0
Clubhouse	0.5 to 8.0	3.5	1.0	0.8
Maintenance and Storage Facilities	0.3 to 0.6	0.4	0.35	0.35
Soft Costs[2]	0.7 to 2.5	1.4	1.1	0.9
Maintenance Equipment	0.3 to 0.5	0.4	0.35	0.35
Maintenance during Grow-In	0.3 to 0.5	0.3	0.3	0.3
Contingencies[3]	0.4 to 1.5	0.5	0.4	0.3
TOTAL	$4.5 to $21.6	$10.5	$7.5	$6.0

[1]Based on a review of projects throughout the United States. Does not include cost of land or development profit.
[2]Includes design fees, overhead, and construction financing.
[3]Approximately 10 percent of course development budget.
Source: Economics Research Associates.

Break-Even Matrix for Greens Fees at a Public Course

Development Cost: Annual Rounds	$6 Million	$8 Million	$10 Million	$12 Million
		Break-Even Greens Fees (per round)		
40,000	$33	$39	$45	$51
50,000	24	29	34	39
60,000	19	23	27	31
70,000	15	18	21	25

Key Assumptions:
- Net combined contribution to gross income (from golf cars, driving range, pro shop, food and beverages, and miscellaneous fees) of $10 per round;
- $1 million annual operating expenses, excluding departmental cost of sales and other expenses;
- 12 percent cost of capital.

Source: Economics Research Associates.

the premise that golf is primarily a fixed-cost business in which operating expenses do not vary significantly with level of play, so that most changes in revenue directly affect performance of the bottom line.

Historically, the cost of developing a golf course was not supported by direct economic performance of the golf course itself. With improved golf market conditions, however, the business of golf has improved significantly. Today, with careful planning and design, many golf courses can support their cost of development as well as generate substantial underlying benefits, such as increased real estate value, enhanced value of nongolf products within the development, and accelerated absorption of real estate products. Real estate development represents an important means of recovering the cost of developing a golf course in addition to the more direct components, such as membership sales, operating income, and disposition of assets.

The developer's idea is expressed in the form of a statement of the developer's position, which describes the goals and objectives or development program for the proposed venture, including a general description of the project in terms of:

■ Type of financial venture (e.g., municipal, private enterprise, or public/private partnership);

■ Scale of venture and of major program elements (total acreage, number of holes, and so on);
■ Type of operational structure (public, private, semiprivate);
■ Type of associated real estate development (e.g., primary, secondary, or retirement residential, resort, commercial, institutional, number and type of real estate units, and so on);
■ A description of the target market, the project's image, and projected schedule;
■ Strategy for disposing of assets.

A project's position in the golf market and the development program can be amended as details are added and information gathered. The developer must constantly reevaluate the project's positioning as conflicts and opportunities arise during planning and design. Ultimately, the development program provides definitive facts and figures to guide design and the subsequent financial analysis of the proposed project.

Because of the risks and substantial sums of money involved in golf-oriented real estate development, a developer rarely commits funds to purchase a site at this stage of the process.

Site acquisition studies should provide important information that is useful for negotiating the purchase price for a site. The cost of land in itself can be a significant factor in the project's feasibility, particularly where land

prices are high, although high land costs do not necessarily preclude golf-oriented real estate development. Instead, different strategies for programming, planning, and design are necessary to offset the high cost of land.

Site Analysis

An obvious physical requirement for a golf-oriented development is a sufficient amount of developable land to accommodate the golf course and associated real estate. Land area required for a golf course is often underestimated. It is influenced by many physical factors, including topography, configuration of the parcel, existing vegetation, drainage, presence of sensitive habitats, and soils. The development program for the course—length of the course, size and capacity of the clubhouse, the driving range, and other facilities—also affects the amount of land required. While 120 to 130 acres might be sufficient for a course with a small practice range and clubhouse on a relatively flat and unconstrained site, the same course and facilities on more difficult terrain might easily require 150 acres or more. No standard formula exists for determining acreage required for a golf course. And the problem becomes more complex when golf-oriented real estate is involved, because allowances must be made for special requirements associated with this type of development. The wisest approach is to involve key design professionals, such as the land planner and golf course architect, in site acquisition studies. Early input of these professionals' expertise and knowledge is necessary for effective risk management. Not only can they obtain and process the essential information about potential sites to determine their suitability, but they can also often see creative solutions for what might otherwise be considered a problem site.

Once a site has been selected, a more rigorous and detailed inventory of the site's existing physical characteristics is undertaken and analyzed in terms of the proposed development program. Typically, a professional landscape architect, land planner, or

Real estate development represents an important means of recovering the cost of developing a golf course. Horseshoe Bay Resort and Conference Club.

golf course architect—or a team comprised of these professionals—who has the knowledge of and capability in the technical and aesthetic aspects of physiographic site analysis and design is retained to perform this study. The specialized training of these professionals is required to translate the information gathered into a usable form for determining feasibility.

The process of recording site data is accomplished on a series of overlay maps, which make it easy to visually determine those areas of the site that are slightly, moderately, or severely constrained for the proposed land use. The site analysis for a typical golf-oriented real estate project includes several factors:

- *Topography/slopes.* Generally, a gently rolling site is easier to develop for both golf courses and real estate. The topography of the site is analyzed in terms of excessively steep or unstable slopes (greater than 15 to 20 percent), which place a constraint on development, and extremely flat areas (0 to 2 percent slope), which could present problems with drainage.
- *Views and vistas.* Topography also provides opportunities and constraints in terms of desirable or undesirable views within the site, panoramic vistas from high points of the site to surrounding areas, and views of the site from outside the site.
- *Drainage/hydrology.* Good drainage is critical for golf courses, and this feature is probably one of the most important ones when this land use is being considered. This analysis of the topography determines drainage patterns of the property, including surface water flow, floodplains, watersheds, and impoundments like ponds, lakes, and reservoirs.
- *Water resources.* The availability of a source of irrigation water is critical for golf courses. This analysis overlaps to some extent with the analysis of hydrology, because information about drainage is used to determine areas of the site that might be suitable for water impoundments. Potential sites for wells are also noted in this analysis.

Physiographic Site Analysis

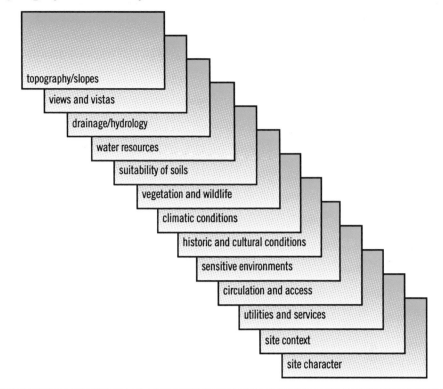

Source: Guy L. Rando & Associates Inc.

- *Suitability of soils.* Several soil suitability analyses must be performed. For real estate development, soils are analyzed for their suitability for building foundations, sanitary septic fields, and roads. For golf courses, additional analyses are necessary, including depth of topsoil, fertility, pH, and drainage.
- *Vegetation and wildlife.* An inventory of existing vegetation and wildlife on the site by type, size, and habitat is necessary. An additional detailed survey to locate positions of significant specimen trees or to delineate sensitive habitats might also be required if endangered or sensitive flora and fauna are located on or adjacent to the site.
- *Climatic conditions.* An analysis of solar orientation, patterns of sun and shade, prevailing winds, temperature, humidity, and rainfall is necessary. An analysis of the site's microclimates (warm or cool slopes, moist valleys, exposed or windy ridges, and so on) might also be necessary when conservation of resources or energy is a major concern.

- *Historic and cultural resources.* Historically or culturally significant features on or near the site could require special consideration. An archeological survey might also be necessary.
- *Sensitive environments.* Development can affect wetlands, sensitive wildlife habitats, and other unusual ecological factors.
- *Circulation and access.* A circulation overlay examines how the site can be reached by pedestrians, and by autos and other modes of transportation.
- *Utilities and services.* The utilities overlay examines accessibility to all utilities—electric power, gas, water, sanitary sewer, telephone, police, fire, ambulance, schools, cultural/social centers, shopping, and other community services.
- *Site context.* A site context overlay describes the surrounding community, proximity to desirable or undesirable features, competitive projects, and existing patterns of land use.
- *Site character.* A description of the site's aesthetic qualities is typically expressed through photographs or sketches of the site.

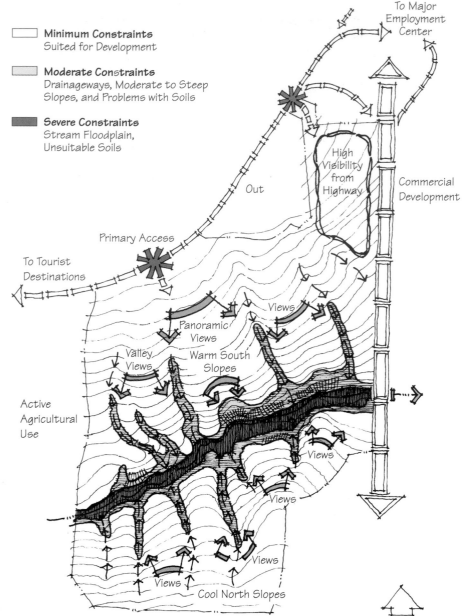

Minimum Constraints
Suited for Development

Moderate Constraints
Drainageways, Moderate to Steep
Slopes, and Problems with Soils

Severe Constraints
Stream Floodplain,
Unsuitable Soils

To Major
Employment
Center

Out

High
Visibility
from
Highway

Commercial
Development

Primary Access

To Tourist
Destinations

Views

Panoramic
Views

Valley
Views

Warm South
Slopes

Active
Agricultural
Use

Views

Views

Views

Views

Cool North Slopes

A synthesis diagram shows at a glance which areas are best for development.
Source: Guy L. Rando & Associates Inc.

Sources of information include the U.S. Geologic Survey, local offices of the Soil Conservation Service, resource management, land planning, and zoning agencies, and private aerial survey and other mapping enterprises. As a general rule, the design professional undertakes on-site reconnaissance and ground surveys to provide a complete, site-specific analysis of the character and resources of the site. Such ground surveys might be required to obtain or verify data such as location of the boundary or property line, delineation of floodplains or wetlands, soils profile or percolation tests, historic or archeologic resources, location of specimen vegetation, or loca-

tion of sensitive or endangered flora and fauna and associated habitats.

In some areas, legal research in coordination with the site analysis might be required to search for and secure water rights—so critical for golf courses. Many states and localities have adopted laws regulating the quantity and quality of water used to irrigate golf courses (see "Irrigation Systems" in Chapter 4).

Information gathered from the site analysis is synthesized into a diagram summarizing the site's opportunities and constraints and delineating areas that are severely, moderately, or minimally constrained for the proposed development.

Informal Market and Marketability Analyses

Informal market and marketability analyses during Stage Two provide the developer with information required to refine the development program and to project a position for a specific project and site. For example, the broad idea of a single-family residential development oriented toward an 18-hole regulation golf course expands into a detailed development program and market strategy with $\frac{1}{3}$- to $\frac{1}{2}$-acre single-family residential lots at least 100 feet wide fronting on the golf course for upscale two- to four-bedroom houses targeted toward the middle- and upper-income markets.

Financial Feasibility

The informal pro forma analyses conducted in Stage One can be used to further refine the idea. The determination of financial feasibility moves another step forward into estimating cash flows during development, which incorporates operating revenues and expenses over a defined period of time, yielding estimated NOI. Estimated projections of cash flow also assign the asset's reversionary value at the conclusion of analysis, and estimated cash flow is used in the financial feasibility analysis of Stage Three to assess the risk and time value of money by applying a discount rate (the discounted cash flow).

Thus, for a golf course or golf-oriented real estate development, all future factors, such as cost of operations, wear and tear, and revenues from sales or rentals, can be put into an equation that reduces all the information to today's dollar value—the Present Value (PV). Future Value (FV) is present value multiplied by one plus the rate of return, including a factor for inflation to compensate for the declining value of the dollar.[3]

$$FV = PV (1 + i)$$

where:

i = real return + inflation factor

The present value for multiple years is equal to the sum of the present values of the future values in all future years. In a summation formula, the values are raised to a power equal to the number of years:

$$\text{Multiyear PV} = \sum_{i=1}^{n} \frac{FV_n}{(1+i)^n}$$

where:

n = number of years

Σ indicates summation from the first to the nth year

The rate of return for a real estate development or golf course is not a definite figure, however. Risk must be considered in the calculations, taking into account the Expected Cash Flow (ECF) in each year. The expected cash flow is derived by projecting NOI as far into the future as possible. When NOI reaches a stable level, sale of the asset is assumed. The expected cash flow is then each year's expected NOI plus the final year's estimated proceeds from the sale. The equation for present value with risk becomes:

$$\text{Multiyear PV} = \sum_{i=1}^{n} \frac{ECF_n}{(1+r)^n}$$

where:

r = i + risk premium

If expected cash flows are certain, the investor can assign a low risk premium to the equation. If the expected cash flows appear questionable, then the investor assigns a high risk premium. High risk does not necessarily mean that the investment is a bad one; some investors might find them attractive if the prospective returns are high enough.

The rate of return investors consider an acceptable return on equity varies. Many investors require a return on equity 12 to 15 percent higher than what could be obtained from a risk-free investment in government bonds. Similarly, a number of factors are considered in assigning a premium for risk. On a low-risk real estate investment, for example, a minimum of 2 to 3 percent might be added to the current rate of return on a government bond.

Pro Forma Annual Net Operating Income for Municipal/Daily Fee Golf Course
(Thousands of Constant 1993 Dollars)

OPERATING REVENUES	Amount[1]
Greens Fees (at $20 per round)	$1,200
Golf Car Rentals (at $4.00 per round)	240
Practice Range (at $2.50 per round)	150
Pro Shop Merchandise (at $3.00 per round)	180
Food and Beverage Services	
Snack Shop (at $2.50 per round)	150
Restaurant/Banquet Facilities	350
Miscellaneous	25
Subtotal	$2,295
Minus: Cost of Sales	
Pro Shop (at 67 percent of department revenue)	120
Food and Beverage Services (at 30 percent of department revenue)	150
Subtotal	$270
GROSS OPERATING PROFIT	$2,025
OPERATING EXPENSES	
Course Operations	
Payroll and Benefits	$250
Services and Supplies	125
Water and Utilities	50
Replacement Reserve (equipment and course)	75
Subtotal	$500
Golf Operations	
Payroll and Benefits	$100
Golf Car Leasing/Replacement Reserve	40
Services and Supplies	30
Practice Range	20
Miscellaneous	25
Subtotal	$215
Food and Beverage Services	
Payroll and Benefits	$175
Services and Supplies	75
Miscellaneous	25
Subtotal	$275
Undistributed Clubhouse Repairs and Maintenance	$50
General and Administrative	
Payroll and Benefits	$90
Insurance	40
Property Taxes	70
Services and Supplies	50
Management Fee	75
Subtotal	$325
TOTAL OPERATING EXPENSES	$1,365
NET OPERATING INCOME	**$660**

[1]Based on 60,000 rounds annually.
Source: Economics Research Associates.

Pro Forma Annual Net Operating Income for Private Nonequity Golf Course
(Thousands of Constant 1993 Dollars)

OPERATING REVENUES	Amount[1]
Dues	
Full Golf Family Membership (300 members at $220 per month)	$800
Full Golf Single Membership (150 members at $165 per month)	300
Social Membership (100 members at $75 per month)	90
Subtotal	$1,190
Guest Greens Fees (6,000 rounds at $30)	180
Golf Car Rentals (at $6.00 per round)	300
Pro Shop (at $5.00 per round)	250
Practice Range (at $2.00 per round)	100
Food and Beverage Services (at $8.00 per round)	400
Membership Transfer Fee (5 percent turnover/20 percent transfer fee)[2]	110
Miscellaneous	25
Subtotal	$1,365
Minus: Cost of Sales	
Pro Shop (at 70 percent of department revenue)	175
Food and Beverage Services (at 40 percent of department revenue)	160
Subtotal	$335
GROSS OPERATING PROFIT	$2,220
OPERATING EXPENSES	
Course Operations	
Payroll and Benefits	$300
Services and Supplies	150
Water and Utilities	50
Replacement Reserve (equipment and course)	85
Subtotal	$585
Golf Operations	
Payroll and Benefits	$150
Golf Car Leasing/Replacement Reserve	50
Services and Supplies	50
Practice Range	10
Miscellaneous	40
Subtotal	$300
Food and Beverage Services	
Payroll and Benefits	$160
Services and Supplies	80
Miscellaneous	25
Subtotal	$265
Undistributed Clubhouse Repairs and Maintenance	$150
Member Services	$100
General and Administrative	
Payroll and Benefits	$125
Insurance	50
Property Taxes	100
Services and Supplies	50
Management Fee	90
Subtotal	$415
TOTAL OPERATING EXPENSES	$1,815
NET OPERATING INCOME	**$405**

[1]Based on 50,000 rounds annually.
[2]Based on 5 percent of 450 members leaving and transfer fee of 20 percent of the average initiation fee ($25,000).
Source: Economics Research Associates.

Formal Market and Marketability Analyses

Methods of market analysis for a golf-oriented residential project differ from those for a golf-oriented resort. All market analyses must address the same basic concerns, however: the market area (the geographic delineation of the primary and secondary market areas), the socioeconomic environment, market demand (demographics), competing products, the capture rate (demand weighed against existing and proposed competition), and employment and absorption rates (used to project demand). A good market analysis should detail the developer's objectives by identifying the targeted market segment, for example, the income or age group targeted. For example, the market for golf-oriented real estate is a submarket that can be defined as a segment or niche whose population has specific characteristics related to income, tenure, age, and lifestyle. The marketability analysis should describe features that will attract the target market. A golf-oriented residential project, for example, should describe preferences for housing-to-price and amenities-to-price ratios, including a description of features and amenities offered by existing and planned competing projects. Additionally, any obstacles that might adversely affect a proposed project should be identified and described, including regulatory restrictions, difficult environmental problems like the presence of hazardous materials or endangered species, or a strong political or community sentiment against certain types of development.

For a golf-oriented real estate project, the formal market analysis must determine the strength and nature of the market for golf as well as the strength and nature of the real estate market. If the project involves residential development, the detail provided by a formal market analysis is critical, because specific market segments and niches for golf developments must be identified and described.[4]

Analyzing the Market for Golf

A thorough understanding of the market for golf is crucial to the marketing strategy and financial feasibility of a golf-oriented real estate development. A no-expenses-spared golf course geared toward tournament players set in a middle-income retirement community obviously conflicts with the marketability and financial feasibility of both the golf course and the real estate development. Although this example is exaggerated, mismatches do occur, and they can pose serious problems that can be avoided through careful analysis of the market.

Like analysis of the real estate market, analysis of the golf market can involve several methods. One method, a three-step process, requires more in-depth assessment for each step. The first two steps consider primarily quantitative factors, the third one important qualitative issues.

1. Compare population to inventory of golf courses in the area.
2. Compare potential demand for golf with supply.
3. Evaluate qualitative issues.

This three-step process is most commonly used to analyze the market for public golf courses, but it also is useful for evaluating private golf courses.

Information about the golf market is usually expressed in number of rounds (a completed circuit or game of golf) per year (or some other time-defined period). A total round of golf is usually expressed in terms of 18-hole equivalents: one 18-hole round or two nine-hole rounds.

The first step compares population to the number of golf courses available in a defined market area. This methodology provides a basic indicator of the relationship between supply and demand but is not sufficient to adequately assess market support for a proposed public golf course.[5]

The extent of the primary market area varies according to a number of factors: the type and scope of the project (resort versus residential, for example), the physiography of the area (road systems, accessibility over mountains, proximity of bridges over rivers,

Estimating the Supporting Market For a Public 18-Hole Regulation Golf Course

Population in the Market Area (age 13 and above):	500,000
Multiplied by: Estimated Golf Participation Rate (adjusted for age and income)	12%
Yields: Number of Golfers	60,000
Multiplied by: Estimated Number of Public Golfers	70%
Yields: Number of Golfers	42,000
Multiplied by: Average Number of Annual Rounds per Golfer[1]	20
Yields: Potential Annual Rounds	840,000
Multiplied by: Number Allocated to Regulation Course	70%
Yields: Potential Annual Rounds	588,000
Divided by: Average Use of Course (annual rounds)[1]	75,000
Yields: Number of Supportable Public Courses	8

[1]Annual rounds for a 12-month course based on statistics from the National Golf Foundation and adjusted for the local market and seasonality.
Source: Economics Research Associates.

and so on), and other market factors (including traffic patterns, proximity to cultural centers, and spillover markets). The primary market area for a nonresort golf course typically is an area within approximately 20 to 30 minutes of driving time, with a secondary market extending up to 45 or 60 minutes—or more—of driving time. Local factors specific to the proposed project should always be considered when defining the primary market area, however.

The second step in analyzing market support for a new golf course is a more detailed, quantitative comparison of the potential demand for golf and current or anticipated supply. The potential demand for golf is based on demographics of the market area (population, income, age) and residents' propensity to play golf. Typically, this analysis includes:

- The number of current rounds of golf played at existing courses (the competition);
- The number of potential rounds of golf within the defined market area around the proposed project;
- The surplus or deficit in rounds of golf within a defined area around the proposed project;

- The anticipated number of rounds of golf that projects in the pipeline in the market area might take up; and
- The average capacity of comparable golf courses in terms of annual rounds.

An inventory of facilities in the primary and secondary market areas identifies and describes existing and planned golf courses by type of operation (municipal, daily fee, private, for example), taking into account reductions in the inventory as a result of conversions to other uses. Although time-consuming, it is an important part of the analysis, and a survey of area planning agencies should generate reliable information. A profile of the local golf market area and the competition should include the following information:

- Number of golf courses open to the public;
- Owner, operator, and year built of those courses;
- Overall quality of the facilities, including the name of the course architect, course slope rating (used to calculate handicaps), and a description of ancillary facilities like the clubhouse and other amenities;
- Greens fees, golf car rental fees, and prices for memberships if applicable;
- Accessibility and geographical sources of players;
- Annual rounds of play by type (public, daily fee, private, and so on);
- Percentage of rounds played by people living outside the market area;
- Weekday versus weekend play;
- Seasonal patterns in demand;
- Trends in amount of play in the market area;
- Gross annual revenue from golf car rentals, the driving range, pro shop, and food and beverage services;
- Average revenue per round of golf at competing facilities;
- Potential revenue per round of golf for the proposed project.

A full evaluation of market support for a golf course requires consideration of several qualitative issues (step 3), based on rational, impartial judgment of factual information. Areas to consider include:

- *Characteristics of the competition.* An analysis of the characteristics and positioning of competing

courses can indicate a specific market niche for a proposed golf course.
- *Fees.* An analysis of the prevailing greens fees in a market area provides information about any constraints on sustainable fees for new courses.
- *Influence of tourists.* A strong tourist trade, both day and overnight visitors, can dramatically influence the demand for golf. This source of demand must be calculated in addition to the traditional analysis of supply and demand.
- *Influence of spillover markets.* In some market areas, supply and demand might appear to be in balance, but a severe shortage of courses in the nearby area could provide significant spillover demand, sufficient to warrant additional golf courses. This factor is particularly important when the area generating the spillover demand has very limited opportunities to add golf courses.
- *Potential of a proposed course to attract players.* Although market conditions appear to favor a proposed course, accessibility and location can mitigate its potential.
- *Conversion of existing public courses to other land uses.* Despite the increasingly favorable economics of golf, escalating land costs and other competitive market forces can result in the future conversion of golf courses to other land uses.
- *Community attitudes and environmental influences.* Although most communities consider a golf course a desirable land use, the approval process can be very difficult, even for a very attractive development package. Thus, initial market research should include taking stock of public attitudes toward golf courses, past failed efforts, environmental protests, wetlands, sources of water, and restrictive land use regulations.
- *Availability and cost of land.* The availability and cost of land strongly affect the supply of golf courses, particularly in more urbanized areas. Many cities accumulated a large amount of parkland during the 1960s but have little money now for capital or operating bud-

gets. Land leases to private golf developers can be viable options, but the market for golf must be very strong to recover costs and lease payments to public agencies.
- *Seasonality and weather.* Seasonality and weather patterns in a market area must be fully considered to project annual rounds. While it might be possible to accommodate 80,000 to 100,000 or more rounds in a 12-month season, 40,000 to 60,000 rounds in a six- to eight-month season is more realistic. In high altitudes, 25,000 to 35,000 rounds might be all that can be generated.
- *Weekend/weekday play.* Filling golf courses on weekends is usually not a problem, but in most markets, weekday play is more difficult to generate consistently, particularly when a course depends on spillover from major secondary markets. The developer might consider promoting tournament play on weekdays and offering specials or discounts (particularly for seniors) as part of the marketing program to increase weekday play.

Quick calculations for step 1 can be helpful in screening areas for potential golf courses, but they are not by themselves sufficient for making critical decisions. The analysis in step 2 provides more detailed market assessment, but the quantitative analysis provided by the first two steps is only an indication of market potential. The evaluation of qualitative issues in step 3 is required to provide a complete analysis of the potential for a new golf course. The applicable issues can have a major effect on the results of market and financial feasibility tests.

Once the demand for golf is projected and the supply of courses serving the market considered, market share for the course can be estimated based on the location and orientation of the course, characteristics of the competition, and other factors.

Financial Analysis of the Golf Course

The pro forma financial analysis of the golf course considers revenues from sales of memberships, operations, and disposition of assets, and

Characteristics of Selected Semiprivate Golf Clubs in Florida

Club	MetroWest	Cypress Creek	Kissimmee Bay	Orange Lake	Poinciana	Schalamar Creek	SunAir	Baytree	Sweetwater
Location	Orlando	Orlando	Kissimmee	Kissimmee	Kissimmee	Lakeland	Haines City	Winter Haven	Haines City
Year Built	1987	1969	1990	1981	1972	1988	1974	1991	1988
Holes/Par	18/72	18/72	18/71	27/72	18/72	18/72	18/71	18/71	18/63
Length (feet)									
Back	7,051	6,952	6,855	6,551	6,701	6,488	6,706	6,688	3,158
Middle	6,467	6,335	6,390	6,186	6,171	5,850	6,096	6,254	2,722
Slope Rating									
Back	126	131	119	132	120	127	131	120	NA
Middle	120	126	114	128	115	121	125	117	NA
Course Architect	R.T. Jones	Lloyd Clifton	Lloyd Clifton	Joe Lee	Bruce Devlin	Ron Garl	Jack Watkins	Dean Refram	NA
Clubhouse (square feet)	23,000	7,000	10,000	NA	17,000	22,000	26,750	NA	10,000
Other Facilities									
Pro Shop	X	X	X	X	X	X	X	X	X
Locker Room	X	X	X	X	X	X	X		X
Snack Bar	X	X	X	X	X	X	X	X	X
Restaurant	X	X	X	X	X	X	X	X	X
Bar	X	X	X	X	X	X	X	X	X
Driving Range	X	X	X	X	X	X	X	X	
Tennis	X	X	X	X	X	X	X		X
Pool	X	X		X	X	X	X		X
Membership Characteristics									
Type					Annual		Annual	Annual	Annual
No. of Golf Members	88	40	270	NA	300	340	270	NA	200
Initiation Fee	$4,500[1]	$1,000	$900	[2]	$250	$1,500[3]	–	–	–
Regular Monthly Dues	$164	$88	$100	[2]	–	$100	–	–	–
Annual Pass (single)	$1,500	No	No	No	$800	No	$910	$900	[4]
Greens/Golf Car Fees									
Winter									
Regular									
Weekday	$52	$40	$40	$52[5]	$38	$25	$25	$25	$10
Weekend	$52	$45	$45	$52[5]	$38	$29	$30	$30	$10
Twilight									
Weekday	$32	$16	$20	$44	$33	$12	$19	$20	$8
Weekend	$32	$16	$20	$44	$33	$12	$22	$20	$8
Summer									
Regular									
Weekday	$52	$25	$25	$25[6]	$23	$20	$15	$18	$9
Weekend	$52	$30	$30	$25[6]	$23	$25	$20	$22	$9
Twilight									
Weekday	$28	$16	$20	$22	$18	$20	$13	$15	NA
Weekend	$28	$16	$20	$22	$18	$25	$17	$15	NA
Florida Residents									
Weekday	$23	$18	$20	$15	$13	$15	$11	$15	NA
Weekend	$29	$22	$20	$15	$13	$15	$11	$15	NA
Total Rounds	50,000	67,000	45,000[7]	65,000	62,500	70,000	60,000	NA	40,000
Seasonal Distribution (percent)									
Winter[8]	38	40	50	45	33	60	50	NA	65
Summer[9]	62	60	50	55	67	40	50	NA	35
Annual Players (percent)									
Members	10	5	38	50[10]	30	75	80	NA	70
Locals[11]	60	80	57	47	30	25	17	NA	30
Nonlocals	30	15	5	3	40	0	3	NA	0

NA = Not available.
[1] Memberships for nonresidents are $7,500.
[2] All membership fees and dues are included with cost of timeshare.
[3] Available to residents only.
[4] Varies from $400 to $900.
[5] $34 for owners.
[6] $19 for owners.
[7] Estimated by Economics Research Associates.
[8] January 1 to April 15.
[9] April 16 to December 31.
[10] Timeshare owners/guests.
[11] Within a 30-minute drive.

Sources: Economics Research Associates and individual clubs.

Average Play at a Public Course

| | Seven-Month Season | | Twelve-Month Season | |
Type of Course	Percent of 18-Hole Rounds	Annual Number of Rounds	Percent of 18-Hole Rounds	Annual Number of Rounds
Municipal	75	50,000	75	100,000
Daily Fee	85	40,000	85	75,000
Resort	90	25,000	90	50,000

Source: Economics Research Associates.

Pro Shop Sales by Type of Course

Course	Average Sales per Round
Municipal	$2 to $3
Daily Fee	$3 to $5
Resort	$10 to $20

Source: Economics Research Associates.

operating expenses, marketing costs, and development costs to estimate the potential economic performance of the development. The measure of revenues varies according to the operational structure of the course (public versus private), as sources of revenue vary according to the type of operation. For public golf courses, whether private or owned by the city, the primary source of revenue is the income generated from daily greens fees, but other sources include the income generated from golf car rentals, use of the driving range, sales in the pro shop, lesson fees, and food and beverage services.

Amount of annual play varies considerably, based on climate, length of season, type, design, and condition of the course, operational efficiency, fee structure, and market strength.

Golf car rentals are an important source of revenue for most golf courses. Use of golf cars can vary from 20 percent to 100 percent of golfers at courses where use of golf cars is mandatory, but the general range is 40 to 60 percent at most public golf courses. With golf car fees of $16 to $20 per round, the average revenue per round, taking into account the golfers who do not use them, would be $3 to $5.

The golf practice range can also be a significant source of revenue. Gross revenues vary depending on the rate structure, use, and availability of night lighting. Annual revenues can range from $4,000 to as much as $10,000 or more per tee station. Typical use at public courses ranges from 20 to 35 percent of total available capacity.

Sales of merchandise in the pro shop vary depending on the type of golfer attracted to the course and the degree of emphasis placed on retailing. Average merchandise sales per round vary substantially by type of business operation.

Sales of food and beverages are directly related to facilities in the clubhouse, location of the golf course, and level of use by nongolfers. Revenues from food and beverages attributable to golfers typically range from $2 to $4 per round. In addition, some public golf courses provide a banquet room, with 80 to 90 percent of the banquet functions used by nongolfers. Depending on the market's size, competition, and accommodations offered (most operators prefer facilities that can accommodate 250 to 300 people at one time), gross banquet revenues can range from $250,000 to $1 million or more per year, with annual revenues of $300,000 to $500,000 usually achieved, according to Economics Research Associates.

An alternative to operating the golf course as a public facility is to sell private club memberships. Typically, a club can accommodate 300 to 500 full golfing memberships, plus social and limited memberships, depending on such factors as size of the golf facilities, the climate (the shorter the golf season, the smaller the acceptable number of memberships), and demographics. In southern Florida, for example, golf is most popular in the winter months when hours of daylight are shorter. Clubs there have a high percentage of retirees; therefore, private clubs in that area can generally accommodate only 300 to 350 members. In contrast, clubs in California suburbs can sometimes accommodate as many as 450 to 500 members.

For a private club with a non-equity membership structure, the golf course and its facilities are run as a for-profit enterprise. Thus, depending on how the membership is structured, revenue can be generated from both membership fees and/or monthly dues. Although the pro forma analysis of NOI during the membership sales period might show an operating deficit, positive NOI is typically achieved at a stabilized level of operation.

For private clubs with an equity membership structure, the golf course and related facilities are generally run as a nonprofit business. Membership dues are set at a level to generate sufficient income to cover all operating expenses and to maintain a reserve fund for replacing capital equipment and improving the course. The developer receives revenue from sales of memberships but must allow for the cost of marketing the memberships (usually 5 to 10 percent of gross sales) and the cost of subsidizing ongoing operations until all memberships are sold. Because the developer is responsible for operating and monitoring the course until ownership of the club reverts to the members, the pro forma analysis of NOI for such an operation generally shows operating losses, which is the cost of the developer's subsidies during the membership sales period. Once most of the memberships are sold, annual dues for members are set at a level sufficient to cover the cost of operating and maintaining the course and clubhouse.

Potential operating revenues for golf car rentals, use of the practice range, pro shop, and food and beverage concessions are determined on the basis of projected use. These revenues vary widely from project to project because of a number of factors: size of the facilities, level of service, and market conditions. Thus, project-specific market studies are necessary to calculate these figures.

Additional sources of revenue at private clubs include fees for services for members (lockers, club storage, for example), greens fees for guests, and membership transfer fees. Guests often account for 5 to 10 percent of total play at private clubs. Membership transfer fees are the share of the proceeds generated from resale of memberships that accrues to the club. They can vary from 10 to 100 percent of the membership resale fee; many private clubs assess a transfer fee of 20 to 30 percent.

Operating expenses vary from project to project as a result of several factors, including design of the course, level of maintenance, climatic conditions, labor costs, utility rates, size of the clubhouse, and so on. Project-specific market research and analysis provide the data required to estimate operating expenses for the golf pro forma.

Standard operating expenses for a golf course include:

- Course Maintenance
  - Payroll and benefits
  - Services and supplies
  - Water and utilities
  - Replacement reserve: Equipment and course
- Golf Operations (Pro Shop, Golf Cars, Driving Range, Lessons)
  - Payroll and benefits
  - Golf car leasing/replacement reserve
  - Maintenance, services, and supplies
  - Driving range
  - Miscellaneous
- Food and Beverages
  - Payroll and benefits
  - Services and supplies
  - Miscellaneous
- Other Undistributed Clubhouse Maintenance and Repair
- Membership Services (Private Courses)
- General and Administrative
  - Payroll and benefits
  - Insurance
  - Property taxes
  - Services and supplies
  - Management fees

Cost of sales represents the cost of products purchased for resale at the golf course. It does not include payroll, services, supplies, and other operating expenses. For pro shops, the cost of sales ranges from 65 to 75 percent of gross revenues. Generally, the higher the percentage of "soft" goods (shirts, sweaters, caps, gloves, and so on), the lower the cost of sales. "Hard" goods (golf clubs, balls, and so on) have a higher cost of sales. The cost of sales for food and beverage operations normally ranges from 30 to 35 percent of gross revenues. The cost can reach 40 percent at private equity clubs, where members' dues often subsidize food and beverage operations.

The value of a golf course is based on annual net cash flow discounted to the present value. The appropriate discount rate (the required annual risk-adjusted rate of return) depends on the cost of capital, development risk, expected inflation, and other such factors. For a public golf course, net cash flow is derived from NOI and disposition of the golf course (value of the asset). For a private nonequity or semiprivate golf course, net cash flow is generated from sales of memberships, NOI, and disposition of the golf course (the reversionary value). For a private equity course, net cash flow is derived from sales of memberships minus marketing costs and operating subsidies required during the membership sales period.

The disposition or reversionary value of a public or private nonequity golf course is based on its potential to produce income. While numerous techniques of valuation are possible, capitalizing stabilized annual pretax NOI at a market-established capitalization rate generally provides a reasonable estimate of value. The capitalization rate (the ratio of annual net income to the asset's value) is established through the investors' criteria for rate of return.

The feasibility of the golf course alone is determined by comparing the course's value with development costs. If the value of the golf course is less than the direct cost of development, the golf course could still be justified when the impact of the course on real estate is considered.

Enhancing Real Estate's Value

Lots and houses in a golf course community bring higher premiums than comparable lots and houses in a nongolf community. Prime sites that front on greens or that enjoy water views or fairway and open-space vistas can command twice the average fairway premium. Property that does not actually front on the course but offers views or partial vistas of it also commands a substantial premium. It is difficult to generalize about the magnitude of the premiums. In percentages, golf's enhancement of land values tends to decrease as the base land value rises.

Historically, private golf courses have created the highest premiums. Regardless of whether it is a private or daily fee operation, premiums for real estate are related directly to the quality of the golf course as consumers perceive it (whether it is well maintained, whether it offers good value to cost, for example). Real estate premiums could also be affected by sales strategies for real estate and the market for a particular project. Market studies play an integral role in determining the premiums that a specific market will bear. Pricing real estate can be based on a number of strategies, including:

- Establishing a base price for an interior unit (nonfrontage, no significant views) and adding a percentage for views and frontage to determine the price.
- Varying sizes of lots or models of housing units to command higher

Golf Real Estate Premiums

	Value of Lot	Value of House
Basic Nongolf Lot[1]	$50,000	$180,000
Golf Course Community		
Interior Lot	$52,500	$185,000
Golf-View Lot	60,000	200,000
Fairway Frontage	75,000	225,000
Prime Golf Frontage[2]	100,000	260,000

[1]An interior lot in a master-planned community without golf.
[2]Lots fronting on greens, lakes, and other particularly desirable features of a golf course.
Source: Based on a review of master-planned communities throughout the United States by Economics Research Associates.

prices for units with a view and frontage. For example, premium golf frontage lots might be slightly larger than interior lots to accommodate larger, more expensive houses targeted to the higher end of the market.

The amount of premium real estate with frontage on the course depends on the design of the golf course and the type of housing or development planned. Land use plans that are designed merely to maximize golf frontage do not necessarily maximize overall real estate values. Land values are maximized by strategic sites for lots that provide a mix of lots fronting on and looking into the course, and by a land use plan that makes the golf component seem to belong to the entire community. In the most economical land use plan, real estate is not allowed to intrude too much on golf. Design strategies for the best real estate values are discussed in detail in Chapter 3.

Golf normally does not create significant premiums for certain types of housing developments, among them moderately priced housing for young families and rental housing. Young families generally look for value per square foot rather than amenities. If a trade-off exists between proximity to a golf course and an extra bedroom or a larger house, these buyers tend to choose the larger house or extra bedroom. Similarly, a golf course usually does not generate sufficient additional rental income to justify its development, although certain exceptions exist, particularly in some retirement and other specialized rental markets.

The value of a golf course often exceeds the cost of its development, particularly when the value of peripheral real estate is considered. In many cases, however, a golf course might not be economically justified, either as a stand-alone venture or as part of a golf-oriented real estate development.

■ *Size of property.* If the golf course consumes a large percentage of developable land, resulting in smaller unit yield for the real estate, the value of the real estate might be unrecoverable.

Prime golf frontage on Mission Hills #18.

■ *Land market.* The area's land market might not support a high enough value for lots or golf course premiums to offset the cost of the course.
■ *Depth of the real estate market.* The area's housing market might not be strong enough to absorb the higher-priced units of a golf development fast enough to enhance the net present value of the real estate program.
■ *Depth of the market for golf.* While overall demand for golf exists in the United States, the distribution of that demand from one region to another is not even. Weakness in an area's market for golf could translate into low membership values, slow sales of memberships, or, in the case of a daily-fee operation, low greens fees and net income from operations. Other factors affecting the value of the golf course include the length of the golfing season, the competition, and maintenance costs.

Increased Value of Real Estate in a Golf Community
(Percent over Base Value)

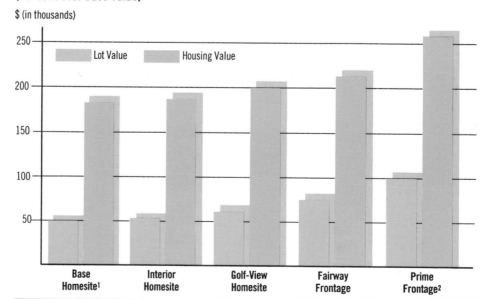

[1]An interior lot in a master-planned community without golf.
[2]Frontage on greens, lakes, and other desirable features of a golf course.
Source: Economics Research Associates.

Typical Percentage of Households Buying Golf Memberships at Private Country Clubs within a Planned Community

Type of Development	Percent of Total
Resort/Second-Home Community	40 to 80
Retirement Community	25 to 50
Family/Primary-Home Community	20 to 30

Source: Economics Research Associates.

■ *Development constraints.* Unfavorable or unusual topographic conditions, drainage requirements, and soil conditions, and the presence of sensitive or endangered environments or stringent environmental regulatory requirements can make the cost of constructing a golf course prohibitive.

The premium attributed to the golf course is normally accrued over several years for absorption or buildout. To calculate present value of such an annual income stream, the premium must be discounted to reflect its present worth.

A second means of cost recovery is achieved through accelerated absorption of the real estate. Houses in golf course developments appeal to both nongolfers and to golfers.[6] The broadening market appeal of golf and its positive effect on a community's image and appearance can speed up overall absorption by 20 to 30 percent or more. Faster absorption translates into a higher net present value for the proceeds of real estate sales.

Public Approval

In some jurisdictions, a proposed golf course might require special permits. The developer not only must determine what regulations affect a proposed project during planning and design of the project, but also must anticipate the effect of regulations that might be enacted at any time during the life of the project. A developer might be required to change the development plan even while the project is under construction or after the project is completed to conform with new regulations.

Golf-oriented real estate development usually involves a large site and a program with several land uses, and it is therefore generally advisable to work within the most flexible zoning category possible, such as that for a planned unit development. Development regulations in most jurisdictions include minimum requirements for open space. Because in most jurisdictions a golf course is considered a type of recreational land use, the area of land the golf course occupies is often qualified for consideration as open space when calculating conformance to regulations governing open space. Flexible zoning categories usually relax requirements for minimum lot or yard sizes so that the allowable densities over the entire project can be clustered in smaller areas, leaving more open space. This arrangement is usually in the best interests of a golf-oriented real estate development, as clusters and other variations in density are integral to design and marketing strategies for such projects.

Project Financing

The developer can pursue different sources of financing for the real estate development and the golf course. Sources of financing for the golf course depend largely on the type of operation planned, that is, municipal or private.

Financing for Private Ventures

For private ventures, sources of financing can include equity funds and/or debt financing. Sources of equity

Aberdeen #14.

© PAUL BARTON

Impact of a Golf Course on the Value of Peripheral Real Estate

	Nongolf	Golf
Total Land Area (acres)	750	750
Residential	600	475
Golf Course	–	150
Roads, Easements, Open Space	150	125
Total Lots (four units per acre)	2,400	1,900
Interior	2,400	1,400
Golf View	–	200
Fairway Frontage	–	300
Average Improved Lot Value		
Interior	$50,000	$52,500
Golf View	–	60,000
Fairway Frontage	–	80,000
Average Site Improvement Cost (per unit)	$28,000	$28,000
Average Annual Absorption (number of units)	250	300
Interior	–	210
Golf View	–	35
Fairway Frontage	–	55
Average Land Cost (per acre)	$15,000	$15,000
Cash Flow Projections (1993 dollars)		
Site Sales	$120,000,000	$109,500,000
Minus:		
Land Costs	11,250,000	11,250,000
Site Improvement Costs	67,200,000	53,200,000
Soft Costs	18,000,000	16,425,000
NET CASH FLOW	$23,550,000	$28,625,000
Net Present Value[1]	$3,300,000	$13,200,000

[1]Projected constant annual cash flow discounted at 10 percent.
Source: Economics Research Associates.

funds include the developer/owner, limited partnerships, and syndicates. Local banks and savings institutions, pension funds, insurance companies, credit companies, and investment banks are potential sources of debt financing. Credit companies and investment banks often provide a combination of both debt and equity financing. In the current economy, a developer might be able to finance only 40 to 60 percent of a new development project, requiring him or her to come up with a substantial amount of equity. In a survey of golf course developers about financing, 34 percent of the courses opened in 1991 were tied to real estate development, and of the courses under construction in 1992, 43 percent were tied to real estate development. Forty-six percent of the courses opened in 1991 borrowed from 40 to 60 percent of their development capital from a lender, 52 percent of those under construction in 1992. An additional 37 percent borrowed more than 60 percent of the development capital

required from a lender.[7] The survey brought home several points:

- Golf courses might be easier to finance if they are part of a larger real estate development.
- Loans for stand-alone golf courses of any type typically require over 40 percent equity.
- Requirements for loan terms and equity are relaxed somewhat if the borrower has a track record.
- Lending institutions prefer personal property and income from unrelated businesses rather than land as collateral.
- An established relationship with the lender is often key to obtaining a loan, as loans are most often made by "local" institutions.
- Limited partnerships are important sources of equity.

No specific guidelines exist for underwriting loans for golf courses; golf courses are treated as conventional real estate. Bank examiners look primarily at the cash flow from the property and

the borrower's cash reserves and secondarily at the property's value if auctioned. Because improvements to a golf course have a low residual value, the lender has no fall-back position if the golf operation fails. Golf is also a service business depending on projected cash flows rather than underlying real estate value as a means of gaining lenders' confidence. As a result, debt financing is easier for addition or expansion of existing golf courses with a track record of cash flow than new golf courses with risky cash flows.

Lenders are becoming more willing to finance golf courses when the requests are well prepared and take into account the lender's needs. According to the National Golf Foundation, informed lenders are eager and willing to lend money to golf courses, and to do so they have:

- Created a loan structure that acknowledges potential negative cash flows in the early years of operation (that is, lenders capitalize requirements for and shortfalls of working capital);
- Required sufficient cash reserves to cover all contingencies; and
- Increasingly offered equity participation to decrease the borrower's requirements for equity and lower the effective interest rate on the debt.

The most attractive investments for institutional investors are those with a proven demand for the asset. Raising debt and equity capital requires preparation of detailed, carefully investigated feasibility studies and formulation of a rational business plan.

The Business Plan

If the feasibility analysis is positive, the developer must then compile detailed project information to incorporate into a business plan. The business plan provides information that lenders and investors will require when the developer seeks debt and equity capital. It addresses the findings of feasibility and market studies, expands on issues related to the development and permitting, and highlights the project's financial potential in greater detail. A typical business plan includes:

The Public Approval Process for Poppy Hills Golf Course

Location: Monterey, California

Owner/Operator: Northern California Golf Association

Golf Course Architect: Robert Trent Jones II

Located on the beautiful Monterey Peninsula, the 166-acre site of this 18-hole golf course is the first golf facility to be built by a regional golf association: the Northern California Golf Association (NCGA). Poppy Hills is the home for NCGA's administrative offices and its major championships. It provides services to approximately 25,000 regular and associate members.

The following chronology details events leading to Poppy Hills's opening.

- *Beginning of an idea.* In 1972, the board of directors of NCGA began to discuss the possibility of constructing an 18-hole golf course.

- *Purchase of land.* In 1976, the NCGA board of directors and staff attended several meetings in the area to explain the proposed concept to delegates of its member clubs. Later that year, a majority of member clubs voted to authorize an annual assessment of $4.00 per member (from membership dues) to help fund the project. Dues were originally $6.00 plus the assessment, a total of $10 per member in 1977. The Pebble Beach Corporation and NCGA signed an agreement to purchase land in April 1977.

- *Selection of an architect.* A committee comprised of broad representation from the golfing industry (golf course superintendents, golf course operators, professionals, club managers) plus two NCGA directors interviewed several architects, selecting Robert Trent Jones II after several interviews, meetings, and conferences.

- *Architectural agreement.* Jones was instructed to work in two phases. Phase 1 consisted of designing the route of play, completing the land study, and determining whether the land fit the requirements of the project. Phase 2 dealt with the design agreement, the completion of specific drawings, and on-site inspections of the golf course up to seeding.

- *Permits.* In 1979, NCGA began the long process of obtaining approval from the various governmental agencies involved. Monterey County required approval from all special districts and state and federal agencies within its jurisdiction, as well as an environmental impact report, to be submitted through the Monterey Planning Department. The approval process continued for four years, and the final permit had 63 conditions attached to it.

Poppy Hills #8.

ROBERT TRENT JONES II

- *Gowan cypress grove.* One of the most significant conditions attached to the permit—and one presenting a major problem—involved a two-acre grove of Gowan (dwarf) cypress trees, which are unique to the area. The cypress had become dwarfed over the years as a result of the shale rock soils and lack of moisture. Environmental consultants recommended rerouting the golf course and completely avoiding the area to increase the chances of receiving final approval.

- *Purchase of additional land.* The environmental consultants' recommendation prompted the purchase of an additional three acres adjacent to the property (where the par-5 12th hole is now located) from the Pebble Beach Corporation.

- *California Coastal Commission.* The property for the golf course fell within the coastal range and therefore was under the jurisdiction of the California Coastal Commission, whose approval was needed for Monterey County to issue final permits. In April 1984, the commission's staff forwarded a favorable recommendation to the full commission to approve the NCGA's project.

- Text on how the course will generate business, get fees, be marketed, and set operational guidelines;
- Conclusions of a credible study of market demand (rounds, fees, net revenues);
- Conclusions of an economic and financial feasibility study;
- Detailed development budgets and a detailed estimated operating budget;
- A projected timetable;
- Qualifications of the management and development teams;
- Financial resources (including equity participation by the developer) and a credit history of the project's principals;
- Environmental analysis;
- Legal considerations;
- A proposed plan to repay the loan; and

- A profile of a comparable project.[8]

In addition, the site analysis must demonstrate careful investigation of legal, environmental, and other property-related issues. Lenders are particularly concerned about:

- Legal issues (entitlements, liens, leases, taxes, easements, zoning, the title search, and insurance for the project);
- Environmental issues (environmental impact report, study of wetlands, Army Corps of Engineers study, study of water use, state and local agency approvals);
- Operational issues (size and shape of the property, terrain, weather, and design); and
- Locational issues (accessibility and location compared to existing golf courses in the market area).

Financing for Municipal Ventures

Sources of financing for a municipal operation can include general budget allocations, the sale of general obligation or revenue bonds, certificates of participation (COPs), and lease/purchase financing. General budget allocations provide surpluses in the budget to fund capital requirements for the golf course. Unfortunately, in these times few public entities can use this method to finance golf courses. General obligation bonds are based on a municipality's taxing powers and established credit and can be subject to approval by the public through a bond referendum. In some municipalities, it might be possible to finance a project through revenue bonds, which are paid out of the golf course's net income. The golf course itself serves as

- *Final approval.* After three months of delay, the project was placed on the July 10, 1984, agenda at 9 A.M. for final approval. After lengthy discussions on numerous topics and conditions, the chair called for a vote at 4 P.M. With the vote standing at six "yes" and five "no," the chair discussed his personal thoughts and in the end voted "yes" to follow the staff's report. The final vote was seven "yes" and five "no," and the chair's vote was significant, as a tie vote would have meant denial of the project. Throughout that day, however, 19 additional conditions were placed on the project.

- *Beginning of construction.* In October 1984, clearing trees began in three phases. After each phase of clearing was completed, grading began immediately (first grading began in March 1985), irrigation was installed, and the ground was seeded. The first seeds were drilled into the ground in October 1985, and seeding was completed in December of the same year.

- *Grand opening.* Poppy Hills Golf Course opened officially for public play on June 1, 1986, 14 years after the project was conceived.

Lessons Learned

The development process and time-consuming public approval process for a golf course require flexibility, diplomacy, and perseverance. Jones, the architect, says "Poppy Hills is a model for all broad-based golfing groups to follow. Located just a chip shot from famed the Pebble Beach, this course has revolutionized the NCGA's golfing activities. Hardly a day goes by without some tournament's or special event's taking place. All the numbers are far beyond our wildest expectations. We encourage other golf associations around the country to design and build their own championship golf course at a central location, creating a destination where thousands of members can gather and play golf and boosting public access to golf."

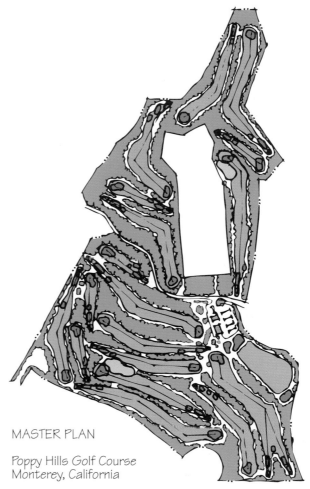

MASTER PLAN

Poppy Hills Golf Course
Monterey, California

Preservation of a two-acre Gowan cypress grove prompted the purchase of an additional three acres (par-5 #12) to reroute the golf course.
Source: Robert Trent Jones II.

collateral, and the revenue bonds are thus usually sold at a higher interest rate than general obligation bonds.

Certificates of participation require the city or county to establish a public development corporation, which contracts with a private developer for design and construction of the facility. The contract calls for a turnkey facility to be delivered at a guaranteed fixed price. The public development corporation uses its financing powers to sell tax-exempt COPs or similar financing vehicles, and debt service is financed from the golf course's positive cash flow. In the event of smaller-than-anticipated revenues, the public agency's general fund provides additional security. Under this arrangement, a management company specializing in golf courses is typically retained to operate the course.

When the bonds are fully repaid, in 20 to 30 years, ownership of the golf course reverts to the city or county.

Lease/purchase financing involves a leasehold contract between a municipality and a financing entity. Like COPs, the contract calls for a turnkey facility to be delivered at a guaranteed fixed price to the municipality. In this case, however, the municipality can

Debt Equity/Business Plan

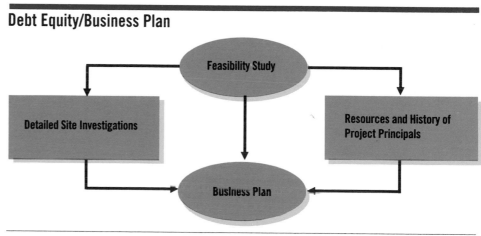

Source: National Golf Foundation.

ask for competitive bids for the construction contract. The municipality agrees to make lease or installment payments on the golf course until its improvements are paid off (usually 20 to 22 years), with installment or lease payments funded from the golf course's net revenues. The city's or county's general fund remains the ultimate guarantor for any smaller-than-expected revenues. Under this alternative, the golf course is developed, and in some cases managed, by a private company. The municipality retains control over the property through the leasehold interest.[9]

Trends in Public/Private Joint Development

One of the most significant trends in the golf industry over the last decade is the privatization of operations at existing public courses. In recent years, the trend has extended to include private participation in the development of public golf courses. Such public/private joint development of public golf courses is not a new phenomenon, for a number of such ventures were completed in the late 1960s and early 1970s, nearly all of them involving development of golf courses by private enterprises on property leased from public agencies. Some term this arrangement "lessee capitalization."

Between the mid-1970s and early 1980s, escalating costs and a reluctance to increase daily greens fees and other fees at public courses resulted in deteriorating economic situations at public golf courses and private enterprises' decreased interest in participating in the development of municipally owned golf courses. Public agencies often subsidized the golf operation, passing the expense of the subsidies on to the taxpayers. With the passage of Proposition 13 in California and other similar legislative revolts against taxes around the nation, public agencies were no longer able to subsidize inefficient operations, golf operations in particular. They thus began to evaluate ways to reduce their role in providing the subsidies, improve the economics of public golf courses, or convert nonperforming assets into income-producing assets. One of the most significant approaches to improve the economics of public golf was the privatization of operations—which more recently has evolved into the privatization of development.

Several fundamental factors have led to the trend toward privatization, but the driving force behind the private sector's interest is the improvement in the economics of public golf courses, generally attributable to the following factors:

■ Increasingly favorable demographics for golf, resulting from an aging population, increasing household income, and increasing interest and participation by women and younger age groups.

■ The rapidly increasing potential or higher revenues resulting from comparatively faster escalation of daily greens fees and golf car fees, along with increasing demand for golf cars and tournament play, which is rising faster than operating expenses.

■ Increased potential for profit with improved marketing and the use of a professional management firm.

■ Constraints on the number of courses as a result of high land and construction costs, and other locally imposed constraints on the development of golf facilities.

■ Public agencies' increased receptiveness to private participation.

From the public sector's viewpoint, the impetus for pursuing public/private golf course development includes the following factors:

■ Most communities are experiencing a strong demand from residents for recreation, including golf. Compared to other recreational facilities, golf is perceived as a game for the wealthy and therefore is of a lower priority in budgeting limited resources.

■ Many public agencies have undeveloped surplus land, but they lack the financial resources and/or experience necessary to develop and operate a golf course.

■ Most public agencies can obtain financing at tax-exempt interest rates that are substantially below commercial market rates. It is also easier for public agencies to secure a debt because of their power of taxation.

■ Public agencies have become increasingly hesitant to incur risks with public funds.

■ The general public is increasingly receptive to the idea of privatizing services that were once considered in the public domain and of allowing private firms to generate a fair profit from such projects.

■ Private operation of a public golf course is often more cost-efficient, as civil service wages and employment practices are more costly than those found in the private sector.

■ The growth in the number and sophistication of private corporations capable of building and operating public golf courses has resulted in a more competitive environment for development.

The economic and political environment is now more conducive to public/private ventures in developing golf courses. As more joint ventures are established, they will play an increasingly important role in the future development of golf courses.

The approaches to public/private development of golf courses entail numerous variations, but the basic concepts can generally be placed in four fundamental approaches: a ground lease of public land, dedication of land, dedication of land and the golf course, and public financing of a privately developed public course.

Ground Lease of Public Land

The most traditional approach to public/private joint ventures is a public agency's ground lease of public land to a private entity for development and operation of a public golf course. The developer is responsible for the construction and operation of a public course. The land is leased for a lengthy term, sufficient for the developer to obtain financing and recover the costs of construction and operation. During the term of the lease, the developer pays rent to the public agency, which typically includes a minimum base figure calculated against a percentage of gross revenue from operation of the course. Upon the lease's expiration,

Ground Lease of Public Land
Mile Square—*Orange County, California*

Mile Square opened in 1968 in the Fountain Valley area of Orange County. It is an 18-hole, par-72, 6,400-yard golf course of moderate quality and one of the original public/private joint ventures. The land is owned by Orange County and leased to the Mile Square Golf Course for 30 years. The course was built by the developer/operator.

Terms of the lease are as follows:

| | | Percentage Rent | |
| | | Greens Fees/ Golf Car Rentals/ Range Fees | Food and Beverage Sales/ Retail Sales |
Year	Minimum Rent		
1	$12,000	7%	3–4%
2	12,000	8	3–4
3	12,000	9	3–4
4	12,000	10	3–4
5–10	12,000	12	3–4
11–30	12,000	14	3–4

Orange County has been one of the fastest-growing regions in the United States for many years, and the demand for golf continues to increase. Currently, Mile Square accommodates approximately 100,000 rounds annually and generates total gross revenues over $2 million per year, over $250,000 of which Orange County receives in lease payments, which go into the county's general fund.

Lessons Learned

Mile Square's percentage rents for the ground lease are about the highest found. While the course struggled during the early years of operation, rising fees and rapidly increasing demand quickly moved the course into a profitable position. In a strong golf market like Orange County, a ground lease is a viable alternative for development.

Source: Economics Research Associates.

the ownership of the course reverts in its entirety to the public agency. While terms of a ground lease vary, features of a typical lease include:

- Thirty- to 50-year leases;
- Minimum fixed annual rent, which typically starts at under $100,000 and increases in steps over the early years of operation, depending on the income and expenses of the golf course;
- Percentage lease payments ranging from 5 to 15 percent of the gross golf revenues (greens fees, golf car fees, use of the driving range, sales, and other fees);
- Percentage payments ranging from 3 to 5 percent of gross food and beverage sales and 5 to 10 percent of gross pro shop sales.

This approach has several advantages:

- It is the simplest approach, in structure, for a public/private joint venture.
- The risk to the public agency is relatively small as long as the developer/operator's financial health is ensured.
- The developer receives the land at no initial cost, and the long-term

lease allows sufficient time to generate a reasonable return on investment and to amortize invested capital.

- Lease payments are tied to gross revenues and generally held low in the first years of operation until play builds to above break-even levels.
- The discounted reversionary value of the course is relatively small and therefore does not play a major role in negotiations.
- The developer retains control over the design of the golf course and any associated real estate development, facilitating coordination between land planning and the golf operation and maximizing the value of both entities without seriously compromising either one.

It also has some disadvantages:

- The approach depends on a strong golf market that can generate sufficient revenues to cover operating expenses, the cost of capital, and a reasonable return on investment.
- The public agency loses some control over operations.

- A working relationship of mutual trust is essential. Because of the lease's lengthy term, both parties must plan with care and negotiate with skill.
- In most cases, low-interest, tax-exempt bonds cannot be used to finance improvements.

Dedication of Land

As part of a golf-oriented real estate development, particularly residential development, a private developer can dedicate land for a public golf course to a public agency in exchange for rights to develop residential uses around the course. Often the land dedicated to the public is, for one reason or another, unsuited for construction of buildings (perhaps the land is in or around a floodplain or other sensitive environment or the soils are unsuited for construction of building foundations or sanitary septic systems). This approach can be used when a public agency does not have sufficient land of its own yet wants a golf course open to the public. Normally, the development and operation of the golf course become the responsibility of the public agency, but not always.

The advantages of this approach are that:

- The developer benefits from the increased land value created by development of an adjacent golf course without the cost of constructing and operating the facility.
- The public agency benefits from acquiring the land at no cost and has an opportunity to provide a public recreational facility, increasing the public agency's assets against which it can secure financing.

The approach's disadvantages are that:

- The public agency assumes the financial risk associated with a major development of this type.
- The public agency must determine the property's suitability for development of a golf course.
- From the developer's standpoint, a public golf course generates a lower premium than a private country club (although premiums generated by the real estate can still be considerable).

29

Dedication of Land
Rancho Solano—*Fairfield, California*

As part of a 1,600-unit residential development called Rancho Solano in Fairfield, California, the developer dedicated 200 acres for the development of an 18-hole, par-72, 7,000-yard golf course. As part of the development agreement, the city built a championship golf course and provided partial funding for a clubhouse with restaurant, cocktail lounge, and pro shop. The city invested $1.25 million for one-quarter ownership of the clubhouse, with the developer putting up the remaining portion. The clubhouse was dedicated to the city, with food and beverage operations leased to an operator for a long-term. The city will share 25 percent of the profit or loss from all operations.

The city retained CCA-Silband to operate the course and clubhouse and contracted with Rancho Solano Country Club and Resort, Inc., to operate the food and beverage services. It issued $7 million in bonds to cover the construction of the course and one-fourth of the clubhouse. The course was completed in 1989.

Lessons Learned

One of the key lessons learned was the importance of the working relationship between the developer and the city. Although the dedication of land was apparently successful, a close working relationship to understand common goals is important. City staff cautioned that this approach might not work in other situations if the working relationship is not healthy. The city's selection of and criteria for qualifications for the golf course architect were also key decisions. Golf courses are very different from parks, and cities need to rely on a competent architect to help manage construction and keep costs down. Before hiring the architect, however, detailed plans and objectives must be established to assist in selecting the right architect. Coordination and communication among the city, the golf course architect, and the developer are crucial. The city of Fairfield also brought in the operator at an early stage—initially as a consultant, later to supervise maintenance during grow-in, and finally as operator. The input from an experienced consultant who would eventually operate the course was very helpful.

Source: Economics Research Associates.

Dedication of Land
Iron Horse Golf Course—*North Richland Hills, Texas*

Richmond Bay Development Company is developing Meadow Lakes, a master-planned residential community in North Richland Hills, a suburb located about 10 miles north of Forth Worth. The developer, electing not to enter the golf course development business, was unsuccessful in attracting a private firm to develop the course. A number of apparent issues concerned these firms, including the tree cover, the terrain and other land features, cost and availability of water, and the limited amount of land area (the 120 acres available would not allow construction of a regulation golf course).

In April 1988, the city of North Richland Hills reached an agreement with the developer to construct a golf course, with the understanding that the course would be a high-quality design. The city assembled three parcels—the 120 acres dedicated at no cost by the developer, a 35-acre parcel acquired for the nominal price of $1.00 from the Federal Savings and Loan Insurance Corporation, and a five-acre parcel leased from an adjoining city—for construction of a regulation course. Most of the land is in a floodplain. The city retained a designer and an operator, and acted as developer, coordinating design and construction. The course opened for play on April 2, 1990.

Construction cost of the golf course was $2 million, total turnkey costs $4.5 million. Tax-exempt bonds totaling $4.25 million were sold to finance the course. The developer contributed $100,000 toward construction, in addition to dedicating the land. Greens fees are $18 Monday through Thursday and $23 Friday through Sunday. The developer has designed a subdivision with approximately 65 lots fronting on the golf course.

Lessons Learned

In this example, a public agency used its powers of land assembly and public financing to accomplish what the private sector was unable to do. With assistance from the golf course architect and golf management firm, the city served as developer, constructing one of the highest-quality municipal golf courses in Texas. In return, the developer received entitlements for a 65-unit subdivision fronting on the course.

Source: Economics Research Associates.

- A close working relationship must be established to coordinate the work of the private developer's land planning and design team with the golf course architect retained by the public agency to ensure that both parties achieve maximum benefits in terms of real estate value and golfing value and that decisions about design do not adversely affect the other entity.

Dedication of Land and Golf Course

An extreme example of the same concept is the dedication of a turnkey public golf course in exchange for development rights to the real estate around the golf course. In this approach, the private developer provides the land and builds a public golf course, then dedicates the project on a turnkey basis to the public agency. The public agency in exchange might assume such responsibilities as the off-site costs associated with the golf course, such as improvements to access roads, utility infrastructure, and the like. This approach generally is realistic only when development is otherwise under strict growth and development controls and the surrounding real estate is a highly valuable residential asset.

Among its advantages are that:

- The public agency benefits from the dedication of a turnkey golf course at little or no cost.
- The developer benefits by having thorough control over the course's design (ensuring maximum real estate value) and from real estate entitlements.

Disadvantages of this approach are that:

- The developer must make a major investment but receives only the development rights and land premiums from that investment. In areas where growth and development controls are stringent, however, it might be the most expeditious means of obtaining development rights.
- The public agency does not control the quality of construction and/or the course's design and therefore has no guarantee that the finished product will not carry high operating costs.

Dedication of Land and Golf Course (Turnkey Development)
Mountain Shadows Golf Course—*Rohnert Park, California*

In 1977, two developers built the north course of the Mountain Shadows Golf Course in return for the right to build 120 houses per developer per year around the course. The city committed $100,000 for the irrigation system. Once completed, the course was dedicated to the city for operation, and in May 1978, the city contracted with a national golf course management firm to operate the course. The course generated $215,000 in revenue to the city in FY 1988. The management contract, which was recently renegotiated, requires the operator to rebuild the clubhouse and to spend a significant amount for other capital improvements. The new contract generated approximately $350,000 in revenue in FY 1989, with the majority of the city's income reserved for construction of new recreational and golf facilities.

Lessons Learned

At the time the idea was conceived, the city of Rohnert Park, in the middle of rapidly growing Sonoma County, had very restrictive growth policies, and the dedication of a multimillion dollar golf course was the only way the developers were able to secure development rights. The golf course has been very successful for all parties, with two particularly positive aspects: the developers' willingness to negotiate and their integrity. Some problems did occur, however. Several holes had to be rerouted because initial planning between lots and the golf course was poor. An important lesson learned is the need to plan and develop the golf course and residences concurrently so that the infrastructure can be coordinated. The land planner and golf course architect should be brought in early to ensure full coordination and to minimize conflicts between adjacent land uses.

Source: Economics Research Associates.

Land Swap
Castle Oaks Golf and Country Club—*Ione, California*

A slightly more complicated version of a joint venture involved the state of California, the city of Ione, and a private developer. In 1989, the city of Ione acquired a fairly large tract of land from the state of California through a land swap as part of an agreement that involved locating a new state prison in the community. The new prison, other regional business development, and development pressure from Sacramento resulted in a need for additional recreational opportunities in the community. Golf was identified as the primary focal point.

To facilitate construction of the golf course, the city entered into a joint venture with a developer that called for the city to lease the land for the course to the developer for $1.00 per year for 25 years. The developer will construct and operate the course during this period and will receive all of the operating revenues. At the end of the lease period, the course will be turned over to the community. In the meantime, the developer may develop and sell the surrounding property. To facilitate development, $12.5 million in bonds has been funded, all of it to be repaid by homebuyers.

A distinctive aspect of this relationship is that the developer retains the right to transfer the public play to another course at any time during the lease period and to convert the existing course to private ownership. The developer has options on adjacent land large enough to construct a second golf course and is tentatively planning to construct the second course once the real estate is nearly all sold.

Lessons Learned

Clear benefits accrued to both the public and the private developer. First, the city will have a golf course to provide recreation for local residents. Second, a golf residential community within the city will help provide an incremental tax base. Third, the provision to issue bonds for the infrastructure enables the developer to accelerate the development of the golf course to include a clubhouse and tennis courts, because the developer's initial financial exposure is minimal. Fourth, the developer gains an advantage in marketing by being able to position the community as a future semiprivate or private development, which should help early absorption and pricing. Fifth, the city can acquire a facility dedicated solely to golf without surrounding real estate if the developer exercises the option to transfer the public play to another course.

Source: Economics Research Associates.

■ The golf market might not be strong enough to generate revenues sufficient to cover operating expenses, thus creating a long-term need for municipal subsidies.

Public Financing of a Privately Developed Golf Course

One of the most prevalent roadblocks to developing public golf courses is the availability of financing—or lack of it. Golf courses require a long construction and "green-up" period during the initial years, when the level of play could be low. With conventional financing, the course might not be able to cover its debt service and generate an adequate return on investment, unless it is in a very strong market.

Public agencies, on the other hand, do not have the same financing constraints as commercial institutions. Because public agencies can borrow funds at tax-exempt interest rates, they are able to accept lower rates of return on investment.

Recent public/private joint ventures serve as the best illustrations of how this public finance/private development approach can be implemented:

■ The public agency establishes a public development corporation, which contracts with a private developer for design and construction of a golf course.

■ The contract calls for a turnkey facility to be delivered at a guaranteed fixed price.

■ The public development corporation uses its financing powers to sell tax-exempt COPs or similar financing vehicles.

■ Debt service is funded from the golf course's net income. The public agency's general fund provides additional security to the bondholders.

■ The public development corporation usually retains a golf course management company to operate the golf course.

■ In 20 to 30 years, when the bonds are fully repaid, ownership of the course reverts to the sponsoring public agency.

The advantages of this approach are that:

31

Public/Private Venture
Rancho Palos Verdes (Marineland) Site—*A Proposed Project*

A major destination resort with a resort-quality, 18-hole, regulation golf course is proposed for the former 100-acre Marineland site on the Palos Verdes peninsula coast in Rancho Palos Verdes. Land for an 18-hole golf course is insufficient on site, however, and off-site options involve significant problems. The golf course is viewed as an integral part of a successful resort, and the city stands to benefit extensively from the resort through occupancy, sales, and property tax revenues generated from its operation.

The city of Rancho Palos Verdes has proposed an unusual public/private joint venture in which adjacent land owned by the city (where former military barracks were converted into city administrative offices), additional privately owned residential coastal land, and a county-owned parcel designated for recreational use would be combined to provide the 150 or so acres necessary for the golf course. The assembled site would be suitable for a high-quality course and appears to be feasible from the standpoint of marketing and potentially capable of generating substantial underlying land value as well. The golf course would be publicly operated, with the city retaining ownership but likely retaining an outside operator. As designed, six holes would be developed on the original site of Marineland, five holes on the private property, one hole on county property, and six holes on city property. The private property allocated for the golf course would be provided through dedication, an easement, or some similar vehicle.

All parties would benefit from this proposal. The resort developer would have a spectacular 18-hole golf course available for hotel guests. The residential developer would retain the overall gross density and gain lots with golf frontage. The city would have the opportunity to construct a golf course that provides public recreation, improves the resort hotel's potential viability and taxes, and affords the construction of new city offices.

The city is considering the use of COPs to finance the golf course. It has been determined that up to one-third of the tee times could be allocated to the hotel without violating the spirit of the guidelines for tax-exempt financing.

Lessons Learned

Although this proposal has not yet been consummated, it represents a special example of cooperative participation between the public and private sectors. Each participating party could achieve its primary objectives at virtually no cost.

Source: Economics Research Associates.

- The public agency can secure financing at a lower tax-exempt interest rate while at the same time using the development skills of the private sector.
- The financing terms, including up to five years of capitalized interest, are more flexible than those for conventional financing.
- Through the use of COPs, the public agency is not required to use a competitive bid to select the developer; thus, the developer can justify the time and cost of predevelopment.

Its disadvantages are that:

- The public agency must ultimately assume the project's financial risk with somewhat limited control over its development.
- While the ability of and procedure for a public agency to borrow funds varies from community to community, the use of COPs is beneficial to the extent that the bonds do not count against the public agency's mandated cap on tax-exempt funding.

Each approach to public/private joint ventures has numerous variations.

The key issues for determining which approach is best suited generally include the availability of land, control over development, control over operations, and financing. The primary goal of public/private joint ventures is to mitigate or overcome problems that otherwise might hinder the development of a public golf course. For any joint venture to work, the market must generate sufficient demand for golf, and the public agency must be strongly committed to a golf course.

Dissolving Ownership of a Golf Course

What happens when a golf course no longer is profitable, when the owner or manager decides to leave the business?[10] Three ways are recognized to exit from an "unquoted" investment:

1. *Float the company on the stock exchange.* To date, few "quoted" golf stocks are available, and it is extremely unusual to float a single golf course on the stock exchange. Thus, this exit route is generally unavailable to a golf course investor, or, if it is, the company is not an attractive candidate because it is too small or has limited prospects for growth, or investors have insufficient interest in this sector.

2. *Sell to a "trade buyer"* (someone already in the golf industry). This route is most likely for exiting a golf investment if the course is a "trophy asset" and buyers are ready to bid an economically unjustifiable price. If the course is average, its chances of finding a buyer are even smaller, although some buyers might be interested because the expensive permitting process for new courses has already been completed.

3. *Refinance the company and use the proceeds to repay the initial equity.* Refinancing the company relies on the course's being able to sustain a higher level of debt (that is, new debt used to repay, or buy back, the initial equity). This course of action relies on the financial markets' being open to golf projects, which at the moment they are not. It is always possible that new investors could buy out the original shareholders, but this random process is not worth the effort of, say, preparing an equity prospectus.

A refinement on the third option is to convert a shareholder-owned course into a members-owned course through the issuance of equity-linked debentures. It is a long and expensive process but, if approached properly, could be a good way to exit the initial investment. Complex measures need to be taken during the transitional phase to ensure that the club functions properly, especially in financial terms.

Exiting a golf investment requires careful preparation, often for two years beforehand. The objective is to maximize "exit value," and valuing a golf company has been an inexact science for far too long. Generally, people have used comparable projects to establish value, but this approach is arbitrary and does not stand up to economic scrutiny. The only real way to value a golf company or golf course is to examine its potential for income.

Venture capitalists always buy a business as a multiple of the cash flow produced (that is, net profits before depreciation, interest, and taxes, or

NPBDIT). Each market or country develops its own benchmark of this multiple. In Japan it could be 50, in the United Kingdom more likely 5. The multiple is relevant only when the club has reached "stabilization" and future cash flow therefore is more certain. This investment brings with it, however, little if any growth in earnings, other than inflation.

How do these comments affect the lender? Normally a business is sold "free and clear of debt"—that is, the investor repays the bank out of the proceeds of sales. It is also possible, however, to roll over the debt to the next shareholder, if that shareholder has an equivalent covenant and the bank agrees to transfer the loan.

If the valuation of the course upon exit is below the level of debt in the company (and therefore the shareholders will receive nothing in the sale), it is likely that the company will have already breached its own covenants. In this case, it is likely that the bank will have taken action to protect its interests and, by trying to, maximize the amount it recovers. Experience suggests that the value of a golf course declines rapidly if it is placed in receivership; nevertheless, banks continue to take this line of action. It would be more sensible to try to trade out of the problem rather than to resort to a fire sale. It makes greater economic sense to hire a first-class manager and con-

tinue trading, unless the bank has decided that the situation is irretrievable.

It is common for banks to seek an alternative source of repayment when agreeing to a loan. For golf courses, this approach is problematic, as they are zoned for one purpose only, and converting them back to agricultural use would be counterproductive. The site's planning provisions and whether hidden value exists or the possibility that other development could take place to help repay the debt should be considered. The most obvious uses would be housing or a much broader leisure use, but if these uses were not considered when permits were initially granted, it is unlikely they will be when the project is in distress. Under these circumstances, it might be best to sell the club to its members and spend more time on the 19th hole reflecting on the mysteries of capitalism.

Notes

1. In standard financial analysis to determine net present value, sale of the asset is assumed at a point where projected net operating income reaches a stable level. See the discussion on multiperiod cash flow analysis for further details.

2. In most markets, the greens fee varies by day of the week, time of day, number of holes, and age of golfer. Because of the various special rates and discounts, the average revenue from greens fees per round

of golf usually approximates the rate for 18 holes on a weekday.

3. Many conservative lenders require DCF analysis to use 0 percent inflation, because a high inflation rate can make a project look better than it might actually be.

4. Specific data about the market for golf are available from industry organizations like the National Golf Foundation and the U.S. Golf Association, from trade journals, and from private market research firms.

5. In 1992, one public golf course existed for every 36,000 in population. Generally, the ratio decreases in lower-density or rural areas and increases in urban areas.

6. According to Economics Research Associates, only one-third of the buyers who purchase houses fronting on a golf course in nonretirement residential projects actually play golf regularly.

7. Richard L. Norton, *Golf Course Financing in the 1990s* (Jupiter, Fla.: National Golf Foundation, 1992).

8. Ibid.

9. Ibid.

10. This discussion is courtesy of Brian Terry.

CHAPTER THREE

Land Planning and Design

A "good" real estate development is built on a foundation of sound land planning and design. Real estate development, with or without golf, whether a residential subdivision, office or industrial park, resort, school, or entire new town, must balance the developer's objectives with the site's physical attributes to support proposed development and the socioeconomic needs and objectives of a community or market. How

Mission Hills.

DESMOND MUIRHEAD, INC.

well the elements of a development meet these basic criteria usually determines whether it is a "good" development. Like the development process, the process of planning and design is rarely a straight line from problem to solution. Land planning involves solving a problem: fitting proposed land uses to a site and coordinating those uses with the environment. As such, it is inherently creative and does not lend itself to set formulas or rubber stamps. Many approaches to solving problems of planning and design have evolved over the years, some of which are specific to the type of development problem. All methodologies for land planning and design share the same basic objective, however: to provide a rational means for solving complex problems.

The Process of Planning And Design

Land planning for real estate development, with or without a golf course, is basically the same. When golf is combined with real estate development, however, a complex interrelationship must be addressed. While golf opens many opportunities for real estate development, the conflicts between golf and real estate can just as easily pose serious and costly problems if improperly addressed. The successful integration of a golf course with a real estate development requires careful planning from the earliest possible moment. The knowledge, talent, and expertise of a number of disciplines are required throughout the planning process. Thus, the active involvement of every team member in all areas of the planning process is critical, especially during the early stages of planning. In any team effort, it is essential that every member have a working knowledge of planning and design and a clear understanding of the goals and objectives for the project. Every team member must also acquire a basic understanding of the role and input of other team members, because few, if any, matters in a golf-oriented real estate development function independently and have no impact on other aspects of the project.

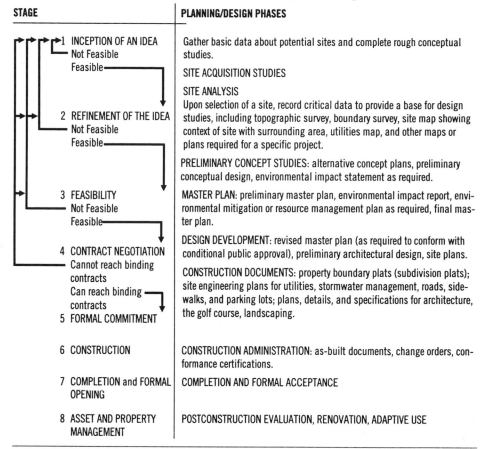

The Eight-Stage Model, Adapted for Planning and Design

STAGE	PLANNING/DESIGN PHASES
1 INCEPTION OF AN IDEA — Not Feasible / Feasible	Gather basic data about potential sites and complete rough conceptual studies. SITE ACQUISITION STUDIES SITE ANALYSIS Upon selection of a site, record critical data to provide a base for design studies, including topographic survey, boundary survey, site map showing context of site with surrounding area, utilities map, and other maps or plans required for a specific project.
2 REFINEMENT OF THE IDEA — Not Feasible / Feasible	PRELIMINARY CONCEPT STUDIES: alternative concept plans, preliminary conceptual design, environmental impact statement as required. MASTER PLAN: preliminary master plan, environmental impact report, environmental mitigation or resource management plan as required, final master plan.
3 FEASIBILITY — Not Feasible / Feasible	DESIGN DEVELOPMENT: revised master plan (as required to conform with conditional public approval), preliminary architectural design, site plans. CONSTRUCTION DOCUMENTS: property boundary plats (subdivision plats); site engineering plans for utilities, stormwater management, roads, sidewalks, and parking lots; plans, details, and specifications for architecture, the golf course, landscaping.
4 CONTRACT NEGOTIATION — Cannot reach binding contracts / Can reach binding contracts 5 FORMAL COMMITMENT	
6 CONSTRUCTION	CONSTRUCTION ADMINISTRATION: as-built documents, change orders, conformance certifications.
7 COMPLETION and FORMAL OPENING	COMPLETION AND FORMAL ACCEPTANCE
8 ASSET AND PROPERTY MANAGEMENT	POSTCONSTRUCTION EVALUATION, RENOVATION, ADAPTIVE USE

Source: Adapted from Mike E. Miles et al., *Real Estate Development Principles and Process* (Washington, D.C.: ULI–the Urban Land Institute, 1991), p.5.

When all team members work in concert, communicating with others, informed decisions can be based on rational criteria. Tight coordination also ensures that neither the golf course nor the real estate side of a project becomes seriously compromised, jeopardizing the entire project.

A great deal of information is exchanged during every phase of planning a project. For example, the on-site reconnaissance team might discover that some physical factor on the site, hydric or nonpercolating soils, for example, precludes its use for development. In that case, the entire design team must swing into action to find alternative solutions to the problem. Solutions might include acquiring additional land, working around or with the soils, or dedicating a portion of the site for permanent open space in exchange for increased density on a portion of the site. Each alternative must be analyzed for its marketability, finan-cial consequences, and technical feasibility so that rational decisions can be made about the development program.

Once the development team establishes a development program, the design team must fit all of the program elements to the site. The development program describes the developer's objectives and market strategies, and details the project's real estate product or products and amenities. For a golf-oriented real estate project, the development program should include:

■ A description of the type of real estate development (commercial, resort, residential, mixed use, for example);

■ A description of the type and quality of amenities to be offered (number of holes, whether private or public, size of the clubhouse, other amenities, such as tennis courts, pools, playgrounds, trails, marinas, or skiing);

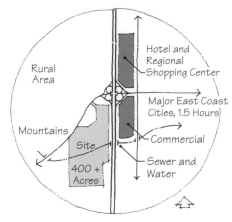

The site context diagram shows the site in relation to surrounding land uses.
Source: Guy L. Rando & Associates Inc.

■ A description of the real estate products to be offered (exclusive, primary residential lots, attached housing, resort or retirement housing, offices, commercial or institutional facilities);

■ A description of the elements and whether they conform with or surpass technical or regulatory guidelines (minimum lot sizes, minimum or maximum lot and building dimensions, road design criteria, utility rights-of-way, public water and sewer service or wells and septic fields, water impounds, and so on).

The development program can be refined or revised many times during the design process as opportunities and problems arise.

Planning and design begins with the analysis of a site for its potential. Typically, design proceeds in phases, facilitating rational decision making from broad issues to design details, and includes:

■ Preliminary conceptual design
■ Master plan
■ Design development
■ Construction documents
■ Construction administration
■ Completion and formal acceptance
■ Postconstruction evaluation, renovation, adaptive use.

Preliminary Conceptual Design

The project's designers translate the development program into preliminary concepts showing various ways that the program elements can be located within the constraints of the

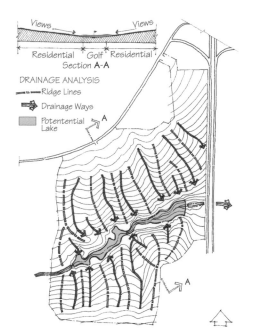

The drainage analysis is one of several physiographic site analyses needed to determine appropriate land uses.
Source: Guy L. Rando & Associates Inc.

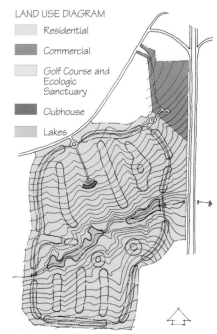

The land use diagram is a diagram of the highest and best land uses based on a synthesis of site analyses.
Source: Guy L. Rando & Associates Inc.

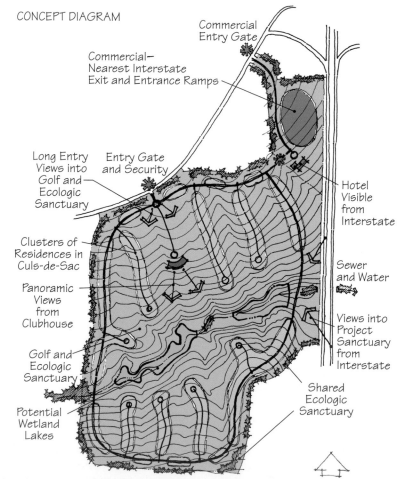

The preliminary concept diagram is one of several alternatives generated to find the best fit between the development program and a site's opportunities and constraints.
Source: Guy L. Rando & Associates Inc.

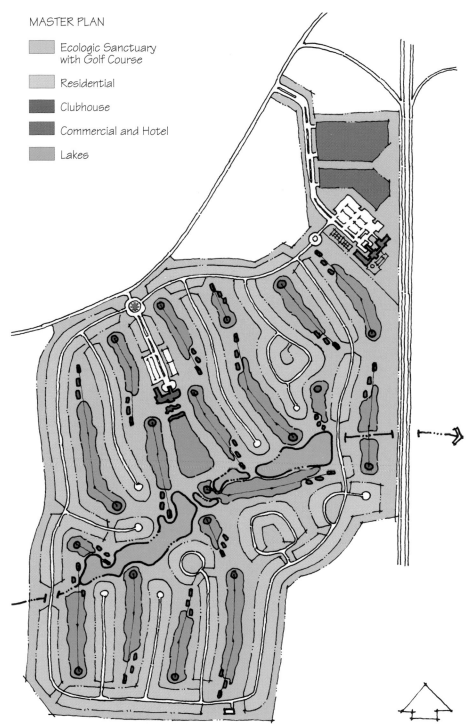

MASTER PLAN

- Ecologic Sanctuary with Golf Course
- Residential
- Clubhouse
- Commercial and Hotel
- Lakes

The master plan is one of several documents that might be required to gain public approval for a proposed project.
Source: Guy L. Rando & Associates Inc.

nary concepts for real estate development are expressed in alternative concept plans that show how development infrastructure and lots or sites can be placed within a site's physical limits. Preliminary design studies for a golf-oriented real estate development delineate alternative golf corridors showing routing plans for the golf course, site concepts for the clubhouse, the maintenance building and service area, other golf buildings, and parking and circulation schemes. Land planning for the real estate and for the golf course should occur simultaneously. A common error in planning a golf-oriented real estate development is to treat the golf course as an afterthought—a way of using "undevelopable" land—or to set aside what appears to be enough land for a golf course without considering its relationship with the real estate, hoping that the golf course architect can make it successful. A common error on the opposite side of the coin occurs when the golf course is designed with little or no regard for the associated real estate development.

The alternative concept plans serve as a basis for preliminary calculations of cost and value and determine areas where rough clearing and grading are needed. (Specific design strategies for golf-oriented real estate developments are discussed in detail later in this chapter.)

Master Plan

The process of design further refines the best features of the preliminary concepts into a master plan. Establishing a working relationship with representatives of regulatory agencies often is advantageous during this phase. When an environmentally sensitive site is involved or an appeal for a zoning variance anticipated, involving key agency personnel in informal reviews of a preliminary master plan includes their input to the team. Concurrent with master planning, preliminary cost estimates are prepared to guide financing and construction phasing.

Comments and input from the review of the preliminary master plan are then incorporated into a final master plan, typically the principal docu-

site. The accompanying examples, from preliminary design studies for a 400+-acre golf-oriented primary residential real estate development in the mid-Atlantic region, can be used to find the best solution for a particular project. These *alternative concept plans* provide a graphic tool that aids in visualizing the project and analyzing the resulting consequences of each

alternative for marketability, financial feasibility, and technical problems.

For a golf-oriented real estate development, the land planner and golf course architect must work together to establish the "golf corridor"—the land area where the golf course will be located—in coordination with roads, stormwater systems, utilities, and objectives for the real estate. Prelimi-

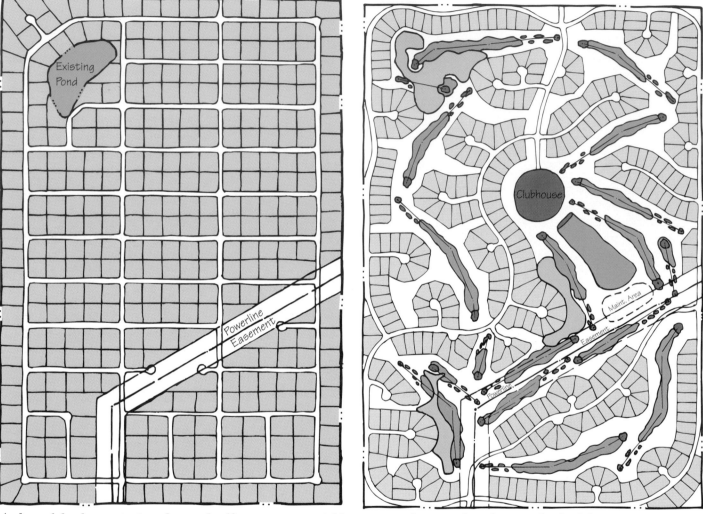

Standard Subdivision Plan comprising 345 single-family lots of at least 40,000 square feet

Single-Family Lots	324.2 acres	(345 lots)
Powerline Easement	25.3 acres	
Existing Pond	7.4 acres	
Miscellaneous Open Space	4.7 acres	
Roads (9.3 miles)	56.2 acres	
	417.8 acres	

Open Space Plan. Reducing the minimum lot up to 50 percent and designating balance in permanent open space yields the same number of residential lots but 15 times more space available for a golf course, lakes, and additional open space.

Single-Family Lots	168.6 acres	(345 lots)
Golf Course, Lakes*	164.1 acres	
Miscellaneous Open Space*	34.1 acres	
Roads (8.4 miles)	51.0 acres	
	417.8 acres	

*Includes powerline easement.

A planned development oriented toward golf or open spaces yields greater real estate values than standard subdivisions.
Source: Walter Stewart/Desmond Muirhead, Inc.

ment that is submitted to regulatory agencies to obtain the necessary approvals and permits. If the project receives the necessary permits, the final master plan is modified to accommodate any conditions that might be placed on the permit. It might also be used to obtain financing and to market the project.

Design Development

After development of the final master plan, the process moves to design development of both the golf course and the real estate. The design program is further refined and detailed in coordination with strategies for phasing and marketing the project. Alternative design details are prepared concurrently with detailed cost estimates.

Construction Documents

Design of the golf course proceeds with refining the course's layout, staking the course in the field, and detailing the course's features and other construction documents that specify how the course will be constructed. Real estate development proceeds with site planning and detailing for construction of the development's features (including roads, layout of lots, utilities, walks, and streetscapes) as well as architectural and engineering drawings for buildings.

Construction Administration

Inevitable changes to the design of the golf course in the field could require adjustments to the boundaries or elements of the surrounding real estate development—or vice versa. Design of both elements must therefore be closely coordinated throughout design and construction. Design professionals

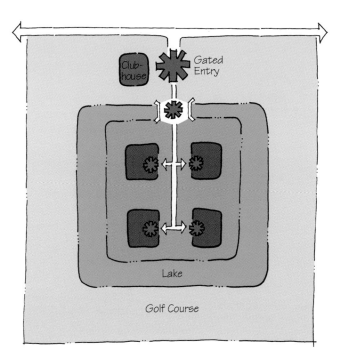

 Controlled Entry

 Clubhouse

High-rise Condominiums

Controlling points of entry and exit to a residential development is important for residents' security. Desert Island was planned for maximum security, with a single entry/exit and two consecutive control points.
Source: Desmond Muirhead, Inc.

Top: The approach drive to Boca Raton Resort & Club creates a strong image for this world-class, five-star destination resort and conference center.

Bottom: Entry drive at Boca Raton Resort & Club.

play a key role in administration, not only to ensure compliance with plans and specifications but also to resolve problems that arise in the field. Design professionals are often involved in preparing change orders and preparing as-built drawings.

Completion and Formal Acceptance

Design professionals are usually responsible for monitoring, verifying, and reporting on construction in progress to the developer or the project manager and for providing a report indicating when a project or phase of a project is complete according to specifications. The developer uses that report to help determine whether the work is acceptable. Most contracts require the developer's formal written acceptance before final payment is released to the contractor.

Postconstruction Evaluation/ Renovation/Adaptive Use

Because real estate development has a relatively long life, adjustments resulting from changes in the market, economic conditions, or regulatory requirements are common. Design professionals continue to play an important role through ongoing evaluations of the project and recommended revisions that will maintain or increase a project's value over its lifetime.

Integrating Golf and Real Estate

Coordination between land planning and design of the course is critical from the earliest stages of the development process to ensure:

■ The most efficient and effective use of land;

■ The maximum real estate value and marketing advantages for the development;

■ Maximum flexibility for development phasing to balance costs with revenue;

■ The maximum use of dual functions for the golf course.

Basic principles of land planning are universally applicable, whether or not a golf course is involved:

■ Controlling the point of entry and exit;

■ Establishing a sense of arrival, orientation, destination, security, and image at the entry;

■ Establishing an easily perceived, understandable, safe, and cost-efficient circulation system for the movement of automobiles, pedestrians, service and support traffic, mass transit systems, joggers, bikers, and equestrians;

■ Maximizing views and other opportunities to enhance real estate values;

39

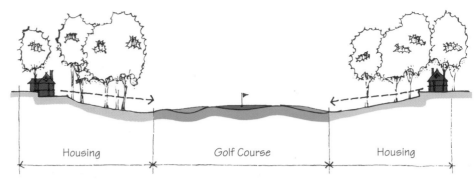

Ideal use of topography for views of the golf course.
Source: Desmond Muirhead, Inc.

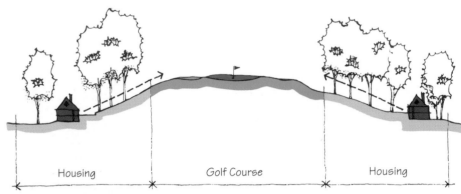

Unsatisfactory use of topography for views of the golf course.
Source: Desmond Muirhead, Inc.

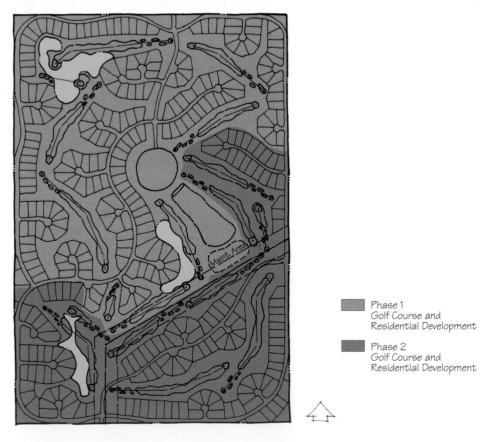

Phase 1
Golf Course and
Residential Development

Phase 2
Golf Course and
Residential Development

The initial nine holes can be constructed and put into play and real estate sales initiated while the second nine holes are under construction.
Source: Desmond Muirhead, Inc.

- Maximizing the use of solar orientation and microclimatic conditions within the site to increase energy efficiency and humans' comfort;
- Maximizing the cost-efficiency of construction by working with rather than against the topography and other physical features;
- Maximizing flexibility for phased development;
- Maximizing the cost-efficiency of infrastructure like utilities and roads;
- Creating a strong sense of community and desirable lifestyle.

The three-tier hierarchy of streets that was pioneered in the new town of Radburn, New Jersey, in the 1920s has proven that hierarchical systems can substantially lower the cost of development infrastructure. Radburn established its hierarchy of streets using the following classifications:

- Arterials (to connect major subdivisions) were 48 to 72 feet wide, in a 100-foot right-of-way;
- Collectors (to carry traffic from arterial streets to minor streets, with no direct access) were 36 to 44 feet wide, in a 60- to 70-foot right-of-way;
- Minor streets (to connect individual units or clusters in low-intensity use, often including loops and culs-de-sac) were 28 to 30 feet wide, in a 50- to 60-foot right-of way.

A hierarchical road system is preferable for a golf-oriented development for several reasons. The branching pattern of a hierarchical system is more cost-efficient, as the length of the road and utilities is less than with other patterns of distribution. Conflicts between automobiles, pedestrians, and other types of transit, including golf cars, can be minimized. Keeping roads to a minimum through the golf corridor is critical; in particular, routing a major collector or arterial road through a golf course should be avoided at all costs and, whenever possible, conflicts between golf and nongolf traffic kept to a minimum. Similarly, nongolfing pedestrians should be restricted from the course for reasons of safety.

The hierarchical system also encourages a greater sense of community, as traffic is kept to a minimum on minor

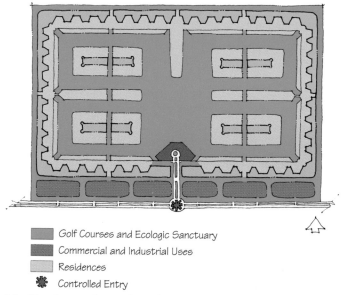

Golf Courses and Ecologic Sanctuary
Commercial and Industrial Uses
Residences
Controlled Entry

Ideal land use relationships for a mixed-use, golf-oriented planned community.
Source: Guy L. Rando & Associates Inc.

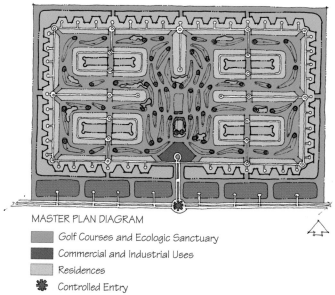

MASTER PLAN DIAGRAM

Golf Courses and Ecologic Sanctuary
Commercial and Industrial Uses
Residences
Controlled Entry

Master plan for an "ideal" mixed-use, golf-oriented planned community.
Source: Guy L. Rando & Associates Inc.

streets. This factor is particularly important in a residential development. Units oriented toward quiet culs-de-sac or cluster loops are generally more conducive to social interaction than units oriented toward high-volume collector roads or arterials.

Most jurisdictions' street classification systems have specific standards and requirements for pavement and right-of-way widths, maximum speeds, minimum sight distances, minimum distances between intersections, maximum lengths of culs-de-sac,

and so on. The land planner or landscape architect must keep these standards in mind during the early phases of design, and input from a traffic engineer might be required, particularly for larger and more complex projects involving major road improvements.

Golf-oriented real estate development entails additional principles of land planning:

- Siting the real estate development in areas of the site with the fewest constraints for that use and the golf course to maximize frontage and views, thus increasing marketability and land value, usually results in routing the golf course along the valleys or lower elevations of the site so that the residential units can overlook the course. The single-fairway, returning-nines configuration (discussed later in this chapter) is often preferable because it provides maximum frontage and views while retaining flexibility in operations.

- Siting the golf course so that potential buyers can see it might include routing parts of the course or locating water features so they are visible from the project's entrance, access roads, and/or primary entrance roads.

- The clubhouse can serve as a major point of orientation, particularly when golf is the major feature of the marketing program. To take ad-

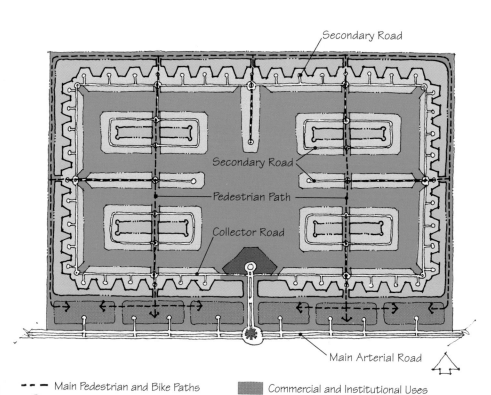

Secondary Road
Secondary Road
Pedestrian Path
Collector Road
Main Arterial Road

- - - Main Pedestrian and Bike Paths
Controlled Entry
Golf Courses and Ecologic Sanctuary
Commercial and Institutional Uses
Residential Use

Hierarchical road systems minimize conflicts between golf and nongolf circulation.
Source: Guy L. Rando & Associates Inc.

Prominent siting and tower of the Cap Rock Clubhouse at Horseshoe Bay Resort and Conference Club provide an orienting landmark.

and reducing peak water demand for irrigation of the golf course.

- Conserving resources like wetlands, endangered or sensitive species, and their habitats as integral parts of the golf course enhances the ecologic value of the golf course and the value of real estate development fronting on open space.

Optimizing the Value of Real Estate

For any real estate development, the value of a unit of real estate, whether a lot for a house or a room at a resort hotel, largely depends on physical and visual accessibility to desirable features. People generally prefer property with views of dramatic landscapes or water. Lots that adjoin open space always sell at a premium. Waterfront property and direct access to or frontage on the rolling expanses of lush, green turf of golf courses enjoy even higher premiums. Easy access to open space or the golf course increases value and commands a premium.

Higher returns can usually be achieved by placing higher densities next to focal features. If the focal feature is a golf course, however, placing high-density units on the course must be done sensitively to minimize the intrusion of development on the golf

vantage of the golf facilities' potential for marketing, the clubhouse should be located in a fairly central site on the project. Clear physical and visual clues should help orient and guide people from the project's entrance to the clubhouse.

- The golf course can serve dual purposes that are advantageous for the golf operation and for the real estate development:

- The golf course can be used to meet open space requirements of regulatory agencies while providing a revenue-producing recreational amenity.
- Stormwater management for the real estate development can be incorporated with the aesthetic use of water features on the golf course, providing water quality control through biologic filtering

Prime real estate frontage on Slick Rock #14 at Horseshoe Bay Resort and Conference Club.

course. Buildings must be set back from the golf course for safety, and the larger or taller the building, the greater the setback from the course.

The two most important factors to remember in integrating housing and golf are to minimize road crossings and to create villages that are well related to the golf facility.

Strategies for Designing Lots

The size and shape of lots determine density and type of real estate unit that can be built. Most jurisdictions have established minimum requirements for lots or yards for various types of residential development. For

Golf Real Estate Premiums

Unit	Base Price	Added Premium (Percent of Base Price)	Total Price[1]
Base Interior Lot (1/3 acre)	$25,000	$0 (0)	$25,000
Lot with Golf View	$25,000	$12,500 (50)	$37,500
Lot With Water View	$25,000	$20,000 (80)	$45,000
Lot Fronting Golf Fairway	$25,000	$50,000 (200)	$75,000
Premium Golf Frontage (Fronting tees, greens, or along view)	$25,000	$55,000 (220)	$80,000
Lake Frontage	$25,000	$75,000 (300)	$100,000
Golf and Lake Frontage	$25,000	$87,500 (350)	$112,500

[1]Excluding variable lot sizes and housing model, and market strategy and project phasing.
Note: This analysis of real estate premiums is for a specific project, a primary residential development in the mid-Atlantic region of the United States that includes an 18-hole regulation golf course. Local market factors and the specific site must always be considered in pricing real estate products.
Source: Guy L. Rando & Associates Inc.

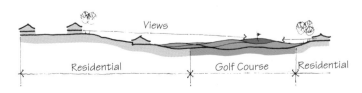

Frontage on or views of a golf course or water enhance real estate values, shown here at Horseshoe Bay Resort and Conference Club.

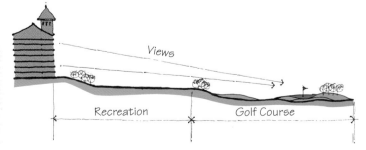

Views of the golf course from a high-rise building.
Source: EDAW, Inc./Christopher Degenhardt, FASLA.

Views of the golf course from low-rise buildings.
Source: EDAW, Inc./Christopher Degenhardt, FASLA.

Buildings should be set back to avoid too much intrusion on the golf course. Tall buildings and high rises should be well set back.
Source: EDAW, Inc./Christopher Degenhardt, FASLA.

a single-family residential development, lot configurations (beyond regulatory requirements) are directly associated with the type of housing that can be built (whether the garage entrance is located to the rear, side, or front of the house, for example). The appearance of a housing subdivision from the street can affect the marketing of the units, and subtle differences in lot widths or building setbacks can make a significant difference in the value the consumer perceives.

Whatever the type of development, general strategies for planning lots should achieve several goals:

- Sufficient buildable area should be allowed for the type of building unit anticipated, so that excessive grading or unusually deep foundations are not required.
- Sufficient usable area for outdoor activity should be available.
- Positive surface drainage away from the building should be adequate.
- Grading lots should be kept to a minimum.
- Specimen trees should be retained.
- Corner lots should be wider than interior lots to permit adequate side yards and setbacks. (Some jurisdictions treat corner lots as two "front" yards, thus requiring larger setbacks than an interior lot.)
- Lots should be reached from minor streets rather than collector or arterial streets.

Many configurations for lots have been developed to increase the number of possible lots and to maximize opportunities for frontage, particularly for residential or resort developments where land prices have escalated. Among some of the more innovative concepts are zero-lot-line or patio homes and Z-lots. Developers must gain the acceptance of both public agencies and consumers when considering these alternatives and pay careful attention to detail in architecture and the streetscape.

The relationship of interior and exterior spaces of the housing units with the golf course is critical. Views from the golf course must be considered with as much care as views of the housing units from the street. Real estate fronting a golf course has two fronts: one facing the street and one facing the golf course. The configuration of lots should consider opportunities to site units to take advantage of the best views to the golf course.

Alternative Configurations For the Golf Corridor

A number of configurations for the layout of a golf course are possible, regardless of variations in design: core course; double fairway, continuous; double fairway, returning nines; single fairway, continuous; and single fairway, returning nines. These basic configurations have been developed primarily to accommodate more efficient operations, and they can be manipulated to fit the course within the boundaries and topography of the site. Often, characteristics of the site or objectives for design for the golf course or the real estate development dictate a combination of configurations. It is not unusual to have a single fairway in some areas and a double fairway in others.

Opportunities for Frontage

For most real estate development projects, a regulation course in a single-fairway, returning nines layout is pre-

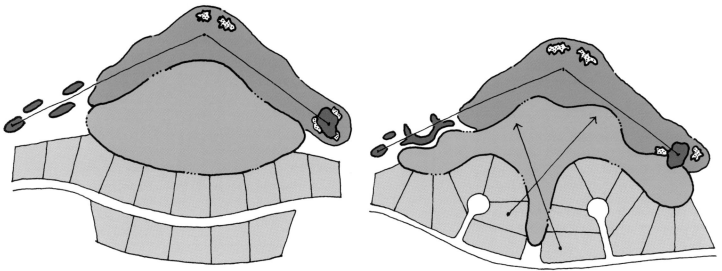

The configuration for the golf hole, lake, and building lots on the left means that only ten of the 15 lots front on the lake or the golf course. The irregular shape of the lake on the right provides long water views from the golf course and lots, as well as the illusion of a larger lake. Clustering lots permits golf and lake views from all lots. In a golf-oriented real estate development, the layout of the course significantly affects potential land values.
Source: Desmond Muirhead, Inc.

Possible Configurations for the Golf Corridor*

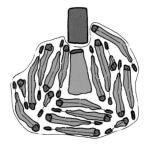

Core golf course: 18 holes. Approximate acreage: 140. Length of lot frontage: ± 10,000 feet.

CORE COURSE

Description: The core course is characterized by clustering the holes together so that the course is an element unto itself. The holes can be arranged in a continuous sequence, with one starting hole and one finishing hole at the clubhouse, or in returning nines, with two starting holes and two finishing holes at the clubhouse.

Advantages: This layout requires the least amount of land, as the periphery of the course is kept to a minimum and much of the safety buffer between the edge of the fairway and the property line is eliminated. This type of course is highly efficient to operate because the holes are closer together, increasing the speed of play and reducing mainte-

nance. The core course also provides the greatest perception of the golf course as an integral open space, as it is uncompromised by real estate development within the course. It is the most popular type of course with golfers.

Disadvantages: The major disadvantage of this configuration is that it results in the minimum amount of golf frontage for development. If the holes are arranged in a continuous sequence (one starting hole), flexible operation is compromised.

Types of Operations: This configuration is best suited for projects where real estate frontage is not an issue, such as a municipal daily-fee course. It is also well suited for projects that will be surrounded by high-density development like high-rise condominiums or offices where the integrity of the open space is important.

Topography: The core course is most adaptable to flat or near flat sites or to bowl-like topography where housing would be located on the steep hillside surrounding the "bowl."

Frontage: Minimum opportunities for frontage.

Double fairway, continuous: 18 holes. Approximate acreage: 150. Length of lot frontage: ± 25,000 feet.

DOUBLE FAIRWAY, CONTINUOUS

Description: This type of layout is characterized by a continuous single loop of adjacent parallel fairways, with one hole starting at the clubhouse and one finishing hole returning to the clubhouse.

Advantages: This configuration might allow some savings in land compared to a single-fairway layout, and it allows a slight reduction in maintenance compared to a single-fairway layout, as the tees and greens are adjacent to each other.

Disadvantages: The single starting hole for an 18-hole course greatly reduces flexibility in operating this type of course. Compared with single-fairway configurations, less

frontage is available for development. And players stand a greater chance of being hit by a golf ball.

Types of Operations: This configuration can be adapted for most types of golf operations. It is least suited to municipal or daily-fee operations.

Topography: This layout is most adaptable for sites with long, narrow valleys or land with potential for development on either side of the golf course.

Frontage: The potential for frontage is fair; it is more suited to medium- to higher-density development where the double-fairway width provides more open space between units or where topography permits good views.

*Diagrams assume a flat, featureless site.

Double fairway, returning nines: 18 holes. Approximate acreage: 150. Length of lot frontage: ± 24,200 feet.

DOUBLE FAIRWAY, RETURNING NINES

Description: This type of layout is characterized by two circuits of nine holes each with adjacent parallel fairways.

Advantages: This configuration allows some savings in land compared to a single-fairway layout. It also requires less maintenance compared to a single-fairway layout, as the tees and greens are closer to each other. With the first and tenth holes at the clubhouse, players can start playing both nines at the same time.

Disadvantages: This configuration allows fewer opportunities for golf frontage than single-fairway configurations.

Types of Operations: It is adaptable for most types of golf operations.

Topography: This layout is most suitable for sites with long, narrow valleys with the potential for development on either side of the golf course.

Frontage: The potential for frontage is fair. It is more suited to medium- to higher-density development where the double-fairway width provides more open space between units or where topography permits good views.

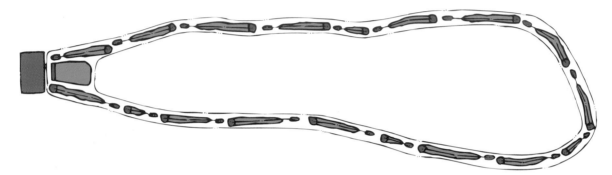

Single fairway, continuous: 18 holes. Approximate acreage: 175. Length of lot frontage: ± 46,800 feet.

SINGLE FAIRWAY, CONTINUOUS

Description: This type of layout is characterized by a single, open loop starting from the clubhouse and returning to the clubhouse.

Advantages: This layout has the greatest flexibility for adaptability to an existing site, as the course has a limited number of fixed elements: a clubhouse, a starting hole, and a finishing hole.

Disadvantages: Of the five basic layouts, this configuration requires the most land, as the holes are stretched out without doubling up to the clubhouse area. Because it offers only one starting hole, flexibility of play is greatly reduced. The number of players that can be accommodated on any given day is reduced, as, with only one starting hole, it can take up to four hours to put the entire course into play. This layout also

presents problems for golfers who want to play only nine holes, because the ninth green is some distance from the clubhouse. Further, the odds of balls' going out of bounds is greater, as the single fairway has out-of-bounds areas on both sides, slowing play physically and psychologically for some players. Maintenance costs for this type of layout could be higher, because the greens and tees are spread out.

Types of Operations: While this configuration can be adapted to any type of operation, it is least suited for municipal or daily-fee courses.

Topography: This configuration is highly adaptable to topography and site conditions.

Frontage: Of the five configurations, this one provides the maximum golf frontage for real estate development, but this fact does not make up for the layout's disadvantages. It is used only as a last resort.

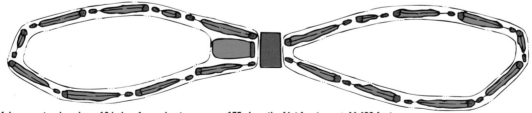

Single fairway, returning nines: 18 holes. Approximate acreage: 175. Length of lot frontage: ± 44,400 feet.

SINGLE FAIRWAY, RETURNING NINES

Description: This layout is characterized by two open loops of returning nines, with the clubhouse in the center.

Advantages: This layout has greater potential for frontage than all the configurations, except the single fairway, continuous. It greatly increases flexibility and efficiency in operation by providing two starting holes. Thus, more players can begin a game, and the entire course can be brought into play in two hours, compared to four hours in a continuous layout with only one starting hole. Further, this layout allows for the option of playing only nine holes.

Disadvantages: Maintenance requirements and costs are higher than for a core course or double fairway, as the greens and tees are spread out.

Types of Operations: This configuration is ideal for any course associated with real estate development.

Topography: It is adaptable for most types of topography.

Frontage: This layout is a close second to the single, continuous fairway in terms of amount of golf frontage for real estate development and amount of land required. The shorter frontage results from bringing the holes back to the clubhouse in two returning loops and the concentration of greens and tees in the clubhouse area.

Source: Guy L. Rando & Associates Inc.

The view from the third floor of the Princess Hotel in Scottsdale, Arizona, illustrates the course's visual access.

Prime Golf and
Water Frontage

Golf Fairway
Frontage

Open Space
Golf Access

Interior Lot

A typical diagram used for analyzing real estate premiums.
Source: Desmond Muirhead, Inc.

ferred. This combination provides the preferred length for the golf course with moderate flexibility in operations and maintenance and maximum golf frontage for real estate development.

Land use plans that are designed merely to maximize golf frontage do not necessarily maximize overall real estate values. A number of other factors must be considered when integrating golf and real estate. The single-fairway, returning nines configuration for an 18-hole golf course is ideal for maximizing golf frontage and therefore maximizing the opportunity to enhance real estate values. In some cases—a hotel resort or high-density development, for example—where real estate values are enhanced by views of the golf course from a high-rise building rather than actual frontage, a core course might provide greater advantages.

Whatever strategy is used to place a value on golf-oriented real estate, valuation must consider local market factors. Comparative marketability studies can aid in determining real estate values and which pricing strategies yield the best results in a particular location.

Safety in the Golf Corridor

One of the most significant factors to consider in delineating the golf corridor is safety. Like many sports, golf is not inherently safe. A well-hit golf ball can reach an initial velocity of 250 feet per second or over 170 miles per hour, and a range of 250 yards or more. The golf ball thus has the potential for greater speed and range than a bullet from a shotgun, and the potential for injury can be considerable. This factor is augmented by the wide range of physical and psychological variables inherent in any golf course and the range of players' abilities. Golf is not easily mastered, and even the most accomplished players can hit a ball poorly. People have been seriously, even fatally, injured by errant golf balls, golf clubs, and golf cars. Being on a golf course during an electrical storm has resulted in many players' being struck by lightning. And the threats are not confined to golfers: pedestri-

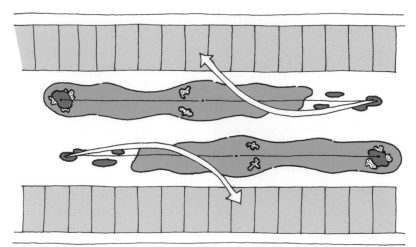

This relationship between fairway and lot should be avoided, because most golfers are right-handed and tend to slice the ball to the right.
Source: Desmond Muirhead, Inc.

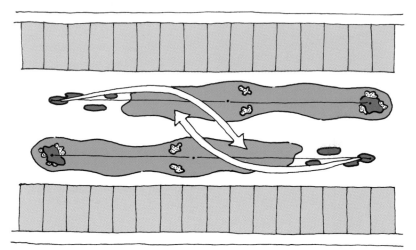

The preferred relationship between fairway and lot allows holes to "slice" into each other rather than into houses.
Source: Desmond Muirhead, Inc.

ans and motorists walking or driving by a course have been struck by errant golf balls. Golf, like life, is a challenge with risks. Thus, safety is a critical concern to anyone involved in the design, development, construction, maintenance, and operation of a golf course, or to anyone charged with responsibility for the safety of people on or near the course, or to anyone who could be injured or suffer damages from golf.

To design a totally risk-free, "safe" golf course is impossible, because numerous factors simply are beyond the control of the designer: the climate, the weather, the ability and skill of individual players. Even if a list of safety criteria could be determined for the design of a totally "safe" golf course, the cost of building such a course would be prohibitive. It is possible, however, to anticipate a few factors

that can present an undue hazard. And it is possible to find economically feasible ways to mitigate the danger.

No hard and fast rules can be associated with safety in golf course design simply because the range of variables from course to course, hole to hole, and even player to player is so vast. The increasing integration of golf courses with adjacent real estate results in conflicts in land use, and safety becomes a greater concern. Today, all areas of the golf course industry, including owners, developers, design professionals, operations and maintenance personnel, managers, material suppliers, equipment manufacturers, and individual players, must address it. Further, technical advances in the design of golf balls and golf clubs have translated into greater speed and distances, with the atten-

dant greater potential for danger from poorly hit balls or slices, hooks, and shanks. All of these factors have influenced the way golf courses are designed today, and a prudent developer would keep the following points in mind:

- *Recognize and understand that land planning and the design of golf courses are intricately related to each other.* The potential impact of one on the other can significantly enhance or diminish the value of a golf-oriented real estate development.
- *The developer or its agent is involved as a key member in planning and design.* The integration of various disciplines is ultimately the developer's responsibility.
- *Regular safety reviews are part of the planning process.* Additional reviews are required after any major change. Safety reviews should be made part of standard operating procedures, and they should involve all members of the design team.
- *Recognize that safety is ongoing.* Include allowances for fine-tuning play of the course in the budget to address any unanticipated issues after the course is put into play.

"Golf course safety" is a relative term, requiring judgment based on some mutually agreed criteria. The following brief overview summarizes a few basic, common-sense criteria for safety in designing golf courses.[1] The design standards developed from these criteria or from the consensus of experienced designers and developers serve only as *guidelines* and must be weighed case by case for specific sites.

- Golfers must use *reasonable care* commensurate with the known hazards inherent in the game.[2]
- Golfers assume *reasonable risk.*[3]
- The design of the golf course should reflect standards that do not expose golfers to undue risk.[4]
- The public has a right to free and unmolested use of the highways. Golf balls landing on or across a highway render the owner liable for maintaining a public nuisance that resulted in injuries from the hazardous condition.[5]
- A golf ball in flight beyond the perimeter of the golf course is the same as

an object falling from a structure, and the liability is comparable.[6]

- A pivotal standard cited in many court cases renders a liability *if the possibility of an accident was clear to the ordinarily prudent eye.*[7]
- Golf-related restrictions on adjacent private property are justifiable for reasons of safety. It is therefore reasonable to restrict the use of private property (building setback lines and so on) adjacent to a golf course.
- Owners of houses and other real estate fronting a golf course assume more risk than the public on a highway but less risk than golfers. The homeowner's uninformed and unsuspecting guests are not included, however.
- Spectators at a golf tournament assume more risk than homeowners but less risk than golfers.

Legal terms like "reasonable care," "reasonable" or "undue" risk, "foreseeable" hazards, and "ordinarily prudent eye" provide criteria for defining and judging safety and for allocating liability. Beyond these legal concepts, however, no measurable design standards can be applied in a blanket formula that satisfies legally defined criteria for safety.

The standard 300-foot through-the-green width that became a rule of thumb in design of a single-fairway layout during the 1960s and 1970s is seriously outdated in terms of current safety concerns. It was rationalized by two concepts:

- The average golfer who hit a ball poorly (did not follow the ideal path as reflected by the centerline) did not hit the ball as forcefully as possible; therefore, the ball would not travel as fast and as far as it might.
- The farther away from the centerline, the less force powering the ball, and therefore the ball will travel even less distance.

In the double-fairway layout, the rule of thumb was that, where possible, the parallel centerlines should be no fewer than 200 feet apart. These dimensional standards are now outdated, however, with the advent of new technology and new designs for golf equipment (particularly golf clubs) to gain

more distance and the desire of many golfers to "smack the ball" as far as they can without regard for safety.

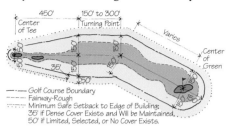

Outdated 1970s single-fairway standards.
Courtesy: Patrick Shane Mulligan.

The standards of the 1960s and 1970s were coupled with caveats to consider such factors as topography, vegetation, elevation, temperature, humidity, wind, location of hazards, and elevated features like tees and greens. They are still critical, but *safety is not a cookie-cutter process.* Defining parameters for safety on a golf course could be a major issue confronting today's golf course developers, and any member of the team could make a decision that would directly affect safety. Golf integrated with real estate development requires the establishment of a team to review every stage of planning and design. The temptation to encroach on the safety perimeter for the golf course to gain frontage for real estate, enhance real estate values, or economize on the golf course is always considerable, and it is heightened by the fact that contemporary golf courses require substantially larger areas of land to accommodate safety in an age of high-tech equipment. Golf course architects and land planners must work with the development team to resolve the problems involved in siting a golf course next to real estate. The professional expertise, knowledge, and experience of every member of the design team must be applied toward ensuring that the public is not exposed to undue risk. In a society prone to litigation, it is in the best interests of any development project to establish the best standards and criteria for safety. Because design and construction often span long periods of time, the intent of the design and safety considerations developed during the planning process should be carefully documented to ensure that it is not compromised by later decisions.

The Safety Perimeter

Defining the safety corridor for a golf course is not necessarily synonymous with establishing the boundary of the golf course, although the two can be related. The following definitions are used in this text. The *golf course boundary* is the legal description of the property boundary for that area of land dedicated to the golf course and its facilities. If the operation were to be sold, this legal description would be used to describe the property in the sales documents. The *golf course safety corridor* is that area of land required to play the game plus the area of land that can be affected or threatened by golfing such that limits are placed on the use of that area. For example, the golf course safety corridor might include the area within the golf course boundary plus an area around that boundary where construction of any buildings is restricted (often called a building setback line or building restriction line). The restrictions on use within the setback area must be clearly stated in legal documents (covenants, for example) describing the affected properties.

Largely because of legal implications, professionals and their attendant organizations have been reluctant to adopt any specific written criteria for golf course safety corridors. The official approach of the American Society of Golf Course Architects (ASGCA) is verbal and very general, and strongly emphasizes site-specific criteria. The prudent course of action is to contract with an experienced, reputable golf course architect early during the planning process.

The following dimensions for the golf course safety corridor are provided solely to illustrate this discussion; *they are not to be applied arbitrarily.* The dimensions are based on an unrestricted flat site, and they must be adjusted to accommodate site-specific features like topography, vegetation, and elevation. Applicable local building and land use regulations could preclude the use of any dimension used in the illustrations, and this information is not a substitute for consultation

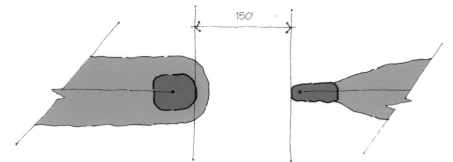

Minimum clearance between the green and the next tee.

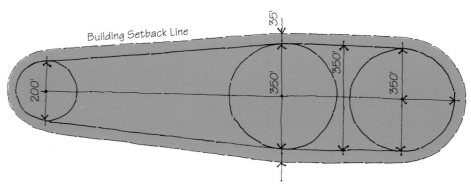

Minimum clearance between adjacent tees and greens.

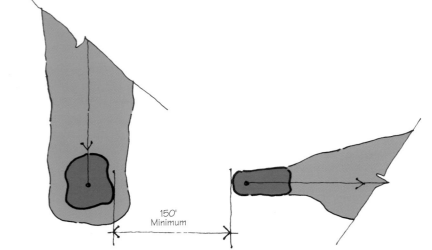

Minimum dimensions for a single-fairway golf corridor.

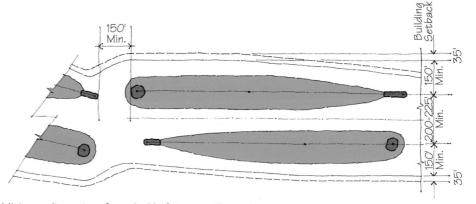

Minimum dimensions for a double-fairway golf corridor.

Minimum safety guidelines for a windless site on flat topography. Other conditions require additional clearances.

Source: Nicklaus Design.

50

with a qualified, experienced golf course architect.

- Minimum horizontal clearance between the green and the next tee is 150 feet. If the adjacent green and tees are separated by a change in elevation, the distance might be greater or less.
- Minimum clearance between adjacent tees and greens is 150 feet.
- Adjacent landing areas should be no less than 200 to 250 feet apart (from centerline to centerline).
- The centerline of a golf hole should be no less than 150 feet from any road right-of-way or boundary.
- The centerline of a golf hole should be no less than 175 feet from any boundary with adjacent development. A setback of no less than 35 feet from the boundary line should also be added.
- The minimum safety corridor for a single-fairway course with development on both sides of the fairway is 420 feet between any building in the landing and greens areas. The minimum safety corridor for a course with surrounding development in other than the landing and greens areas is 370 feet, which allows for a 300-foot corridor with 35-foot building setbacks on either side.
- On a double-fairway course, the centerlines of parallel fairways should be no less than 200 to 225 feet apart in wooded areas (where vegetation is present between the fairways) and no less than 250 feet apart in open areas (no buffering vegetation between fairways). Adding a minimum of 150 feet from each centerline to the property line yields a minimum corridor of 500 to 550 feet for a double-fairway course. If the course is surrounded by development, a building setback of 35 feet from the property line on either side yields a total minimum safety corridor of 570 to 620 feet. The safety corridor can be narrower in the area between the green and the next tee—approximately 400 feet (a 100-foot buffer off the center point of the tee, a 150-foot minimum on the green's centerline, and 150 feet between the green and the next tee).[8]

Safety on the Golf Course

The responsibility of a golfer for the safety of others, such as shouting "Fore!" to warn that a ball is approaching, is defined by rules of etiquette and enforced by golf associations. These rules and responsibilities should be posted in a readily visible location on the golf course. Handbooks specifically addressing rules and responsibilities should also be made available to every golfer and key points printed directly on scorecards. Designing a safe golf course includes not only concern for the safety of players, but also for guests, maintenance personnel, and spectators. Many design guidelines involve common sense:

- Blind shots should be avoided, and holes should be designed so that players can clearly see the target area, hazards, and other players on the course. While several mitigating measures to reduce the risk of blind shots have been developed—special flags, caddies as target indicators, and even traffic lights—they are at best only mitigating measures.
- Shelters should be provided at key locations on the course for golfers seeking safe shelter from inclement weather, particularly lightning storms.
- Specific safety guidelines and procedures regarding lightning storms should be readily visible to every golfer, employee, or visitor.
- Circulation patterns should be readily apparent and organized to minimize conflicts between autos and pedestrians, golf cars and pedestrians, maintenance vehicles or equipment and golfers, and golfers and nongolfers, for example. A golf course, for example, is not a safe or appropriate place for a nature walk while play is in progress. Security measures should be in place to prevent intentional or unintentional trespassing on the golf course by nongolfers while play is in progress.
- Paths for golf cars should be specifically engineered as *roads* for vehicular traffic, not sidewalks, but the fact that the path is often a hard surface (usually asphalt or concrete) should be given due consideration when locating it. Such paths are potentially dangerous if a ball bounces or ricochets off the pavement, and for this reason it is inadvisable to have the car path cross the fairway. The path should be out of the area of play (see further discussion later in this chapter).
- If spectator galleries are anticipated, the course's design should specifically provide for them. Measures should be implemented to make the inherent risks of watching golf on the golf course readily apparent to the ordinarily prudent eye.
- Buildings of any type should not be used as the obstacle that forces a dogleg hole, and the inside angle of a dogleg hole should be treated as a hazardous zone. Obstacles or barriers of sufficient height, density, and width should be located on the inside angle of the dogleg to prevent players from attempting to hit the ball across the inside angle. Housing or any other buildings, playgrounds, recreational facilities, paths, or parking lots should *never* be located on the inside angle of a dogleg where injury or damage to property is possible!
- Clear sightlines and visibility of players on the course should be maintained, particularly near landing areas and paths for golf cars.
- Signs, benches, tee markers, and other furnishings can cause a ball to ricochet, injuring people or damaging property. Their placement on the golf course and design should be seriously considered and constantly reviewed for safety.

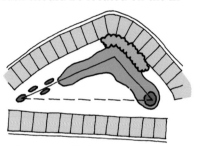

A. An acceptable design but wastes land. Trees protect lots, but golfers are likely to drive the green.

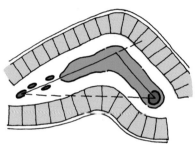

B. A layout to be avoided. Golfers are likely to overshoot the landing area or drive the green.

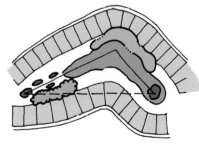

C. An acceptable layout if trees are large and dense. Some golfers might still drive the green, putting lots at risk.

D. An acceptable design but wastes land. Lake protects lots, but most golfers are likely to drive the green.

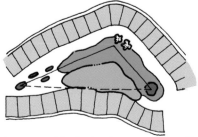

E. An acceptable design, because traps discourage overshooting the landing area and the lake adds value while discouraging driving the green.

Hazards must be considered when development surrounds a dogleg hole.
Source: Walter Stewart/Desmond Muirhead, Inc.

■ Trees should not be considered an effective means of catching errant balls, particularly between the golf course and adjacent real estate development.

Topography and Safety

A sloped lie directly affects the distance and direction a golf ball will fly. The more severe the slope, the greater the impact on the distance and direction of the ball. Therefore, the design of a golf hole and its associated safety corridor must be adjusted to accommodate the tendencies for balls to fly right, left, short, or long despite a golfer's best efforts.

On long approach shots, the ball's trajectory tends to be low, and the ball tends to bounce and roll on impact unless the golfer can put a backspin on the ball. If a long approach shot is coupled with a downhill lie, the ball tends to travel lower and farther than if the lie is flat. The inherent danger of overshooting the target must be considered and the safety clearance between the green and the next tee or land use beyond the green increased accordingly. On short approach shots, the ball's trajectory tends to be high and to bounce and roll little on impact. If a

short approach shot is coupled with a downhill lie, the ball tends to fly lower and farther than for a flat lie. Again, the margin of safety must be increased.

On side-sloping lies, the ball tends to fly left or right, depending on whether the ball is above or below, respectively, the golfer's feet. The margin of safety between adjacent fairways and between the golf course and adjacent land uses must be increased and configured to accommodate the ball's flight pattern.

Paths for Golf Cars

The driving ability of golfers varies with the number of individuals playing golf, and it is virtually impossible to judge their ability to drive a golf car on appearance alone. Understanding the abilities, limitations, and tendencies of both vehicles and drivers provides some basis for planning and designing safe paths for golf cars.

Golfers tend to drive golf cars along the path of least resistance—along the most direct route to where the ball lands, whether paved or not—and sometimes the chosen route is not the safest route. The sensible guideline therefore is to align the path where

most golfers will find it convenient and to provide physical and regulatory means to encourage golfers to stay on the path. A majority of players are right-handed and tend to slice the ball (to the right), particularly off the first tee. Therefore, paths for golf cars should generally be aligned to the right side of the fairway, where most golfers hit their shots. An exception occurs when the hole is designed to encourage play toward the left of the fairway—where a water hazard is located on the right side of the fairway, for example. In this case, aligning the path to the left side of the fairway would be more convenient. The National Golf Foundation suggests that the path be located at least 25 feet from the edge of the fairway, a compromise between keeping the path out of play but close enough for convenient use.

The shared use of a path between two adjacent golf holes might appear to be an economical and more cost-efficient means of accommodating golf cars, but it is highly unadvisable. Shared use of a path presents a higher risk of unsafe conditions, and rarely does the shared path serve both holes with the same convenience for both golfers. If the path is not conveniently

Additional Thoughts on Safety

Include an insurance underwriter as a member of the development team.

The developer might wish to forge a link with the insurance company that will provide public liability insurance for the golf course. While no substitute exists for safe design criteria, to the extent that risks are unavoidable, perhaps they can also be insurable. Having a representative of an insurance company involved at the inception increases the likelihood that appropriate coverage can be obtained. Input from the insurance company can shed light on safety criteria based on actual claims as well as information about costs for budgeting. It is important to select a representative who is actually involved in underwriting and claims rather than a sales broker whose primary interest is a commission.

Give thought during planning to defenses for negligence.

Part of the application for a golf course adjacent to a public road, for example, should point out the issue of errant golf balls and the built-in safety criteria to minimize this risk. After entitlements are received, a planning department's signing off can be characterized as an impartial judgment of a safe design. Similarly, regarding the sale of houses adjoining a golf course, a part of the purchase agreement should be the acknowledgment of the proximity of the golf course and an assumption of the buyer's risk and/or waiver of claims. This type of provision can also be built into a community's covenants and restrictions, which attach to the title and bind succeeding owners.

Publish rules and regulations governing conduct on the course.

Consider prohibiting or limiting the consumption of alcoholic beverages on the course. Post signs prohibiting nonlicensed drivers from operating golf cars.

Alert golfers to potentially unsafe areas without admitting to an unsafe condition.

For example, a sign might say "Reduce Speed–Downhill Grade" rather than "Dangerous Grade" or "Snakes in Stream" rather than "Watch for Poisonous Snakes."

Physical safety features are generally more effective than cautionary signs alone.

Speed bumps or textured rumble strips should be considered where control of golf cars' speed is needed. On long downhill grades, safety features like "turnouts" for runaway golf cars should be considered, similar to gravel turnouts for runaway tractor-trailers on long downhill grades.

The factory's safety criteria and performance specifications for golf cars should be considered during design of the course.

If a manufacturer has published safety guidelines for the operation of its product, then the design team should consider them during design.

Safety should be an integral part of employee training programs.

Employees should be required to attend regular meetings on safety policies and practices. They should provide written acknowledgment that they understand all policies, procedures, and rules, including wearing hard hats on the course, who is permitted to handle chemicals, and the procedures for handling them.

Source: John B. Miles, McDermott, Will & Emery, Newport Beach, California.

located, golfers will not use it and the purpose of shared paths is defeated.

From the standpoint of safety, vertical and horizontal alignments should be based on the vehicle's physical capabilities to maintain controlled speed and direction of travel. The path should be intentionally designed to assist drivers in maintaining control over the vehicle, regardless of their skill in operating it. For example:

- Grades (the vertical alignment) should not be so steep as to cause the vehicle to slip backward while going uphill or to attain uncontrolled speed while going downhill.
- Horizontal curves should be gentle and sweeping rather than sharp and abrupt to maintain control around curves.
- The path should include no abrupt dips or bumps that might cause the driver to lose control; grades should be carefully engineered.
- Curves at the beginning, end, or middle of an incline should be engineered to help the driver maintain control.
- Pavement on the path should be crowned or sloped for proper drainage, as excess water on the surface can cause the driver to lose control.

Design of a safe path for golf cars requires that the path be engineered and designed for vehicular travel, just like roads for automobiles, considering such factors as:

- The vehicle's physical capabilities (turning radius, speed, braking distance, et cetera);
- Design speed (maximum desired vehicle speed);
- Friction (ability of the surface to hold the vehicle in place);
- Centrifugal force (the tendency of a vehicle to leave a path on a curve);
- Sight distance and average eye height;
- Grade (percentage of slope);
- Minimum safe radius for curves;
- Rate of superelevation of curves (the banking curve to help hold the vehicle to the pavement);
- Maximum safe slope;
- Maximum safe length of a slope;
- Minimum safe sight distance; and
- Minimum width of the recovery area (an unobstructed, relatively even area next to the pavement that provides

an opportunity to bring an out-of-control vehicle back onto the pavement).

Typical paths are constructed of a hard surface like concrete or asphalt, but the hard surface also presents safety hazards from balls ricocheting off the pavement. Other pavement materials might present less risk but have other consequences in terms of cost and maintenance. Such alternatives include loose materials like gravel, stone dust, or ground shells for paths and open-celled paving units or geotextiles designed to support vehicular traffic that permit grass to grow as part of the pavement surface.

Special attention must be given to the routing of foot traffic and golf cars on slopes. Slopes are prone to wear and tear and to erosion, and the problems and conflicts with safety increase with severity of the slope. Generally, gently ramped paths should be provided for both golf cars and foot traffic in steep areas. Gentle switchbacks can be used to provide adequate horizontal distance to negotiate the vertical change in elevation. A sufficient turning radius and leveling or grading at regular intervals must be provided to help maintain the golf car's speed and direction of travel.

Intended versus Perceived Line of Play

The centerline of a golf course is not an engineered, fixed line, and no white line is painted down the middle of the fairway. The centerline is one of several ideal flight lines, or the mean of several flight lines, of an ideally struck golf ball responding to the challenge of a particular hole. The challenge might include forced carries over water, an unplayable rough, bunkers, trees, and other vegetation. The golf course architect must take into account all the implications of these elements and others that might affect golfers' responses. For a golfer, the ideal line of play is largely a psychological perception, and the player's perception of the line of play is highly vulnerable to change, with its significant implications for safety. Seemingly minor operational procedures, such as the position of tee markers or the mowing pattern of the turf, can dramati-

cally affect a golfer's perception of a hole and how he or she decides to address the challenge. A major change to the course, such as expansion of a stormwater retention pond toward an adjacent fairway, also affects the perceived centerline of play. Whenever the design of a hole is changed, the resulting impact on safety must be analyzed. Ongoing reviews of safety should be an integral part of every phase of planning, design, construction, and operation.

Other Safety Issues

The range of safety issues of concern to any type of real estate development—with or without golf—includes compliance with all federal, state, and local regulations covering employees' safety, building codes, environmental protection regulations, and the like. Some of them involve design, others operational and management policies and procedures. Dangerous conditions can be the result of oversight, ignorance, negligence, or choice.

The restriction of nongolfing and unauthorized uses of a golf course can still find a developer liable for untoward events. The *attractive nuisance* of a large pond on a hot day can invite swimmers, and the slopes of that pond's banks should anticipate the possibility of a child's attempting to wade into the pond. Another potential exposure to liability is the "Central-Park-at-night syndrome," in which the operator of a golf course was found responsible for not warning golfers in a remote location that muggers might be an additional hazard during off-peak hours. Inappropriate access and abuse during construction and when a course is in operation are always of concern.

While compromising safety might have some short-term "benefits," such as reduced costs or increased developable real estate, it is without question an unacceptable approach to responsible design. The benefits are usually illusory and the results often counterproductive. The burden is on the developer and the team to ensure that no such conditions are created. The starting point is to be aware of the potential problems and to address the issues effectively during planning and design.

Types of Golf-Oriented Real Estate Development

Residential

Perhaps the most common golf-oriented real estate development is residential, and it includes many variations and types. The accompanying feature boxes describing The Woods and Desert Island cite some lessons to be learned.

Resorts

Like residential development projects, a number of different types of resort operations target different market segments. For purposes of planning and design, resorts can be categorized into the following basic types:

- The *destination golf resort*, where golf is the primary focus of the resort's amenities, and
- The *multiple-use resort*, in which golf is only one of several major amenities offered.

In either type, the sale of real estate (lots for vacation homes, condominiums, timeshares, or vacation club memberships, and so on) might or might not be part of the resort's program. The ideal configuration for a resort varies according to whether or not real estate sales are to be part of the program. The basic principles of golf course design, land planning, and architectural design still apply to resort golf developments, however, regardless of type of resort or whether real estate sales are part of the program. The key difference between planning and design for a resort and other types of development comes down to a marked difference in *market expectations* and *market demand,* including the target market's heightened expectations for distinctive and challenging golf or recreation and for a significantly higher quality of service.

Resort golfers, for example, *expect* that the golf course will be meticulously maintained, challenging, exceptionally beautiful, and fun beyond anything at home. They want an experi-

ence to remember. Typical resort patrons seek value and recreation. They expect to be provided with a full complement of services that will allow them to make the most of their leisure time. The target market for a resort development is generally much broader than for other developments, both in geographical reach and in social, cultural, and economic profiles. Commensurate with the broader market is the need to maintain a competitive edge over similar resorts, often regionally if not nationally or internationally, to ensure financial success. Resort golfers are sophisticated customers who can exercise personal choices within a highly competitive market. Like no other golf operations, resorts must meet the highest standards of perfection. Subsequently, their operations tend to be more complex than private clubs or daily-fee golf courses. But while resorts have the potential for comparatively higher returns than private clubs or daily-fee operations, they also require higher investments, from initial planning through operation.

Early morning on the #14 green of Princeville's Prince Course in Kauai, Hawaii. The golf course is a feature of the resort. Pockets of residential development will eventually be added.

Market studies during the early stages of project planning are mandatory for a resort. Similarly, the application of basic principles of "ideal" golf course design and land planning is also significantly more critical for a resort. Responses to problems in design must be heightened proportionately to accommodate greater market expectations and demand. For example, the project's entrance as *the* point of identity, image, orientation, and security control is even more critical at a resort than at other types of development. Therefore, the design of a resort should include greater visibility of the golf course or dramatic water and landscape features at the project's entrance to establish an image or dramatic sense of place. Other design features acknowledge the heightened expectations and demands of resort golfers and make the greatest use of marketing opportunities:

- Establishment of a theme that enhances the resort's image as a special place and can be carried through to design of the golf course to reinforce its one-of-a-kind image.
- The use of distinctive, highly dramatic, exceptionally challenging, and/or unusual signature holes to capitalize on opportunities for marketing and draw attention to the resort.
- Particular attention to the details of high-image areas, such as entrances, arrival areas, and lobbies, to meet expectations of quality and to heighten the sense of orientation, comfort, security, and drama.
- Provision for space for additional elements to accommodate the higher level of service that resort guests expect (booths for valet parking attendants and golf bag attendants, accommodations for guest service employees, larger pro shop retail sales areas, and so on).

- Ability of the golf course to accommodate a wide range of players' abilities, from the novice to the professional tournament player. It must be sufficiently flexible so that each player can decide how much challenge to take on. For these reasons, the resort course usually emphasizes the multiple-tee system to accommodate varying abilities. Resorts might also offer play on more than one course, each providing a different level of challenge.
- Because resort golfers generally expect the course to be ideal, accommodations for equipment and personnel to maintain the course in top condition must be provided.
- If a resort's program includes hosting major golf tournaments, consideration must be given to accommodations for spectators, television and other media coverage, security, traffic control, parking and trans-

The #17 green of the Palms Course at Marriott's Desert Springs is a dramatic presentation of a tee and green located at the project's entrance. It creates a magnificent gateway to the resort without dominating the entrance drive. The dramatic hole surrounded by water gains multiple value for the resort.

The Woods Resort

Location: Hedgesville, West Virginia

Developer: Potomac Valley Properties, Inc.

Operator: The Woods Club, Inc.

Owner: Potomac Valley Properties, Inc./Ray Johnston

Golf Course Architects: Ray Johnston and Guy L. Rando

The Woods Resort is a vacation and second-home retirement community 90 miles northwest of Washington, D.C., in scenic West Virginia. The 1,800-acre development includes an 800-acre, 566-home resort built between 1976 and 1986. In 1987, construction began on an additional 1,000 acres that will eventually include 500 single-family detached houses, 200 townhouses, and 100 luxury apartments oriented around a 27-hole golf course, driving range, and clubhouse. Besides golf, the resort's facilities include swimming pools, tennis courts, an indoor recreation center with racquetball and tennis courts, a fitness and exercise center, an indoor pool, and a sauna, ponds, and trails within the resort and connecting to an adjacent state forest. The resort also includes conference, lodge, and restaurant facilities.

The golf course and real estate developments were designed concurrently to maximize opportunities for golf frontage and the site's physical attributes. A single-fairway, returning nines configuration was adapted to fit the steeply rolling terrain. For the most part, roads and houses follow ridgelines, and the golf course winds its way along the valleys and side slopes to afford the best views from housing units. Thus, 75 percent of the units front on the golf course. The remaining lots are generously sized to attract single-family detached houses.

The developer recognized his market to be comprised mostly of fair to competent golfers, and the golf course was designed to be fair to competent golfers and challenging for skilled golfers using the back tees. (Less than 5 percent of play on the 18-hole course is from the back tees.) Efforts were focused on providing fun and rewarding all parts of the game (accuracy and chipping as much as distance and putting). Ponds and lakes serve multiple duties: to create opportunities for real estate units fronting on water, to add challenge to the play, to manage stormwater, to irrigate the golf course, and to enhance views.

Lessons Learned

According to the developer, the golf course is the keystone to a very successful residential development. Over 300 houses were sold in the first five years. The public's acceptance of the course has been positive, reflected in a consistent annual increase in rounds of play during a time when play at competing courses in the area was declining.

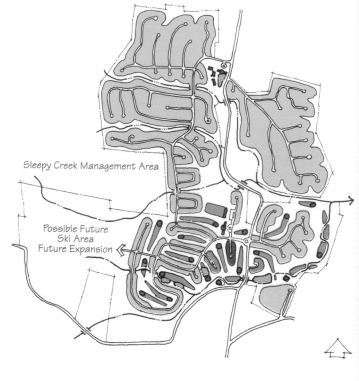

Sleepy Creek Management Area

Possible Future Ski Area Future Expansion

■ Main Complex and Clubhouse

□ Single-Family Residences

▨ Townhouses

■ High-Rise Condominiums

Master plan for The Woods.
Source: Guy L. Rando & Associates Inc.

#18 green and fairway at The Woods.

#5 green at The Woods.

Desert Island

Location: Rancho Mirage, California

Developer: Safero Insurance

Engineer: Webb Engineering Company

Land Planner and Architect: Desmond Muirhead, Inc.

Golf Course Architect: Desmond Muirhead

Desert Island is distinctive in the world of golf-oriented real estate development. The 155-acre development consists of four seven-story midrise condominium/apartments (388 units) that form the "core" of the project. A 27-acre manmade lake forms a moat around the residences. The 18-hole, par-72 golf course rims the site, providing both a buffer and a spectacular view. The lake comes into play on five of the holes, while also serving as a recreational amenity. The lake also adds an invaluable sense of security for the island.

Security was a primary concern for this development and the primary force behind its unusual concept of land planning. During the summer, temperatures in Palm Springs can reach 130 degrees Fahrenheit, and many residents leave their houses. Securing the residences during extended absences thus became a primary concern for homeowners. The moat effectively limits access to the island, and the development has several security points: the guarded gate at the entrance to the project, which is completely surrounded by an eight-foot fence, the bridge between the lake and the island, and the entrance to each building. According to its designers, "No prospective thief has yet tried to swim the moat with a television set on his shoulders," and, in fact, a burglary has never occurred on Desert Island.

The 6,684-yard course covers only 99 acres but imparts the sense of spaciousness because the real estate development is confined to the 25-acre island beyond the lake rather than the fringes of the fairways.

The site was zoned for 700 single-family residences, but designers recognized that the Palm Springs market is comprised largely of people who travel and do not want to be bothered with a big house and garden. Thus, they decided to concentrate density into spacious condominiums, lowering the density from 700 residences to 388 units. The dedication of all the land beyond the 25-acre island for recreational open space (the lake and the golf course) set the project apart from typical residential subdivisions. Another feature reinforcing the concept of open space was to place parking garages under the buildings, allowing room for tennis courts and generous landscaped gardens. The resulting density is four units per acre. The units range from 1,900 to 2,620 square feet of indoor living area plus generous balconies where most people spend their time, which in some cases add another 50 percent of livable outdoor space. Every unit has views of the lake and surrounding golf course and the dramatic mountains beyond.

The Desert Island Country Club and golf course are operated separately from the residential development. The club is private, with an equity membership structure.

Lessons Learned

The owners consider the project an outstanding success, and the golf course has not been changed except for some extra tees to lengthen it. The fairways and greens are 60 yards plus wide and are divided by six- to eight-foot mounds, with trees on top. In over 20 years, there has never been a lawsuit involving a golfer hit by a golf ball at Desert Island.

Aerial view of Desert Island.

On the debit side, the two newer buildings could have been located at a greater angle to secure better views. The roofs, which were originally tar paper, have been changed to urethane on the newest building, which is much more durable. The hallways were reduced to seven feet in the third building, but seven feet is not considered spacious enough and in the new building they will be eight feet, like the old building.

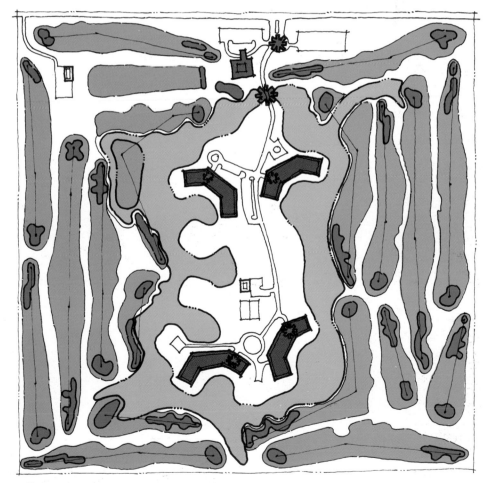

Controlled Entry

Clubhouse

Residences

Master plan for Desert Island.
Source: Desmond Muirhead, Inc.

Boca #5, the signature hole.

portation, staff offices and control centers, and the like on the course. An experienced events planner could be included as part of the planning and design team, if such events are anticipated.

While a golf course provides significant market attraction, it is by no means the only component of a resort. The lodging or guest accommodations, convention, conference, or meeting facilities, nongolf recreational amenities, local transportation and other guest services, and real estate products (condominiums, second homes, vacation clubs, for example) must all be programmed and designed to meet the market's demand for value in quality and service. In the highly competitive resort business, repeat customers are necessary.

The accompanying feature box about Horseshoe Bay Resort and Conference Club illustrates how design and land use planning for a golf course can provide a resort with greater potential and opportunities for profitable operations.

Golf Academies

A *golf academy* is a facility specifically designed to provide adequate practice areas for a full-range golf teaching curriculum. It might be a freestanding facility or associated with an existing golf course, destination resort, hotel, office park, or other planned land use. Target markets for a golf academy could include specific programs for club members (lessons, clinics, and

Views from the golf course complement the impact of the 486-room Hyatt Gainey Ranch resort hotel and extensive water playgrounds.

Horseshoe Bay Resort and Conference Club

Location:	Horseshoe Bay, Texas
Owners/Developers:	Norman C. Hurd and Wayne Hurd
Operation of Amenities:	Lake LBJ Investment Corporation
Real Estate Sales:	Lake LBJ Improvement Corporation
Primary Land Planners:	Robert Trent Jones, Sr., Willis Environmental Engineering, Norman C. Hurd, and Wayne Hurd
Land Planners:	Phillips, Proctor & Bowers
Primary Architect:	The Architects Partnership
Golf Course Architect:	Robert Trent Jones, Sr.
Consultants:	Guy L. Rando & Associates Inc.

Panoramic view of Horseshoe Bay and Lake Lyndon B. Johnson from a golf tee.

Horseshoe Bay is a major land development of 4,500 acres inside the Golden Triangle of Texas—an area formed by the cities of Houston, Dallas, and San Antonio, where the majority of Texas's population and wealth resides. Horseshoe Bay sits along the shores of Lake Lyndon B. Johnson, one of the largest constant-level lakes in Texas, five miles from the town of Marble Falls and approximately 40 miles from major shopping and cultural facilities and higher education institutions located in Austin.

The resort's privately owned 6,000-foot paved and lighted airstrip and country club–style terminal make the resort's amenities available to members through virtually every means of private air travel. The resort's airstrip can accommodate corporate jets up to the size of a DC-9 and offers a complete fueling facility, rental car assistance, on-site people movers, covered auto parking, and overnight hangar space.

Horseshoe Bay Resort and Conference Club focuses on three award-winning 18-hole golf courses designed by Robert Trent Jones, Sr., and two clubhouses. Other facilities include a 300-slip marina and yacht club and a 17-acre tennis complex. The yacht club is a lavish private dining room that includes three separate and distinctive dining experiences. It is also home to the Anchor Lounge, a black marble basin pool, lakeside beaches, a food and beverage cabana, decks, waterfalls, fountains, sculptures, and a one-of-a-kind adult spa and waterscape surrounded by billion-year-old granite outcroppings. The yacht club features a multiuse sports court and observation garden. The marina allows its members and guests to enjoy power boating, water skiing, and fishing. The full-service marina includes a full-line ship store and lakeside hospitality lounge for private functions.

The resort's tennis complex includes 12 tennis courts, four of them under a glass dome. Tennis was designed to be an event, not merely a game. It includes acres of careful landscaping and oriental water gardens featuring fountains, waterfalls, statuary, and underwater lighting. The Racquet Clubhouse features a pro shop, separate lockers and exercise areas for men and women, saunas, a whirlpool, and a glass-paneled atrium-style lounge on the second story overlooking the fitness trails and covered tennis courts. In addition, the resort's equestrian center offers individual and group guided trail rides along Slick Rock Creek.

Living accommodations include 84 hotel-style accommodations and a wide variety of privately owned one-, two-, and three-bedroom townhouses and condominiums. An additional 100-room hotel is planned as part

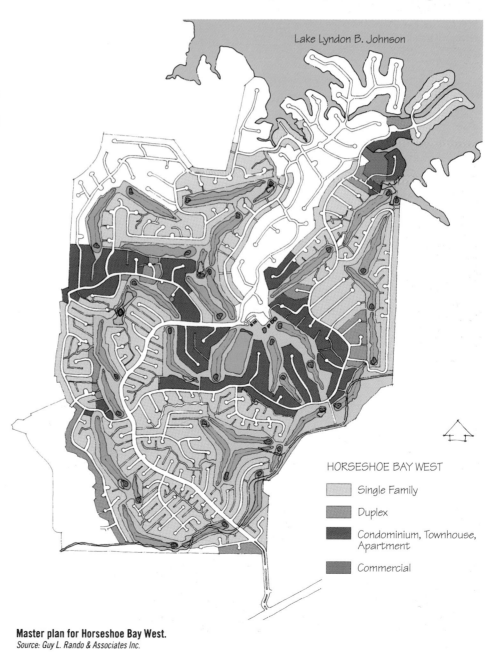

Master plan for Horseshoe Bay West.
Source: Guy L. Rando & Associates Inc.

HORSESHOE BAY WEST

- Single Family
- Duplex
- Condominium, Townhouse, Apartment
- Commercial

View over the #3 green and #4 island hole of the Ram Rock Course at Horseshoe Bay Resort and Conference Club.

Cap Rock Clubhouse at Horseshoe Bay enjoys spectacular views of two golf courses and Lake Lyndon B. Johnson.

of a major health and fitness center and new conference complex. The owners and operators of the resort consider the development's amenity package only 35 percent complete, and they have purchased additional land for golf-related projects.

The developers' objective was to create a major destination resort that would equal or surpass any such resort in the United States. The developers formed two separate companies, one to own and operate the amenities (Lake LBJ Investment Corporation [LBJIC]) and one to own and sell the lots (Lake LBJ Improvement Corporation [LBJ]). LBJIC, through its wholly owned subsidiary, operates the resort as "Horseshoe Bay Resort and Conference Club." Horseshoe Bay Resort and Conference Club will be the surviving company that continues operation of the resort and its amenities.

To remain a purely destination resort, LBJIC in no way participates in the sale of lots or encourages its members or guests to purchase lots or housing. Horseshoe Bay Resort and Conference Club is a private, nonequity club, and use of its amenities is restricted to members and their guests. Any person renting one of the club's units is considered a temporary member of the resort during that stay. Horseshoe Bay has over 7,000 property owners from 48 states, 34 foreign countries, and seven Canadian provinces. The resort and conference center currently has over 4,000 individual members.

Land planning was designed to allow phased development of the resort and real estate development. Although the resort and real estate development are two distinct operations, master planning for the real estate and for the golf courses was carried out concurrently to ensure harmony between real estate development and golf/resort uses. The land planning team included the tightly coordinated, active involvement of the owners, golf course architect, engineers, architects, and land planning consultants. The real estate development program for Horseshoe Bay includes single-family, duplex, and condominium units and commercial development. Some 20 percent of the development area was set aside as permanent open space and recreational use, and a 24-acre nature preserve remains permanent, undisturbed open space along the spring-fed Horseshoe Creek, which runs through the interior of the property.

The golf courses were laid out to open up the interior of the property, increasing the value of nonwaterfront lots. The developers have title to the 700 acres of lake bottom fronting the development. The lake is controlled and maintained at a constant level, enabling the developers to build to and into the lake.

The three golf courses—Slick Rock, Ram Rock, and Apple Rock—together take up 513 acres of the property. The 18-hole, par-72, 6,839-yard Slick Rock Course, built in 1971, was the first course to be completed. It covers approximately 170 acres and provides 33,700 feet of salable golf frontage (excluding the practice range) for real estate development, which includes 299 single-family lots, 17 ¾-acre multifamily tracts, and seven 5,000-square-foot commercial lots. Slick Rock is served by a 3,560-square-foot clubhouse and pro shop. The second course, Ram Rock, was constructed in 1981. This 18-hole, par-71 course is 6,946 yards from the championship tees and covers approximately 196 acres. It provides 40,200 feet of salable frontage (excluding the practice range) for real estate development, which includes 242 single-family lots, 53 ¾-acre multifamily tracts, and 31 duplex lots. The third course, the 147-acre Apple Rock, was built in 1986. It provides 18 holes of par-72 golf. The 6,999-yard course covers approximately 147 acres. It provides 46,540 feet of salable

frontage for real estate development, which includes 318 single-family lots, 55 ¾-acre multifamily lots, 21 duplex lots, and 53 zero-lot-line lots. Ram Rock and Apple Rock Courses are served by the 7,632-square-foot Cap Rock Clubhouse, which houses the pro shop, poolhouses, and swimming pools. Slick Rock and Apple Rock Courses are basically single-fairway, returning nines configurations, while Ram Rock is a continuous loop. These layouts maximize real estate frontage.

Lessons Learned

With its high quality of amenities and operations, Horseshoe Bay Resort and Conference Club has been profitable for the past decade, surviving four recessions since its inception. Texas golf professionals have rated all three golf courses, designed by Robert Trent Jones, Sr., as among the top ten courses in the state, and *Golf Digest* and other leading golf magazines in the United States and Europe recognize them as among the best golf courses in the nation. During each of the past ten years, the resort's operations have grown in business over the previous year. The owners have consistently reinvested funds from the operating cash flow into additional amenities and plan to continue doing so for the next decade. The amenity owner's debt to asset ratio is 1:52. The land sales company has also been profitable since the project's inception, having sold approximately 85 percent of available lots as of 1992. Some of the project's success can be attributed to the fact that it is a family-owned business and the owners live in the development. Members can easily see their long-term commitment to the community, their consistent reinvestment, and the personal risks they take to protect the project's value and viability. The quality of management and the staff's dedication reflect the owner's commitment to excellence.

Another distinctive aspect of Horseshoe Bay's concept for development is that it makes virtually no demands on public institutions. It builds and maintains it own streets and utility systems and maintains its own fire, emergency, and police services. The developers formed a municipal utility district and installed one of the first tertiary sewage treatment plants in Texas and the first major pressurized sewage collection system in the United States. Sewage effluent is used to irrigate the golf courses. The development of Horseshoe Bay has resulted in many benefits to the surrounding community. Before its development, the land where it is located was assessed for ad valorem taxes at less than 1 percent of the total assessed value of Llano County. Today, with only 0.66 percent of the land area in Llano County and generating less than 2 percent of the public school population, it pays about 46 percent of county and school taxes. Horseshoe Bay's assessed valuation is now 2.5 times the combined valuation of the county seats of Llano and Burnet counties (a minor portion of the site is in Burnet County). Local businesses have experienced considerable growth as a result of the development, including Marble Falls's principal bank, which realized an increase in deposits of 1000 percent during the first half of the period that Horseshoe Bay was under development. The resort and conference center is now the largest employer in the immediate six-county area.

Horseshoe Bay's success can also be attributed to the fostering of community spirit by the development's property owners, who donated an interdenominational chapel constructed on a valuable promontory overlooking the entire site.

leagues for juniors or tots, day or evening sessions, for example), summer camps and holiday camps for adults and juniors, family vacation camps, school programs, organized programs for condominium or apartment residents, celebrity and tour professional exhibitions, or specialty entertainment exhibitions. A variety of programs and curricula can appeal to golfers at all levels, from novice to professional. Comprehensive packages might include lodging, instruction, food and beverages, miscellaneous gifts, and sometimes travel arrangements. Golf academies rely on a well-trained staff of instructors current in teaching techniques and methods of relaying information in a stimulating manner.

Golf academies are usually planned as an integral core operation, with all the elements located close to each other, and they are best suited for small to moderate sites of 12 to 65 acres. A 16-acre site can generally accommodate a program that includes a double-ended driving range (tee stations on both ends of the range) with target greens and chipping greens, a

Guidelines for Land Area for a Golf Academy

	Minimum Acreage Required
Range Only (including target greens, chipping green(s), and bunker practice area)	12
Double-Ended Range	13.3
18-Hole Putting Course	2
Putting Course, Double-Ended Range, Clubhouse with Parking, and Maintenance Area	16
Putting Course, Double-Ended Range, Clubhouse with Parking, Maintenance Area, and 2,400-Yard, 9-Hole, Par-33 Course	66

Source: Palmer Course Design Company.

putting course, a full-service clubhouse with video teaching facilities, parking, and a maintenance area. A site with more than 16 acres provides opportunities to expand the program to include a nine-hole, par-3 course or an executive or full regulation nine-hole course. The addition of night lighting and covered tee stations for use of the driving range during inclement weather maximizes the facility's use and profitability. The par-3 course might also be lighted.

Master planning and the basic principles of planning and design for a golf academy are the same as those for a regulation golf course. Certain design parameters are unique to a golf academy, however.

Entry

Like any development project, a clearly defined entry is essential to direct attention to a facility and to orient visitors. The circulation pattern, signage, lighting, and landscaping should be carefully planned and designed to satisfy these requirements. "Drive-by" use of the academy is usually encouraged to generate business; thus, the design of the entry should reflect an upscale quality to distinguish the golf academy from ordinary driving ranges.

For a stand-alone golf academy, the entry should be easily accessible from the main road. For a golf academy that is part of other golf facilities, the main clubhouse can be used as the primary focal point, or clear directional signage can be used to direct traffic to the golf academy.

Parking

A covered area at the clubhouse's entry, large enough to accommodate a golf bag drop-off area, is strongly recommended. The parking area for the academy should accommodate 75 to 125 cars plus a separate bus parking area in proportion to the size and capacity of the academy. Staff parking can be incorporated with the maintenance area, if it is included as part of the facilities.

Clubhouse

A well-equipped clubhouse is essential for the promotion and operation of a golf academy. If the academy is part of a larger golf facility, it might be possible to incorporate the areas required to support the academy with the main clubhouse. A stand-alone golf academy requires a clubhouse that includes a lobby/reception area/information center for greeting members and guests, a registration center for lessons and activities, locker rooms with

Master plan for the Arnold Palmer Golf Academy in Orlando, Florida.
Source: Palmer Course Design Company.

61

Target green at the Palmer Golf Academy.

Pit lights at the Palmer Golf Academy.

restrooms and showers, a laundry room, storage facilities, a pro shop, meeting and audiovisual rooms, administrative offices, a restaurant and lounge or snack bar, and golf car and/ or golf cart storage, maintenance, and staging areas. An architect with experience in designing clubhouses would be the best choice to design the clubhouse for a golf academy.

Practice Range

A double-ended practice range (tees at both ends) includes:

- At least 1,050 feet of length (including the tee area);
- At least 550 feet of width serving 75 10-foot-wide practice stations distributed over both ends;
- A minimum depth of 100 feet at the tees to accommodate rotation of the hitting area;
- An artificial hitting pad along the back edge of the tee area for use when the turf is to be rested or is wet;
- Contouring the tee area with varying heights of grass to simulate actual lies encountered on a golf course;
- Several graded target greens with framing sand bunkers located 100 to 250 yards from the tee area;
- Chipping greens and bunker practice areas located adjacent to or near the tee area;
- A private instruction area on all tee areas;
- Covered hitting areas ranging from a temporary tent to a multistory

structure in the tee area for use during inclement weather;
- Lighting for night use (Typically, 1,500-watt metal halide fixtures are mounted on poles 40 feet above grade, but a pit lighting system, with fixtures mounted below grade and concealed by mounds, is also effective.);
- Safety netting (one-inch mesh) along the perimeter of the range.

Putting Green or Putting Course

The availability of space generally dictates whether a putting green or putting course can be accommodated. Both the putting green and putting course are designed through surface contours and multiple pin locations to

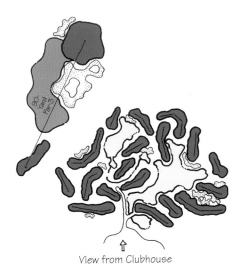

18-hole putting course on a two-acre site.
Source: Palmer Course Design Company.

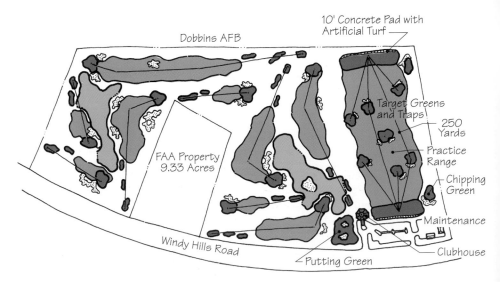

Master plan for the golf academy in Atlanta, Georgia.
Source: Palmer Course Design Company.

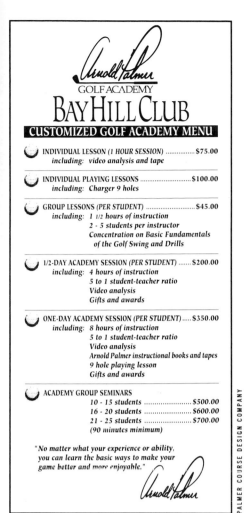

Customized golf academy menu for the Bay Hill Club.

simulate a variety of putting situations that might be found on a course. The putting course offers a wider variety for practice and can serve as a separate profit center. The practice putting green should be at least 6,000 square feet, avoiding steep slopes and extreme contouring. The putting course should consist of 18 holes with landscaping and water features to simulate actual putting greens on a course.

Projected Construction Costs for a 40-Acre Site in South Florida

Engineering	
Topo, 100 scale, boundary, centerline, pads (3)	$ 5,000
Surveying	10,000
Miscellaneous Engineering	15,000
Topsoil	
Stripping/Stockpiling/Replacing, 45,000 cu. yd. @ $2.70/cu. yd.	121,500
Earthmoving and Rough Shaping	
On-Site Cut and Fill, 125,000 cu. yd. @ $1.75/cu. yd.	218,750
Drainage and Support Structures	45,000
Irrigation	
40 Acres, 300 heads @ $500/head	150,000
Pump Station and Filtration	30,000
Finish Grading and Seedbed Preparation	150,000
Grassing	
32 Acres, 419 Bermuda stolons	22,000
2 Acres, 419 Bermuda sod	20,000
54,000 sq. ft., Tifdwarf stolons	4,000
Materials and Construction	
Fairway Drainage (rock and tile)	20,000
Championship Putting Course plus Nine Greens (rock, tile, grassmix)	400,000
Bunkers	25,000
Covered Tee Shelter	
2-Tier Modular Concrete or Steel (18 ft. x 200 ft.) (other less expensive sizes and types available)	150,000
150 Simulated-Turf Driving Stations ($300 each)	45,000
Clubhouse	
Pro Shop/Snack Bar/Locker Rooms/Offices (10,000 sq. ft., two-level modular) @ $55/sq. ft.	550,000
Furniture, Fixtures, and Equipment @ $35/sq. ft.	350,000
Maintenance Building (3,000 sq. ft., modular metal) @ $30/sq. ft.	90,000
Maintenance Equipment (mowers, sprayers, etc.)	100,000
Specialty Items (cart paths, bridges, bulkheads, etc.)	50,000
Lighting (perimeter, pit/course)	75,000
Parking Lot, Entrance Paving (125 cars)	125,000
Landscaping	100,000
Fencing, Ball Net	
Ball Net (25 ft. high), 600 ft. @ $25/ft.	15,000
TOTAL HARD COSTS (including construction fees)	$2,886,250

Note: Includes practice range, nine-hole, par-3 course, putting course, clubhouse, parking, and maintenance area but not land acquisition.
Source: Palmer Course Design Company.

PALMER COURSE DESIGN COMPANY

Notes

1. The court rulings cited should not in any way be construed as a legal interpretation, as they might have been overturned. The information should be used only for purposes intended in this publication.

2. *Hornstein* v. *State of New York*, 46 Misc. 2d 486, 259 N.Y.S.2d 902 (1965).

3. Ibid.

4. Ibid.

5. *Townsley* v. *State of New York*, 6 Misc. 2d 557, 164 N.Y.S.2d 804 (1957).

6. *Gleason* v. *Hillcrest Golf Course, Inc.*, 148 Misc. 246, 256 N.Y.S. 886 (1933).

7. *Palsgraf* v. *The Long Island Railroad Company*, 248 N.Y. 339, 162 N.E. 99, 59 A.L.R. 1253 (1928).

8. Nicklaus Design.

Design Of the Golf Course

The object of the game of golf is fairly simple: to hit a ball with a club into a hole with the fewest possible strokes. Planning and designing a golf course, however, is a far more complex process, requiring technical expertise and artistic skills. The artistry of golf course architecture results in the impression that building a golf course simply involves laying carpets of turf onto a piece of dramatic or scenic landscape.

Deer at Horseshoe Bay.

GUY L. RANDO & ASSOCIATES INC.

Golf Nomenclature

Golf Course: The whole area within which play is permitted, comprised of *holes* played in a specific sequence. ("Hole" is a general term used to describe the entire area between and including the tee and the green.)

Course Length: A measurement of horizontal distance expressed in yards from the middle of the tee area to the center of the putting green, following the line of play planned by the architect.

Putting Green: Ground specially prepared for putting.

Bunker: A hazard consisting of a prepared area of ground from which turf or soil has been removed and replaced with sand or a similar material.

Water Hazard: Any sea, lake, pond, river, ditch, surface drainage ditch, or open water course (whether or not containing water), and anything of a similar nature.

Through the Green: The whole area of the course except for the teeing ground, the putting green, and hazards. Although the term "fairway" is not defined in *Rules of Golf,* through the green is close to what is commonly referred to as "the fairway." The generally accepted use of "fairway" refers to the area of the course that is maintained to reward a well-hit shot—usually an area of closely mown turf. The fairway is often surrounded by an area called the "rough"—an area where the turf is maintained at a greater height than the fairway that might include shrubs, trees, and other plants. The fairway and rough are both included in through the green.

Teeing Ground: The starting place for a hole to be played, the teeing ground is a rectangular area two club lengths in depth, with front and side outside limits defined by tee markers.

The Hole: The destination for the golf ball. It must be $4\frac{1}{4}$ inches in diameter and at least four inches deep. Any lining must be sunk at least one inch below the surface unless the nature of the soil makes it impractical to do so.

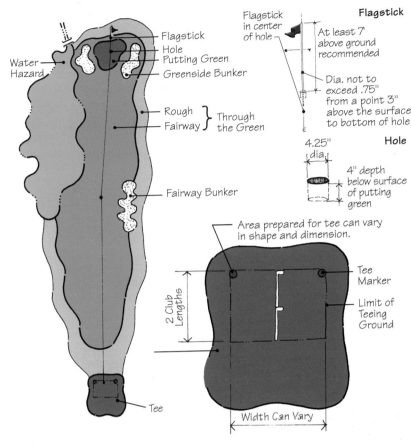

Flagstick: A movable, straight indicator with or without bunting or material attached, centered in the hole to show its position.

Source: USGA Rules of Golf.

In actuality, building a golf course involves hundreds of hours of design and engineering to direct the movement of thousands of tons of earth, laying miles of drainage pipes and irrigation lines, and clearing, replanting, and planting many acres of trees and landscape materials.

This chapter focuses on the principles of designing golf courses to aid the understanding of the physical requirements of the game and their implications for design. This fundamental understanding should result in rational decisions about whether the design of a golf course meets the needs and goals of a development project.

The Basics

Nomenclature

The language of golf includes an extensive vocabulary of terms specific to the game, many of which have no "official" definition and thus cause some confusion. *USGA Rules of Golf*[1] governs play on most golf courses in the United States. Designing a golf course involves the intelligent arrangement of these elements on a site. A successful design combines playability, adaptability, and mental, sensual, and aesthetic fulfillment for the golfer.

Design Criteria

The developer who wants to add a golf course to a project should have some basic understanding of the game of golf to allow the development of rational criteria that can be used to select a golf course architect, the design professional with specialized technical training and artistic expertise whose work can make or break a project. The owner or client must work closely with the golf course architect at all times, reviewing work and making decisions. The design criteria for a golf course are directly affected by a number of factors:

- Regional or local environmental factors;
- Preferences of the target market;
- Physical restrictions of the site;
- Regulatory requirements or restrictions affecting land use;
- Budget constraints and/or financial performance goals;
- Goals and objectives of associated real estate programs;
- Goals and objectives of the operational aspects of the course.

These factors vary greatly from one project to another, but all golf courses must meet one universal criterion to be successful: *playability*. A course's playability directly affects its financial potential, for if a course is not playable, it cannot be marketed and the operation's potential to earn revenue might never be realized. The most dramatic and beautiful site cannot make up for an unplayable course. An unplayable course diminishes the real estate value of any associated land development.

In the United States, playability is defined by a number of factors, most of them controllable through design of the golf course:

- *Overall course length, number of holes, and their par value.* While the designs of courses vary widely, a regulation course (see the following section) is generally preferred for a course associated with real estate development.
- *The variety of challenges* over the course, achieved by:
  - varying the par from one hole to the next;
  - varying the length of holes over the course so that golfers have the opportunity to use every club in their bags at some point on the course (see "Distance and Use of Clubs" later in this chapter).
- *A reasonable challenge for all players*, regardless of their ability, by:
  - providing multiple tee positions to adjust length of the course for players of varying levels of ability;
  - taking into account visibility and the size of landing areas and elbow points;
  - being aware of solar and wind orientation;
  - strategically positioning bunkers and water hazards.
- *Safety on the course and around the course.* While the game carries inherent risks, the course should be designed with safety margins. (See "Safety in the Golf Corridor" in Chapter 3.)
- *Opportunities for strategic play.* Golf is as much a mental game as a physical sport. Players should have ample opportunity for strategic play so they can choose the level of challenge they prefer. (See "Styles of Holes" later in this chapter.)
- *Operational flexibility and ease of maintenance.* The designs of certain areas lend themselves to operational flexibility and cost-effective maintenance:
  - size and design of tees;
  - size and design of greens;
  - size and design of bunkers and water hazards;
  - roughs;
  - irrigation systems.

Once the criteria for playability have been met, other design strategies can amplify or enhance the potential value of a golf course: sculpturing earth, siting and framing views, landscaping, and heightening a course's aesthetic qualities through water features, bridges, retaining walls, and other structures. The costs of such aesthetic improvements, however, must be weighed against the benefits gained in marketability and enhanced value.

When a golf course is part of a real estate development project, design of the course must be integrated with adjacent land uses and must meet additional criteria for marketability and economic performance. The layout of the golf course to maximize real estate values becomes a critical factor in real estate development projects (see Chapter 3). Playability is still a mandatory requirement, however, and should not be compromised by planning for the real estate portion. Such a compromise would defeat the purpose of building a golf course.

The Regulation Golf Course

One of the first considerations in designing a playing field for outdoor sports is its physical dimensions based on the rules or regulations governing the sport. The playing field for golf, however, has no standard dimensions except for the size of the hole the ball must eventually enter. The number of holes and the length, width, and configuration of a golf course can all vary. Add the variety of terrains, climates, and settings found in the United States alone, and the possibilities for design become endless.

The evolution of golf in the United States has included an effort to standardize golf courses to make them safe, to make the game enjoyable for all players, regardless of their ability, and to accommodate tournament or competitive play for players of varying capabilities. The *regulation course* is the result of this effort toward standardization, although no formal rules define exactly what qualifies as a regulation course other than some parameters for the length of a course set by the NGF. Some variations in design, such as *executive courses* and *par-3 courses*, are defined by length of the course, and other variations, such as *championship* or *tournament courses*, define the quality of the course and the type of play on it.

The range of variables and lack of standardized measurements often lead to confusion in terms describing golf courses, particularly "championship" and "regulation," which are often used interchangeably. A regulation course might sometimes be called a championship course simply because championship tournaments are held there, with no consideration of the course's length or quality. Many prefer, however, that the term "championship" be reserved for courses that "by virtue of their design and maintenance are capable of providing an exacting challenge and excellent playing conditions for superior golfers in regional, state, or national competition."[2] In any case, the term "championship" has no officially accepted definition and should

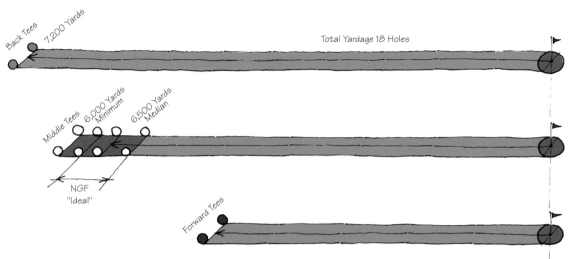

Distance is measured horizontally from the center of the tee area to the center of the putting green along the line of intended play.

Back Tees 7,200 Yards

Total Yardage 18 Holes

Middle Tees 6,000 Yards Minimum 6,500 Yards Median

NGF "Ideal"

Forward Tees

Understanding distance for an NGF regulation course.
Source: Guy L. Rando & Associates Inc.

therefore *not* be used to describe the caliber of a course.

The NGF cites the regulation course as the "best-balanced, well-rounded test of golf in its truest form, as the origins of its composition are found in early Scottish courses."[3] The regulation course is the most popular in the United States, and it is often considered the standard to achieve when a golf course is associated with real estate development. While a regulation course is not in itself a guarantee of a playable course, it is a popular standard by which a course's perceived playability is often judged.

No official rules define a regulation course, but golf course architects customarily use certain guidelines and concepts when designing a regulation course:

■ 18 holes;
■ Par 72;
■ A course length of at least 6,000 yards from the middle tees, with 6,300 to 6,700 yards desirable and 6,500 yards a good median;
■ Provision for front and back tees to give an effective course length of 5,200 to 7,200 yards.

Par 72 should be achieved by including 10 par-4 holes, four par-3 holes, and four par-5 holes. Each nine holes should include five par-4 holes, two par-3 holes, and two par-5 holes.

Par

Par is an expression of scoring related to horizontal distance. The definition of par is based on the USGA's guidelines for computing the par of a hole based on horizontal distance in yards. The USGA defines "par" as:

> ...the score a scratch golfer would be expected to make for a given hole. Par means errorless play without flukes and under ordinary weather conditions, allowing two strokes on the putting green.[4]

Thus, a par-3 hole allows for one shot off the tee to reach the putting green plus two strokes on the putting green, a par-4 hole allows for two shots to reach the putting green plus two strokes on the putting green,

and a par-5 hole allows for three shots to reach the putting green plus two strokes on the putting green.

The USGA suggests the following yardages for computing par:

Par	Men	Women
3	Up to 250	Up to 210
4	251 to 470	211 to 400
5	471 and over	401 to 575
6	–	576 and over

According to USGA, par is a range of horizontal distances for men and for women, which should not be applied arbitrarily. "Allowance should be made for the configuration of the ground, any difficult or unusual conditions, and the severity of the hazards."[5]

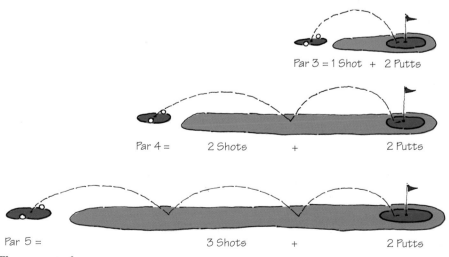

Par 3 = 1 Shot + 2 Putts

Par 4 =   2 Shots   +   2 Putts

Par 5 =   3 Shots   +   2 Putts

The concept of par.
Source: Guy L. Rando & Associates Inc.

Yardage Rating, Course Rating, And Slope Rating

The USGA's suggested yardage[6] for computing par should not be confused with the "course rating" or "yardage rating" described in the USGA's golf handicap system. "Yardage rating" is the evaluation of a course's difficulty of play based solely on yardage. It is the score a "scratch golfer" is expected to make when playing a course of average difficulty using distance as the primary consideration in rating.

The difficulty of obstacles and hazards encountered on the golf course also must be considered when rating a golf course. Therefore, "course rating" was developed to evaluate the playing difficulty of a course compared with other rated courses to establish a uniform, sound basis on which to compute handicaps. Course rating is based on yardage and other obstacles to the extent that they affect a scratch player's scoring ability. The more difficult the course for a scratch golfer, the higher the course's rating.

Not many golfers, however, are scratch players or better. Thus, USGA developed "slope rating," which defines the golf course's degree of difficulty for an *average* golfer. The higher the slope, the more difficult an average player finds the course. Slope rating also makes it possible for golfers to play matches away from their "home" course, making a golfer's handicap portable. More strokes are given on courses with a higher slope rating than the golfer's home course, fewer on courses with a lower slope rating.

Par Sequencing

For an 18-hole regulation course, the NGF suggests that holes be distributed evenly between two circuits of nine holes each with a par of 36 and similar total yardage. The holes should start and end at the clubhouse (with the last nine holes the returning nines). This even distribution can be translated as a par sequence of 4–5–4–3–4–5–4–3–4 for each of the nine holes, although the sequence can vary.

According to the NGF, while par 72 is "ideal," traditional, and balanced, pars of 70 or 71 are "acceptable" if the nature of the terrain or size of the property prevents the layout of four par-5 holes. In this case, the reduction in total par should result from replacing one or two par-5 holes with par-4 holes, as a regulation course should *always* have four par-3 holes. While sequencing par is a method of providing variety over a course and is one of several factors affecting a course's playability, it should be noted that some of the world's most famous courses do not have balanced pars or even a par of 72.

Other parameters must be considered in designing a playable golf course. Those born entirely of operational efficiency, for example, include the guideline that the starting holes (number 1 and number 10) should be midlength par-4s. This guideline takes certain tendencies of players into consideration:

- Players tend to think of a par-4 hole as a good warm-up before confronting a more challenging par-3 or par-5 hole.
- Golfers can play a par-4 hole in less time than a par-3 or par-5 hole; therefore, starting with a par-4 hole is more efficient in getting the maximum number of players into active play over the entire course.

Other parameters arise from the demand for variety in challenges over a course. Further, contemporary golf courses must accommodate a wide range of abilities among players. Thus evolved variations in lengths of holes over the length of a course and multiple tee systems.

Distance and Use of Clubs

The concept of variation in the lengths of holes over the entire course is based on the premise that a course should be designed so as to allow a golfer to use every club in his or her bag at some point on the course. A full set of 14 clubs, the limit imposed by USGA on the number of clubs a player is allowed to carry, consists of a driver, two fairway woods, irons numbered from 2 to 9, a pitching wedge, a sand wedge, and a putter. Thus, to apply the principle of using every club in the bag, one must understand the relationship between the club used and distance. The distance one can expect to hit a ball with a given club is related to the degree of loft designed for the club and to the player's ability and strength. Long hitters generally get more distance from the same club than the "average" player, while short hitters and women generally get less distance than the average. But beyond players' varying abilities, other factors, such as wind, humidity, temperature, topography, and condition of the course, result in varying distances an individual golfer might achieve with a given club. Each golfer develops his or her own strategy for which club to use based on individual ability and condition of the course.

The design of a course can accommodate a variety of play by the architect's manipulating the length of holes, so that the course contains both long and short shots to the target. For example, the first, par-4 hole might require a full drive off the tee with a driver, and a shot with a number 6 iron to reach the green. The following hole, par-5, might require a full drive off the tee with a driver, a number 3 wood to the second landing area, and a number 8 iron to the green. The next par-4 hole might require the driver off the tee and a number 3 iron to reach the green. The driver or number 1 wood is always used for the first shot off the tee on par-4 and par-5 holes and on long par-3 holes.

Multiple Tees

The position of multiple tees is the primary method that a golf course architect can use to adjust the length of holes to accommodate players of varying abilities. According to *USGA Rules of Golf*, a three-tee system uses standard colors and terms for tee markers to determine the course rating used to determine handicap.

Many golf course architects advocate the addition of a gold tee or for-

USGA Course Rating

Tees	Color/Descriptive Term	Men's Rating	Women's Rating
Back	Blue or Championship Course	72.0	—
Middle	White Course	71.3	73.7
Forward	Red Course or Women's Tee	69.5	72.0

ward tees to the standard blue/white/red to provide for a wider range of players' abilities than this three-tee system can accommodate. Some golf course architects, however, prefer that the nomenclature for the tees remain gender neutral, while others term the forward tees "women's tees," as in the two-tee system advocated for women golfers by Alice Dye. The gold tee has been used both as the back tee for long hitters or tournament play and as a tee for seniors in a forward position between the white and red tees. Neither the USGA's *Rules of Golf* nor its handicap system includes a standard definition for the gold tee. The NGF suggests placement of the gold tee behind the blue (championship) tee.

The number and placement of tees are not restricted by any regulation. In locating tees, the golf course architect determines the distance that various players can hit the ball on average with a certain club or combination of clubs, then locates the tee accordingly based on level of ability. For example, if a par-4 hole is designed to be played with a full drive off the tee and a medium number 6 iron to the green, the architect can calculate the distances a typical player of a certain ability can cover with those clubs. Thus, a five-tee system can accommodate a professional tournament player (the tournament tee), a long hitter (the championship or blue tee), an average hitter (the middle, member's, or white tee), a short hitter (the senior or forward

tee), and a woman or junior golfer (the women's or red tee). The corresponding tee for each player is located at the intended design distance for that level player from the green. To implement this multiple-tee system over an otherwise regulation course, the same concept of design for maximum variance in hole lengths to permit use of all the clubs in a typical set over an 18-hole regulation course can be applied for players of each level.

Alice Dye, a well-known golf course architect, has become a strong advocate of a two-tee system for women golfers, many of whom are not comfortable with the average 5,800-yard course. According to Dye:

■ One in four golfers is a woman, and 41 percent of new golfers are women.

■ The *average* woman drives the ball 130 yards.

■ The national average course length for women is 5,800 yards, for men 6,400 yards. Women with low handicaps hit the ball 85 percent as far as men; an average woman hits the ball 75 percent as far as a man. Thus, a low-handicap woman golfer would be most comfortable playing a course approximately 5,440 yards long, and the average woman golfer would find a course of 4,800 yards most comfortable—both of them considerably shorter than the average 5,800-yard course available to women.

■ Today's lush, irrigated golf courses have reduced the "roll" of the ball that was expected when many holes were originally designed. Formerly, on a firm fairway, an expected roll of 33 percent was designed into the hole.

Thus, the average woman needs a more manageable 4,800- to 5,200-yard course, without sacrificing the

longer yardage for women capable of playing the longer distance. The accompanying chart lists the distances Dye suggests for placement of back tees and forward tees for women.

The longer-yardage tees should provide a course of 5,400 to 5,800 yards, the shorter-yardage tees a course of 4,600 to 5,400 yards.

Dye notes that par-5 holes meeting USGA guidelines for length (401 to 575 yards) are virtually unreachable for the average woman player. With an average drive of 130 yards, a second wood shot of about 120 yards, and a third wood shot of 120 yards, the average woman player could attain a total distance of only 370 yards. Thus, the same concepts for other multiple-tee systems can be used to locate additional tees for women. Note that Dye does not advocate replacing existing forward tees but adding a forward tee or tees to make a course more playable for women.

Dye's two-tee system includes additional guidelines for distances on par-3 holes:

■ A forced carry over water or a ravine should not exceed 75 yards. While the yardage can be longer, the distance over the hazard should not exceed 75 yards.

■ A par-3 hole completely guarded by a sand bunker should not require a carry of more than 100 yards.

■ Par-3 holes with a fairway and an entrance to the green can reach 150 yards. While many women will not reach the green from the tee shot at this distance, they can reach the green with an additional short pitch shot from a fairway lie. The average woman golfer does not like all short par-3 holes, and many women golfers find a 150-yard, par-3 hole an acceptable challenge.

NGF Tee Placement Guide

Tee	Drive (yards)	Second Shot (yards)
Gold	250	225
Blue	225	200
White	175	150
Red	150	125

Two-Tee System for Women

Par	USGA Guideline (yards)	Women's Back Tee (yards)	Women's Forward Tee (yards)
3	Up to 210	120–200	60–150
4	211–400	300–380	240–340
5	401–575	420–540	401–420

Planning for Women Golfers

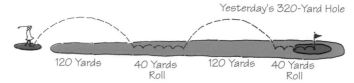

Yesterday's 320-Yard Hole

120 Yards — 40 Yards Roll — 120 Yards — 40 Yards Roll

When fairways were more firm, a woman golfer could reach a 320-yard hole in two shots, because the ball tended to roll as much as 40 yards after landing.

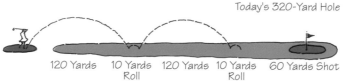

Today's 320-Yard Hole

120 Yards — 10 Yards Roll — 120 Yards — 10 Yards Roll — 60 Yards Shot

With today's lush, irrigated fairways, the ball does not roll far after landing and a woman golfer needs three shots to reach a 320-yard hole.

The concept of roll.

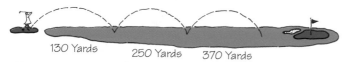

130 Yards — 250 Yards — 370 Yards

The average woman golfer usually cannot reach a par-5 hole in three shots. Par-5s for women should not be much longer than the regulation 401 yards from the forward women's tee.

A par-5 hole for a woman golfer.

A. Correct Forward Tee
B. Position for Back Tee for Women
C. Incorrect Position for Forward Tee

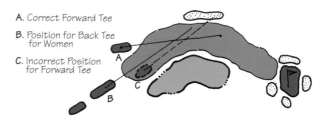

Place the tee on the side that diminishes the dogleg so that a longer shot does not go through the fairway.

75 Yards

A par-3 hole with a forced carry over water or a ravine should not require more than a 75-yard carry for women.

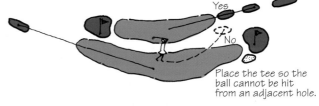

Yes / No

Place the tee so the ball cannot be hit from an adjacent hole.

100 Yards

Par-3 holes with a sand bunker completely guarding the green should not require more than a 100-yard carry for women. Failure to make the carry might not result in a penalty stroke, as most women are able to hit out of a sand bunker.

Car Path

New Tee

Place the new tee so that women golfers do not cross in front of the back tee.

150 Yards

Par-3 holes with a fairway and an entrance to the green can be as long as 150 yards. The average woman golfer might not reach the green with the tee shot, but it is a reasonable challenge and would require only a short pitch from a fairway lie if the tee shot falls short.

Par-3 holes for a woman golfer.

Lake

120 Yards

Place the tee beside water, not behind it.

Position of new forward tees.

Source: Alice O. Dye.

The placement of the additional tees for women must include the same considerations of safety, circulation, and playability for any tee. In particular, the following guidelines should be used to position new forward tees.

■ The tee should be placed to diminish a dogleg and encourage the proper playing angle on dogleg holes so that a longer shot does not go through the fairway.

■ The ball should not be capable of being hit from an adjacent hole.

■ New tees should be placed as close to the preceding green as possible, near the golf car path, and out of the line of vision of the back tees. The new tee should be positioned so that players do not cross in front of the back tee.

■ The tee should fit the natural contour of the ground.

■ The tee should be placed beside water instead of behind it.

Any variation of a multiple-tee system can achieve greater playability on a regulation course. Multiple-tee systems have several advantages:

■ Accommodation of a broader range of players' abilities;

■ Greater opportunity for variation in play from day to day simply by moving the position of tee markers;

■ Greater opportunity for recovery of tee surfaces where tee markers are frequently moved to alternate locations.

Such advantages are particularly useful for courses that are used intensively, have a target market whose players cover a broad range of abilities, or whose repeat players seek variety on the course from one visit to the next.

The USGA's handicap system makes it possible for golfers to play a match from different tees. The golfer playing from the higher course rating gets extra strokes in addition to the difference in course handicaps.[7] The same system applies when men and women compete together; in this case, the women's course rating is compared to the men's course rating for the respective tees they are using, and the extra strokes are calculated accordingly.

Tees can be any shape from rectangular to free-form curves. They can vary in size and, in many cases, can equal or exceed the total area of the green to make the course more playable. Whatever their size or shape, however, tees should be oriented so as to assist players in visualizing the intended line of play. The orientation and placement of tees play a significant role in a player's perception of a course's fairness. A novice player confronted with a golf course whose distances are beyond any reasonable chance of achieving a par score, even if every shot is hit well, will perceive the course as unfair and unplayable. Similarly, if the orientation of the tee and tee markers encourages play in a direction other than the intended line of play, fairness is compromised. Regardless of the method used to determine the placement of tees, the overriding consideration is whether they have been located to provide *playability and fairness* for all golfers, regardless of ability.

Design Criteria for Fair Play

Whether a player considers a course to be fair largely depends on that player's perception of whether he or she has a reasonable chance to successfully overcome the challenges presented by the course. Perhaps the best rule of fairness is that a well-hit ball should not be penalized. The orientation and placement of features other than tees also affect a course's playability in terms of a fair challenge for all players, regardless of their ability. Several criteria should be considered in determining whether a golf course offers fairness in playability. Beyond playability, the principal design criteria for today's golf courses should be accuracy, comfort, excitement, achievement, and fun. The real essence of the game is in its physical and *mental* challenge.

Solar and Wind Orientation

The orientation of a golf hole should not allow players to be blinded by the sun when shooting toward their target. The designer should remember that the majority of players start

a round of golf in the morning and finish in the afternoon.

■ Whenever possible, orient the starting holes (number 1 and number

Ball Lost in Sun

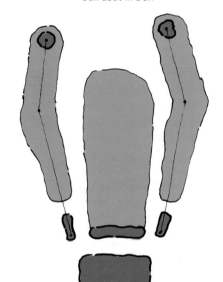

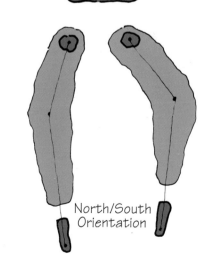

North/South Orientation

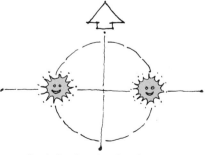

Source: Guy L. Rando & Associates Inc.

10) and finishing holes (number 9 and number 18) in a generally north/south direction.

- Avoid orienting the outgoing holes (number 1 and number 10) toward the morning sun.
- Avoid orienting the incoming holes (number 9 and number 18) toward the afternoon sun.

The solar orientations should be adjusted, however, according to a site's particular location.

The wind can also add a significant challenge for players, particularly novice players who have not yet learned to compensate for the effect of wind on the direction and distance of shots. On sites where the prevailing winds significantly alter the direction of a well-hit ball from the forward tees, the designer should consider providing physical and visual markers to help players determine the direction and strength of the wind.

Landing Areas and Elbow Points

Landing areas include all of the points along the centerline of intended play where a well-hit ball should land from back, middle, and forward tees. These points are also called "elbow points," because at these points the intended centerline

of play can be turned on an angle to form a dogleg. On a par-4 hole, the landing area is defined by the points where a full drive with a driver or number 1 wood off each tee is expected to land, including an allowance for the ball's bounce and roll after it hits the ground. The landing area from each tee position varies according to players' abilities. A par-5 hole has two landing areas, the first defined by a full drive off the tee, like the par-4 hole, and the second defined by a well-hit shot using a fairway wood or long iron from the first landing area. And because the landing area from each tee position varies, the distance achieved by different levels of players to the second landing area can result in a different landing area for each level of player.

The landing areas are in essence target points en route to the final target—the putting green. As targets, how landing areas are designed directly affects the course's fairness

and playability. Landing areas should be designed with certain criteria in mind:

- Landing areas should be visible from the tee or, in the case of a par-5 hole, from both the tee and the first landing area. To provide greater visibility, the fairway is usually wider in the landing areas. In some cases, the landing area from the forward tees is wider than the landing area from the back tees to accommodate less experienced players while still challenging better players. The fairway is oriented fairly symmetrically over the centerline of the hole between the tee and green, beginning about 50 to 75 yards in front of the middle tee, and varies from 35 to 60 yards wide, with 50 yards typical. The width of the fairway affects the difficulty of a hole and the strategy for playing it. At landing areas, the fairway should be at least 40 yards wide, with public

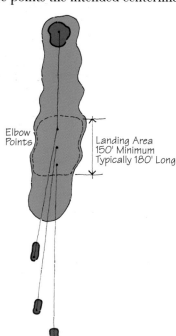

Landing areas include all the points along the centerline of play where a well-hit ball should land from the tees.
Source: Guy L. Rando & Associates Inc.

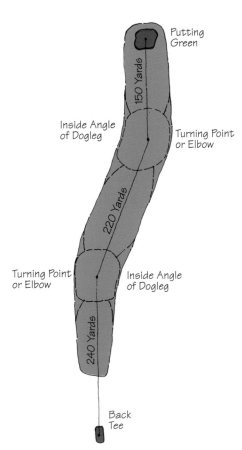

A par-5 hole has two landing areas.
Source: Guy L. Rando & Associates Inc.

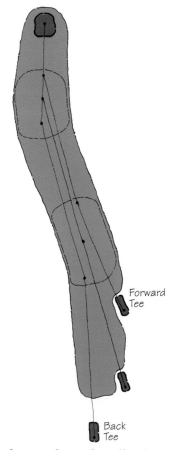

Doglegs can be used to offset forward tees out of the centerline of play from the back tees.
Source: Guy L. Rando & Associates Inc.

72

course operators preferring 45 yards.[8] If the fairway runs through heavy woods, the cleared areas generally should range from 175 to 200 feet wide[9] to allow a wider margin of error on the tee shot for an average golfer where heavy woods represent a severe penalty. Some cases, such as for a par-3 hole, might not include a fairway at all. These dimensions are for the fairway only, not including roughs or safety buffers. The boundary of the golf hole can be substantially wider than the fairway for safety.

- In no case should the landing area be in a blind area so that a player on the tee cannot see a player in the landing area ahead.
- Most landing areas should be graded to provide a fair lie, particularly for novice or less experienced players.
- Ideally, the green should be provided with a backdrop to provide a visually defining setting for the target. Setting the green against a hill or trees provides an effective backdrop that adds to visibility and depth perception for golfers.

The dogleg adds variety and an element of playing strategy to a hole. The most fundamental use of a dogleg is to change the direction of play on a hole. Thus, the design can accommodate a number of physical factors, such as topography (by bending the hole around the side of a hill), vegetation and trees to be preserved, or other obstacles. A dogleg can also be introduced to offset the centerline of play from a back or middle tee where the forward tee would otherwise be very close to the first landing area, thus providing a small margin of safety as well as possible strategic values.

The Strategic Use of Hazards and Bunkers

A hazard is an obstacle on a golf course that makes play more challenging. A *water* hazard is "any sea, lake, pond, river, ditch, surface drainage ditch, or other open water course (whether or not containing water) and anything of similar na-

Stone Harbour's #7 is a classic example of a "no fairway" par-3 hole.

PAUL BARTON

ture."[10] Thus, roads, paths, ground under repair or cultivation, mud or extreme wetness, bare patches, mounds, and vegetation are not hazards under this definition but "obstructions." A bunker, also known as a "sand trap," is "a hazard consisting of a prepared area of ground, often hollow, from which turf or soil has been removed and replaced with sand or the like."[11] Grass-covered ground bordering or within a bunker is not part of the bunker. Objects that define "out of bounds," such as walls, fences, stakes, and railings, are considered part of the ground on which play is prohibited (to their innermost point at ground level). While trees and topographic features like mounds and depressions are not by definition hazards, they are often used to create a strategic situation similar to a hazard.

The strategic use of bunkers at Wakagi's #14.

Hazards are incorporated in the design of a hole for several reasons:

■ To provide the opportunity for strategic play;
■ To provide visual clues that allow players to better judge distance or depth;
■ To direct the strategic placement of shots;

■ To direct traffic patterns of players and golf cars;
■ To penalize poorly placed shots;
■ To help absorb the impact of errant balls (sand decreases the ball's bounce);
■ To add aesthetic interest and variety to the landscape of the course.

Hazards should consist of natural site features—bodies of water, existing sand areas, rough depressions, ridges—whenever possible. Such physical features offer opportunities to shape the hole inexpensively to fit the potential hazard. Water hazards and bunkers can add significantly to the cost of construction and maintenance; therefore, they are best located where they have a critical role in playing strategy. The guiding principle for placement and design of hazards is to provide a reasonable chance to avoid them or, if in a bunker, to play out of it. In general:

■ Hazards should not be placed in the middle of a fairway so as to inhibit fair play. In particular, hazards should not be located in landing areas unless options to play around the hazard are provided (see "Styles of Holes" later in this chapter). Similarly, trees, vegetation, and obstructions should not be located in the middle of a fairway unless they influence the direction of play.
■ Excessively deep bunkers from which recovery is close to impossible and more a matter of luck than skill should be avoided. Such a hazard serves no useful purpose.
■ On par-4 holes, the longer the approach, the wider the opening between hazards at the front of the green should be. For a par-4 hole under 400 yards long, the opening should be at least 40 feet wide. For

Selective use of trees for strategic play at The Woods.

The pit of despair.
Source: *Guy L. Rando & Associates Inc.*

par-4 holes over 400 yards, the opening should be 80 feet wide.

■ On holes designed for a long approach shot to the green, the hazard should not be placed directly across the centerline of play (a frontal hazard). Because of the low trajectory of a long shot, a frontal hazard requires that a golfer play all the way to the putting green with enough backspin to hold the ball on the green. While accomplished golfers can handle this situation, an average golfer usually must reach the green by rolling the ball up to the green, making a frontal hazard particularly daunting. Therefore, frontal hazards should usually be reserved for short approach shots in which golfers use short irons for greater loft—for example, a par-3, short par-4, or par-5 hole.[12]

The #12 hole of the Apple Rock Course at Horseshoe Bay Resort and Conference Club contains a frontal hazard (water).

Sand is considered a traditional part of the game of golf, and the dramatic contrast of white sand against green turf contributes greatly to a course's aesthetic appeal. On the classic courses of Scotland, it is believed that bunkers were formed by sheep seeking shelter from the wind in the hollows. Sand bunkers add significantly to the challenge and the visual impression of a course, and, to many, a course without sand is unacceptable or at best inferior.[13] As a hazard, sand is particularly compatible with the strategic aspect of the game, for it provides a reasonable opportunity to recover or escape. A water hazard requires a penalty stroke, but sand allows the possibility that a skilled golfer can make the shot without losing a stroke.

The two basic types of bunkers are the fairway bunker (located along the fairway) and the greenside bunker (located around the green). The location of the fairway bunker is usually related to distance from the back or championship tees. On par-4

Classic greenside bunkers on #10 at Ram Rock Course, Horseshoe Bay Resort and Conference Club.

This water feature at Boca Rio Club at Boca Raton, Florida, provides a dramatic focal point and aids in maintaining a healthy pond by aerating and circulating the water.

holes, the bunker is usually a strategic part of all golfers' play, regardless of the ability or the tee's position. Green-side bunkers must be carefully located, for they affect more than the strategy of how the hole is played. They serve a critical role in directing the heavy traffic that occurs around the green, and they can also serve as a safety measure, as the sand bunker helps to trap errant balls, keeping them from bouncing onto adjacent tees or greens. On heavily used courses, a wider, bunker-free entrance to the green allows faster play, because fewer players are likely to be caught in a bunker as the result of a poor approach shot.

The size and shape of bunkers have no set limits. But because the primary purpose of a bunker is to penalize a badly placed shot, a bunker should be large enough and deep enough to make it more difficult to play out of the hazard than if the ball landed on the fairway or green. As a rule, greenside bunkers are deeper than fairway bunkers, permitting a golfer to use a longer iron or wood to escape the shallower fairway bunker and precluding escape with a putter from the deeper greenside bunker. In either case, the bunker should be configured so as not to interfere with a golfer's backswing.

Water features are unquestionably one of the most desirable aesthetic elements of a golf course. Existing bodies of water and water features provide one of the most economical means of introducing beauty and strategy to the design of a golf hole or golf course. Large bodies of water in the United States are required to store irrigation water, so water features can also serve a very practical use.

A water hazard offers no opportunity for recovery, and a penalty stroke is the only outcome of a ball that lands in one. Because of the heavy penalty and potential loss of balls that water hazards represent to players of all skills, water always causes golfers to think about how to negotiate the hazard. While water presents an opportunity for a dramatic shot by an accomplished player, less skilled players can be thoroughly frustrated and intimidated by a water hazard. For this reason, holes with water hazards must be carefully designed. The water hazard must be clearly visible to golfers, and an alternative route must be provided for players who do not feel capable of negotiating such a challenge.

Water hazards fall into two categories: water across the line of play and lateral water. The more dramatic of the two is water across the line of play, which requires a player to make a dramatic shot across the water on the tee shot or on the approach to the green. Lateral water, which runs along the line of play, represents a different challenge and requires a more defensive strategy. A hook or slice into a lateral water hazard results in a penalty stroke. In general:

■ Water hazards should be placed to be fully a part of the play rather than simply penalizing a bad shot.

Slick Rock #14 at Horseshoe Bay Resort and Conference Club requires a drive across a dramatic waterfall.

A lateral water hazard on Ram Rock #11 at Horseshoe Bay Resort and Conference Club.

Retaining wall made of railroad ties.

- A water hazard should never be placed in a landing area or where it is not visible to players.
- Water hazards directly in front of the tees have no value. They do not test good players, but if a ball lands in one, it slows play.

Topography and a Fair Lie

Working with the challenges presented by topography and lie (the relationship between the terrain and the position of the ball) is one of the great talents required of golf course architects. A perfectly flat lie is rare on golf courses, except on the tees, where the flat lie allows a player to take a full, unobstructed swing on the drive shot off the tee. Playing on sloping lies requires golfers to alter their stance and the way they address the ball to compensate for the slope. The topography or lie of landing areas is particularly important. A slope that is too extreme, causing the ball to roll into a hazard or off the course, is unfair. In this case, the slope should be graded or contoured to provide a fair lie for a well-hit ball. Retaining walls and geotextile slope stabilizers can be used to make the transition from one elevation to another within a limited horizontal distance, but retaining walls must be carefully designed to minimize balls' ricocheting off the surface.

Mounding and other detailed contouring (or "earth sculpting") of the fairway can provide aesthetic excitement and an exacting challenge for low-handicap, tournament, or professional golfers. Contouring should be limited to what fairway mowing equipment can handle without scalping the turf. Extreme contouring that requires special hand maintenance can be costly and should therefore be used only selectively.

Sloping lies directly affect the direction and distance of the ball's travel, despite compensation by the golfer. On a side slope where the ball

A model of Segovia's #8 hole shows how earth sculpting can be used for both challenge and beauty on the golf course.

A typical sideslope fairway at Spokane Country Club.

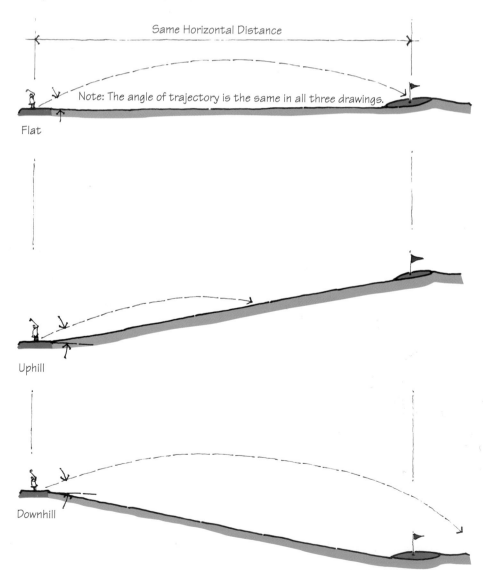

Same Horizontal Distance

Note: The angle of trajectory is the same in all three drawings.

Flat

Uphill

Downhill

Effect of topography on distance of balls hit with the same angle of trajectory.
Source: Guy L. Rando & Associates Inc.

travel, despite compensation by the golfer. On a side slope where the ball is above the golfer's feet, for example, the ball tends to fly to the left, but on a side slope where the ball is below the golfer's feet, the ball tends to fly to the right. The more severe the side slope, the greater the tendency for the ball to hook or slice.

On an uphill lie, the ball naturally tends to fly higher and shorter than on a flat lie. Hence, uphill holes are said to "play longer" than the actual horizontal distance they cover, and uphill orientations of golf holes are generally avoided because of poor visibility, players' fatigue, and longer playing time. Average golfers, however, tend to favor a slight uphill lie, because the position of the ball facilitates contact of the club with the ball before the club makes contact with the ground.

On a downhill lie, the ball tends to fly lower and longer than on a flat lie. Hence, downhill holes are said to "play shorter" than the actual horizontal distance they cover. A downhill orientation of golf holes is often preferred, primarily because it offers greater visibility and faster play. An average golfer, however, often finds a downhill lie, particularly a steep downhill lie, more difficult, because of the tendency to hit the ground ahead of the ball.

Generally, the more severe the slope, the greater the effect on the ball's trajectory. The golf course architect must consider all of these factors in designing a hole. The design must allow for the effect of topography on the ball's trajectory to ensure the hole's fairness, playability, and safety for players.

Styles of Holes

As the design of golf courses evolved, three basic philosophies emerged, expressed in the style of the holes or the course and how they tested the abilities of golfers: penal, strategic, and heroic.

A penal golf hole is characterized by many sand traps or water hazards placed to penalize a poorly played or errant shot. Most of the golf holes built on the country's earliest courses are penal, largely because the holes were patterned after British golf courses where naturally occurring hazards would be scattered randomly through the course. This style is infrequently used today, as the numerous hazards that characterize this style are often placed unfairly for golfers of average ability. A penal golf hole rewards only those who can hit straight, true, and long shots. It tends to slow down play and to discourage average recreational golfers;

thus, is not recommended for golf courses serving anyone other than the most proficient golfers.

A strategic hole is designed so that a golfer must play position to score well. Poorly played or errant shots are not severely punished. Often called a "thinking player's lay-out," the hazards are located on the fairway and green so that taking the riskier shot off the tee is rewarded with an easier shot to the green (no hazards), while taking the more conservative shot off the tee results in a more challenging approach to the green (usually requiring play over a hazard to the green).[14]

A heroic golf hole is characterized by alternative routes of play, with one route significantly more difficult than the other. The difficult, or "heroic," route rewards a well-played long shot with a chance for a birdie or at least par while promising disaster if the shot is not perfectly executed. The safer alternative route comes at the expense of an extra stroke.

Contemporary golf courses are designed to offer golfers choices as to the placement, direction, and length of a golf shot and usually follow the strategic or heroic philosophy or a combination of the two. Each golfer can thus select the strategy best suited to his or her own ability. A less accurate golfer might choose the longer route with fewer hazards and more strokes, while an accurate golfer would take the shorter route requiring long distances over or between hazards with fewer strokes.

← Green tilts toward bunker

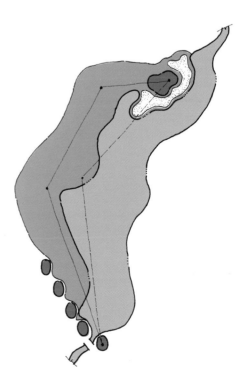

Penal, strategic, and heroic holes (left to right) test golfers' abilities in various ways.
Source: Guy L. Rando & Associates Inc.

Source: Desmond Muirhead, Inc.

Beyond these basic design criteria for fair play, the golf course of today should emphasize accuracy of shots, comfort, excitement, achievement, and *fun*. The real essence of the game is in the physical and *mental* challenge.

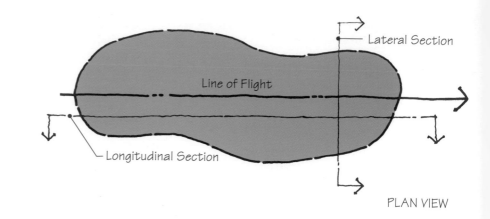

PLAN VIEW

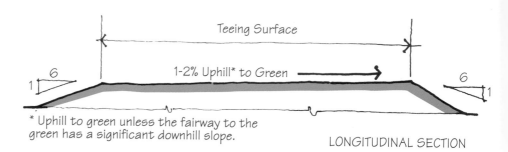

* Uphill to green unless the fairway to the green has a significant downhill slope.

LONGITUDINAL SECTION

Design Strategies for Operational Flexibility and Easy Maintenance

The size and design of features like tees, greens, bunkers, fairways, and roughs can greatly affect a golf course's operational flexibility and ease of maintenance. The ability to maintain a course in a playable condition begins with designs that allow cost-effective operation and maintenance. Long-term costs are a significant concern for any golf operation.

Size and Detail of Tees

For golf courses today, the tee is considered an area of ground that has been specifically designed for the first shot on a hole. The tee includes the "teeing ground" defined by tee markers and can be rectangular, square, circular, or irregular.

A tee generally is elevated to allow optimum drainage required to maintain healthy turf in an area of heavy, concentrated traffic and to provide good visibility for golfers. The tee is usually pitched to drain front to back or side to side, depending on the surrounding topography, but otherwise the tee surface appears flat.

Early golf courses usually had small rectangular tees in scale with the low levels of play typical during the time. As the popularity of golf boomed in the 1950s and 1960s, tees became larger to accommodate frequent relocation of the tee markers. The frequent relocation of tee markers actually makes maintaining the turf easier despite the intense play, because excessive wear of any one area is reduced and time needed for the turf to recover is hastened. Usually the tee is longest along the axis of the fairway, and the golfer tees off at various locations each day. Tees that

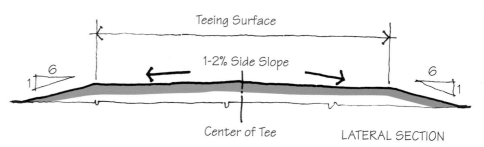

LATERAL SECTION

A typical tee.
Source: Robert Muir Graves, Ltd.

are wider than they are long offer more opportunities for variety in play.

Contemporary courses place a much greater emphasis on tees as a convenient and inexpensive means of introducing flexibility, variety, and interest to the course's layout and play of a hole. Constructing several tees or one very large tee allows the length of the hole to be revised as desired. The opportunity to move tee markers to different locations on a large tee provides the returning golfer some variety in playing the same hole and permits rejuvenation of worn spots without closing down the hole. Inexpensive "winter tees" on many courses permit work on the regular tee without closing the hole (as well as extending the golfing season).

Size and Detail of Greens

Putting greens on contemporary courses are usually elevated to provide drainage and better visibility to the target for approaching players. Greens vary in size, shape, and contouring based on the specific setting and characteristics of play intended for the hole.

Some courses have developed a two-green or alternate greens system to protect greens from long-term damage where climate permits play over a long season or year-round. The two-green system, more commonly used in Japan than in the United States, includes one green for summer use (with Bermuda grasses) and another for winter use (with bent grasses). The two-green system allows flexible maintenance without interrupting play and can be particularly advantageous for golf courses that are used intensively. The alternate greens system provides a temporary, smaller green to the front or side of the regular green where play is possible during repair of the regular green or during the winter.

The putting green can range from as small as 1,200 square feet to over 27,000 square feet. In the United States, typical putting greens range from 5,000 to 8,000 square feet. On intensively used courses, greens should be at least 6,500 square feet.[15] Not long ago, large greens became popular to permit pins to be moved frequently, allowing turf to recover from high traffic and to provide variety for players. The size, shape, and contour of the green are specific to every hole and affect strategy and difficulty of play. In general:

- The longer the approach shot, the deeper the green along the line of play to allow for the ball's low trajectory and its tendency to roll on landing.
- The smaller the green, the smaller the target and thus the more difficult the hole.
- Greens should be large enough to accommodate variable contours and challenges.
- Greens should be large enough to accommodate flexibility in placing the cup, thus enabling movement of traffic and giving the turf a chance to recover.
- Every green should have at least six areas for placement of pins with varying degrees of difficulty.
- Pins should be located at least 12 feet from the edge of the putting surface, with 15 feet from the edge preferred.[16]
- While the green should be contoured to "hold" the approaching shot, its contours should also allow rapid surface drainage and be free of any depressions where water can collect. Preferably, a few gentle swales should direct the surface water off to the sides, but draining all the surface water toward the front of the green where a high

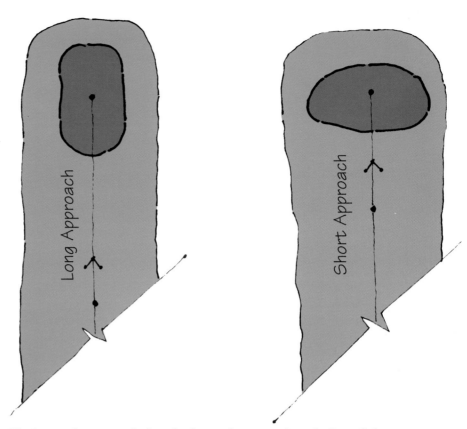

The longer the approach shot, the deeper the green along the line of play.
Source: Guy L. Rando & Associates Inc.

concentration of foot traffic occurs should be avoided because of the associated wear on the turf and problems of compaction. It is also disconcerting to a golfer to have a shot that is slightly short get stuck in soggy soil.
- Contours should be fairly gentle, with a slope of 2 to 4 percent where the cup is set. Special effects—small areas with slopes from 4 to 20 percent to form bumps or rolls in the surface—can be incorporated. Significant changes in contour, however, should be associated with different pin placement areas, should permit economical maintenance, and should allow golfers a reasonable opportunity to put the approach putt close to the cup.
- The green should generally be "tilted," with the back higher than the front, so that the green is visible to golfers. If the hole is located on tight or poorly drained subsoils or in an area where the water table is high, the green should be elevated over the existing grade to al-

low for optimum drainage and aeration of the putting area.

Location and Detail of Bunkers

From the standpoint of maintenance, greenside bunkers should be configured to allow a sufficiently wide area of turf for golfers to enter the green and exit to the next tee to reduce the wear and compaction associated with heavy foot traffic. Also from the standpoint of maintenance, the bunkers should be located no closer than 10 to 12 feet from the putting surface (the collar) to allow the use of larger mowing equipment with sufficient room to operate and to turn. This allowance also prevents sand blasted out of a bunker from a shot from getting onto the green and damaging its surface and the equipment used to maintain it. The designer must also consider surface and subsurface drainage in deciding where to locate bunkers, as bunkers require excellent drainage. Surface drainage must be directed so that water does

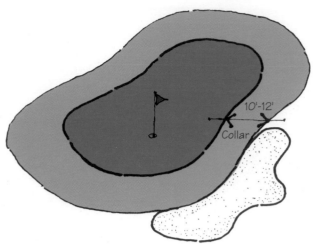

Allow 10 to 12 feet clearance between the bunker and green for easier maintenance.
Source: Guy L. Rando & Associates Inc.

not flow into the bunkers, and the bunker should not cause water to get trapped on the green or fairway. Any water that falls onto the bunker must drain away quickly and freely. In areas with tightly compacted subsoils or high water tables, the floor of the bunker must be elevated to ensure positive drainage.

The basic components of a bunker are the "lip," the "face," and the "base." The lip is found primarily on greenside bunkers; it is often defined by a vertical area of turf that forms over the sand and facing the putting green so as to prevent a player from putting out of the bunker. The lip also prevents balls from rolling out of the bunker and defines the edge of the bunker for maintenance operations. The face is the sloped area of the bunker normally visible to players. While it was originally intended to make getting out of the bunker difficult, today's sand wedges and strategic play mean a bunker serves more as a highly visible obstacle that makes players plan their shots. For maintenance and to avoid the ten-

dency of sand to slip down excessively steep slopes, the maximum slope of the bunker face should not exceed 35 percent or a 3:1 slope. The base of the bunker is the generally flatter area at the toe of the face, farthest from the green or fairway.

Bunkers come in several basic designs. Typical at the turn of the century were pot bunkers or pits, cross bunkers, and grass-faced bunkers. Of the three types, pot bunkers are the smallest—sometimes barely large enough for a person to stand in—and are generally round and deep. Cross bunkers are long and narrow and cross the fairway or are placed in front of the green. They were often associated with a heroic shot off the tee. Grass-faced bunkers are steep mounds with grass growing down the face to the base of the slope where it meets sand.[17] These earlier bunkers characterize what could be done in an era when moving earth was very limited and often accomplished with great effort by horse-drawn scoops. The heavy equipment used to construct courses today and the large

mowers used to maintain them make these bunkers all but extinct on contemporary courses.

The most common types of bunkers found on contemporary courses are the flash trap or sand-faced bunker, the cape-and-bay bunker, and the boarded bunker. The flash trap is the most popular bunker used on contemporary courses. Characterized by gently curved contours and gently upward sloping sand built at or slightly above grade, the bunker is plainly visible to golfers. It is easy to construct and maintain with power equipment and simple to drain, making it particularly economical.

The cape-and-bay bunker is a modified imitation of the grass and sand dunes of the Scottish seacoast, where long grass overhangs the edge of sand rises. It is regarded as the most dramatic and artistic of the types of bunkers: varying heights, widths, and depths of sand contrast against grass capes in a visually and aesthetically effective bunker. While these bunkers are popular with golfers because of their aesthetic appeal and association with the wild landscapes of the Scottish seacoast, cape-and-bay bunkers cost considerably more to maintain because the grass cape must be mowed by hand. And while maintenance costs can be reduced by allowing the capes to take on a shaggy, wild appearance, the advantage is offset by slower play, which might not be acceptable on heavily used courses.

The concept of boarded bunkers is borrowed from the oldest Scottish courses, where wooden railroad ties, sandbags, or stone was used to support the face of the bunkers. This type of bunker should be designed and used with caution, as a ball can easily rebound off the hard surface and hit a player. Generally, when railroad ties or other hard surfaces are used to face a bunker, they should be designed to form a line along the direction of play, not *across* the line of play. If railroad ties or other hard retaining walls are used to front a bunker, requiring players to hit over the wall, the face of the wall should be laid back suffi-

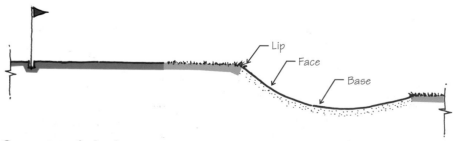

Components of a bunker.
Source: Guy L. Rando & Associates Inc.

Typical sand-faced bunkers on Shinyo #12.

ciently to eliminate a ball's ricocheting off the wall into a player.

Bunkers can range from small, deep pot bunkers barely large enough for a person to stand in to expansive areas of sand where the only turf areas are the tees, fairways, and greens. On courses in the United States, they typically range from 1,000 to 3,000 square feet for greenside bunkers and 2,500 to 4,000 square feet or more for fairway bunkers.[18] Generally, the wider the fairway, the larger the bunker can be and still maintain fair play and prevent backups on heavily used courses. A contempo-

rary 18-hole golf course averages 40 to 80 bunkers over the course, although the trend has been toward fewer bunkers because of their high maintenance costs.[19]

Size and Detail of Water Hazards

Ponds, lakes, reservoirs, and other water features serve many functions on the golf course, including stormwater management, water quality control, and storage of irrigation water. How large they should be depends on capacity required and other engineering factors. The design

of the water's edge directly affects the playability of adjacent surfaces and the ease of maintenance. Some finishes that could be used include:

- Turf to the water's edge;
- A shallow area to support growth of emergent water plants;
- Gravel or sand banks;
- Timbers or railroad ties;
- Concrete, stone, or another form of masonry;
- Geotextile mats to retain and stabilize the slope.

The use of bulkheads provides freeboard (the vertical distance be-

A large bunker at Horseshoe Bay Resort and Conference Club.

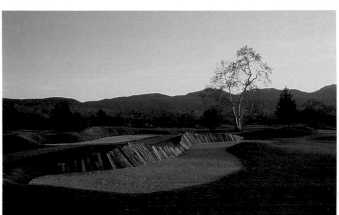

Bunker faced with railroad ties at Carlton Oaks #9.

83

tween the water line and the playing surface) for water storage, allowing the water level to fluctuate with minimal detrimental impact on playable areas of adjacent golf holes. Impoundments of stormwater that serve to enhance flood control by accepting, retaining, and re-releasing stormwater runoff at a slower rate can realize dramatic fluctuations in water levels. Without freeboard, the adjacent fairway, roughs, and other playing areas of the golf course can become inundated as the water level rises during a storm. Bulkheads provide a relatively maintenance-free treatment of the edge for bodies of water with fluctuating water levels. Turf adjacent to the water does not become saturated and spongy as a result of the inherent capillary action of soil typically found in shallow, sloped bodies of water. This fact might help reduce long-term costs of maintenance, as mowing does not have to be altered to accommodate wet or unstable soils typically found

near the water line. Bulkheads also provide a means of taking up vertical elevations between water and adjacent playing surfaces, particularly useful when the horizontal distance is inadequate to take up the slope adjacent to the water, resulting in an excessively steep lie that deflects the ball into the water. The bulkhead can be designed to provide sufficient vertical height to ease the toe of the slope and reduce the tendency of the ball to roll toward the water. Bulkheads can also be used to control the points where stormwater runoff enters bodies of water. Timber or railroad tie bulkheads provide a relatively affordable, easily constructed means of providing freeboard. While masonry bulkheads might provide greater durability over the long term, their initial cost can be two to three times greater than timber or railroad tie bulkheads.

The rise and fall of water levels tend to result in siltation and accumulation of debris along shallow,

sloped edges. Therefore, gently sloped water edges are more appropriate for bodies of water that will have a fairly constant water level and/or for impoundments designed to function as biologic filters. A constant shallow water depth is required for optimum growth of the emergent and rooted surface plants that play a critical role in removing waterborne nutrients, sediments, and toxicants. (See "Environmental Issues" later in this chapter.)

The Rough

The fairway can extend from treeline to treeline (commonly called a "wall-to-wall fairway") on a wooded or heavily vegetated site, or the perimeter of the fairway can be defined by an area of turf that is mowed to a higher height than the fairway, or "rough." The rough serves two main purposes: to define the limits of the fairway, and to create a strategic element of play by penalizing a poorly placed shot. The rough can vary in

Railroad tie lake bulkhead at Carlton Oaks #12.

Contrasting roughs at Sea Ranch Golf Course.

as a strategic or penal element has supporters and opponents. From one point of view, the rough is designed and maintained with progressively taller or denser grass or vegetation the farther the golfer gets from the fairway so that the greater the error in the shot, the more difficult it is to get out of the rough. Because average or novice players are more apt to hit an uncontrolled shot into the rough than more accomplished ones, however, the use of the rough as a penal element runs against the principles of strategic golf. Deep roughs are generally considered more appropriate for courses frequented by better or accomplished golfers, such as those where professional tournaments are played. Roughs are often eliminated on intensely used public courses serving a wide range of abilities to reduce the number of lost balls and keep up or increase the speed of play.

Courses that include roughs can include both a primary rough and a secondary rough, with the primary rough closer to the fairway where errant balls are most likely to land. In both cases, the terms indicate different mowing heights for the turf. The secondary rough can simply be higher than the primary rough or can include vegetation and woods. Whether or not a course includes roughs depends on a variety of factors, including available land area, proximity of trees and hazards, and market de-

mand. With golf courses' increasing impact on the environment, how roughs are designed and managed has taken on greater importance in the design of a course (see "Environmental Issues" later in this chapter). The primary rough can range from 10 to 15 yards wide; its sharply defined height makes the edge of the fairway easy to see.

The Driving Range and Practice Greens

A driving range and practice putting greens are typically included as part of a golf course operation. They are generally located near the clubhouse for the golf pro's easy access.

The driving range is approximately 350 yards long by a width depending on the desired capacity of the range. Its capacity can vary, depending on the size of the membership or the market. Generally, it includes at least 10 10- to 12-foot-wide teeing stations. In some cases, the driving range could have teeing stations at both ends, in which case it must be at least 330 yards long (see "Golf Academies" in Chapter 3). The primary purpose of a driving range is to provide a controlled area where golfers can practice drives. Target "greens" can be provided on the driving range to challenge accuracy. Some driving ranges also include teeing areas that simulate a variety of fairway lies, chipping greens, and practice bunkers. A driving range is ideally oriented along a north/south axis, with golfers driving toward the north, offering the least amount of conflict between visibility and the sun. When possible, the driving range should also be oriented so that shots are taken into the prevailing wind.

A practice putting green is often located near the clubhouse. It is usually large enough to accommodate several pin positions and contoured to provide a variety of challenges. The practice green can be extended to form a "putting course" (see "Golf Academies" in Chapter 3).

Putting course at Horseshoe Bay Resort and Conference Club.

Variations in Golf Courses

The 18-hole standard for a golf course originated at the Royal and Ancient Golf Club in 1764, when the number of holes at St. Andrews was reduced from 22 to 18. It occurred when the Royal and Ancient Club was writing rules for play, and members agreed on the 18-hole standard by common consent. Variations on the 18-hole standard have evolved for many reasons, among them accommodating the game on a restricted site or accommodating the demands of a specific market.

Among the variations that have been developed are executive courses, par-3 courses, compact courses, and nine-hole courses. They are basically modifications in course length to accommodate the game on a restricted site or for a specific market, such as lunchtime golfers, resorts, or golf schools. Another variation of a short course that was developed for smaller sites is Cayman golf, in which the golf ball is modified so that it travels only half the distance of a regular golf ball. On the other end of the scale are 18+3 courses and 27-hole, 36-hole, and 54-hole courses, which can accommodate greater volume

and variety of play. The stadium course is specifically designed to accommodate large galleries for PGA tours or other professional tournaments.

The Executive Course

The executive course is shorter than the traditional regulation course. It generally includes a total par of 28 to 33 for a nine-hole course, with a course length of 1,500 to 2,300 yards *or* a total par of 55 to 67 for an 18-hole course, with a course length of 3,000 to 4,500 yards. It generally consists of par-3 and par-4 holes, with a par-5 hole possible only within the constraints of the site. The holes are shorter than those typically found in a regulation course, but all the criteria for playability should still be met.

Because the executive course is shorter, it requires less land than a regulation course, usually 60 to 95 acres; thus, it is useful on sites where acreage might be insufficient to accommodate a regulation course. It is also useful in urban areas where land costs are high.

While the term "executive course" was probably coined to appeal to business executives, the shorter course appeals to many other market sectors,

including novice golfers, junior golfers, seniors, and women. Some golf course architects have therefore advocated the use of the term "challenge course" instead. The shorter length is generally less intimidating to players, because even a player with a high handicap can shoot a lower score. The game can be taken less seriously on most executive courses, making it especially appealing to occasional players. An executive course might also appeal to:

- Players with a limited amount of time available to play a round of golf, as the shorter course can be played in less time than a regulation course;
- Players with physical limitations, who might find a shorter course easier to walk;
- Players with limited disposable incomes, as greens fees are usually lower on executive courses.

The Par-3 Course

A par-3 course consists of all par-3 holes. An 18-hole, par-3 course thus has a total par of 54 and usually ranges from 2,000 to 2,400 yards. To provide variety on a par-3 course,

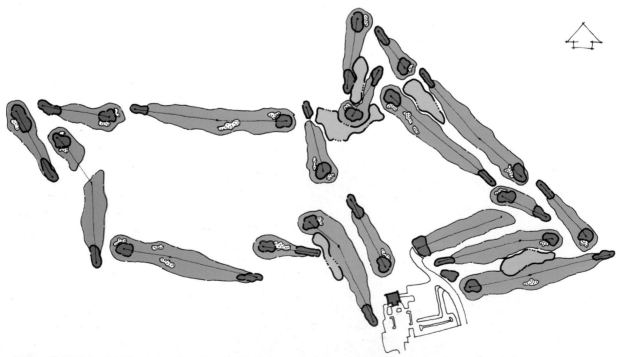

Hidden Lakes Golf Course in New Smyrna Beach, Florida, is an 18-hole, par-62 executive course playing at 4,400 yards from the blue tees, 4,001 yards from the white tees, and 3,569 yards from the red tees.
Source: William W. Amick.

individual holes should vary from 75 to 240 yards. Courses with only very short holes intended for play with wedges and number 9 irons (75 to 130 yards) are often called "pitch-and-putt courses." A nine-hole pitch-and-putt course can range from 700 to 1,100 yards, an 18-hole pitch-and-putt course from 1,400 to 2,200 yards.

The market appeal of a par-3 course is generally the same as for an executive course, except it is particularly attractive to less dedicated and experienced golfers. Most par-3 courses have little appeal for strong, highly skilled golfers, except for occasional play. Many par-3 courses also have a driving range to attract a broader market.

The major advantages of a par-3 course are the substantially smaller requirement for land and the lower costs associated with the smaller facility. A par-3 course is particularly useful when the site has tight boundaries or includes difficult terrain, as the shorter lengths and narrower fairways associated with par-3 holes make it possible to fit a course more easily than one with par-4 or par-5 holes. A nine-hole pitch-and-putt course, for example, might require only 10 acres of land on a relatively flat site, while an 18-hole, par-3 course with lengths similar to those found on par-3 holes on a regulation course (75 to 240 yards) might require up to 50 acres.

Location near a populated area with good highway exposure is helpful for generating play on this type of course. The small size could make lighting for evening play feasible, but night lighting can be objectionable if the course is located in a residential community.

Compact Courses

Compact courses are more popular in Europe than in the United States. No standards exist for compact courses; they basically include whatever is desired and whatever the situation permits. The course can be any number of holes of any length in any sequence. They might be a variation on an executive or a par-3 course, with the distinction of being built on the existing terrain. Courses that are built with little modification of existing terrain are reminiscent of the historic Scottish links, which consisted of areas where rich alluvial deposits of soil were left on sand dunes by a river as it flowed into the sea.[20] Bunkers and hazards were formed by the erosion of wind and rain and by hollows formed by sheep and birds seeking shelter from the weather. The terrain of the land dictated the route the player would follow, with rabbit holes reputedly serving as target holes. In the contemporary translation of the Scottish links, compact courses might do little more than

prepare the existing grade for a playable surface.

In addition to the advantages of the executive and par-3 courses, compact courses can provide:

- A place where beginners or juniors can gain some experience and competency before venturing onto the main course;
- A place for lessons in golf, particularly at a golf academy;
- A fast round of lunchtime or twilight golf;
- A way to accommodate play when the main course is full;
- A place where seniors or people who cannot negotiate a full course can play;
- A marketing tool to introduce prospective buyers or members to play while the main course is still under construction;
- A means of continuing play while the main course is under repair or renovation.

Like other short courses, compact courses require less land, are quicker to build, and are less expensive to construct and maintain. Such courses could also make a golf course possible where environmental conditions or regulations otherwise preclude such a land use—a golf course in a desert environment, for example.

Cayman Golf

"Cayman golf" is the popular term for what is otherwise known as "modified golf." Its name is derived from the site of its introduction on the Cayman Islands, Britannia Resort. The basis of Cayman golf is a lightweight golf ball introduced in 1985 that travels a little more than half the distance of a regular golf ball. Players still hit all the shots they normally would, using the same full range of golf clubs they use on a regular course. As a result, the Cayman golf course can be considerably shorter, in theory about half the length of a regulation course. Further, it might be possible to have narrower fairways than for a regular golf course, because errant Cayman balls do not travel as far and presumably

#6 at Hidden Lakes Golf Course.

are not as dangerous. Like executive, par-3, and compact courses, Cayman golf courses provide a means of accommodating the game of golf on smaller sites or on sites constrained by topography or sensitive environments. For a real estate developer, a Cayman course might provide a savings in areas where land costs are high, but it does not necessarily represent a savings in construction or long-term maintenance costs. The costs of constructing and maintaining the tees and greens for a Cayman course are, for the most part, the same as those for a regulation course. Its supporters believe that Cayman golf is a viable option for the future, as a Cayman ball can also be used on executive and par-3 courses and thus might also accommodate safer playing conditions on existing short courses with inadequate safety margins. Others are more reserved about its future potential, for players' acceptance and experience with the game are limited. Golfers seem to prefer hitting the ball twice as far, not half as far.

Other Supplemental Courses

While short courses have many advantages, they might not be financially feasible in certain markets, particularly if the market for golf is weak. Often, a golf course operation uses a variety of a short course as a *supplement* to a regulation course rather than the primary course to expand operational flexibility, market appeal, and capacity of play. One variation is the "18+3 course," which combines a regulation 18-hole course with a compact three-hole course. In this configuration, the three-hole compact course could be used for lessons, a quick round at lunchtime, or beginners and juniors without disrupting operations and play on the regulation course. The 18+3 configuration also can provide greater operational flexibility while one or more holes on the regulation course are under repair. The three-hole course can be designed to permit rerouting of the 18-hole course sequence so that the holes in need of

repair or rest and recovery can be temporarily taken out of play with minimal disruption.

Other combinations and variations include 27-hole, 36-hole, and 54-hole courses, which are combinations of nine-hole and 18-hole courses varying in length, difficulty, and style to offer golfers a number of choices.

Point-to-Point Golf™ [21]

Over the past few decades, the game of golf, golf courses, and golf equipment have evolved to reward long hitters. Every golfer dreams of "smacking the ball a mile." Going

for distance has become a popular notion among golfers with the televising of professional golf tournaments. It is not unusual to see a golf pro hit a drive well over 300 yards, to the delight and admiration of golfing fans. This drive for distance has presented significant problems in golf course design, however. Many existing golf courses were not designed for such long drives. Designers of new courses must consider this tendency toward the drive for distance and design courses with larger margins for safety than in the past, taking serious risks and liabilities into consideration. Consequently, larger

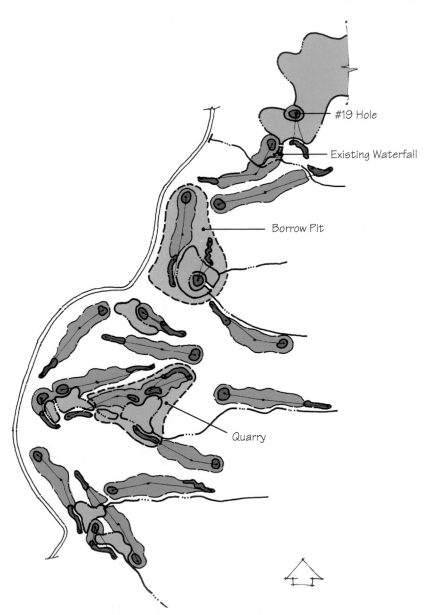

Holly Forest Golf Course in Sapphire Valley, North Carolina, is a 19-hole golf course for a resort community in the Great Smoky Mountains.
Source: Guy L. Rando & Associates Inc.

areas of land could be required to accommodate a new course with wider safety margins. Existing courses could require major renovations and adjustments in layout and design to meet the challenge. The problem is further exacerbated when real estate development is oriented around a golf course. Developers are faced with the costs of complying with regulations for environmental protection, high land costs, scarce financing, and a society prone to litigate. Difficult compromises must often be considered to contain the cost of developing a golf course and maintain reasonable objectives.

Point-to-Point Golf™ was invented to provide a new direction for the game of golf and the design of golf courses of the future. Its main objective is to change the game to minimize the conflicts and compromises while increasing options and opportunities. Its features include:

- A reward for accuracy and finesse rather than distance;
- The ability to play from existing tees and greens with minor modifications;
- Challenging play on shorter courses with adaptability for regulation courses;
- Use of existing course rating and handicap systems to accommodate equitable play regardless of golfers' ability;
- Play with existing equipment;
- Encouragement for players to use every club in their bag at some point on the course;
- A challenge for low-handicap (back-tee) golfers combined with fun alternatives for beginners and high-handicap (forward-tee) golfers;
- An optional challenge. Players can play the course with or without taking on the challenge of Point-to-Point Golf™. A group of players can individually opt to play point-to-point on individual holes or over the entire course without affecting the conventional game. If one player in a group opts to play point-to-point, the other players in the group need not play. Point-to-point scoring can be in addition to or in place of conventional golf scoring for par.

Design of the point-to-point course involves specially designed "point zones" within the fairways and greens, strategically located to challenge accuracy and finesse, *not* distance. Each point zone contains "hot points."

The object of Point-to-Point Golf™ is to land the shot within the point zone, as close to the hot point as possible. Points are awarded for landing within the point zone, and the closer the ball to the hot spot, the more points awarded. Scoring is cumulative. If the game is played for the hole, the player with the highest point score for that hole wins the hole. If the game is played over the entire course or selected holes on the course, the player with the highest cumulative point score over the course wins the game. A variation of Point-to-Point Golf™ is to trade in points against strokes taken on the hole.

Note that point zones are located to reward shorter drives off the back tees than conventional golf course designs normally accommodate.

A number of design details are used to visually define the point zones and hot points, including topographic features, distinctive landscaping, markers and pins, patterns of mowing and mowing heights, and a contrast in color or texture of zone turf or other surface material.

Point zones can have one or more hot points. Hot points are designed to be flexible, capable of being moved from day to day. Additionally, different hot points can be designated for each tee position.

Point-to-Point Golf™ provides a viable alternative for developers of golf courses and particularly for developers of golf-oriented real estate projects. It has become increasingly difficult and costly to acquire the larger areas of land required to ac-

The concept plan for stadium golf in Japan shows a 36-hole golf course consisting of 12 returning threes to accommodate a wide variety of play combinations and quick rounds of golf.
Source: Guy L. Rando & Associates Inc.

commodate safety and environmental features and to accommodate a regulation golf course on limited and/or expensive land. Supporters of shorter-length golf courses note that the majority of golfers prefer the shorter courses because they have a better chance to get a decent score. From the standpoint of operational cost-efficiency, shorter courses play faster and can be walked more easily, reducing demand for golf cars and paths. But few have enthusiastically embraced short courses as a standard over regulation or championship courses. It has yet to be determined whether shorter courses are significantly less costly than regulation courses in terms of construction cost or long-term maintenance, or whether the golf market will readily accept shorter courses over regulation courses. Developers of golf courses and golf-oriented real estate must capture the broadest market possible to ensure financial success. Short courses lack appeal to a small yet vocal segment of the golf market—the professional or low-handicap golfer.

#19 at Holly Forest Golf Course in Fairfield Sapphire Valley is a challenging water-carry tie-breaker "final bet" hole.

Thus, short courses have been regarded as a *compromise* rather than as the preferred choice.

While Point-to-Point Golf™ can be played on any existing course, it is particularly suited to the development of new shorter courses without the problem of limited market appeal. Point-to-Point Golf™ challenges professional or low-handicap players by requiring skilled play rather than the ability to smack the ball as hard as possible. Distance is no longer the primary objective;

therefore, course length is no longer the primary design criterion. Point-to-Point Golf™ also provides average, beginner, junior, or occasional golfers of varying skills with a wider range of options that challenge skills in a variety of ways. It might best be summarized as a return to the original spirit of the game, when the mind was the tool of the game to be mastered.

Irrigation Systems

A properly engineered and installed irrigation system is necessary to sustain a playable golf course in many

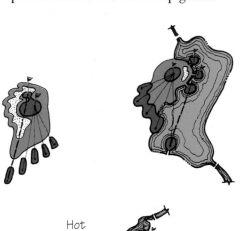

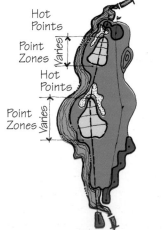

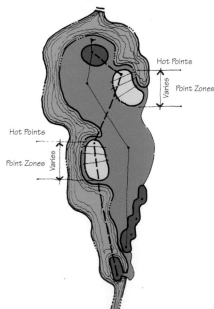

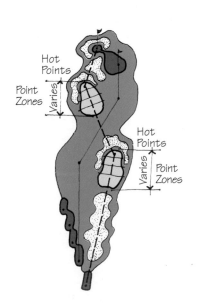

Concepts used in Point-to-Point Golf™.
Source: Guy L. Rando & Associates Inc.

arid areas of the world. Other areas where the climate is moist and temperate, like the British Isles, seemingly require a minimum amount of irrigation. The range of uncontrollable variables, however, makes reliance on rainfall very risky. Irrigation provides a precise way to regulate and control the rate and duration of water needed to germinate grass seed and maintain the turf in a playable condition. If real estate sales are associated with a golf course, the condition and appearance of the turf can make or break a sale. It can be said that irrigation systems provide a form of insurance.

For a golf-oriented real estate development, the irrigation specialist is an important member of the planning and design team, and that input is important from the early stages of site feasibility studies through construction and initial course management. The design process for the irrigation system must be tightly coordinated with all other design activities. Thus, the irrigation specialist is often a member of the golf course architect's staff or works directly with the golf course architect. The process of designing an irrigation system requires several steps:

- *Determine water needs.* Based on climatic data and the physical site, water demand is usually expressed in terms of inches per week. The demand can be referred to as "evapotranspiration," the sum of the evaporation of water and transpiration of turf plants per unit of time (day, week, or month). The analysis is based on data such as:
  - the frequency, intensity, and duration of rainfall;
  - seasonal, daily, and hourly fluctuations in climate, temperature, and humidity;
  - physical factors like slope and the ability of soils and plants to absorb and retain moisture.
- *Determine water sources and water rights.* Many sites have some source of surface water, such as a stream, river, lake, or pond, but their storage capacity, rate of flow, history of water fluctuation, and the rate and conditions under which

other users draw water must be investigated. Legal counsel might be involved in researching and securing water rights. Water rights might or might not allow stormwater runoff to be captured in ponds or lakes as a source of irrigation water. If a well is planned, necessary permits and certifications of delivery rate must be secured.
- *Determine water quality.* Once sources and water rights are established, the quality of the water supply and its suitability for irrigating turf must be determined by a qualified laboratory. Such tests will reveal any problems, such as the presence of pollutants or contaminants that could be toxic to turf. If effluent is a source of water for irrigation, the quality of the effluent must be determined, because it will directly influence the depth of building setbacks or buffer zones between effluent-irrigated turf and surrounding development or other land uses.
- *Determine requirements for water storage.*
- *Prepare preliminary design and cost estimates* based on the golf course architect's master plan, delineating the areas of turf and landscaping that will require irrigation. Prepare conceptual plans for location of the pump house, main irrigation lines, sprinkler heads, and control units as well as preliminary cost estimates.
- *Begin the approval process.* Some states regulate the quantity and quality of water used to irrigate golf courses. In Arizona, for example, irrigation plans for a proposed golf course must show that use of water will not exceed 4.8 acre-feet per acre of turf, and the total irrigated turf area may not exceed 90 acres. Maryland is in the process of formulating regulations for maximum water use based on historical data. Florida is in the process of requiring effluent as a source of irrigation water, and proposed legislation requires a developer to cover the cost of improvements required to bring the effluent from the public utility to the project site. De-

pending on local regulations, documentation must be prepared to demonstrate the design's compliance with regulatory requirements.
- *Prepare construction documents,* including:
  - fully detailed mechanical diagrams
  - programming instructions
  - electrical details
  - diagram for the pump station
  - detailed component schematics
  - specifications.
- *Monitor construction.* Changes to positions of tees, greens, and other elements of the golf course are inevitable during construction. When changes occur, the irrigation system must also be modified. Typically, the irrigation system designer is responsible for installation and modification of the system to the full original intent. To ensure that the system will operate as designed, the irrigation designer must be on hand in the field to make decisions and to conduct field surveys of the project throughout construction. During the field survey, the designer marks the positions of irrigation heads, controllers, and main-line routing. Any changes are documented on the as-built drawings. The designer also monitors construction to ensure that the system is being installed according to specifications and that components meet specified quality standards.
- *Demonstrate the system's operation.* The designer has the opportunity to set up the system and demonstrate that it will operate within the design parameters for the site.

Design Parameters for the Irrigation System

Irrigation systems are defined by method of coverage and type of control system, as shown in the accompanying feature box. Generally, single-row or double-row systems are used for courses in the eastern United States. The additional coverage and flexibility of a triple-row system are often advantageous during critical periods when turf is growing in and during droughts. In the western United States and in golf-oriented real estate developments that put a premium on green turf up to the lot line, wall-to-wall systems are the standard. The confinement system is common in courses located in arid regions where water resources are extremely limited, such as Arizona and Nevada.

Control systems are discussed on the facing page. Semiautomatic and automatic systems include various means of sending signals from the central control device to the field switching devices. Signals can be sent over standard electrical wiring or a special communications cable, or by radio signal, phone line, or a ground/space satellite system. Selection of the most cost-efficient communication system largely depends on specific site conditions, cost of initial construction, and long-term operation.

The Pump Station

All irrigation pumps work by means of centrifugal force and are thus called "centrifugal pumps." Water enters the center of the impeller and is pushed out in a circular motion to the outside. The force created is measured in pounds per square inch.

The location of the pump house directly affects installation and long-

Irrigation Pumps

The *vertical turbine* is generally used when the irrigation water is pumped from a reservoir like a pond or lake. The impeller is located in the water. A series of bowls creates the pressure required to lift the water out of the reservoir and into the irrigation lines.

The *well/submersible turbine* is similar to the vertical turbine, except that the pump is placed in a casing and totally submerged in the water. The motor is located on the bottom of the impellers and moves the water in an upward or pushing motion. This type of system is generally used when the source of water is a well, the water level is very close to the ground, or a pump house cannot be built.

The *booster/centrifugal pump* is typically used when the source of water is away from the project site and is supplied by another entity, such as a city water main or a remote effluent site.

term operating costs. Ideally, the pump house should be located in the middle of the golf course to disburse the water as quickly and in as many directions as possible. Doing so keeps the size of the pipes to a minimum. The central location usually translates to an area near holes number 1, 9, 10, or 18.

Location of Storage Reservoirs

Most golf courses provide a reservoir for storing irrigation water regardless of the source. Water is usually stored during the day for use at night. Use of a reservoir reduces the supply rate by one-half to one-third that of direct supply. For instance, a system that requires 1 million gallons per day (gpd) would require 2,083 gallons per minute (gpm) over an eight-hour irrigation period in a direct-supply system. The reservoir system, however, requires only 700 gpm over a 24-hour period to fill the reservoir for the daily requirement. To save electrical and pumping costs, the storage reservoir ideally should be located at the highest elevation possible on the site, allowing gravity to help maintain pressure and flow through the distribution system with a minimum of intermediate pumps and motors. If stormwater runoff is collected as a source of irrigation water, impoundments should be located at the lowest elevation on the site, requiring a transfer pump system to move the water from the stormwater impoundments to the storage reservoir.

Irrigation Systems

Single-Row System

A *single-row system* contains one row of sprinklers or quick-coupling valves down the center of the fairway. It generally covers up to 90 feet wide, leaving a "scalloped" outer edge between sprinkler outlets.

Pros: Lower initial cost.

Cons: Limited coverage in center of fairway. A good shot is penalized because the lush, irrigated turf in the center of the fairway prevents the ball from rolling as far as a ball hit to the unirrigated edge of the fairway or rough.

Double-Row System

A *double-row system* contains two rows of sprinkler outlets, with a row following each edge of the fairway. This concept evolved from the single-row system to prevent the scalloped edge and to provide better turf over a wider area of the fairway (about 120 to 150 feet).

Pros: More coverage.

Cons: The center of the fairway receives twice the water of the outside, perhaps resulting in overwatered fairways to get adequate irrigation for the roughs.

Triple-Row System

A *triple-row system* contains three rows of sprinkler outlets providing coverage of both the fairway and roughs. A center row is located in the middle of the fairway

and the outside rows in the intermediate rough area. It generally covers 120 to 225 feet.

Pros: Probably the most efficient of the single-, double-, or triple-row systems. If water is restricted, the flow to the outside two rows can be reduced, saving water while still irrigating the turf adequately.

Cons: Higher initial cost.

Wall-to-Wall System

The *wall-to-wall system* provides maximum, uniform coverage from boundary line to boundary line.

Pros: Provides maximum coverage for golf courses that serve as a visual extension of the real estate elements of a golf-oriented development.

Cons: High initial cost and high water use.

The Confinement/Desert System

The *confinement/desert system* limits the area of coverage by providing part-circle sprinklers along the perimeter of the area defined for irrigation.

Pros: Coverage can be selectively restricted and/or directed, providing more efficient use of water. Includes a weather station driven by a central computer that monitors every drop of water and where it is applied.

Cons: The golf course and irrigation system must be designed concurrently to ensure the most effective use of water while providing maximum playability.

Control Systems

Manual System

The *manual system* involves opening and closing control valves by hand. Typical of golf courses built before 1960, most have since been converted to automatic systems to reduce the amount of labor required.

Pros: Low initial cost.

Cons: Extremely labor intensive and not cost-efficient for contemporary operations.

Semiautomatic System

A *semiautomatic system* is the most basic contemporary control system. A central clock sends signals to start field controllers, initiating an irrigation cycle. If the irrigation cycle must be terminated for any reason (a rainstorm or excessive runoff, for example), a signal can be sent to terminate the cycle.

Pros: Low initial cost and easy operation.

Cons: Moderate control over water use requires the superintendent and grounds crews to monitor the system in the field.

Automatic System

An *automatic system* includes a weather station driven from a central computer and provides highly accurate control. Such control is mandatory for golf courses with environmental concerns, high energy costs, limited water supply, and/or high demand for premium turf. Automatic systems are being further refined to include sensors for ground moisture, temperature, and other environmental factors.

Pros: Precise control allows for most efficient operation.

Cons: High initial cost.

Cost Estimates for the Irrigation System

As a general rule, the normal installation cost for an irrigation system in 1993 ranged from $700 to $900 per sprinkler. The estimate must also consider the spacing of sprinkler heads and the definition of the area to be covered and the cost of the pump and pump station. For general cost estimates, $8,000 to $11,000 (1993 dollars) can be anticipated per acre of irrigated area. A pond type turbine station with intake structure and pad costs approximately $100,000. As for the golf course, more detailed cost estimates can be made as design progresses.

Environmental Issues

One of the most significant trends in the development industry has been the growing public awareness of environmental issues, resulting in the adoption of protective legislation at all levels of government. A commitment to a healthy environment has become an increasingly mandatory requirement for the granting of land use permits for golf courses in many municipalities throughout the United States. Public perception of golf courses as an environmental asset or an environmental liability varies from community to community. Major environmental concerns generally focus on the following issues:

- A change in land use patterns to accommodate a golf course and any related real estate develop-

ment that can result in loss, damage, or fragmentation of sensitive wildlife habitats or other valued environments;
- Soil erosion from construction of the golf course;
- Contaminated soil from the use of chemical fertilizers and pesticides;
- Contamination or degradation of water resources from the use of chemical fertilizers and pesticides;
- Harmful effects of chemical pesticides on nontargeted organisms and wildlife;
- High water demand associated with irrigation.

Golfers argue that golf courses, with their carefully managed turf, trees, and other vegetation, are by most standards environmental assets. An average 18-hole golf course with about 150 acres of vegetation is said to be capable of providing enough oxygen through photosynthesis for 10,350 people per day during the growing season.[22] Photosynthesis is also responsible for reducing large quantities of carbon dioxide, and for absorbing and detoxifying sulfur dioxide, ammonia, nitrogen oxide, and other noxious pollutants associated with urbanization. Plants also play an important role in moderating air temperature and humidity, wind velocity, and ability of soils to absorb water and withstand impact erosion from rain. Additionally, independent research shows that well-managed turf can contribute dramatically to water quality.[23] Golf courses can also serve a valuable role in water conser-

vation and water quality improvement programs.

Other research and technical advances in environmental management have resulted in measures that can be applied on golf courses to significantly enhance environmental quality. Few would argue against the environmental benefit of a golf course compared to a complex of, say, industrial warehouses. But if the choice is between a golf course and other types of open spaces, such as a multiple-use recreational park or a nature preserve, then room exists for questioning the environmental benefits of a golf course to a community. Because of the public's growing support for protection of environmental resources, it has become increasingly more difficult to build a golf course in some localities, where protective legislation restricts this land use and requires an increasingly complex permitting procedure. Such restrictive legislation and cumbersome permitting processes often drive the cost of time and capital for planning such a project beyond the capability of developers and investors to finance it. In such locations, the market for golf must be strong enough to value this land use as an asset to the community. And, if so, the developer must be demonstrably committed to environmentally sensitive planning, design, and operation of the golf course, often acting as an educator to gain public acceptance and to dispel any myths or misconceptions about the sport and the impact of a golf course

The 2,500-acre Elkhorn Valley Resort in Sun Valley, Idaho, features a golf course, tennis courts, plaza, and water features. It is an excellent example of the possibilities for careful stewardship of the land in conjunction with an exciting outdoor environment for people.

on the environment. The golf industry has maintained a continuing commitment toward research and technical development that make golf courses more environmentally sound and more cost-effective as a result of new technology in their design and operation.

The guiding criteria for deciding what strategies, policies, and procedures are suited to a particular project are *Best Available Technology* (BAT) and *Best Management Practices* (BMPs), terms common in environmental law and often referred to in regulatory legislation that has performance requirements. Often such performance requirements call for an environmental impact report or mitigation plan to address environmental issues.

Any environmental program or mitigation plan is based on an understanding of the various ecologic systems involved and their interactions and interdependencies. Landscape

architects are generally the professionals who have the training, knowledge, and experience required to undertake the inventory of resources and site analysis to determine what impacts a golf course might have on the immediate site and in relation to an overall environmental plan. Some localities require the additional input of environmental specialists, particularly if sensitive or endangered flora and fauna or habitats will be impacted by the golf course. In most cases, the public approval process for a golf course requires an environmental impact statement (EIS), which states the potential adverse impacts of a proposed golf course, and/or an environmental impact report (EIR), which states both potential impacts and ways to mitigate them.[24] Basic information for the EIS and EIR is available from a number of independent organizations and government agencies. Although many sources of information

are not directly associated with golf courses, they can be just as valuable as specific golf-oriented research:

- Publications from federal agencies involved in various aspects of the environment, such as the design of ponds, stormwater management systems, alternative wastewater treatment systems, wetlands, and the like;
- Publications and other materials available from private organizations, such as the U.S. Golf Association, the National Wildlife Federation, the Audubon Society, and The Nature Conservancy;
- An inventory of resources and its analysis by local municipal agencies;
- Information from private enterprises, such as turf growers and seed suppliers;
- Professional journals, trade publications, and newsletters;
- Research reports and publications by educational institutions.

An environmental mitigation plan typically includes:

- A statement of goals and objectives for the project;
- An inventory of resources and analysis of their impact;
- A description of strategies to mitigate the effects of the proposed project through planning and design;
- A description of management policies to be implemented;
- A description of operational procedures to be implemented.

Horror stories abound of development projects brought to a standstill by the discovery of an endangered species on the site or failure to consider the sentiment of the public toward a particular resource. Sound environmental design and practice are not only necessary, but also *cost-effective*.

Golf Courses as Ecologic Sanctuaries™[25]

Golf Courses as Ecologic Sanctuaries™ is based on the premise that golf courses, as major landscape elements, offer special opportunities and potential to combine a recreational amenity with programs to improve environmental quality. The thousands of acres of land being converted to golf courses every year in the United States should be planned within the context of broad-scale and long-range planning and design of open space and environmental systems. The quality of life and the quality of the environment are interdependent and share the same goals. It logically follows that golf courses should be planned not as isolated recreational amenities but as integral parts of a larger network of open space on a broad context ranging from relationships with adjacent open space to a regional ecosystem.

The concept of Golf Courses as Ecologic Sanctuaries™ provides a basic approach to planning and designing a golf course, coupling it with the application of current research, technology, and management practices. The goal of this approach is to make the most of potential environmental benefits from a golf course in long-

range improvements to the quality of life. New advances are being made every day, both in the golf industry and in other fields, and continual inquiry, review, and study should be part of the golf industry's ongoing commitment to environmental awareness and stewardship.

Methodology

Golf Courses as Ecologic Sanctuaries™ involves strategies in every stage of a project, from initial planning to daily operation and management. The concept can be applied at three basic levels:

- Planning and design strategies;
- Management policies and objectives;
- Operational strategies.

Complete and thorough site analysis and an inventory of resources provide the foundation for planning a golf course as an ecologic sanctuary. The analysis of the site from an ecologic point of view examines land

use patterns beyond the site's boundaries, anticipating long-range or future patterns of development and seeking opportunities to dedicate the open space and golf course as contiguous parts of a larger open space network. Often, these opportunities arise along natural drainageways and water courses (wetlands, streams, rivers, and so on), where land use regulations or restrictions preclude development. The restrictions against development in wetlands or floodplains subsequently result in dedication of these ribbons of land centered around water courses as permanent open space. The developer must also analyze opportunities for and benefits of integrating the golf course to create greenbelt buffers or reclaim environmentally damaged land.

Once the contextual relationship of the golf course ecologic sanctuary is established through studies of alternative land uses, the layout of the

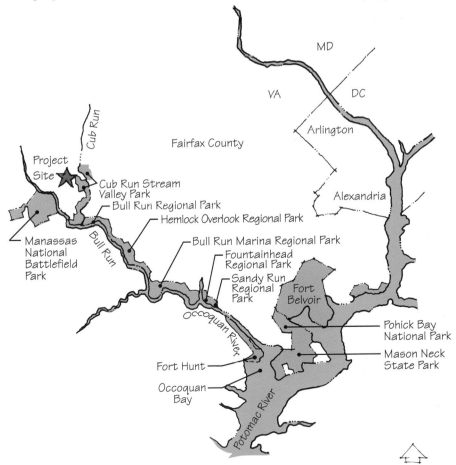

Project context map for a Golf Course as Ecologic Sanctuary™. A potential project site was considered in context with the regional open space system along a major watershed in northern Virginia.
Source: Guy L. Rando & Associates Inc.

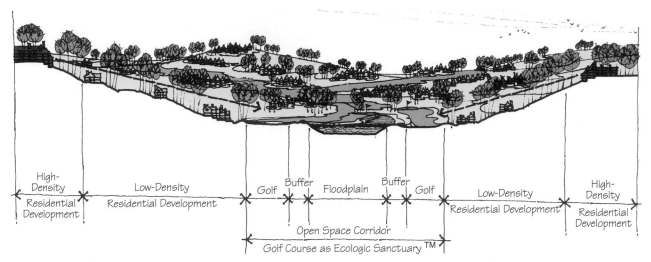

Open space system along a water course.
Source: Guy L. Rando & Associates Inc.

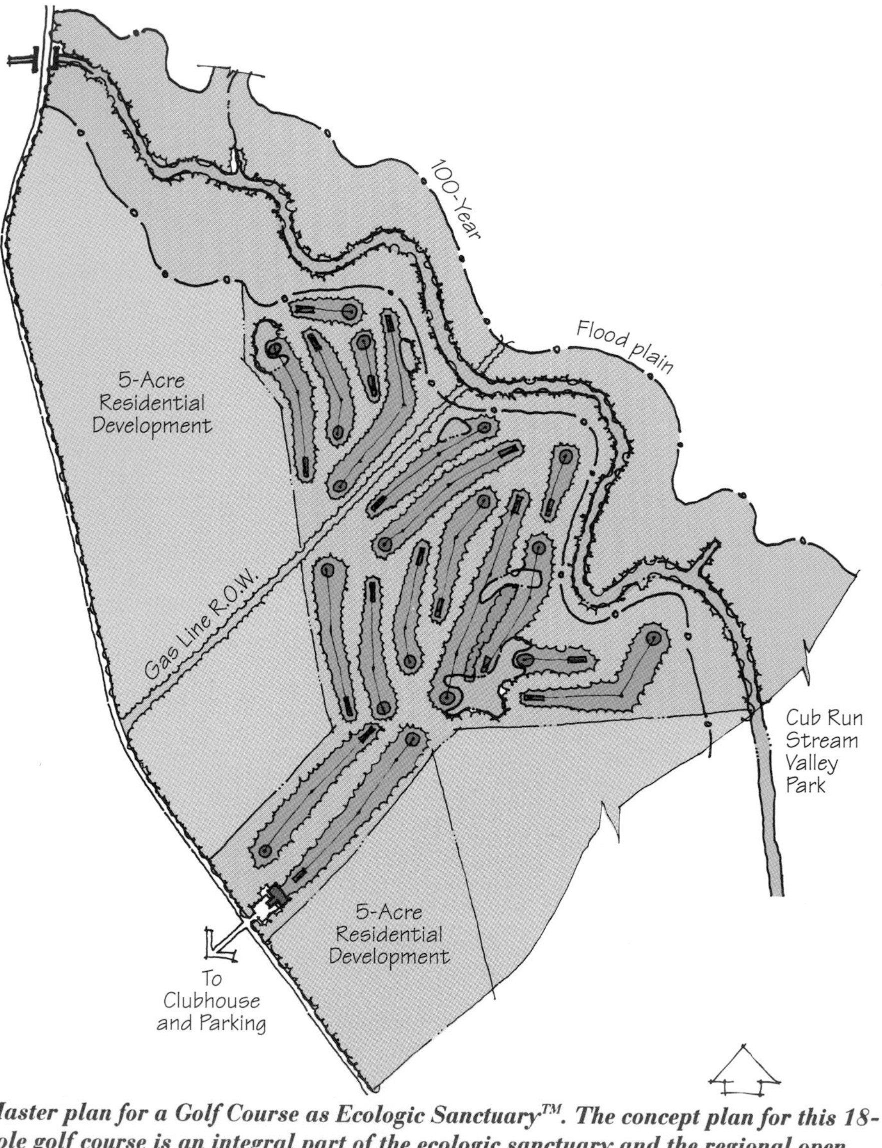

Master plan for a Golf Course as Ecologic Sanctuary™. The concept plan for this 18-hole golf course is an integral part of the ecologic sanctuary and the regional open space network.
Source: Guy L. Rando & Associates Inc.

(labels within lower map:)
100-Year
Flood plain
5-Acre Residential Development
Gas Line R.O.W.
Cub Run Stream Valley Park
5-Acre Residential Development
To Clubhouse and Parking

(labels within upper section diagram:)
High-Density Residential Development
Low-Density Residential Development
Golf
Buffer
Floodplain
Buffer
Golf
Low-Density Residential Development
High-Density Residential Development
Open Space Corridor
Golf Course as Ecologic Sanctuary™

course further reinforces the concept by maintaining strong, contiguous connections to the overall open space network by delineating ecological zones that relate to the various types of habitats found on a golf course and the level of management that occurs within each zone:

- Preservation areas;
- Conservation areas;
- Reestablishment/enhancement areas;
- Maintained turf areas.

Preservation areas are to remain undisturbed by development, receiving the highest level of protection consistent with local regulations and BMPs. They typically include all areas delineated by a local jurisdiction to preclude or otherwise restrict development for whatever reason, as well as areas deemed too sensitive for development by site analysis and/or special environmental surveys. *Conservation areas* are those areas where existing vegetative cover is to be preserved as much as possible with limited but planned management to ensure compliance with goals for quality of water and habitat (such as addition of vegetative buffer strips, soil erosion controls, or brush piles or nesting boxes for sheltering wildlife). *Reestablishment/enhancement areas* include areas disrupted by development in which vegetative cover is to be reestablished. Such areas are designed for more intensive management than conservation areas to enrich the diversity of both species and habitats.

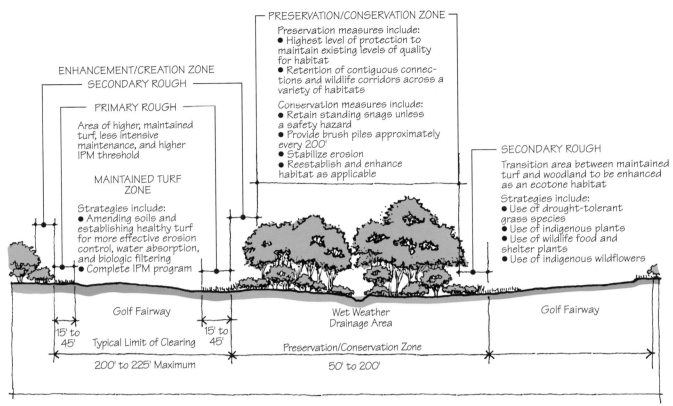

ENHANCEMENT/CREATION ZONE
SECONDARY ROUGH

PRIMARY ROUGH

Area of higher, maintained turf, less intensive maintenance, and higher IPM threshold

MAINTAINED TURF ZONE

Strategies include:
● Amending soils and establishing healthy turf for more effective erosion control, water absorption, and biologic filtering
● Complete IPM program

PRESERVATION/CONSERVATION ZONE

Preservation measures include:
● Highest level of protection to maintain existing levels of quality for habitat
● Retention of contiguous connections and wildlife corridors across a variety of habitats

Conservation measures include:
● Retain standing snags unless a safety hazard
● Provide brush piles approximately every 200'
● Stabilize erosion
● Reestablish and enhance habitat as applicable

SECONDARY ROUGH

Transition area between maintained turf and woodland to be enhanced as an ecotone habitat

Strategies include:
● Use of drought-tolerant grass species
● Use of indigenous plants
● Use of wildlife food and shelter plants
● Use of indigenous wildflowers

Golf Fairway

Wet Weather Drainage Area

Golf Fairway

15' to 45'   Typical Limit of Clearing   15' to 45'

Preservation/Conservation Zone

200' to 225' Maximum

50' to 200'

Typical concept section for wet weather drainage areas.
Source: Guy L. Rando & Associates Inc.

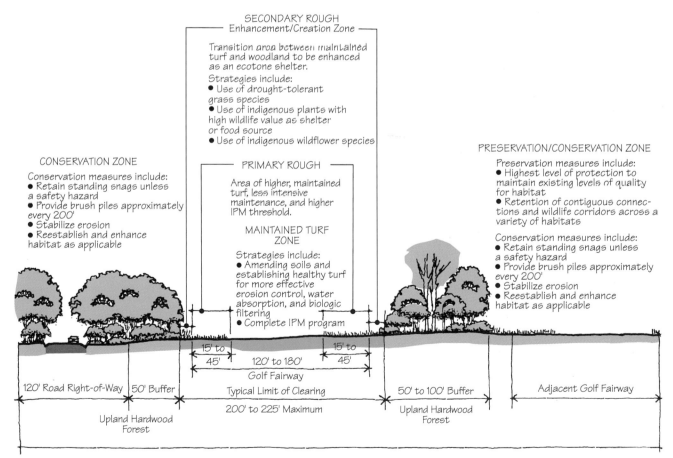

SECONDARY ROUGH
Enhancement/Creation Zone

Transition area between maintained turf and woodland to be enhanced as an ecotone shelter.
Strategies include:
● Use of drought-tolerant grass species
● Use of indigenous plants with high wildlife value as shelter or food source
● Use of indigenous wildflower species

PRIMARY ROUGH

Area of higher, maintained turf, less intensive maintenance, and higher IPM threshold.

MAINTAINED TURF ZONE

Strategies include:
● Amending soils and establishing healthy turf for more effective erosion control, water absorption, and biologic filtering
● Complete IPM program

CONSERVATION ZONE

Conservation measures include:
● Retain standing snags unless a safety hazard
● Provide brush piles approximately every 200'
● Stabilize erosion
● Reestablish and enhance habitat as applicable

PRESERVATION/CONSERVATION ZONE

Preservation measures include:
● Highest level of protection to maintain existing levels of quality for habitat
● Retention of contiguous connections and wildlife corridors across a variety of habitats

Conservation measures include:
● Retain standing snags unless a safety hazard
● Provide brush piles approximately every 200'
● Stabilize erosion
● Reestablish and enhance habitat as applicable

15' to 45'   120' to 180'   15' to 45'

Golf Fairway

120' Road Right-of-Way   50' Buffer   Typical Limit of Clearing   50' to 100' Buffer   Adjacent Golf Fairway

200' to 225' Maximum

Upland Hardwood Forest

Upland Hardwood Forest

Typical concept section for adjacent fairways.
Source: Guy L. Rando & Associates Inc.

Emphasis is placed on the use of indigenous plant materials that are useful to wildlife for food and shelter. They might also include additional areas on or off site where vegetation is to be enhanced or wetlands or habitats improved as a mitigation for sensitive areas lost to golf course or real estate development. *Maintained turf areas* include all areas of managed turf for both the golf course and grounds (such as lawns around the clubhouse). On the golf course, they include the turf areas for the tees, greens, and fairways as well as the primary and secondary roughs.

Best Available Technology and Best Management Practices

Within the zone system, the concept of ecologic sanctuary incorporates various strategies that address the major environmental concerns related to golf courses. The strategies vary according to individual sites and available technology at a given time; thus, the selection of appropriate technologies and practices for application to a particular project should be part of the development team's decision-making process, with guidance and input by environmental specialists. Several current BATs and BMPs are consistent with Golf Courses as Ecologic Sanctuaries™:

- Protecting habitat;
- Protecting endangered or sensitive species and habitats;
- Conservation management;
- Controlling soil erosion;
- Integrated pest management;
- Selecting turf;
- Retention ponds;
- Conserving water resources.

None of these strategies should be applied without consideration of the specific site and its conditions. Each project must consider indigenous aspects of the local ecology and environment.

Mitigating Loss or Fragmentation of Habitat

Building golf courses involves the manipulation of land and vegetation over large areas. The most significant potential environmental impacts include the loss and fragmentation of existing habitats. The manicured turf of golf courses has little if any value to wildlife as food and shelter, and the most serious impact from a change in land use to accommodate a golf course is the loss of contiguous habitat.

Mitigating the loss of habitat focuses on preservation and conservation strategies at all levels, including design, and preparation of performance specifications, operational guidelines and procedures, and management policies. Such strategies might include:

- Preserving and/or conserving continuous wildlife corridors throughout the site, incorporating a variety of habitats;
- Reducing the width of fairways by incorporating primary roughs of less intensively maintained turf (a higher height and higher tolerance for pest or weed invasion) and secondary roughs as ecotone habitats of meadow and indigenous shrubs that provide diverse habitats and species for food and shelter for wildlife;
- Increasing the width of roughs and buffer areas between adjacent fairways along important habitat corridors to maintain contiguous connections with undisturbed habitats and provide ecologic sanctuaries throughout the golf course.

Protecting Endangered or Sensitive Species and Habitats

Other design measures can be implemented to protect water resources and habitats:

- Using vegetated filter strips as buffers between the treated golf course turf and adjacent sensitive environments within preservation/conservation areas;
- Providing stormwater management ponds to collect, filter, and trap any waterborne contaminants in stormwater runoff from the golf course and associated development;
- Using vegetated berms and mounds to redirect or contain surface runoff away from sensitive environments;
- Providing storage reservoirs for irrigation water to reduce fluctuations in peak demand and stress on groundwater resources.

Where endangered or sensitive species of flora or fauna have been identified, knowledgeable experts must cooperate closely with regulatory agencies to formulate acceptable means of protecting them and their associated habitats. Many factors must be considered to determine the extent and configuration of contiguous habitats required to protect and support a specific species or ecologic habitat. Sensitive or endangered species should be identified and responses determined as early during project planning as possible so as not to cause delays late in the development process or after ground is broken. The consequences of rushing through a site analysis or cutting corners can be costly in terms of delays and lost or additional hours for redesigning and repairing physical and public relations damage. Every person in a responsible position must be educated about the goals for protecting species and habitats to avoid blunders that can cause irrevocable damage, expensive delays, or punitive costs. The following performance specifications and procedural guidelines can be implemented to ensure the maximum protection of endangered or sensitive species.

- Include drawings, photographs, and other information that helps to identify endangered or sensitive species and their associated habitats as part of the construction documents.
- Provide for qualified professionals (a landscape architect or golf course architect or an independent expert) to monitor all staking and clearing operations. Provide a procedure for tagging and protecting any endangered or sensitive flora that might be found on the site.
- Physically delineate (with protective fencing or flags) areas to remain undisturbed, with the delineation to remain in place until it is decided whether to reroute the clearing or arrange for transplanting specimens to an alternate location or construction is complete.

- Provide clear and detailed specifications for transplanting sensitive flora by a qualified landscape contractor.
- Provide clear guidelines and instructions for reports and protection in the event the contractor, employees, or consultants identify a possible endangered or sensitive species. Create a positive environment and incentives for identifying and reporting such species.
- Provide a written record of located sensitive species and transplant sites, if applicable, to be prepared by the landscape architect or appropriate professional consultant for inclusion with the management and operations documents for the golf course.
- Provide written recommendations for the care, management, and monitoring of endangered or sensitive species that have been located or transplanted, to be prepared by the landscape architect or appropriate professional consultant for inclusion with the management and operations documents for the golf course, perhaps in cooperation with local conservancy groups.

Conservation Management

The primary goals of conservation management are to protect the quality of wildlife habitat and to enhance the diversity of species and habitats. Conservation management is recommended for both the conservation and restoration/enhancement zones of a project. Such strategies might include:

- Retaining snags (dead or partially dead trees whose leaves and most of the limbs have fallen) in various stages and in a variety of habitat associations. As they gradually decay, snags are an important source of food and shelter for a wide variety of wildlife and an important component of a diverse habitat.
- Monitoring snag habitats for safety and development of undesirable pests.
- Using brush from clearing operations to create piles within conservation areas as shelters, nesting sites, and food sources for wildlife.

- Creating "hedgerow"-type habitats along critical wildlife corridors of indigenous plant materials that supply food and shelter for wildlife.
- Restoring indigenous plant materials in appropriate habitats.
- Enhancing the diversity of habitats and species by using plants that have value for wildlife throughout buffer areas of the golf course.
- Providing nesting boxes and/or feed stations as appropriate.

Controlling Soil Erosion

Soil erosion during construction of a golf course can adversely affect the quality of both water and habitats. Measures to control soil erosion include:

- Phasing construction to minimize the extent of the site's exposure at any given time;
- Preserving or conserving vegetated buffer strips around sensitive environments;
- Using siltation control devices;
- Selecting turf and other vegetation that will rapidly restabilize exposed soils;
- Applying BMPs during construction and the growing period.

The developer should meet all local regulations for erosion control, without exception.

Controlling Pests

A major public concern is the potentially harmful effects associated with pest control, particularly potential contamination of soil or water resources or harm to untargeted organisms. The U.S. Environmental Protection Agency (EPA) developed an integrated pest management (IPM) system, which it defines as "the coordinated use of pest and environmental information with available pest control methods to prevent unacceptable...pest damage by the most economical means and with the least possible hazard to people, property, and the environment."[26] The goal of this approach is to manage pests and the environment so as to balance costs, benefits, the public health, and environmental quality. IPM systems use all available techni-

cal information on pests and their interaction with the environment. Because IPM programs apply a holistic approach to pest management, they take advantage of all appropriate options, including but not limited to the use of pesticides. Thus, IPM is:

- A system of using multiple methods to combat pests;
- A decision-making process;
- A risk-reduction system;
- An information-intensive, cost-effective, site-specific system.[27]

The development of IPM systems for turf and in particular for golf courses is rather recent, and systems are continually being updated as more information and research become available. The following components make up an IPM system, as defined by the EPA:

- Define the roles of all people involved in the pest management system to ensure their understanding and to establish communications between people.
- Determine the management objectives for each area of the site as a basis for deciding possible methods of control.
- Set "action thresholds," the points when pest populations or environmental conditions indicate that some action must be taken. Take no action until that point is reached.
- Monitor the site and pest populations periodically and consistently to determine when the action threshold is reached and whether the action taken is effective.
- Take action that modifies the pests' habitat to reduce the site's carrying capacity, exclude the pest, or otherwise make the site inhospitable to the pest.
- Apply appropriate pesticides, with the preferred pesticide the one with the longest dwell time in contact with the pest while presenting the least possible hazard to people, property, and the environment.
- Evaluate the results of modifications of the habitat and pesticidal treatment by periodically monitoring the site and its pest population.
- Maintain written records of management objectives, monitoring

and data collection, actions taken, and results obtained.[28]

The use of IPM systems for turf management on golf courses is relatively new, but new information should be implemented constantly. An IPM system for any golf course therefore involves a commitment to adapt and implement the system continuously as information becomes available. Current recommended strategies include:

- Selecting pest-resistant varieties of grass suitable to the site, climate, and use.
- Filtering, trapping, and neutralizing waterborne nutrients and pesticides in specifically designed stormwater management impoundments.
- Using vegetated filter strips as buffers between treated turf and adjacent sensitive environments.
- Establishing a list of pesticides that are prohibited on the site by local regulations and current research data, which rate pesticides in terms of potential toxicity or hazards to wildlife (by the New York Adirondack Park Agency, for example). The use of persistent pesticides (those that are slow to break down into harmless products and persist in the environment for a long time) should be restricted or prohibited completely.
- Using bacterial or biochemical control, such as plant growth regulators.
- Using biological controls for pest management, such as nematodes for control of white grubs and pest-resistant, endophytic-enhanced grasses.
- Increasing mowing heights and reducing the frequency of watering to reduce weeds and fungus; evaluating problem areas and the need for drainage control and/or improvements in the irrigation system; using slow-release fertilizers; controlling accumulation of thatch and compacted soil.
- Using caning and syringing to reduce stress and the threat of fungus damage in summer.
- Using fungicides on a strict schedule that uses computerized monitoring and diagnostic tests to determine potential disease; selecting the least invasive but effective fungicidal treatment; rotating fungicides to reduce the buildup of resistance.
- Monitoring changes, beneficial and destructive, in populations of flora and fauna.
- Educating the public and the course's management about the strategies used at the site. Make environmental responsibility part of a written policy and part of the job descriptions for all positions. A certificate is a minimal requirement for anyone dealing with or handling chemicals, and ongoing education should be a necessary part of employment policy.
- Posting information about chemicals used on the golf course where it is readily accessible to golfers, employees, guests, visitors, and anyone else who might come into contact with the chemicals used. Supervisors must be fully informed about the chemicals used and their dangers and carefully monitor their use.

Turf Nutrients and the Environment

This section includes more detail about a few current technologies and management practices addressing environmental concerns.

A major environmental concern regarding turf on golf courses is the degradation of water quality as a result of the use of high rates of fertilizers, which is often cited as incompatible with management strategies for both groundwater and surface water. Nitrogen and phosphorus (common components of turf fertilizers) are the cause of most concern. Nitrogen (nitrates) is the component in fertilizer that promotes leaf growth and the green color. Phosphorus (phosphates) and potassium (potash) promote root development. It is a common *misconception* that golf courses are a major source of pollution from nitrates and phosphates as a result of surface runoff that carries applied fertilizers or leaches these nutrients into the groundwater. Another popular misconception is that the soil with a high sand content is especially prone to heavy nitrate leaching. In fact, research and studies have shown that the well-managed turf of golf courses does not contaminate water, either from nutrients borne in surface runoff or from leaching of nutrients into the groundwater. Unlike intensive agricultural practices where fertilizers and other chemicals are applied on open soil, golf courses are covered with healthy, well-managed turf that has a remarkable ability to absorb and retain stormwater and nutrients. And the amount of fertilizer used on golf courses is much less than the public's perception.

Studies at the University of Maryland[29] of surface runoff from turf evaluated the effects of rainfall intensity and turf seeding rate (density) on runoff initiation time, runoff rate, and sediment loss (including total movement of nitrogen and phosphates). The research showed that surface runoff, sediment loss, and total nitrogen and phosphate movement were *dramatically lower* than agricultural uses. Other studies at Pennsylvania State University investigated surface runoff on managed turf relative to contamination by both pesticides and fertilizers. Researchers concluded that managed turf grasses do *not* display a high potential for movement of pesticides or fertilizers by runoff or percolation. The ability of well-managed turf to absorb and hold water and nutrients in the tests conducted at Penn State was dramatic. Measurable runoff on the test sites could not even be induced until researchers had irrigated the test slopes at more than twice the intensity of a 100- to 125-year storm. Infiltration of the turf slopes was sufficient to virtually eliminate runoff. And what runoff they were able to induce under the highly unlikely conditions of six inches per hour of rainfall showed that the average concentrations of nutrients, particularly nitrates and nitrogen, in both the runoff and leachate were consistently well below the standard for public drinking water.[30]

Studies by Dr. A. Martin Petrovic of Cornell University looked specifically into the effects of management of turf on the quality of groundwater, with emphasis on nitrate/nitrogen leaching. The study examined two types of nitrogen sources: the highly water-soluble sources known as urea, and slow-release sources like ureaformaldehyde, plastic-coated urea, and activated sewage sludge. Common practices of turf management on golf courses involve the use of the slow-release sources, which are more cost-effective. The Cornell studies, applied to both sandy sites and the less sandy soils associated with fairways, tees, roughs, and other general areas, showed no leaching of nitrates/nitrogen from slow-release sources, supporting the hypothesis that golf courses do not contaminate groundwater with high levels of nitrates.[31] The Cornell studies were further supported by similar research funded by EPA, known as the Cape Cod Study. The area of sandy soil on several golf courses in Cape Cod were monitored, and researchers found "no evidence of groundwater leaching of currently used golf course chemicals."[32]

Phosphorus leaching through the soil is noted only when the capability of the biotic mass of plant materials and soils to absorb and retain phosphate is exceeded. The key to mitigating this situation is to implement an IPM program, that is, to determine the need for a phosphorus supplement and apply it only at the rates indicated by test procedures.

Recent research also has shown that biostimulants like cytokinins and other growth stimulants are effective for promoting increased root growth while reducing the need for fertilizer containing phosphorus and nitrogen. Applications of iron to turf have been shown to increase chlorophyll content, carbohydrates, and rooting and to decrease respiration rates. Midsummer application of iron has been shown to be an effective means of achieving "green up," and late fall applications on cool-season grasses have produced earlier spring greening and enhanced rooting.[33]

The following additional strategies may be applied to mitigate any possibility of nutrients' contaminating water resources:

- Selecting turf and other plants suitable for the site;
- Selecting turf and other plants requiring low applications of nitrogen;
- Reducing heavily managed areas of the course (by incorporating primary and secondary roughs) and using less energy-demanding plants wherever possible;
- Collecting, treating, and recycling drainage water in stormwater management ponds designed to act as biologic filters that prevent the movement of nutrients into surface water courses and groundwater;
- Amending soils in managed turf areas and vegetative interceptor strips to reduce runoff and to retain nutrients;
- Using conservative irrigation practices to reduce water use and the potential for leaching;
- Practicing IPM diagnostic procedures to determine whether and when application of nutrients is appropriate and what rates of application are needed;
- Avoiding the application of fertilizer when turf naturally grows slowly (cool weather);
- Using slow-release sources of nitrogen applied frequently and lightly only when needed and at rates indicated by tests and diagnoses;
- Applying phosphorus only when needed and at rates indicated by tests and diagnoses;
- Using alternative biostimulants as appropriate.

Retention Ponds for Removal of Nutrients, Sediments, and Toxicants

Stormwater management and irrigation reservoir ponds and other water impoundments can serve dual purposes: as biologic filter systems to maintain high-quality water and habitat, and as aesthetic hazards that come into play on the golf course.

In a biologic filtering system, all surface runoff and all subsurface drains below golf course features like sand bunkers, greens, and tees are diverted into a series of strategically located retention ponds. No runoff water or drainage from the golf course is allowed to enter sensitive habitats or open water courses (streams or rivers) without first being biologically filtered by the retention pond system. Vegetated berms and/or vegetated filter strips can be provided where the limits of grading or clearing would otherwise make it difficult to divert the flow of surface runoff from the golf course to the retention ponds. The basic concept is to use the biologic processes of the pond ecologic system to "polish" or filter the water. The filtered water can then be returned to the hydrologic cycle through irrigation of the golf course. The mechanics of irrigation aerate the water, while biologic processes in the soil and plants purify the water additionally. The following principles guide the design and engineering of the stormwater management impoundments, golf course drainage system, and irrigation storage reservoirs.

- *Removal and Transformation of Nutrients*
  The retention pond system provides for removal of nitrogen, ammonium, and phosphorus from surface runoff and drainage system waters. Nitrogen and phosphorus are removed by trapping and sinking nutrients, which occurs by slowing down the incoming flow and retaining nutrient-rich water in the pond. *Nitrogen fixation* occurs by conversion or fixation of gaseous nitrogen into an inorganic form by bacteria and blue-green algae in the pond's plant system. Additional nitrogen is removed from the water during nutrient uptake of the emergent and aquatic vegetation. Phosphorus is immobilized through adsorption and precipitation reactions in the saturated soils and sediments of the pond's bottom. Soils with a high level of fine minerals like calcium, aluminum, and iron that provide high rates of ions for such reactions with phosphorus are specified for the pond substrate. Permanent saturation of the soils favors the re-

tention of phosphorus. The rapid fluctuation of anaerobic and aerobic conditions in saturated soils also favors the removal of nitrogen. Thus, retention ponds should be designed as "wet" ponds, with a permanently flooded basin.

Ammonium is also removed as part of the process of removing nitrogen. This abiotic process, known as "ammonium volatilization," results in removal by evaporation of ammonium at high temperatures and pH levels greater than 7.5.

■ *Retention of Sediments and Toxicants* Temporary removal of sediments and toxicants, including pesticides and other water- or sediment-borne chemicals, occurs by the deposit of sediment in retention ponds. The velocity of incoming surface runoff or drainage is slowed by restricting the pond outlet and by adding vegetation to the pond. The process of depositing sediment is further facilitated by shallow water and minimal "fetch" or wind expo-

sure. Complete removal of the toxicants occurs through chemical breakdown, assimilation in plant and animal tissue, or burial. The use of soils with a high organic content and high levels of fine minerals facilitates the trapping and breakdown of many toxicants.

Ponds are designed for long retention and therefore are engineered to retard infiltration of water from the pond into the subsoil and groundwater. The groundwater is recharged when the biologically processed water from the retention ponds is recycled onto the maintained turf of the golf course by irrigation, with the water further purified as it is aerated during irrigation.

The pond's profile is designed to enhance the diversity of plant forms, and a typical pond plant community includes trees and shrubs above the pond's normal water level, emergent plants in water to one foot deep, rooted surface plants in water from one to two feet deep,

and rooted submerged plants in water from 1.5 to 6.5 feet deep. Because nutrient uptake is generally higher in emergent plants, highly dense and diverse persistent emergent plants (more than 50 stems per square meter) should be provided. These plants provide frictional resistance in the water, take up nutrients, and bind the sediment to favor retention of nutrients. Persistent emergent species should be selected according to the local climate and site.

The biotic mass of the ponds can be harvested periodically, composted, and used to amend soil on the golf course or landscaped areas around the course.

The pond's location, size, configuration, depth, and other specific details are engineered to conform with requirements of the stormwater management system for the specific watershed area of each pond or impoundment.

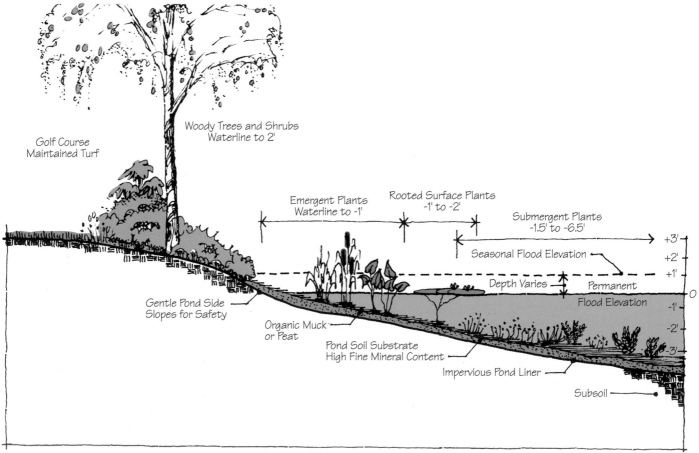

Typical concept section for a retention pond as biologic filter.
Source: *Guy L. Rando & Associates Inc.*

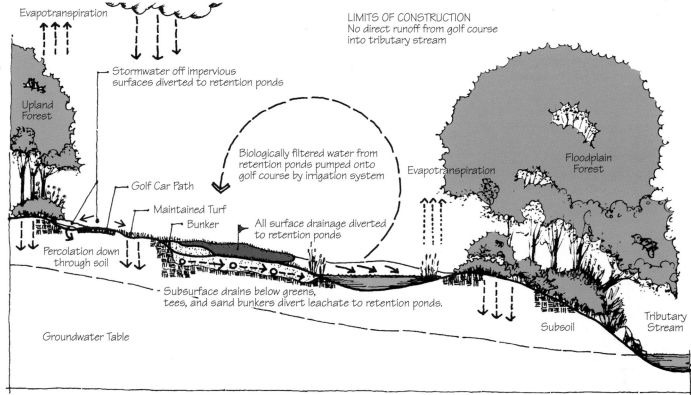

Evapotranspiration

LIMITS OF CONSTRUCTION
No direct runoff from golf course
into tributary stream

Upland
Forest

Stormwater off impervious
surfaces diverted to retention ponds

Biologically filtered water from
retention ponds pumped onto
golf course by irrigation system

Evapotranspiration

Floodplain
Forest

Golf Car Path

Maintained Turf

Bunker

All surface drainage diverted
to retention ponds

Percolation down
through soil

Subsurface drains below greens,
tees, and sand bunkers divert leachate to retention ponds.

Groundwater Table

Subsoil

Tributary
Stream

Typical concept section for the hydrologic cycle of a golf course.
Source: Guy L. Rando & Associates Inc.

Conserving Water Resources

One of the primary environmental issues related to golf courses is the
high demand for water associated
with irrigating fairways, tees, and
greens. Several strategies have been
devised to reduce the demand for
water and conserve resources:

■ Selecting low-water-demand,
drought-tolerant turf grass and
landscape materials.

■ Using a series of stormwater retention ponds to store storm runoff as
a source of irrigation water, thus
reducing the peak demand on water
resources by maintaining a constant level of available water. Sup-
plemental water can be provided
during anticipated dry periods by
pumping water from wells or other
sources into irrigation ponds,
where it can be held until needed.
Such ponds can be engineered to
biologically filter stormwater.
Groundwater is recharged through
redistribution of the processed
stormwater onto the golf course.

■ Using dry stormwater ponds as an
alternative method to recharge

groundwater. These dry ponds reduce stormwater surge and aid in
biologic filtering. BATs and BMPs
guide the design of such ponds to
conform with regulatory requirements.

■ Selecting an irrigation system that
provides highly accurate control
and monitoring of water use. In
keeping with objectives for the
IPM system, irrigation is limited to
the extent necessary to maintain
healthy turf. Other ways to reduce
stress on the turf during drought,
such as mowing it higher, are given
priority over irrigation in the typical IPM system.

■ Using wastewater effluent as a
source of water for irrigation. Effluent from primary and secondary
sanitary treatment plants can be
an important source of water for irrigation in many regions. Distributing the effluent over the turf is an
effective means of further processing the effluent. The combination
of sun, aeration (during irrigation), turf, and soil effectively puri-
fies the effluent. If effluent is used
as a source for irrigation, it is usu-

ally pumped into a storage reservoir, where it is held until needed.
It is critical to establish a testing
program to determine the quality
of the effluent and the presence of
any contaminants that could be
toxic or detrimental to turf. In
some jurisdictions, the quality of
the effluent directly affects the
minimum setback required between irrigated turf and adjacent
land uses. A storage reservoir system can provide biologic filtering
to improve the quality of the effluent before it is used for irrigation.

■ Using principles of Xeriscape™[34]
to minimize the demand for water:

  ■ Selecting low-water-demand and
  drought-tolerant plants (including the selective use of turf) appropriate to site-specific climatic
  conditions;

  ■ Using plant materials to moderate
  the microclimate and provide
  easy maintenance;

  ■ Providing conditions that will
  support healthy plant growth,
  such as amending soils with organic materials;

- Using mulches to retain moisture and promote the establishment of strong, deep root systems;
- Using efficient irrigation systems;
- Providing appropriate maintenance and care.

Initial implementation of these concepts is not necessarily inexpensive in terms of labor and materials. Rather, its cost-effectiveness is realized in the long-term benefits of reduced requirements for water and energy to maintain the landscape.

Land Reclamation and Golf Courses

One positive influence of golf courses is in land reclamation projects—the conversion of sanitary landfill sites, mining sites, and other "spoiled land," for example. Golf course projects using reclaimed land require a highly technical approach to design, and, while the cost of land for these sites might be low, the cost of building a golf course can be very expensive.

Almost every town or city has a landfill. Landfills are generally viewed as a liability to the community rather than an asset, and they tend to lower the value of nearby property. Landfills are usually reclaimed for use as wildlife sanctuaries or recreation, but otherwise they do not produce income once the landfill is closed. Sanitary landfills, however, can make good sites for golf courses because of the relatively large area of land that is typically involved and its low value. The reclamation of landfills for use as golf courses benefits the community by converting a liabil-

Water: Nature's Renewable Resource

If you asked the beleaguered City of Chicago Department of the Underground how much rainwater we saw last summer [1991], they probably would not recall last year's drought.

As this article is written, the unfortunate Loop buildings are still flooded, business is not as usual, and the heart of our beloved city is a disaster area.

Although this much attention is not usually paid to our water supply, Chicagoland is in fact a "water-rich" area with an immense supply of the golden liquid within easy reach. Many western suburbs, however, may not agree that we, as a region, are water rich. We have rivers, a fairly shallow aquifer, and Lake Michigan. Sure, we occasionally have to go easy on our lawns, but we are in great shape compared to other parts of the nation and the world.

In Saudi Arabia, King Fahd ordered the construction of several huge water desalination plants costing the royal family billions of dollars. The immense plants provide water to the oil-rich, but water-poor, citizens.

In the desert areas of the Southwest, golf courses dig deeper than 100 feet for water. Grass lawns are a luxury not even the rich can afford. The mighty Colorado River has even run dry because of the upstream demands for water.

Local Restrictions

At the local level, lawn sprinkling restrictions are routine, and outright bans on watering are commonplace. Local golf courses, too, have seen restrictions placed on course watering. We saw evidence last summer when many courses suffered a disturbing case of brown fairways.

The need to treat water as a valuable resource is not new. It is a need that is accepted more readily by people in water-poor environments than here. But, it is a growing need and one that deserves more attention in the Chicago area.

An often-overlooked water source is wastewater. That's right. Wastewater. Sewage. We have a tremendous resource in wastewater generated by hundreds of millions of gallons each day. Water reclamation and reuse, as it is called by industry insiders, is an answer to many course irrigation problems.

It is also an answer to crop irrigation. It may not be the answer for every course, but it has its place in golf course development and irrigation.

Ed Partyka is the grounds superintendent for White Pines Golf Club in Bensenville. White Pines is a public course irrigating with municipal wastewater. Since the treated water is used first in homes and businesses and secondly on the golf course, "we do not pay a water bill, we just supply the pumps and electricity," said Partyka.

Palm Desert, California

Marriott's Desert Springs Resort and Spa in Palm Desert, a 110,000-round-per-year, 36-hole facility, takes advantage of wastewater in a similar fashion. Dan Gieseler is the grounds superintendent for the facility.

The system Marriott uses in Palm Desert is similar to the one White Pines uses in Bensenville. Both take water directly from the municipal wastewater treatment plant. These plants treat the water conventionally through filtration, settling, and disinfection.

Gieseler's courses take up to 2.5 million gallons per day from the Cochella Water Valley Water District. The district is in charge of managing the Cochella Valley aquifer that supplies much of the water used by the region. An aquifer is the underground water supply.

Gieseler's operation takes half of its water as effluent (treated wastewater) from the local sewage treatment plant and the other half from the aquifer. He has drilled a 1,300-foot-deep well on the property. Because the effluent has a higher concentration of salt, he mixes the clean well water with the saltier effluent. The result is a mix that does not harm the grass plant.

"One more step and you could drink it," said Gieseler.

Cochella Water District

The annual cost of irrigating the two Marriott golf courses is a whopping $350,000. The Cochella Water District discharges water at the top of the aquifer to replace all of the water used by its various customers. The district has done a good job, because in the last 10 years, the water level in the aquifer has remained steady. The Cochella Water District pulls the water it uses to recharge the aquifer from the Colorado River.

Just because Gieseler uses so much water, he doesn't waste it.

"We want to use the least amount of water, because grass grows better and the course takes less of a beating," Gieseler said.

Another type of effluent is being used regularly now, too. The reclaimed water discussed above was processed at a water treatment plant. Wynstone, the North Barrington championship course designed by Jack Nicklaus, uses a more environmentally sensitive process.

Wynstone Golf Club

Wynstone Golf Club in North Barrington is home to John Malloy, the grounds superintendent. Included among Malloy's many duties is the responsibility for the water reclamation system designed by engineers at Scheaffer & Roland, Inc.

Scheaffer & Roland maintains offices in Wheaton and specializes in the design and construction of water reclamation systems.

"Why dump the nutrients in the rivers when you can dump them on land?" Malloy asks.

Effluent is a nutrient-rich water. Sodium, nitrogen, phosphorus, and potassium are all found in various concentrations in reclaimed water.

"My office is 40 yards from the aeration lagoon. I have never smelled anything," added Malloy.

ity into an asset—with the added potential for producing income.

Not every landfill site is suited for development of a golf course. Several criteria can be used to evaluate a landfill for use as a golf course:

- Sufficient size to support an 18-hole regulation course;
- Accessibility to a sizable golf market;
- Availability of water for irrigation;
- Availability of power and other utilities.

The nature and history of the landfill itself are also important determinants of suitability:

- What type of refuse went into the fill?
- Are any toxic or hazardous wastes present?
- How was the refuse layered and compacted daily?
- What are the depth, density, and final contour of the landfill's cap?
- What system was used to collect and vent liquid and gas by-products of decomposition?

Generally, the best landfill sites for golf courses are those with the lowest fill height (20 feet ideally, with up to 35 feet acceptable) that have been aged 20 years or more after the landfill was closed. The establishment of strong plant populations over the site is generally a good indication of the site's suitability.

Traditionally, water that is treated by local governments is discharged into the local water network. It makes its way to the mighty Mississippi River and eventually the Gulf of Mexico. Reuse of the treated water by golf courses is a great way to take advantage of the water resource.

Malloy feels good about using reclaimed water because of environmental responsibility. It makes good common and economic sense to process waste on site and reuse the water. Scheaffer & Roland has based a successful engineering practice by selling this good-sense process to developers, who need such a service with increased government restrictions.

The Reclamation Process

Malloy's system at Wynstone is a typical sewer collection system. Sewer pipes run from the homes, offices, and clubhouse at Wynstone. The wastewater is then pumped to the lagoon 40 yards from Malloy's office. Air is continually pumped by air compressors from the base of the lagoon. The air rises to the top and aerates the sewage as it rises.

This process is known as aeration. It allows natural settling to occur. Large non-biodegradable particles, grit, and organic matter are removed by coagulation and settling. This process creates sludge, which requires removal only every 20 years or so.

The water spends an average of 36 days in the aerated lagoon and is then pumped to a reservoir, which can hold up to a four-month supply of water. The water then goes through a sand filtration process similar to the process that occurs in the City of Chicago's Jardine lakewater treatment facility near Navy Pier.

The water is treated with chlorine to kill harmful bacteria. The water is then ready for irrigation on Wynstone's beautiful grounds. The water is now reclaimed. Although irrigation water is safe, the government agencies controlling this reclamation method do not allow it to be used for drinking water.

Malloy does not have the opportunity to mix the reclaimed water with well water like Gieseler does at Marriott. The saline content of the Scheaffer & Roland system is high, just like the reclaimed water from the wastewater treatment plants. Malloy is required to apply a chemical to counteract the high sodium content.

The best news of the day for Wynstone's budget was expressed well by Malloy.

"We don't have a water bill," he said.

The Final Filter

Even though the water is not potable after the final step of the reclamation process, it is clean enough to use for irrigation of golf courses, corn crops, and vegetable fields.

Grass and soil combine to form a living filter for the reused wastewater. The grass absorbs the moisture, microorganisms attack any bacteria, the soil filters the

Marriott's Desert Springs Resort in Palm Desert, a 110,000-round-per-year, 36-hole facility, uses treated municipal wastewater for irrigation.

water, the air oxidizes it, and the sun radiates it. These combined natural processes actually exceed the benefits of traditional sewage treatment.

Third Time is a Charm

Wayne Cowlishaw from Scheaffer & Roland worked on an exciting municipal project in Lubbock, Texas, where the town uses the same drop of water three times. The city's wastewater is treated by the reclamation process and pumped to a 4,000-acre cornfield, where it is used for irrigation.

A series of wells drilled beneath the 4,000 acres of corn collect the water. The water is then pumped to the headwaters of a local river, where it is used for aesthetics and recreation.

More developments and courses should discover what Malloy, Gieseler, Partyka, and Cowlishaw already know. It is very safe, and, most important, reuse of the water resource is environmentally responsible.

The environmental issues associated with water reclamation and reuse should make the use of reclaimed water a more widely accepted practice.

Source: Peter Dyke, "Water: Nature's Renewable Resource," *Chicagoland Golf*, May 1992, pp. 10–11. Reprinted with permission.

Rough grading of #18 around an existing waterfall.

Final shaping of #18.

#18 in play.

The #2 hole is located in the quarry's former borrow pit.

An old quarry site in Fairfield Sapphire Valley was reclaimed for the Holly Forest Golf Course and recreational open space.

Three basic problems must be resolved in the development of a landfill site:

■ The development of gases (primarily methane) that tend to migrate upward within the soil and are toxic to plants, combustible, and malodorous;
■ Uneven settling or subsidence;
■ Toxic liquid outflows.

Specially trained civil engineers can address these problems, and qualified engineers are essential members of the design team that is considering a landfill for a golf course. An engineering assessment of a landfill is necessary to determine the limitations on design, construction, and operation for a proposed golf course.

Projects involving the reclamation of a landfill include certain limits on design:

■ Cutting or excavating the landfill cap (a dense clay cover that seals the top of the landfill) is usually prohibited. Therefore, the golf course must be shaped entirely of fill material brought in from off site. Gas barriers must be installed under all tees, greens, and key turf areas. Fairways must be built up to allow irrigation and drainage lines to be buried without breaking the landfill cap. Special roads for hauling must be built over unstable fill areas. These factors can add substantially to the cost of constructing the golf course.
■ The golf course must be routed around gas collection or venting systems where excessive subsidence is expected, "hot" pockets of gas or liquid, cleansing ponds, and unstable soil.

■ The clubhouse and other structures cannot be built on the landfill itself because of the lack of stable conditions for building foundations and the dangers presented by gases. Similarly, utilities, parking lots, driveways, golf car paths, sidewalks, bridges, walls, water features, sanitary septic leachfields, and irrigation pumping stations cannot be located on the landfill itself.

Other limitations must be considered:

■ Safety precautions must be posted to alert golfers about the potential for igniting the methane and possible allergic reactions some individuals might have to by-products of the landfill.
■ All employees, workers, and operators must be specially trained to recognize potentially hazardous or hazardous situations.
■ Obnoxious odors can occur under certain weather conditions.

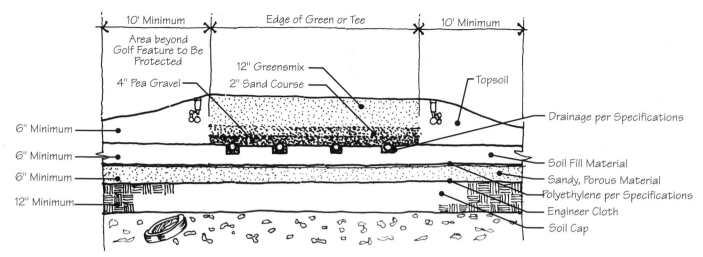

A green constructed over a landfill.
Source: Michael J. Hurdzan, Ph.D.

- All vehicles used on the course, including maintenance vehicles and golf cars, must be equipped with modified exhaust systems to reduce the potential for igniting the methane. In addition, they often need high-flotation tires to minimize compaction, which can cause subsidence and poor surface drainage.
- Irrigation can accelerate decomposition and the formation of by-products.

Despite the limitations and problems associated with building a golf course on a landfill, the results can be highly rewarding in terms of environmental quality for a community. The best way to integrate golf courses and landfills is to design for both simultaneously. In other words, the golf course should be anticipated when the landfill is being designed. Such joint planning allows the landfill systems to be designed to fit around the golf course rather than vice versa. The placement of fill and shape of the cap can be designed to match the intended contours for the golf course. The methane gas collection system can be designed to minimize conflicts with the golf course and might even be designed to capture the gas as a source of energy. With foresight, such joint planning can turn a negative land use into a positive one with few conflicts and maximum cost-effectiveness.

Another approach to integrating golf courses and landfills is to use the golf course as a greenbelt around a landfill, providing a buffer between the landfill and adjacent land uses while providing an opportunity for recreational uses. The golf course increases the value of adjacent land and can make the landfill more acceptable to its neighbors. At the same time, the landfill can be designed for eventual use as a golf course. This second golf course, scheduled for construction after the landfill has been closed and aged, could be designed to be served from the same clubhouse as the one on the greenbelt.

For any land reclamation project, the golf course serves not only as an income-producing recreational amenity, but also as an opportunity to reestablish a healthy ecosystem in which the golf course is but one element. The concept of Golf Courses as Ecologic Sanctuaries™ provides tools for transforming spoiled land with little or no value into an environmental asset whose value can be calculated in terms of both increased land value and quality of life.

The Audubon Cooperative Sanctuary Program for Golf Courses

The Audubon Cooperative Sanctuary Program, sponsored by USGA, is administered by the Audubon Society of New York State. Its main purposes are to:

- Protect and enhance wildlife habitats on existing and planned golf courses;
- Recognize the importance of golf courses as open spaces and educate the public about their environmental benefits;
- Encourage all those associated with golf to learn about environmental issues and practice conservation.

The program distributes publications, offers telephone consultations, and makes on-site visits. A questionnaire and inventory of resources for golf course owners and operators can be returned to the program's offices for review and recommendations about appropriate conservation actions to take. Golf course owners or operators who wish to have their facility certified a "cooperative sanctuary" under this program must develop an environmental plan of action and appoint a committee to oversee implementation of the plan. Such certification makes the project eligible for regional and national awards.

The Clubhouse

Although it is generally recognized that the game of golf dates back to the 17th century in Scotland, the contemporary golf clubhouse, as the center of the golf club, has evolved primarily in the United States during the last century (although a clubhouse was built at St. Andrews about 1850). European golf clubhouses were born of necessity, their fundamental purpose being simply to house members' golf equipment and to provide a workroom for the pro to manufacture golf sticks.

Early clubhouses were built outside the largest metropolitan areas of the United States in the late 19th century. The first "clubhouse" for John Reid's St. Andrews Club in Yonkers, New York, consisted of little more than boards set on two barrels, with tubs of ice and water kept under the boards. It was later expanded to the permanence of a tent. A few years later, the city built a road through the meadow, requiring the St. Andrews golf club to move to a 34-acre apple orchard a few blocks north on the Weston estate. This site featured a steep slope to the valley and panoramic views of the Hudson River and New Jersey Palisades. The members hung their coats and lunch baskets and a wicker basket of scotch in the branches of a tree located near the first tee and the sixth and final green. A crude bench encircled the trunk, providing a place to gather and relax in the shade of the tree. Thus, the group became known as the "Apple Tree Gang."

At the outset, club memberships were small. Members used their resources to buy farm property, often converting the original farmhouse into the clubhouse. One of the first buildings specifically designed as a golf clubhouse was at Shinnecock Hills, in Southampton, Long Island. Designed by Stanford White (who happened to be a member of the St. Andrews Club and of the architectural firm McKim, Meade and White), that clubhouse is a classic example of the shingle-covered style prevalent in the

Cap Rock Clubhouse at Horseshoe Bay.

late 19th century for both residential and recreational buildings in the Northeast. Although the building has since been expanded, it remains true to White's original concept of a linear arrangement that stretches the clubhouse along the golf course. Sited among the tees of starting holes 1 and 10 and the greens of finishing holes 9 and 18 and close to the practice green and range, the clubhouse at Shinnecock Hills exemplifies an ideal relationship between clubhouse and golf course. The dining porch overlooks the #9 green.

The development of resorts in the late 19th century through the 1920s spread the popularity of golf as sport that was both fashionable and fun. Clubhouses have since been created in every architectural style, bridging the gap between commercial and residential architecture to achieve the presence appropriate to the status associated with a golf club, while still offering the familiarity and comfort of a home setting.

The clubhouse, then and now, serves as a portal between the realm of golf and the outside world. It has the capability to modify initial perceptions about a golf course and to punctuate the experience upon leaving the course. It also serves as the most visible and tangible element on the landscape of a golf course, conveying ideas about the character and

quality of the golf course. The building supports the game of golf and often other recreational or social activities as well.

Fitting the Clubhouse To Users' Needs

Typically, the clubhouse architect's role is to determine the needs of the client and to establish a design program and relationships between various elements of the building and its surroundings. The clubhouse is a highly specialized building that must serve many functions. Cost-efficiency is a major factor in programming and designing a clubhouse. The most common error cited by course owners, operators, developers, and architects is that the clubhouse is too large for its membership: it is too expensive to operate given the income it generates. Members' needs and desires must be analyzed critically compared to the *actual* needs of a clubhouse for a specific course and its membership within the constraints of realistic budgets for construction, operation, and maintenance. The goal of the clubhouse architect in today's economy is to meet the needs of as many users as possible cost-effectively.

The design of a clubhouse is driven by its use within the project site. Its needs and functions vary with the type of golf course operation and membership structure (daily fee, municipally owned; daily fee, privately owned; semiprivate; private equity or nonequity club; and so on). Other amenities to be integrated with the clubhouse (tennis, swimming, a health club, a resort, for example) could also affect the design of the clubhouse. Except in rare instances, real estate sales and marketing should *not* take place in the clubhouse.

For a daily-fee course, whether municipally or privately owned, the clubhouse's primary function is as a point of control for starting players and collecting fees, capable of handling high volumes of traffic. The food and beverage concessions are generally minimal or limited to light fare. The clubhouse might also serve as a point of control for other recreational facilities like the tennis courts and swimming pool and other amenities like a shop for sale or rental of sports equipment. Lockers and showers are usually limited, largely because many daily-fee courses cater to high-volume traffic and players tend to limit the use of the clubhouse to changing clothes and eating a snack before returning home.

In contrast, the clubhouse for a private golf course tends to be as much a center for social gatherings as it is a facility that supports both golf and a variety of other recreational amenities. Thus, social spaces like dining rooms and other food and beverage facilities, card rooms, party rooms, lounges, and the like are given considerably more importance in the design of the clubhouse. Locker rooms tend to be larger and include social spaces like the traditional card room and optional amenities like saunas, fitness rooms, massage rooms, and so on. A multipurpose club might provide a separate entrance to the pro shop or locker rooms to reduce traffic through the main lobby. The building generally includes offices for key personnel, including the club manager, chef, superintendent, golf pro, and social director. Social and recreational amenities for nongolfing family members are important elements of the clubhouse's program.

A clubhouse for a resort must take into account the high level of service expected by guests, including the special requirements for club storage and handling and the logistics of coordinating check-in and check-out with resort operations. Each resort must develop a program and design specific to the project that are integral parts of the entire resort operation. Of equal concern is barrier-free accessibility to all clubhouse and course facilities, and today's designer must take into account the Americans with Disabilities Act (ADA), passed in 1990.

The ADA sets forth a goal for social policy that requires the removal of barriers so that individuals with disabilities can enjoy the same bene-

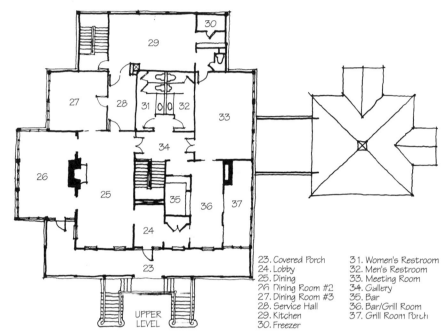

The upper level at Wachesaw Plantation.
Source: W. Wade Setliff, Architectural Design Group, Inc.

23. Covered Porch	31. Women's Restroom
24. Lobby	32. Men's Restroom
25. Dining	33. Meeting Room
26. Dining Room #2	34. Gallery
27. Dining Room #3	35. Bar
28. Service Hall	36. Bar/Grill Room
29. Kitchen	37. Grill Room Porch
30. Freezer	

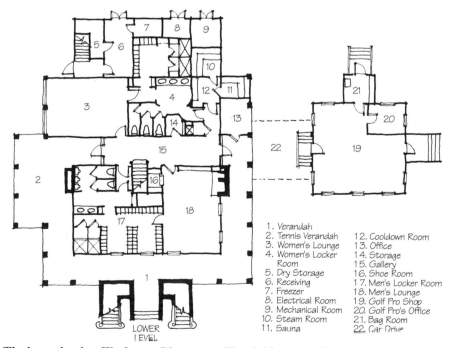

1. Verandah	12. Cooldown Room
2. Tennis Verandah	13. Office
3. Women's Lounge	14. Storage
4. Women's Locker Room	15. Gallery
5. Dry Storage	16. Shoe Room
6. Receiving	17. Men's Locker Room
7. Freezer	18. Men's Lounge
8. Electrical Room	19. Golf Pro Shop
9. Mechanical Room	20. Golf Pro's Office
10. Steam Room	21. Bag Room
11. Sauna	22. Car Drive

The lower level at Wachesaw Plantation. The clubhouse at Wachesaw Plantation in Murrells Inlet, South Carolina, incorporates old brick from a turn-of-the-century factory.
Source: W. Wade Setliff, Architectural Design Group, Inc.

fits and opportunities that those without disabilities have always enjoyed. Sections of the ADA bear directly on the accessibility of clubhouses and other buildings and on hiring practices; eventually, the law will also cover accessibility of the golf course. The ADA is very precise about how facilities are to comply with its requirements, but it has yet to provide detailed physical specifications for golf courses. In the meantime, owners and operators of golf courses must show intent to comply with the law. Several golf organizations have taken steps to create industry guidelines for barrier-free golf courses. Research and reports by golf organizations and by public, private, or institutional research groups and planning and design firms bear watching.

ADA was implemented in four phases:

- By January 26, 1992, existing public accommodations were to be accessible for the disabled when modifications could be reasonably achieved.

- By July 26, 1992, discrimination based on disability became unlawful for businesses with 25 or more employees.

- New public accommodations intended for occupancy after January 26, 1993, must be accessible to the disabled.

- After July 26, 1994, discrimination based on disability becomes unlawful for businesses with 15 or more employees.[35]

Clubhouses and other buildings built before January 26, 1992, must comply with ADA if the modifications are "easily accomplishable and able to be carried out without much difficulty or expense." Buildings that began construction after January 26, 1992, must comply with ADA without exception. The ADA clearly specifies guidelines regarding architectural and transportation barriers. Operators and owners should examine hiring and employment procedures and practices to determine whether current practices discriminate or exclude the disabled.[36]

Golf *should* be accessible to any individual regardless of ability or disability, gender, or age, and anyone willing to rise to the challenge of golf should be afforded the opportunity to try. The sport offers challenges to even the most physically fit individual, but it can be said that in this curious sport where luck often plays a greater role than skill, we are all "handicapped." The handicap system was specifically devised to allow players of various abilities to play on "equal" terms. Barriers to accessibility come in many forms, and the designer must consider those who have difficulty walking or negotiating stairs, those who are visually challenged, those who cannot hear or speak, those who have difficulty breathing or performing manual tasks, and those who have difficulty caring for themselves. Removing barriers involves not only physical changes to a building, course, or equipment, but also changes in the perceptions and attitudes of society and individuals. The designer must remember, however, that those who are physically, mentally, or spiritually challenged do not want to be singled out. They do not want places designed "for the blind," "for the deaf," or "for the wheelchair." A distinction can be made between barriers and challenges: remove the former, not the latter. In the end, design should enrich experiences for all.

The Site for the Clubhouse

The ideal location for the clubhouse is in the center of the golf course with easy access to and within sight of the #1, #9, #10, and #18 holes, practice green, and driving range. In addition to control points for the golf course, the site should take into consideration such factors as the orientation of the building for views and solar and climatic conditions. Siting must also consider the vehicular approach (for golf cars and automobiles) and the experience of golfers or patrons coming to, entering, going through, and leaving the clubhouse. In Asia, which is a rapidly growing golf market, the *feng shui* of the site must be considered in locating the

clubhouse and arranging features on and around the golf course.[37] The arrangement of elements like approach drives, parking, and sidewalks should be carefully considered to make the layout easy to "read" and thus comfortable for the user. The golf course architect, land planner, landscape architect, civil engineer, and clubhouse architect should work together on the siting of the clubhouse. In general:

- Soil conditions, locations of trees, accessibility to utilities, water, and sewer lines, distance of the driveway from the main road, and similar factors should be considered.

- Conflicts between automobiles, golf cars, and pedestrians can present a safety hazard. An analysis of different circulation patterns for autos, golf cars, pedestrians, golfing guests, nongolfing guests, and employees early during design can avoid serious conflicts and expensive solutions later.

- Service traffic should be separated from traffic generated by patrons if at all possible. Service traffic and service areas should be screened from public view, and cross traffic with automobiles, golf cars, or pedestrians should be avoided.

- The entrance drive should be welcoming and provide strong visual clues to orient and direct guests to the clubhouse.

- An arrival area should be provided where drivers can drop off guests in a comfortable, sheltered area at the clubhouse entrance, then proceed to the parking area.

- Parking should be located a short walking distance from the clubhouse, screened from view from the clubhouse or course. For some golf operations, particularly resorts, valet parking should be considered at the arrival area of the clubhouse entrance.

- The clubhouse should be located to minimize the distance for golfers from the ninth green and 10th tee if the clubhouse is to serve as a "halfway house" to speed up play.

- The club should be located on high ground to maximize views to the

The clubhouse at Grand Cypress Golf Course in Orlando, Florida.

golf course and other amenities and take advantage of long vistas whenever possible. Views of the first and 10th tees and the driving range from the pro shop are desirable. Views of the incoming greens and outgoing tees from the dining areas, the 19th hole, and other social areas are also valuable.

■ The clubhouse should be sited to take advantage of solar and wind orientation to reduce energy costs and to permit enjoyment of a variety of comfortable indoor and outdoor settings for patrons. Porches or terraces should be shielded from the afternoon sun.

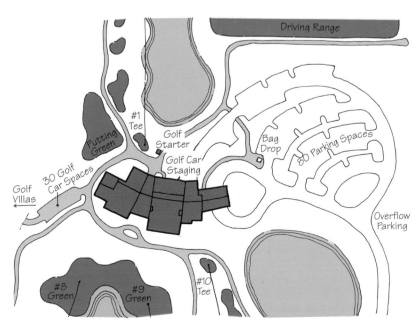

Site plan for the clubhouse at Grand Cypress Golf Course.
Source: Richard J. Diedrich.

111

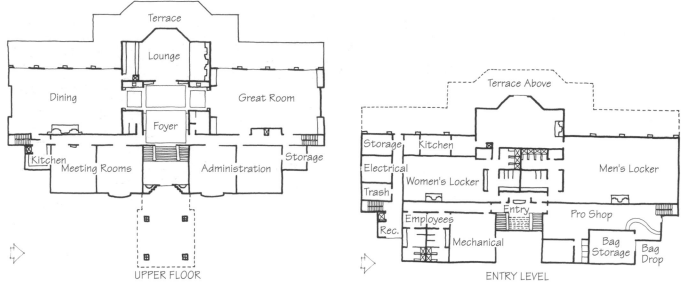

UPPER FLOOR

ENTRY LEVEL

At the Marlboro Golf and Country Club in Monmouth County, New Jersey, shaded terraces provide a variety of comfortable settings for patrons.
Source: Craig Roberts/Desmond Muirhead, Inc.

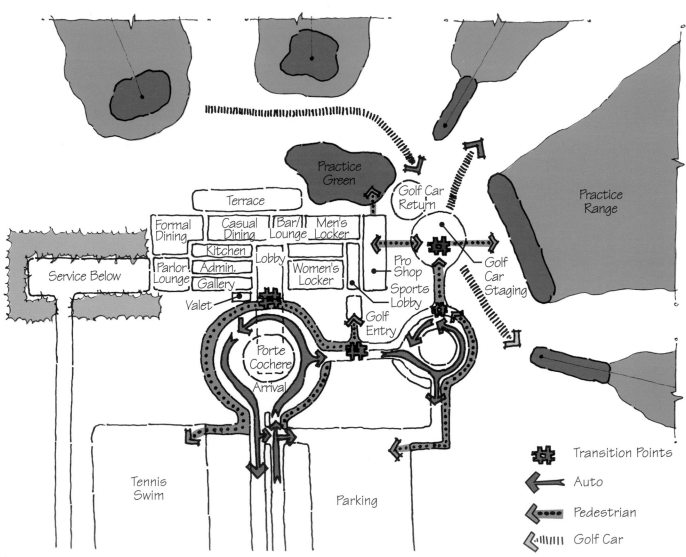

Typical entry and circulation.
Source: Richard J. Diedrich.

The Clubhouse's Facilities

As noted earlier, the golf clubhouse houses functions unique to the sport and social aspects of golf. The size and inclusion of some of the spaces discussed in this section vary according to the needs of a particular golf operation.

Arrival Area

The arrival area provides a transition from the automobile to the pedestrian environment; it is a place of first impressions. It must respond to the needs of both golfers and non-golfers, particularly at resorts and private clubs where the clubhouse serves multiple social and recreational functions. For daily-fee operations, the provision of simple amenities, such as a place to drop golf bags before parking the car, is an important consideration. A comfortable, sheltered area for golfers to wait is desirable. At a resort where guests expect a high level of service, valet service and an attendant at the arrival area to greet guests, take care of golf bags, park cars, provide information or directions, and so on are often necessary. When the clubhouse serves multiple purposes, providing a second entrance for golfers should be considered to allow direct access to the pro shop or locker area and reduce traffic through the main lobby. Often, the arrival area is under a roof (a porte cochere) so that members and guests can proceed in comfort, despite the weather. This amenity is especially important when the clubhouse also serves as a social or community gathering place.

Admirals Cove Clubhouse, Jupiter, Florida.

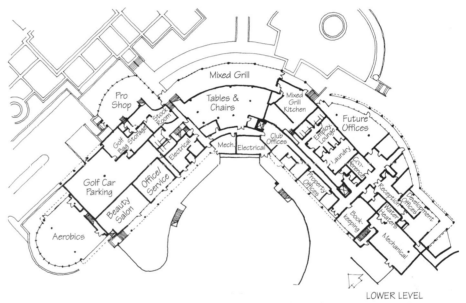

First floor plan, Admirals Cove Clubhouse.
Source: Richard J. Diedrich.

Second floor plan, Admirals Cove Clubhouse.
Source: Richard J. Diedrich.

113

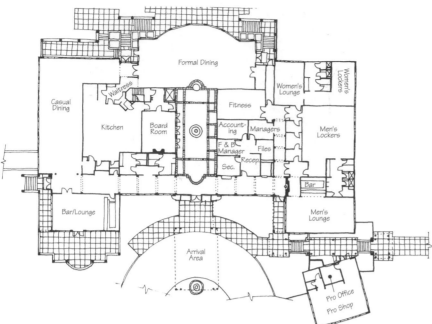

Floor plan, Hammock Dunes Golf Clubhouse, Palm Coast, Florida.
Source: Richard J. Diedrich.

Lobby/Entry

The lobby can range from 200 to several thousand square feet, depending on the type of operation, the overall number of members, the complexity of functions offered, and the desired aesthetic character for the clubhouse.

The lobby demands specific attention, particularly for private clubs and resort operations, for several reasons:

■ It provides most members' and guests' first impressions, setting the tone or ambience of the facilities.

■ It is a hub within the clubhouse, leading to other activity areas, and should clearly direct members and guests to various destinations. In most cases, a receptionist in the lobby can offer directions.

■ The lobby is a support area for the club's social areas, providing access to coat storage, restrooms, telephones, and other comforts.

■ The lobby is a staging area for groups using adjoining social or dining rooms.

Administrative Offices

Administrative offices can be located anywhere in the clubhouse, but they are usually located near the lobby so that the club manager and/or receptionist are readily available to members or guests. They support the club's day-to-day operations. Administrative offices can vary from 400 square feet for a manager's and secretary's office in a daily-fee clubhouse to accommodations for several staff members at a private club. A larger club typically includes an office for the food and beverage manager and other managers, such as those for

The lobby of Isleworth Clubhouse.

The lobby of Hammock Dunes Golf Clubhouse.

114

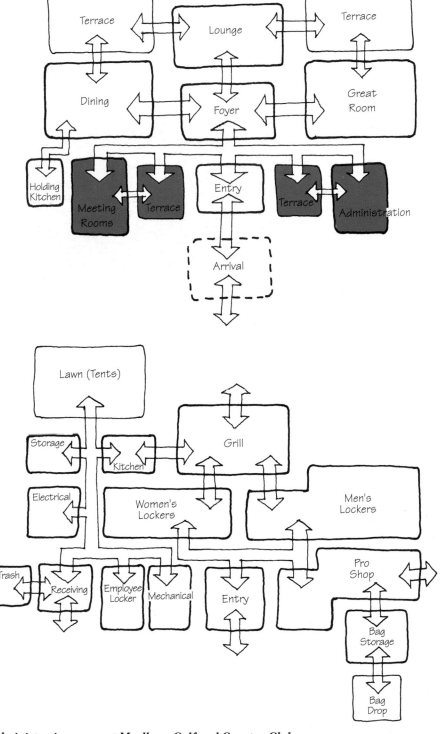

Administration areas at Marlboro Golf and Country Club.
Source: Tim Casey/Desmond Muirhead, Inc.

banquets, sales, membership, and activities. These offices should provide easy access for patrons, in contrast to the office where a chef plans meals. An office for the accounting staff and a common workroom or board-

room for conferences and meetings might also be included.

Locker Rooms
Certain traditions and social patterns peculiar to the sport of golf make

clubhouse locker rooms different from other recreational locker rooms. For most daily-fee operations, the locker room is a small area with restrooms and a place to change shoes. For private clubs, however, the locker room serves as more than just a place to change clothing and clean up. It is actually the principal social center for the clubhouse.

Three basic areas are associated with the "locker rooms": the locker area proper, the washroom area, and the lounge area. The locker area proper varies in size, depending on the size, spacing, and number of lockers. Lockers range from a 12-inch-wide shoe locker that can be stacked several units high to an 18- to 24-inch-wide, full-height locker. A 42-inch-high, three-quarter locker can be stacked two high and comfortably accommodate a hanging sports jacket. Lockers are at least 20 inches deep, although users decidedly prefer a 24-inch-deep locker. Members of a private club most often demand a full-sized personal locker. The cost of the equipment and space required to include a locker for every member plus guests, however, must be weighed against the benefits of stacked lockers or a shared locker system that requires less space. The classic locker arrangement is a full-height unit with a bench seat in front that can be lifted to reach a shoe locker underneath. The designer planning a locker area should allow 10.5 square feet for each 18-inch-wide, full-height locker and include a comfortable changing space.

Even stacked, the number of lockers in a private club can appear cramped and confining, even with ample changing space. Higher ceilings, skylights, and clerestories can create an impression of greater volume and relieve the confining, maze-like feeling created by banks of lockers. The problem in every clubhouse is to keep the locker space from taking over the clubhouse.

Historically, the ratio of women's to men's lockers has been about one in three, but recent experience shows an increasing demand for expanded women's facilities and services, as

Locker   3 Square Feet

Changing Area 6 Square Feet
Aisle   1.4 Square Feet

Area per Locker 10.4, Say 10.5 Square Feet

Typical diagram of locker area with 18-inch full-height lockers.
Source: Richard J. Diedrich.

Men's locker room at Adios.

W. WADE SETLIFF, ARCHITECTURAL DESIGN GROUP, INC.

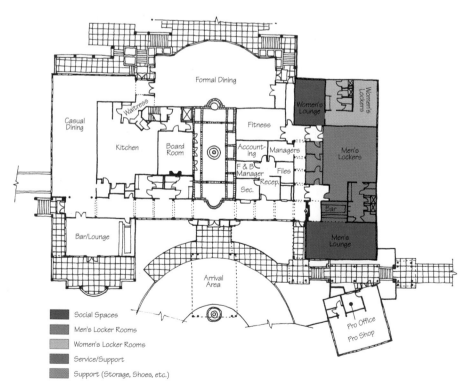

Social Spaces
Men's Locker Rooms
Women's Locker Rooms
Service/Support
Support (Storage, Shoes, etc.)

Locker rooms and social spaces at Hammock Dunes Golf Clubhouse.
Source: Richard J. Diedrich.

women make up the fastest-growing segment of new golfers in today's market. The equalization of men's and women's golf facilities and services has become a sensitive issue and requires careful attention. Men's locker rooms, for example, have traditionally included card rooms—either a separate room adjacent to the locker room or an open area among the lockers themselves. For women, however, an area to play cards is provided in the lounge or other social area. Changing attitudes and demands should be carefully considered. By rights, members who pay equal initiation fees should be entitled to equal services and facilities, regardless of gender. Perhaps the place to start is to distinguish between golfing and nongolfing members or spouses rather than to refer to people by gender. Few will argue the need for separate men's and women's facilities, but providing equal facilities for both genders remains an issue.

The washroom or "wet" area of the locker room typically ranges from

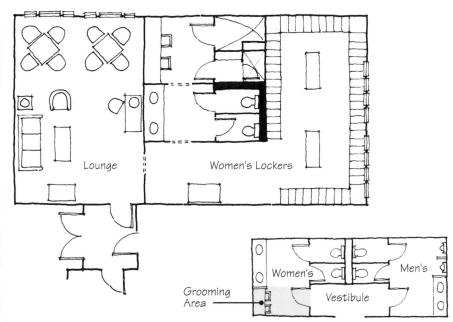

The lounge often serves as a separate anteroom to the restroom area.
Source: Richard J. Diedrich.

400 to 600 square feet, again depending on users' needs. Over time, the trend has been toward more compartmentalized showers that provide greater privacy. The wet area might include showers, a whirlpool, steam bath, sauna, and toilet areas. Showers are seldom used in residential communities or daily-fee operations, because golfers tend to simply change shoes and return home for a shower. Showers are seldom used in resort communities, as golfers can easily return to their rooms to clean up. Showers are more in demand in private urban clubs where members come from work to play golf.

The number of toilet fixtures is determined by local building and plumbing codes. In a smaller clubhouse, like that for a daily-fee operation, the restrooms in the locker might serve the entire building, including social areas. Thus, restrooms should be accessible without going through the locker room and should be finished and furnished commensurate with the quality of the clubhouse.

The lounge area of both the women's and men's locker rooms should include a grooming area. The lounge often serves as a separate anteroom to the restroom area, particularly in an upscale private club. A separate lounge provides an opportu-nity to communicate the quality of the clubhouse that should not be discounted. Particular attention should be paid to the proper quality of lighting in the grooming area.

At some clubs, particularly private and resort operations, the locker room attendant offers shoe service. If such a service is to be provided, an appropriate space (at least 120 square feet at a private club) for the attendant should be located where service can be offered to both the men's and women's locker rooms. It must accommodate space for a sink, workspace with a shoe buffer, shoe racks, and counters for storage. Bar service in the locker room might also be handled by a commonly located, behind-the-scenes service bar. The place where service is offered must work for a bartender of either sex.

The Pro Shop

The pro shop serves as home base for the resident golf pro and is the command center for the golf and related retail operation at the clubhouse. Thus, good visibility of the golf course and driving range is highly desirable to aid in monitoring traffic to and from the golf car staging area, the practice range and green, the #1 and #10 tees, and other outgoing tees for larger golf courses. In most cases, this requirement generally translates into many windows that provide expansive views of the course for these areas. If, however, a minimum amount of supervision of the course from the pro shop is likely, the emphasis is on retailing, translating into more solid walls suited for displaying merchandise. As a retail center, the pro shop should be highly visible, located to encourage traffic and sales. Its ideal location is between the locker rooms and access to the parking areas and other destinations inside the clubhouse.

The size of the pro shop varies, largely depending on the importance of the retail operation—from as small as 400 to 700 square feet for daily-fee operations catering to repeat local golfers to 2,500 square feet or more where retail sales are more important, such as resorts. Typical golfers at a daily-fee course tend to look for the best buy in town and do not purchase golf equipment or soft goods at the clubhouse. Conversely, members of a private club generally purchase their golf equipment and soft goods from their golf pro, so a retail space of 1,000 to 2,000 square feet might be required to display merchandise.[38] At resorts, the majority of purchases are soft goods rather than golf bags and sets of clubs. In general, if the course is known for its design or designer and is located to draw golfers from a wide market, then the sales area should be large enough to accommodate the display of a wide assortment of merchandise with the course's logo, as golfers will want a memento of their play. Such merchandise with logos has replaced name brands as the chief sales item in many pro shops.

For example, the golf shop at a clubhouse on Hilton Head offering 54 holes of golf in a resort community has a sales area of 3,000 square feet. In contrast, the entire clubhouse serving a municipal golf course in metropolitan Atlanta is 3,500 square feet, 1,600 square feet of which the golf shop shares with the grill.

In addition to the retail area, the pro shop should include the following elements:

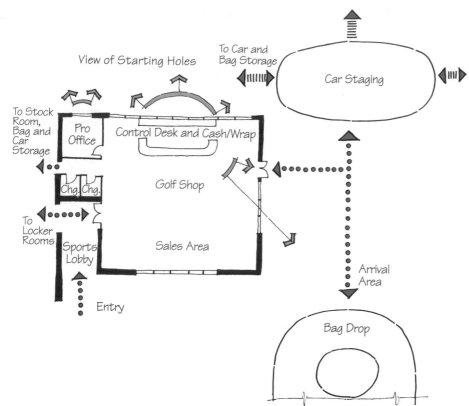

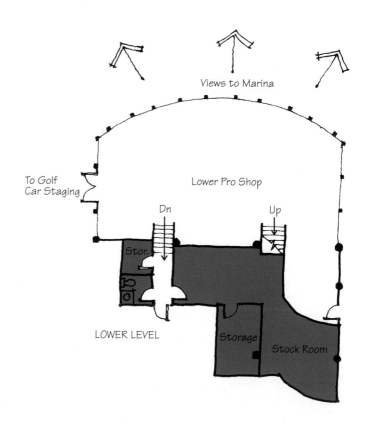

- Offices for the golf pro and assistant pro (as applicable);
- An area for storing inventory and for marking and ordering merchandise;
- Changing rooms for customers to try on clothing.

If golf lessons are a major offering, then a small classroom with room for video equipment and an indoor hitting station are desirable.

The majority of pro shops are located inside the clubhouse, but they could also be housed in a separate building. Such a location has an advantage in the possible reduction of the initial construction cost, as the pro shop can be appointed less luxuriously than the clubhouse. A separate pro shop also opens opportunities for phasing the project. The disadvantages include the loss of impulse buying when members pass through the clubhouse, which can often be a substantial part of the pro shop's business. This disadvantage can be overcome, however, if the pro shop is located between the club-

The pro shop should allow visibility of the golf course when it serves as a command center for the golf pro.
Source: Richard J. Diedrich.

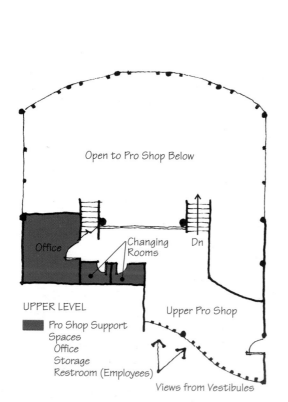

The pro shop at Admirals Cove Clubhouse.
Source: Richard J. Diedrich.

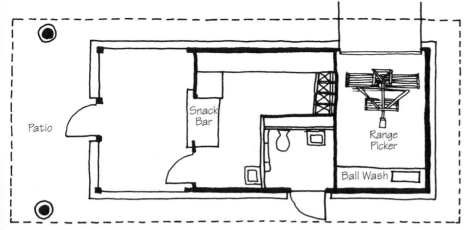

Plan for a turnstand/range house.
Source: Richard J. Diedrich.

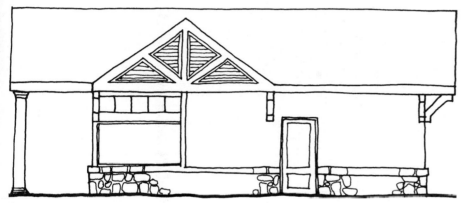

Elevation for a turnstand/range house.
Source: Richard J. Diedrich.

house and the first tee. The NGF notes that if the pro shop is located more than 200 feet from the clubhouse or main building, it often becomes too inconvenient or uncomfortable for golfers, significantly reducing sales for the golf pro.[39]

A "starter shack" might be needed if the starting holes are remote or cannot otherwise be controlled from the pro shop. It can be especially appropriate at a daily-fee or resort course where a high volume of play demands control of foursomes' meeting their appointed tee times. A similar subcenter is the "range shack," which monitors, maintains, and supplies buckets of balls for the practice range. It should be large enough to house the range picker as well as ball cleaning and storage equipment.

Golf Car Storage

A golfer can travel around a golf course with a golf bag by several means:

- Driving a golf car, a two-seat, two-bag gas or electric vehicle (often incorrectly called a "golf cart").
- Walking with a golf cart, a hand-pulled, two-wheel carrier for a single bag. In Japan, a four-bag motorized golf cart pulled by a female caddie has become common on mountainous courses.
- Walking with a golf caddie, an employee of the club with specific service-oriented tasks that include carrying the golf bag. In most of the United States, caddies are a dying breed, as the pressure to speed up play has caused most courses to require the use of golf cars.

The most common means of conveyance around U.S. golf courses is the golf car. An area for storing and maintaining them has therefore be-

come a standard part of the design for a clubhouse.

The size of a storage area for golf cars is largely determined by the number of holes of golf served. For example, an 18-hole course at capacity could serve two foursomes or four cars on each hole, resulting in a maximum of 72 golf cars on the course. Three additional golf cars are generally provided to cover those requiring maintenance, bringing the total to 75 golf cars that must be accommodated. Peak demand in a particular situation must always be kept in mind.

If residents of a golf community are allowed to have their own cars, they normally store them in their own garages, so the size of the golf car storage area can be adjusted accordingly. Even in this case, however, golf cars might be needed and rented for large events like tournaments.

For planning, a golf car parking space should be five feet wide by eight feet deep, with a minimum access aisle 12 feet wide. The cars can be stored in a number of different arrangements, ranging from an allowance of 40 square feet per car to twice as much space. A compromise is a double-loaded aisle with double-stacked parking (55 to 60 square feet per car). A second common compromise is a double-loaded aisle with tandem parking of a row up to five cars deep between two aisles. This arrangement allows for head-in and drive-through parking for all the tandem spaces. The efficiency of this arrangement varies with the number of cars in tandem, but for planning, the designer should allow 70 square feet per car.

While a closely packed arrangement saves a substantial amount of space, it is unsuitable for operators who require access to any car at any time with minimal damage to the cars. A double-loaded aisle, single-depth parking arrangement allows operators to reach any of the cars without disturbing the others. The criteria for deciding the best arrangement for storing golf cars should include the initial construction costs versus long-term operational costs

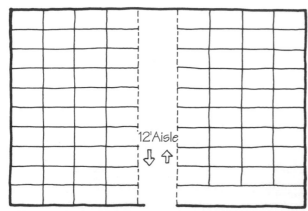

A golf car parking area allowing for 76 cars and maintenance, with 40 square feet per car.
Source: W. Wade Setliff, Architectural Design Group, Inc.

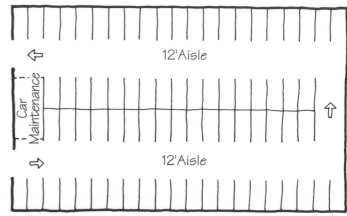

A golf car parking area allowing for 76 cars and maintenance, with 80 square feet per car.
Source: W. Wade Setliff, Architectural Design Group, Inc.

that come with the inevitable damage to cars being jockeyed through storage facilities. Backing golf cars in and out are difficult maneuvers even for skillful drivers. Therefore, the traffic flow pattern through the car storage facility has an important role in avoiding damage to cars. In the tandem-row arrangement, a curb or rail between tandem rows can act as a guide, providing inexpensive insurance against damage to cars.

The traffic flow through the storage area should be arranged to provide for unloading golf bags, cleaning and maintaining cars as they enter the facility, and loading golf bags and other equipment as they leave. The maintenance area should accommodate two cars with space to work around them. A workbench, secured tool locker, and parts storage should also be provided in this area, requiring approximately 300 square feet for the service area plus storage and workbench. A washing area for golf cars could be located in a screened area outside the building or inside the building in an area separated from other car traffic. In either case, space for a small high-pressure washer with proper drainage must be provided.

A staging area provides space where a number of cars can be prepared to handle a large volume of play more efficiently. Generally, this paved area should be able to accommodate cars ready for going onto or coming off the course for 30 minutes at any one time. For high-volume

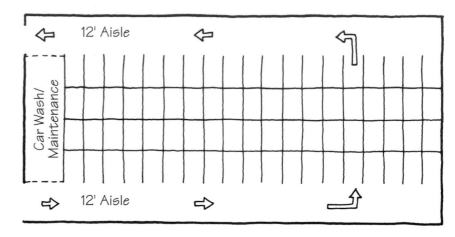

A golf car parking area allowing for 76 cars and maintenance, with 55 to 60 square feet per car.
Source: W. Wade Setliff, Architectural Design Group, Inc.

play, golf car paths should be widened to provide sufficient room for an entire course full of cars, facilitating the "shotgun start." The designer needs to consider the staging area's location, type of pavement, and landscaping to minimize objectionable views from dining and social rooms in the clubhouse.

As for any facility housing motorized vehicles, safety should be a fundamental criterion. Care must be taken to avoid conflicts between entering and exiting cars, and between pedestrians and cars. Blind intersections and corners should be avoided.

In addition to traffic safety, a primary concern in designing a golf car storage facility, regardless of whether it houses gas or electric vehicles, is the provision of positive ventilation to eliminate a concentration of

fumes. A broader issue is the location of the storage facility. Storing a full complement of golf cars for an 18-hole course quickly adds up to a requirement of 5,000 or more square feet, making the storage facility one of the largest elements in the clubhouse. The storage area could be located in a separate, one-story building or in the basement of the main clubhouse. Each plan has advantages and disadvantages.

If the site for the clubhouse is ample and the immediate area is not heavily constrained by other elements, a one-story detached building has several advantages:

- Construction costs might be lower as a result of less stringent structural and fire codes. In some localities, the storage of golf cars below habitable areas is not permitted.

- The roof of a one-story building can be structured to allow a clear span for storing and maneuvering cars, allowing greater flexibility in the storage layout.
- In general, future expansion would be possible without disrupting the club's operations.

While a detached storage facility allows for its remote location from the clubhouse, the requirement to shuttle cars back and forth like trains can seriously compromise the efficiency of the golf operation. Therefore, its location should be convenient to the clubhouse—dictating architecture that relates to the clubhouse. Although the interior can be spartan and minimally appointed, the budget must include enough funds so the exterior architectural treatment is consistent with that of the clubhouse. If the storage area is a semidetached or attached wing of the clubhouse with a common wall between the storage area and the clubhouse, that wall must be a rated fire wall.

Using the lower level or basement of the clubhouse to store golf cars also has advantages:

- Operational cost-efficiency is greater because the golf cars are closer to the pro shop and its personnel. The pro shop could be on the same level as the storage area. If the pro shop is on a higher level, a staging area should be provided on a middle level between the pro shop and the storage area, as it is much easier to move a golf car vertically on short ramps than for golfers, wearing spikes, to negotiate stairs (which are also more expensive in terms of materials and maintenance costs).
- Upper levels of the clubhouse can be elevated above the golf car storage area, taking advantage of enhanced views and longer vistas from dining rooms and other social areas.
- The exterior building elevation becomes more prominent, providing better visibility of the clubhouse from the course.
- Less land for buildings is required.

- Views from the clubhouse are not obstructed by the storage facility.

The disadvantage of locating the storage area on the lower level is that the storage arrangement for cars must be worked around the structural columns that support the main clubhouse above. The efficient layout of the main clubhouse spaces above should be given priority and the storage area worked to conform with the structural system.

Decisions about the appropriate location for golf car storage depend on the overall clubhouse program, topography, land use, phasing, and cost, among other considerations.

Golf Carts and Caddies
The use of golf carts must be accommodated at clubs where the use of golf cars is not mandatory. Generally, golf carts can be stored in the bag storage area. Some facilities store bags on the cart, while others provide separate racks for bags. Shelves at least 24 inches deep are required to store golf carts on shelves. For planning, four square feet per cart (including aisle space) should be allowed. The four-bag motorized, caddie-tended golf cart that has become popular in Japan is sometimes guided on an electronic track. These

carts require a storage area of approximately 15 square feet per cart.

The traditional caddie is still in evidence in older clubs and is appearing in some newer, upscale clubs. If caddies are part of the club's operations, space should be provided for a sheltered waiting area, toilet facilities, showers, and changing areas. The caddie waiting area should be close to the bag and golf car storage areas.

Bag Storage
A bag storage area is usually closely associated with or located between the pro shop and the car staging area. It is a temperature- and humidity-controlled area with a fixed or movable bag rack system. It should also include an area for cleaning and repairing bags and clubs, with a rack to hold 12 to 16 bags, a deep sink, and counter space for storing supplies. When towel or ice service is offered, the related equipment and storage spaces are provided in the bag storage facility, and a washer and dryer are often conveniently located in this area to wash towels from golf cars.

For a daily-fee operation, golfers generally carry their clubs in the trunk of their car, requiring a bag drop-off area, preferably near the ar-

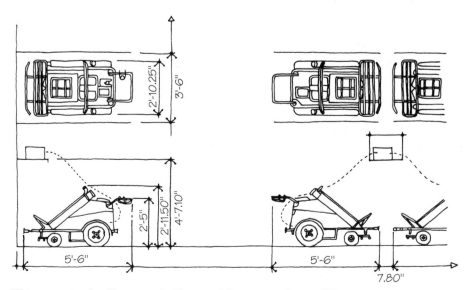

This motorized golf cart tended by a caddie carries four golf bags.
Source: Richard J. Diedrich.

rival and/or parking area in direct view of the starting or staging area. The need for storing bags at a daily-fee operation is much less than for a private club, where members generally store their equipment at the clubhouse. Storage facilities must be sized according to the number of members and their family members, and guests. At a resort, guests generally store their equipment at the clubhouse, and storage facilities must be sized to accommodate the number of guests as well as rental equipment. Requirements for rental equipment at resorts and at daily-fee courses can be significant. A major resort like the Grand Cypress in Orlando with three full-length courses, for example, might maintain an inventory of 100 sets of clubs for rentals.

If a fixed-rack system is used, bags can be stored vertically on two levels of metal or wood racks flanking the access aisle. An allowance of two square feet per bag is the general rule for this type of storage system.

If a movable-rack system is used, an allowance of one to $1\frac{1}{2}$ square feet per bag is the rule. While movable racks allow a substantial savings in space, the expense for the rack equipment is higher than for fixed racks. The designer must compare the cost of constructing added building space with the cost of the mobile racks to determine whether the savings in space will offset the cost of the equipment. Movable racks are time-consuming and sometimes cumbersome for the bag attendant. A compromise is to use fixed racks initially and replace them with mobile racks as membership and demand increase.

The social area at Grand Cypress Golf Clubhouse in Orlando, Florida.

Social Areas

Although a strong trend toward smaller clubhouses is apparent in the 1990s, private clubs sometimes provide a variety of social areas, a room for billiards, a library, a sitting room, a ballroom, or a boardroom among the possibilities.

A consideration for a multipurpose, family-oriented club is the provision of social spaces specifically for junior members or children of members. Reducing the conflicts between children's and adults' activities has its advantages, but appropriate supervision of the children must be provided. While the concept of separate space might be popular with parents, older children often do not use such spaces in private clubs, because the club is not considered the "in" place if friends who are not members are excluded.

Food and Beverage Facilities

Even the smallest golf clubhouse offers some form of food and beverage service, and the sale of food and beverages is one of the main income-generating profit centers of a golf course, regardless of the type of operation. The need for refreshment is

not only basic, particularly on a hot, sunny day, it is also very much a part of the social aspects of golfing. Food and beverage facilities range from a minimal vending area and snack bar for a municipal daily-fee operation to a full complement of formal and casual dining rooms, banquet halls, bar/lounges, and lunch counters at a multipurpose community or resort clubhouse. Decisions about the space to set aside for a food service program should consider re-

The lounge at #19 at Isleworth.

The formal dining room at Hammock Dunes Golf Clubhouse in Palm Coast, Florida.

The formal dining room at Country Club of the South in Atlanta, Georgia.

quirements for capacity, flexibility, and the type of dining (formal or casual).

Generally, approximately 17 or 18 square feet per seat should be allowed for a casual dining area, except for a small room (50-seat capacity), where the requirement tends toward 20 square feet per seat. Outdoor patios or decks can be used to expand the capacity of the dining area, but they should be offset or lowered so that the view from the interior dining room is not obstructed.

For a private club, food and beverage services can be a lucrative profit center, and the clubhouse therefore usually includes various types of dining facilities in response to market demand and members' needs. At the very least, it provides a casual dining facility, such as the "mixed grill." Some operations provide both casual and formal dining accommodations, in a number of combinations: two separate dining facilities operating simultaneously, two separate dining facilities operating at different times (perhaps a casual grill serving breakfast and lunch and a formal dining room serving dinner only), or one dining facility serving both formal and informal meals. The latter might offer informal dining during the day, then change table settings, menus, and service for more formal, evening dining. While the latter option sacrifices flexibility, it is

more economical. Generally, a formal dining room allows 22 to 24 square feet per diner.

Although today the use of a separate formal dining room does not usually warrant its cost, some operators of private clubs with a multipurpose clubhouse might determine that a formal dining room is a desirable amenity. If a club is to provide space for special functions, such as wedding receptions, dinner dances, or banquets, a separate facility for large parties should be provided away from the casual dining area so it does not interfere with golfers. Such rooms can be sized to accommodate any number of seats, but they must include space for a dance floor, band or entertainment, and storage of tables and chairs. Banquet seating usually involves larger tables and closer seating than other dining facilities, requiring an area of approximately 1,700 square feet for 140 seats. Large banquet or function rooms can be subdivided for smaller groups with operable walls and alternate furnishings, but the designer should keep in mind that such flexibility comes at the expense of adequate acoustics. And the "conference meeting room" look associated with operable walls is often contrary to the desired atmosphere of the clubhouse's interior design.

Kitchen

The heart of the food service operation is the kitchen, and the kitchen in each clubhouse is distinctive. Its goal, however, is always the same: to provide the highest-quality dining experience for the least effort and expense. The best design provides a smooth traffic flow within the kitchen, from the kitchen to the dining areas, and between the kitchen and support areas. The flow between kitchen and dining rooms is particularly important. Sight lines and transmission of noise from the kitchen to the dining areas and cross traffic between service personnel should be minimized. Effective planning minimizes the duplication of facilities and staff so that the food service operation can be cost-effective.

The layout of the food service components within the clubhouse is affected by some basic guidelines:

- The kitchen must be served by delivery of food and removal of trash, but because the clubhouse has numerous outdoor elements, an appropriate location for a service yard is usually difficult. The service area must be well-screened from view.
- Service traffic (delivery trucks, garbage trucks, and so on) to the kitchen should not cross the traffic flow from golfers.
- Delivery and maintenance personnel to and from the kitchen should

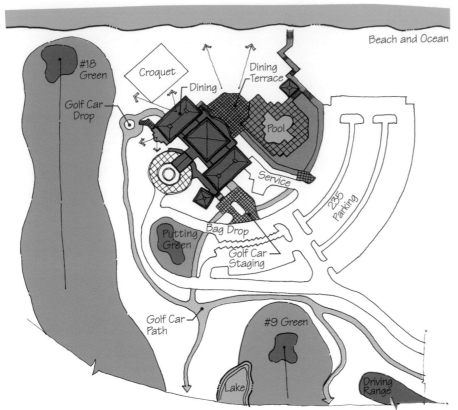

The dining areas at Hammock Dunes Golf Clubhouse are oriented to take advantage of views of the golf course.
Source: Richard J. Diedrich.

experience in clubhouses (rather than hotels) is extremely important. The following general space requirements can be used for conceptual planning and programming.

Type of Kitchen	Space Required (square feet)
Snack Bar	400
Grill Kitchen	1,000–1,400
A la Carte Kitchen	1,400–1,800
A la Carte Kitchen with Limited Banquet Service	1,600–1,800
A la Carte Kitchen with Full Banquet Service	2,000+

It is advisable to have a conceptual equipment layout prepared by the kitchen consultant as early as possible to test the space's configuration.

Service and the Back of the House

In addition to the kitchen, the following service areas are necessary:

- A receiving dock under the roof;
- Bulk storage areas, including space for receiving and checking deliveries, dry goods, a walk-in cooler and freezer, chilled beverages and liquor, linens, china, and serviceware, and chairs and tables;
- General storage, usually 2 to 4 percent of the club's gross area;
- Banquet preparation, service, and storage areas, with an area approximately 20 percent of the floor space of the banquet areas for storing tables and chairs adjacent to the banquet room;
- A soda system;

not cross patrons entering the dining facilities.

- Parking areas and service areas should not infringe on views of the course from the clubhouse. They are usually located on the opposite side of the clubhouse from the finishing holes.
- The dining areas should offer a view of the golf course, one of the clubhouse's greatest assets. The view should be unobstructed by mullions or spandrels in the windows so that views of the #18 green can flood into the clubhouse.

The kitchen's size is based more on the type of menu than on the number of seats served, although capacity can be a factor. Input from a food and beverage consultant with

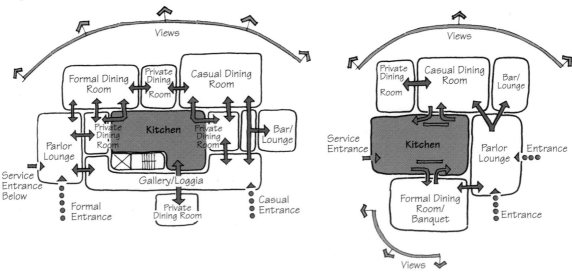

Left: Central kitchen. Right: Corner kitchen.
Source: Richard J. Diedrich.

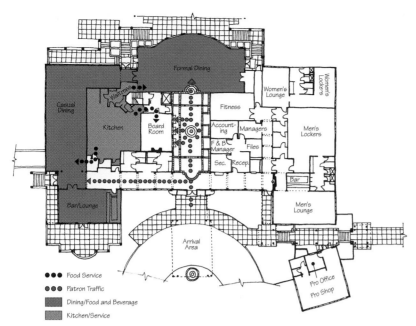

Food service traffic at Hammock Dunes Golf Clubhouse does not conflict with patrons.
Source: Richard J. Diedrich.

- Sanitary facilities, lockers, and a lounge for employees;
- Storage for janitorial equipment and supplies;
- An in-house laundry if an outside laundry service is not used;
- Mechanical and electrical rooms, generally 6 to 8 percent of the club's gross area;
- Trash/garbage area (sometimes refrigerated).

Phasing Clubhouse Construction

The initial financial burden of a clubhouse for a private golf facility could be reduced by phasing construction of the clubhouse, building the essential support and revenue-generating spaces first and secondary support and revenue-generating spaces when membership and financial support are sufficient. For example, the first phase could include the locker rooms, showers, sanitary facilities, pro shop, bag and golf car storage, and limited food and beverage services. The second phase could include the kitchen, grill, dining room, lounge, and administrative offices.

Interior Furnishings and Finishes

Design of the clubhouse's interior is a balance between function, economy, and aesthetics. Regardless of the finish, one fact is paramount: golfers wear spiked shoes. Not only do spiked shoes present maintenance problems and wear and tear on flooring surfaces; they also present a problem of safety and comfort for the wearer, which can be affected by the type of flooring. Walking across hard, polished surfaces in spiked shoes is both a slippery hazard and a noisy, uncomfortable, bone-jarring experience for the wearer.

In general:

- Use spike-proof carpets or rubber matting in areas where spiked shoes are inevitable or even probable: the locker rooms, pro shop, grill, and hallways connecting golf activity areas.
- Avoid polished, hard surfaces like marble, granite, or tile in areas where people will wear spiked shoes.

In large clubhouses, golf spikes are usually restricted to golf-related areas. In small clubs, spike-proof flooring is recommended throughout the building. Certain carpeting is suitable for golf clubhouses:

- Wool or wool and nylon blend makes the most versatile, wearable—and costly—carpet suited for use in a golf clubhouse. Usually available in limitless patterns in true, rich colors, such carpets can be custom-designed and are especially suited for tartan plaid patterns.
- Tufted graphic designs available in midpriced carpet are available in stock patterns, including plaids (although all are on a bias). They are especially suited for a small

Guidelines for Spike-Proof Carpeting

Avoid solid color carpets (except for borders). Light carpet shows soil and wear, and dark colors tend to highlight tracked-in grass. For overall serviceability, a midrange, patterned color is recommended. Borders are helpful for their aesthetic value, to define spaces, and to make variances along possibly crooked walls less noticeable.

The color of carpeting changes with available lighting, and carpeting should therefore be selected in the type of light where it will be used (fluorescent, incandescent, or natural). Some manufacturers provide an actual sample of the carpet to test its colors and density.

Spike-proof carpet should always be a cut pile, for loops can trip a golfer in golf shoes.

Carpet should be glued directly to the floor. Pads lead to early wear in heavily trafficked areas and an undesirable rippling of the carpet. Some carpet warranties are not valid if a pad is used.

Hemp or synthetic carpet backings provide more "play" to assist in matching carpet installations. They can increase the mismatch in a large installation, however.

All clubhouse textiles should be Class B fire-rated. Most jurisdictions require certification of fire-rating, which the mill should provide.

Fifty-two-, 60-, and 72-ounce carpeting is typical for spike-proof installations, although commercial office (30-ounce) carpeting can be used. The weight refers to the density of the pile and amount of twist per inch. If a lighter-weight, non-spike-proof carpet must meet a spike-proof carpet at a seam, the installer should be instructed to coat the floor so that the two heights are even.

Source: Jane Baxter/Country Club Designs, Knickers, Inc.

Wool carpet at Hawks Nest Golf Club.

Tufted graphic carpet at TPC Avenel.

area, as custom carpet must frequently be ordered in lots of 100 to 200 yards.
- Printed carpets offer the most style for the dollar. The pattern is screened onto a solid background, one color at a time from light to dark. A wide range of patterns is available.

Golfers should not be required to negotiate stairs in spiked shoes, and alternative means of negotiating vertical distances, such as carpeted or matted ramps, should be provided for safety and easier maintenance. If no other alternative is available, stair treads should be covered with spike-proof carpeting or nonslip matting.

Relationship of the Clubhouse With Other Amenities

When a clubhouse also serves other recreational and social uses—from tennis courts and swimming pools to fitness or exercise rooms, an aerobics room, racquetball and handball courts, basketball or multipurpose courts, lawn croquet, and shuffleboard—the relationship of these facilities among themselves and with the clubhouse must be considered. The impacts of vehicular, pedestrian, and service traffic and the effects of visibility of and noise from the different activities that could conflict with the clubhouse's other functions must be evaluated.

A swimming pool and bathhouse are often located close to the clubhouse, with shared parking facilities, but separated from golf facilities to avoid conflicts, especially noise. It is generally not advisable to provide

shared locker rooms for golfers and swimmers, because their needs are different. For example, pool locker rooms must provide flooring that can safely accommodate wet feet, while golf locker rooms must provide flooring that can accommodate spiked shoes.

Like the swimming pool, the tennis courts and facilities are often separated from golf facilities to avoid conflicts. Large operations might include a separate pro shop, locker room, and vending area, as golfers seldom play tennis and vice versa.

A recent trend to accommodate the growing market of women golfers and the demand for more family-oriented facilities includes services and amenities, such as:

- Supervised child-care facilities, which might range from a playroom and playground for younger children to a full-scale day camp for both older and younger children in a large community or resort operation;
- Family game rooms;
- Family-oriented recreation like a miniature golf course, which can be highly profitable in itself.

Other Golf Buildings

Maintenance Compound

The maintenance facilities for a golf course serve several functions:

- Storage area for maintenance equipment;
- Service area for maintenance equipment;
- Receiving and storage of materials, including pesticides, fertilizers, top-

Maintenance compound at Horseshoe Bay Resort and Conference Club.

126

soil, sand, and reserve landscape materials;

- Office/administrative center for the golf superintendent;
- Changing rooms and sanitary facilities for the grounds crew;
- Unusual requests, such as occasional storage of a resident's oversize vehicle.

Maintenance buildings can range from 5,000 to 12,000 square feet, depending on the size of the course and maintenance required. Typically, an 18-hole golf course requires a building of 10,000 to 12,000 square feet. The golf course architect is usually the best judge of determining the proper size in consultation with the golf course superintendent.

As an area where potentially hazardous chemicals and petroleum products are stored and handled, the maintenance area must be designed to meet all federal, state, and local regulations. Stringent regulations often must be followed to protect the public safety and to prevent contamination of soil and water. Handling stormwater runoff in the maintenance compound must also be carefully considered, because the chemicals that are stored and handled there could contaminate soil and water.

The maintenance compound should be close to the golf course but visually screened from it and surrounding development. It should be located adjacent to a perimeter road for service access and to avoid conflicts between golf activities and service traffic. Because they are used to store chemicals, maintenance facilities should be located where flooding is unlikely and sited downwind and downhill from ponds, play areas, and housing.

Sanitary septic leaching fields are inappropriate for disposing of rinsate, which could contain any number of the chemicals associated with maintenance operations. Thus, maintenance facilities must be located where they can be served by a sanitary sewer or other appropriate system.

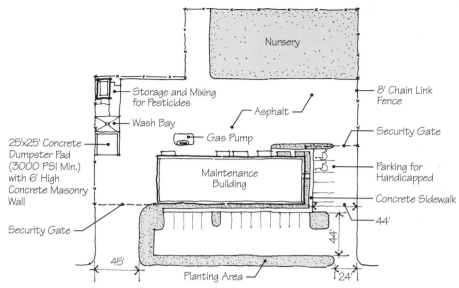

Site plan for a typical maintenance compound.
Source: Nicklaus Design.

LEGEND

- Floor Drain
- Ceiling Mount Ion Type Detector
- Eyewash Unit
- Safety Shower
- Industrial Type First Aid Kit
- [F] Wall Mount 10# ABC Fire Extinguisher
- "Danger: Pesticide Storage" Sign

NOTE: All doors metal fire rated with fire rated jambs and keyed locks.
All electrical (not shown) explosion-proof type and all outlets weather protected.

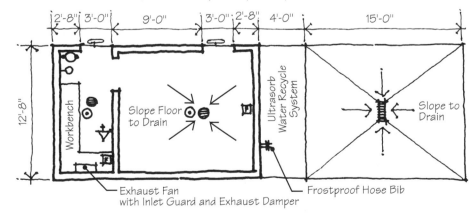

Floor plan for a typical pesticide storage building and washdown area.
Source: Nicklaus Design.

Halfway house at Horseshoe Bay Resort and Conference Club.

GUY L. RANDO & ASSOCIATES INC.

Golf Shelters

Shelters are often provided for golfers' protection during inclement weather—particularly thunder and lightning—and for comfort at key locations along the course when distance to the clubhouse is too great.

Irrigation Pump House

Housing for the irrigation pumping equipment is strategically located on the course. Because it is often visible

to golfers, it should be compatible with other architectural elements or visually screened with landscaping or other devices.

Construction of the Golf Course

The Construction Process

To understand the costs of constructing a golf course, it is necessary to have some understanding of the construction process itself. This complex topic requires a publication of its own, and the following brief overview provides only a general outline of the knowledge necessary to make informed decisions as part of the design team.

Construction of the golf course in a golf-oriented real estate development should be coordinated with construction of the real estate. Considerable costs can be saved when operations like clearing and rough grading are done simultaneously. While construction of golf courses is a specialized field of work, some construction operations for a golf course, such as clearing and grading, can be done by the same contractor or sub-

contractor handling the construction of the real estate. Coordination is critical to minimize conflicts between construction of the golf course and the real estate. For example, access to a section of the real estate development might require moving materials and equipment through the area for the golf course. Or the area for the golf course might no longer be accessible once construction of the real estate has reached a certain point. These logistical issues must be resolved jointly. Coordinated construction allows efficient resolution of any conflicts that arise in the field.

The construction process typically begins with the appointment of the contractor after bids are accepted and one is selected. The entire contract might be awarded to a single contractor, or portions of the contract might be awarded to several contractors. For a golf-oriented real estate development, a contractor with specific experience and expertise in construction of golf courses must be sought.

The contractor first enters into a simple agreement that describes the work involved, the time schedule to complete the work, the amount of the contract and the payment schedule, and other responsibilities and

Plan for a golf shelter.
Source: Richard J. Diedrich.

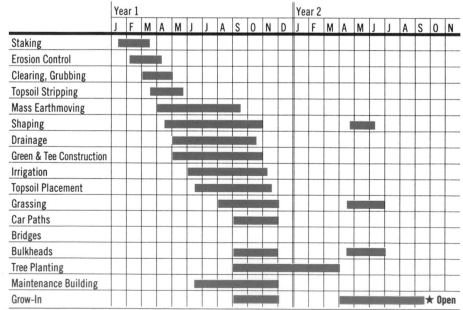

Proposed Construction Schedule

	Year 1												Year 2											
	J	F	M	A	M	J	J	A	S	O	N	D	J	F	M	A	M	J	J	A	S	O	N
Staking		▬																					
Erosion Control			▬																				
Clearing, Grubbing				▬	▬																		
Topsoil Stripping					▬																		
Mass Earthmoving						▬	▬	▬	▬	▬													
Shaping						▬	▬	▬	▬	▬							▬						
Drainage						▬	▬	▬	▬														
Green & Tee Construction							▬	▬	▬	▬													
Irrigation							▬	▬	▬	▬													
Topsoil Placement								▬	▬	▬													
Grassing									▬	▬								▬					
Car Paths									▬														
Bridges																							
Bulkheads									▬	▬								▬					
Tree Planting									▬	▬	▬												
Maintenance Building								▬	▬	▬													
Grow-In													▬	▬	▬	▬	▬	▬	▬	▬			★ Open

Source: Desmond Muirhead, Inc.

Elevation for a golf shelter.
Source: Richard J. Diedrich.

provisions. The contractor's agreement refers to the general and special conditions for the work expressed in the design plans, detailed drawings, technical specifications, and other construction documents.

Once the contractor or contractors are appointed, the construction time schedule generated during design must be reviewed and finalized. This schedule outlines the step-by-step progression of each construction activity.

Construction schedules typically take the form of a flow chart based on the *critical path method* (CPM), which makes visual interpretation easy. This method of scheduling is particularly useful for construction of golf courses, as most regions must consider the seasonal conditions that likely make certain times of the year more conducive for construction or planting. The CPM is also helpful for understanding such factors as procuring materials, permit and inspection schedules, and the like.

The golf course architect's involvement in the project continues throughout all phases of construction, until every item has been satisfactorily completed. This period could range from six months to two years or more. The role of the golf course architect (or a representative) includes periodically monitoring all construction activities to verify their conformance with plans and specifications and making the adjustments that are an inevitable part of any construction project. In some instances, the developer or owner retains a construction inspector or "clerk of the works" as its representative to inform the golf course architect if any construction is not to specifications. Unlike the golf course architect, the clerk of the works has no supervisory capacity over the contractor. Sometimes the architect has a full-time representative on the job.

Construction proceeds according to the following outline, with some tasks occurring simultaneously:

- Surveying, staking, and flagging†
- Erosion control and environmental protection†

- Utilities (electricity, water, and sewer lines)*†
- Clearing, grubbing, and disposal*†
- Removing and storing topsoil*†
- Earthmoving*†
- Surface and subsurface storm drainage†
- Constructing ponds, lakes, and other water impoundments*†
- Rough shaping†
- Constructing greens
- Constructing tees
- Constructing bunkers
- Respreading topsoil
- Irrigation system
- Final shaping
- Preparing the seedbed and sowing grass seed
- Constructing bridges, bulkheads, abutments, and other features
- Golf car paths
- Landscaping*†

Procedure can be done by other than a golf course contractor.
†*Procedure should be done in coordination with real estate construction in golf-oriented real estate projects.*

Surveying, Staking, and Flagging

This first stage of construction involves laying out the golf course architect's plan onto the site through controlled surveying and marking or staking of the course's boundaries or property lines and the centerline of each golf hole at the tee, turning point, and green. It *must* be done by licensed surveyors because accuracy in relation to the housing lots is essential. The stakes must be readily visible and last throughout construction. Long sections of pipes made of polyvinyl chloride should be used for stakes; once the stakes are in place, they should not be moved until the course is completed, because information on the drawings is keyed to these reference points. Surveyor's flagging, a plastic ribbon available in several bright and easily visible colors, is used to indicate sites to be cleared or adjustments and changes in the field. To ensure conformity and consistency in surveying and flagging information, all persons involved in the design, layout, and construction of the course should be consulted

about the colors used and their respective identities and purpose.

Typically, the golf course architect or a representative is intimately involved in this phase of construction, because this critical point is where drawing is transformed to site. At this stage, adjustments can be indicated to allow the incorporation of certain physical features that were not previously indicated on the maps, perhaps an area of vegetation or an outcrop of rocks.

Erosion Control and Environmental Protection

Most jurisdictions have regulations to control soil erosion and siltation on a construction site. The project's civil engineers usually prepare such plans; they include control devices like sediment basins, silt fences, and other structures that conform with guidelines and regulations. The contractor puts these measures in place before beginning clearing and grading. They are especially important in mountainous locations.

Utilities

The installation of utilities must be coordinated between construction of the golf course and the real estate, particularly if below-grade utility lines are anticipated in the golf corridor.

Clearing and Grubbing

Clearing and grubbing varies according to the region and a site's physical attributes. In a desert, for example, clearing could involve transplanting established plants more than actual clearing. In areas with vegetation, clearing a path along the centerlines of the golf holes might be required; if so, it is accomplished in stages. Careful monitoring of clearing operations is a necessity, particularly if the site is heavily wooded, as the course's anticipated "look" can be irreparably damaged during clearing operations. With the introduction of heavy equipment on the site, contractors must be informed of the routes and corridors where they can work to avoid damaging completed areas. They should be made responsible for repairing damage to important trees,

129

Clearing at Mt. Kinabalu Golf Course in Malaysia.

which should be done immediately with surgery and tree paint.

Clearing is done in four stages to allow for adjustments to plans by the golf course architect:

1. *Clearing Centerlines and Flagging*

This phase involves clearing the centerline for all holes and the driving range, beginning at the tee and continuing to the green. Twenty-five feet on each side of the centerline should be cleared. Flagging the limits of the clearing and minor adjustments are made under the golf course architect's guidance. Any trees or other natural features deemed necessary for aesthetic or strategic value should be flagged and saved until the golf course architect can assess their worth. Care must be taken to prevent damage by equipment to the trunks, branches, and root structure of trees to be saved. (These procedures typically are spelled out in performance specifications accompanying the construction documents.) After

the centerlines are cleared, the golf course architect or a representative walks the site to determine whether additional initial clearing is necessary. All fallen trees and cleared vegetation should be stacked out of sight to maintain a clear view along the centerline to each of the stakes that mark tees, turning points, and greens.

2. *Clearing and Grubbing*

With the limits of clearing flagged, the clearing contractor can proceed with full-fledged clearing, grubbing, and disposal operations. Grubbing involves removing roots and other vegetation from the soil in the area of the clearing operation. (See "Disposal" later in this section.) Clearing for lakes and other features is also carried out in this phase. At this point, the playing characteristics of the holes and the significance of trees that have been flagged for preservation should become apparent. Typically, other work occurs simultaneously with this stage, perhaps removing topsoil and rough earthwork.

3. *Selective Clearing*

This phase includes additional expansion of the width and length of the holes by selective clearing. At this point, trees or vegetation that was tagged for saving might be eliminated or retained, based on the golf course architect's determinations.

4. *Selective Pruning and Clearing Roughs*

This final phase involves the selective clearing and pruning of the vegetation in the roughs, often with close monitoring by the golf course architect. It is a delicate clearing operation, usually performed with small equipment or hand tools. Particular attention is given to not damaging root systems or tree trunks.

Protecting Existing Vegetation or Trees

Specifications should call for the protection of all existing vegetation on the site, except that specifically marked for removal. No plants should be removed before the golf course architect's inspection and spe-

130

Trees Competing with Turf for Attention

The presence of a tree on a golf course means different things to different people. To some, trees can help create the most beautiful setting that one has seen all year. To others, a tree is the sole obstacle standing between a career-best round and a major disappointment.

President Dwight D. Eisenhower used to play golf at Minocqua Country Club in northern Wisconsin. According to local legend, there once was a tree in the center of the fairway on the first hole, a beautiful par-4. He constantly complained about the strategic position of the tree and how unfair it was. Apparently, Ike hit it most every time he played the hole.

One night under the cloak of darkness, an unknown someone cut the tree down and left it lying in the middle of the fairway. Of course, when asked, the President said he knew nothing about how it happened.

And even if that story is a myth, then the one about Ike's battles with the fabled "Eisenhower Tree" certainly is not.

Without question, trees play varying roles on golf courses. Golf course superintendents and golfers interact with trees daily. Whether it is a 100-year-old mature oak tree or a newly planted three-inch-diameter maple sapling, trees need air and water to survive.

Tree Roles

The late David Gill was a golf course architect who loved trees and respected their need for space and ability to create a beautiful environment. Architects use trees to define holes and to protect homes, tees, and greens. They also create shade and help to beautify the grounds.

Trees are also used to protect the dogleg on longer holes. Clearly, strategy is decided each time golfers play a wooded course, because trees and tree clusters are intentionally located.

Silent Enemies

At first glance, our view of the golf course is one of a special place where nature and man exist in harmony after man has built the course. The most visible components of the views we enjoy are any changes in elevation, plus the grass and trees.

As much as we would like to think that grass and trees are always compatible, they are not. The "greenspace" that we know and love is really a battleground. The mature trees are fighting the bent grass every day.

"Turf and trees are not friends, because they both compete for crucial water, nutrients, and space," says Chuck Stewart, president of Urban Forest Management in suburban Wheeling.

The critical tree roots are located directly below the grass roots, which is the problem. Unfortunately for the trees, grass is first in line for water and nutrients.

During dry periods, grass picks up water before it makes it to the lower tree roots. Only after the first few inches of topsoil are fully saturated will the area below the grass roots receive any water.

As a drought continues, the lack of water and nutrients makes the tree become less resistant to disease and insects. And problems with trees might not show up for months or even years. Trees that are stressed bear less fruit, change color early in the fall, and have fewer buds the following spring.

In Terms of Trees

We all know what a "trunk" is, but what about "crown"? I used to think that the crown was similar to zenith, apex, pinnacle, peak—the "top."

Wrong. The crown is the top of the tree including everything but the trunk. Twigs, branches, and limbs are part of the crown.

The roots are obvious, but the "critical root zone" is that area immediately beneath the soil where the tree absorbs moisture and obtains air. The critical root zone is generally considered to extend 12 to 18 inches below the surface.

Healthy grass roots typically do not extend beyond 12 inches. Nearer trees, the root structures generally do not extend eight to 10 inches and in heavily shaded areas, the roots can be as shallow as two inches.

The "drip line" is identified by establishing a line from the outermost twigs straight down to the ground. The drip line is important because if root damage occurs inside the drip line, a tree has a good chance of dying.

Once construction vehicles and fill encroach upon the drip line, the tree's odds for survival decrease dramatically. The roots of most trees usually extend outward twice as far as the height of the tree. Thus, the roots critical for survival are within the drip line.

Tree Cuts

During design, the architect needs to look at existing trees on the property to see whether he wants to keep them in place, move them to a new location, or clear them.

An attempt is made to save many trees, but some must be cleared to make room for fairways, buildings, and other features.

Chuck Stewart's specialty is helping clients decide what trees to save and how to save them. He also provides tree maintenance programs.

When advising clients who are building new courses, Stewart uses his PCM Program. PCM stands for planning, construction, and maintenance, the three categories that need attention to keep the trees alive.

"Trees have trouble adjusting to abrupt changes," he said. "They do, however, adjust well to changes occurring over time.

"You need a well-qualified team to advise the clients. During the planning phase, we let clients know how to protect the trees during construction."

Part of the planning program calls for recommending fences around both individual trees and tree clusters. He also feels that it is important that the contractors understand the rules.

Important trees have to be identified, then fences are installed to prevent vehicular traffic within the drip line. Monitoring the site by a tree expert is critical during construction, as fences need to be maintained during grading of the course.

If a road needs to be built along with curbs and gutters, tree roots could be severed in the process. Stewart plans strategic "cuts" in the roots so the tree survives the ordeal. If the developer allows heavy machine operators to remove any roots, the tree could be killed because the roots could be ripped up all the way to the base of the tree.

"Our company policy gives extreme concern to existing vegetation," says Brent Wadsworth, president of Wadsworth Construction Company in Plainfield, one of the most respected golf course construction companies in the world. He instills his philosophy in his site superintendents and operators.

"Nothing is harmed unless it has been formally approved by the developer, owner, or designer," he says.

Sometimes that philosophy causes problems and/or is extremely costly.

Wadsworth recalls a Florida golf course project where his crews were working in a wetland area. They were not permitted to disturb or damage the wetlands in any way, but they needed to get fill into an area surrounded by wetlands to build the back tee for a hole. They used a helicopter to deliver dirt to the site.

Grading

Grading includes both the act of cutting into the earth and filling in low areas or building up high areas. "Fill" is an all-encompassing term used to describe the act of placing dirt over ground. Fill is used to create hills, mounds, berms, sand traps, and changes in grade.

Stewart claims "cutting"—removing original soil—injures more trees on a construction site than any other activity. Vehicle operators cut to create different topography, including slopes, bunkers, and mounds. When an operator cuts within the drip line of a tree, he could injure the roots within the critical root zone.

Wadsworth's operators are very meticulous about avoiding injuries to trees. He says that if the architect and developer do not address the issue, his workers take the initiative to stake and fence trees on their own.

There is another side to the "save the trees" argument on new course sites, however.

"Sometimes architects and owners are too timid," Wadsworth says, pointing out there are times when clearing a tree is appropriate.

"The beauty of the surrounding vegetation might be shielded from view," he says, adding there is a happy medium.

Compaction

Heavy construction vehicles sometimes drive through the drip line of trees, compacting the soil within the critical root zone. This compaction can physically damage the roots.

After the construction phase is over, compaction can also be caused by golf cars and the body weight of golfers. Soil compaction is particularly damaging because the denser soil does not allow air and water to pass through easily. This prevention of absorption increases runoff and makes it difficult to fertilize effectively.

Tree and grass roots do not grow as well in compacted soil for another reason. The space between the soil particles is reduced, preventing the roots from growing. Roots, like branches, regenerate. As old or damaged roots die, new roots take their place.

During the fall golf season, superintendents aggressively aerate fairways and greens. This process reduces compaction and thatch problems.

"Interestingly enough," Stewart says, "aeration is about the only thing superintendents do for grass that helps the trees." The holes make it easy for air, water, and nutrients to get down to the roots.

Normal Maintenance

The "M" part of Stewart's PCM Program is for maintenance.

"Typically, golf course superintendents are turf guys," he says. Most pay attention to trees, but it is a safe bet they are not "tree people." If grass is going to get a lot of attention, maybe the trees should get some, too.

An obvious part of the maintenance program is pruning. Pruning is conducted for three essential reasons: 1) to repair a tree after wind or storm damage, 2) to eliminate dead and diseased limbs on a routine bases, and 3) to increase playability, for example, a branch hanging over a green.

A good maintenance schedule can control overall tree quality on a golf course. Routine pruning really needs to take place only every four to seven years.

Stewart uses a tree-quality rating system based on a scale of one to six. A tree receiving a six is about to die, while a tree rated one is a perfect specimen.

There are two essential components to applying the grading scale.

The first is "vigor." A high vigor assessment indicates that the tree is a healthy tree for that species. Disease, insects, and people can all affect a tree's vigor.

The second is "form." A tree might be healthy, but if it has an unusual or ugly shape, it might not be desirable.

A tree inventory can be important to a tree management program. Country clubs and public courses maintain tree inventories. The trees need to be evaluated so that preventive maintenance can be conducted and disease and insect problems dealt with. Often, maintenance programs are designed following the tree inventory. It makes sense to set up a program once the extent of the tree population is determined.

Critical Trees

The important trees are usually apparent to the golfer. They are the ones that affect club selection and shot strategy from the fairway. More specifically, critical trees are those trees that if lost would dramatically change strategy, alter aesthetics, change the definition, or no longer protect a natural or manmade feature.

It makes sense, then, that critical trees be evaluated as to their vigor and form in case they need maintenance.

Let's look at an example. If an oak tree protects the right side of a green, the approach shot would be significantly easier if the tree were lost. Upon inspection, it is discovered that the tree is unhealthy, but has good form.

Insects have invaded several dead branches, and as insects and disease go hand-in-hand, rotten branches are discovered. The tree receives a rating of three, which means it will survive, but needs some help.

Let's take that same tree and assume it receives a rating of five, its ability to survive questionable.

It survives for 10 more years and dies. One or more trees could have been planted adjacent to the questionable tree 10 years ago, so that when it finally is lost, its younger brethren could carry on with the act of protecting the green.

The superintendent might also want to consider lightning protection for critical trees. Trees are natural lightning rods, as they tower above level ground. Lightning rods have been place in trees all over the country to protect critical trees from loss.

As you can see, the need for an ongoing tree evaluation and maintenance program is essential.

In addition, identification of and care for critical trees is a nonnegotiable requirement for courses today.

Source: Peter Dyke, "Trees Competing with Turf for Attention," *Chicagoland Golf*, Fall 1991, pp. 12–13. Reprinted with permission.

cific direction. All plants that are not to be removed should be protected from injury to roots and tops for at least three feet beyond the drip line. No grading, trenching, pruning, or storage of materials should be allowed in these areas except that approved by the golf course architect or a representative.

Disposal

The options available for disposing of cleared materials vary according to what is permissible under local regulations. While larger trees are generally logged for timber or pulp wood, the clearing contractor must dispose of the other vegetation by one of the following methods:

- *Burning* requires special cautions by the contractor to control the fire

and ensure that no damage occurs to surrounding vegetation or trees that are to be saved. Burning must conform with local regulations or guidelines, and permits are usually necessary. Any residue from the burning is buried according to specifications. Burning or burying vegetation is permitted only in the roughs.

- *Burying* is generally more expensive than burning and can lead to future maintenance problems as a result of uneven settlement and underground production of methane gas from decomposition. If burying is permitted by local regulation, then it should be in accordance with specifications and *never* occur under fairways, playing areas, or building sites.

- *Hauling* materials off the site has become virtually obsolete because of the associated high costs. Costs should be weighed against the benefits of alternative methods.
- *Chipping, mulching, and composting* can be viable, environmentally sensitive means for disposing of brush. Debris is reduced in volume by chipping or shredding, and the chipped or shredded material can be used as a mulch or composted for later use as organic soil or nutrient supplement. Another alternative is the use of debris to create brush piles to provide food and shelter for wildlife (see "Environmental Issues" earlier in this chapter).

Removing and Storing Topsoil

A laboratory specializing in turf development should analyze samples of the topsoil for quality and amendments to provide a suitable medium for turf culture. The quality of the topsoil available on the site is essential for success during the grassing phase of construction. If topsoil on the site is insufficient, topsoil can be brought in from other sources, although this method is very expensive and it too must be analyzed. The removal and storage of topsoil generally follows the following sequence:

- Removing all vegetation in the stripping zone (the area where topsoil is to be stripped or excavated), including carefully shaking off the excess soil clinging to the roots of vegetation that is removed.
- Using scrapers, pans, loaders, and/or bulldozers to excavate the topsoil to the depth indicated by specifications. Ideally, it is done when the topsoil is dry.
- Stockpiling topsoil in established areas, removed from construction activities. This stockpiling area

should be leveled and smoothed, without depressions, to preclude the soil's saturation, particularly if the storage period will include seasonal changes. Dry topsoil is much easier to handle. Consideration must be given to installing drainage and maintaining suitable erosion control devices around the stockpiles. Typically, these areas are placed in several key locations to make redistribution easier and reduce hauling distances.

Earthmoving

Earthwork consists of all the excavation and filling of earth—the cut and fill—to meet the design specifications for changes in the topography of the site to accommodate the golf course. This phase of work represents the largest expenditure of time and labor for the contractor, because great quantities of material are removed, hauled, and placed by the largest machinery and the costliest employees. Typically, the designer has already calculated the volume of cut and fill for the project so that the amount of cut is balanced with the amount of fill. Further, the grading plan is designed to reduce the quantity of materials that need to be moved, minimizing hauling distances. On flat sites, excavations for ponds or lakes are often a major source of fill material.

Fill should be clean and free of organic material. If major rock excavations and fill are required, the excavated rock should be reduced in size and/or mixed with soil to minimize the potential for settlement in fill areas. If the soil is deep enough, grading can be localized for short-haul bulldozer work, and grading can be effected by moving earth on individual fairways.

Elevations and grades must be checked periodically throughout this phase to ensure that adequate volumes of fill are being placed in the correct locations. The surveyor's role is critical in verifying and certifying the volumes of excavated materials moved, providing certifications to the owner and generally to the golf course architect. A plan for moving earth that shows the hauling distance can save hundreds of thousands of dollars, for very few contractors move the correct amount of earth if they are not carefully checked.

Surface and Subsurface Storm Drainage

The storm drainage system is designed to conform with local regulations regarding upstream and downstream watersheds, and nonconformance to plans without written review and approval can result in civil and criminal actions against all parties involved in the project. Work on the storm drainage system generally begins concurrently with rough shaping as major earthwork is completed. It involves locating and installing all components of the system on the surface and below the surface in conformance with plans drawn by the project's civil engineer. Surface drainage work could include grading and shaping drainage swales, stabilizing stream banks, and constructing overflow structures and drainage structures that connect ponds or lakes. Subsurface work might include installing storm drain lines, catch basins, and other structures.

The vertical elevations of storm drain lines are expressed as "invert elevations" (vertical elevation measured at the bottom of the interior of the pipe or drainage structure) and are directly related to the final elevations of playing surfaces. Any change to invert elevations could seriously affect the course's playability and maintenance.

Constructing Water Impoundments And Water Features

Lakes, ponds, and other water impoundments are often integral parts of the stormwater management system and supply of water for irrigation of a golf course. The project's of a concrete, rock, or wooden bulkhead. All treatments must allow for periodic changes in water level.

The course's design might call for the construction of an artificial stream, waterfall, or other water feature that requires recirculation pumps and installation by specialized subcontractors.

Rough Shaping

During this phase, the sculptural aspects of golf course design come into play. The subgrade is shaped to the proposed final contour for the golf course architect's review, and it is not unusual to have the land forms shaped several times to get exactly the right effect. Some golf course architects provide detailed plans, with surveyors assisting to ensure that the drawings are followed precisely. Other golf course architects prefer to work on site with specialized equipment operators ("shapers") who contour the subgrade under the golf course architect's direction. The shaper's ability can be important to the success of the course, as the contour of the subgrade sets the shape of future greens, tees, and bunkers. It is important to remember that when the course is in operation, it will receive 200 to 300 inches of irrigation water on land that might have received only 15 to 40 inches of natural rainfall before. Wet pockets will inevitably result; therefore, the slope of the ground must always exceed 2 percent, and tile drains are likely to be needed for many years.

Constructing Greens

After the golf course architect approves rough shaping of the subgrade for the greens, the contractor can proceed with cutting the drainage trenches in the subgrade, sometimes called "cutting the green cavity." This work is typically done with a trencher or small backhoe, and climatic conditions and conditions of the subgrade soils are critical at this point. If the subgrade soils are wet or heavy rain is anticipated, the work should be delayed until conditions are favorable.

The drains are laid out in a herringbone pattern with a discharge to

Rough shaping at Mt. Kinabalu Golf Course in Malaysia.

civil engineer should already have prepared construction drawings in conformance with regulatory standards for construction of dams, overflow structures, and inlet and outlet structures. Water impoundments should be shaped and graded concurrently with other construction. They are then lined with impervious materials, such as clay soils if locally available, bentonite, or polyethylene, according to design specifications. Treatment of the water's edge is particularly important; depending on the design, edges could range from grass to the waterline to construction

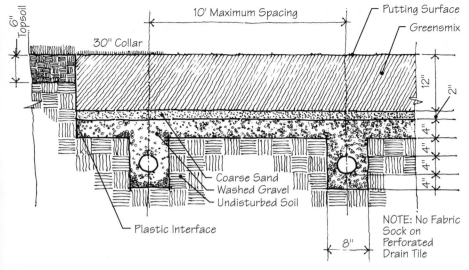

Typical section of green.
Source: Nicklaus Design.

(labels in figure: 6" Topsoil, 30" Collar, 10' Maximum Spacing, Putting Surface, Greensmix, 12", 2", 4", 4", 4", 4", Coarse Sand, Washed Gravel, Undisturbed Soil, Plastic Interface, NOTE: No Fabric Sock on Perforated Drain Tile, 8")

nearby ponds, streams, swales, or catch basins. Perforated drainpipe is placed in the trenches and surrounded by clean gravel, with a four-inch layer of the same gravel placed over the entire subgrade, carefully following the established contours. This gravel must be clean and free of any native soils or clay particles that could block drain pipes. On top of this gravel is spread a two-inch layer of coarse sand, sometimes called the "choker sand," again carefully following the established contours. A 12- to 14-inch layer of *greensmix* or *root zone mix* is added on top of this coarse sand, shaped, compacted, and prepared for seeding. Drainage in areas where soil is very sandy is often unnecessary.

The greensmix or root zone mix is a mixture of sand and peat moss specially formulated according to exact specifications of the golf course architect (typically based on standards developed by USGA). The USGA's Physical Soil Test Laboratory determines the percentage of each component of the mix required to meet its precise standards, and following USGA's recommendations is critical. Testing determines the physical properties of sand samples, such as infiltration and percolation capacity, porosity, bulk density, water retention capacity, and size of the particles. Sometimes several sources must be tested to find a sand

with the appropriate properties for the greensmix. Sand is mixed with the other ingredients off site, and during unloading, trucks must remain off the greens, with their tires outside the cavity, to avoid damage to existing layers and pipes.

Constructing Tees

Because of concentrated use, tees take more abuse per square foot than any other part of the golf course; tees must therefore be constructed to the same exacting specifications as the greens. Well-drained, virtually flat (with a 1 percent slope to the left and a 1 percent slope to the back) surfaces free of any depressions that can hold water are essential for durability and playability. The golf course architect determines the size and location of the tees, and it is common for tees to be constructed like the greens, with the same kind of drainage system, layers of the subgrade, and greensmix for the surface.

Constructing Bunkers

Bunkers are the most common hazard incorporated on a course to create the opportunity for strategic play. Proper construction is critical

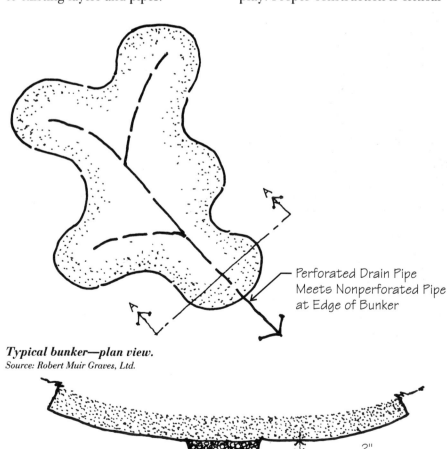

Typical bunker—plan view.
Source: Robert Muir Graves, Ltd.

(labels in figure: Perforated Drain Pipe Meets Nonperforated Pipe at Edge of Bunker)

Typical bunker drain—section A–A.
Source: Robert Muir Graves, Ltd.

(labels in figure: Perforated Drain Pipe, 2", 4", 1")

to avoid costly maintenance problems later. Sand appropriate for use in bunkers should drain well, play well, and be consistent with the course's aesthetic qualities. The golf course architect must approve the sand, considering guidelines for size of particles, purity, shape, composition, and color.

Final Shaping

Final shaping of the subgrade provides the opportunity to ensure that the course is shaped as close to the original specifications as possible. Particular attention is paid to surface drainage and correction of any settlement that has occurred around the edges of greens, pipe lines, inlets, irrigation heads, and valves, and along the edges of the golf car paths.

Installing the Irrigation System

Installing the irrigation system can begin after shaping and major drainage systems have been completed. It is often done as each set of two or three holes is graded. In some cases, irrigation lines are installed after the topsoil has been respread to avoid damage to the irrigation lines from equipment. The designer of the system generally has a major say in when the system should be installed, considering other construction activities. The irrigation system *must* be in place and operational before planting begins. If it is operational, the system can sometimes be used to assist in settling the greensmix or root zone mix during final finishing and preparation of the seedbed for greens and tees.

The following general procedures are used to install the selected irrigation system:

- The irrigation designer stakes out the location of the sprinkler heads along the entire golf hole.
- The irrigation contractor installs a main line (usually to one side of the fairway), usually with a backhoe.
- Lateral irrigation lines are installed with trenchers and connected from the main line to individual sprinkler heads.
- If an electronic valve system is selected to operate irrigation heads, the valves are wired to control

boxes located at each hole. The control boxes are then linked to a central controller in the maintenance building.

- The pump system is installed. An electrical pump system is generally installed early during the construction process to allow time for local power companies to supply power to the pump house.

Respreading Topsoil

After final shaping of the subgrade and construction of features are completed, the golf course architect has approved them, and the irrigation system has been installed, topsoil can be respread. The equipment usually includes front-end loaders, dump trucks, and mid- to small-size bulldozers. Because of the potential damage from equipment, this phase is sometimes specified for completion *before* irrigation is installed. Particular attention must be paid to preserving the final shaping and to a consistent depth.

The topsoil must be spread evenly over all prepared subgrade areas except the surfaces of tees and greens. The generally accepted standards are a minimum of six inches of topsoil over all fairways, tee slopes, green slopes, and mounds, and a minimum of four inches over the roughs. If the topsoil is imported, the golf course architect must specify structure consistent with native soils. If the soil is heavy clay, six to eight inches of sand could be necessary on top.

Preparing the Seedbed

This phase of work involves the preparation of the soil for sowing grass seed. The analysis of soils provides information about any soil amendments that will be required.

Preparation generally proceeds as follows:

- Disk or harrow the soil to a depth of six inches.
- Rake the soil to remove all rocks, sticks, and stones larger than one-half inch in diameter to a depth of four inches. A tractor-driven specialty rake is used for picking up rocks. It places the rocks into

rows, which can then be picked up by a machine that screens out the rocks from the soil.

- Add any necessary soil amendments at this time to the upper few inches of soil.
- Use tractors and various attachments to apply a final finish to the soil's surface by grading and floating to ensure positive surface drainage and to eliminate any depressions that could hold water. Greens, tees, and fairways are floated with a tractor and box attachment.
- Secure the golf course architect's final approval of the finished grading before beginning grassing.

Grassing and Grow-In

Once the final grading is complete, the area must be planted as quickly as possible before rain, wind, traffic, or other conditions damage the seedbed. If the seedbed is damaged, the surface must be carefully reshaped. The type of grass specified will determine the method of planting. Grasses planted during cool seasons are usually planted with a mechanical device pulled by a tractor that drops seeds into the ground, or "hydroseeded." Bermuda grass is planted using live stolons or sprigs. A special machine is attached to a tractor to ensure the sprigs are planted evenly. Another method is "hydrosprigging" with a special hydromulching machine. Zoysia grass is typically installed in plugs or as sod.

In areas especially prone to erosion, such as steep slopes and the area immediately surrounding a bunker, sod should be specified.

Immediately after grassing, a critical period of specialized maintenance occurs to ensure survival and healthy growth of the turf and other landscaping. Responsibility during that phase is usually turned over to the golf superintendent as sections of the course are completed.

Landscaping

The landscape architect or golf course architect might specify additional landscape plants on and around the golf course to define spaces, improve aesthetics, buffer or screen adjacent holes or between the golf course and surrounding elements, stabilize the soil, or enhance or mitigate the quality of the ecologic habitat. This work is typically assigned to a qualified landscape contractor with experience in handling live plants. Landscape planting must be coordinated with other construction operations—for both the golf course and the real estate development. In some cases, landscape materials can be planted before the seedbed is prepared and the course grassed to minimize potential damage. In other cases, landscape materials could be planted after grassing if workers are cautioned about damaging the turf.

Landscape planting generally proceeds as follows:

- Staking positions of landscape materials for approval by the landscape architect and/or the golf course architect;
- Preparing planting beds or tree pits according to specifications prepared by the landscape architect, including necessary soil amendments based on specifications and soil tests;
- Placing plant materials and adjusting them as directed by the landscape architect or golf course architect;
- Backfilling, planting, and watering plant materials according to specifications;
- Staking and wiring trees according to specifications to stabilize them during their establishment;
- Applying mulching or other finishes to plant beds according to specifications;
- Selective pruning as directed by the landscape architect.

A program for care of landscape materials during the critical establishment period (the time it takes for newly installed plants to develop adequate root structures and to grow enough to ensure survival) is generally part of the responsibilities of the course superintendent or specialized personnel under the superintendent's direction.

Golf Car Paths

If a full golf car path system is anticipated as part of the initial construc-

tion, grading, preparation of the subgrade, and surfacing of the path should be coordinated with the corresponding phases of constructing the course. If, however, golf car paths are installed after the course is constructed, they generally are constructed in phases to minimize disruption of play on the course and of the budget. Worn areas of the turf are usually given priority. Directing and restricting construction traffic must be carefully considered to prevent damage to drainage or irrigation lines.

Construction generally proceeds as follows:

- Surveying and staking both horizontal and vertical alignments of the path for the golf course architect's review, approval, and/or adjustments as necessary. Marking all below-grade utility lines in the construction area;
- Stripping and stockpiling topsoil;
- Excavation, fill, and grading;
- Compacting and preparing the subgrade, usually including the installation of a gravel layer over the compacted subgrade;
- Installing the surface material according to specifications and de-

pending on the type of surface material used;
- Respreading topsoil over exposed subgrade areas around the path;
- Preparing and grassing the seedbed.

Buildings, Bridges, and Other Features

Construction of the clubhouse, maintenance compound, shelters, bridges, signs, and other features must be coordinated with construction of the course and real estate. Temporary bridges for construction equipment might be required to reach work areas. The maintenance compound is often built early in the process so it can be used as a staging area for construction materials and equipment.

Cost Estimates for Construction Of a Golf Course

Cost estimates typically are generated throughout the development process, starting with very general figures and progressively becoming more detailed as more information becomes available.

Many variables affect the cost of constructing a golf course: local climate, soils, rocks, amount of earth to be moved, vegetation, environmental

Preliminary Construction Cost Estimate

	Alternative A: 18-Hole Course	Alternative B: 36-Hole Course
Staking	$ 25,000	$ 40,000
Clearing	150,000	250,000
Rough Grading/Fine Grading	612,500	1,120,000
Drainage and Lakes	195,000	350,000
Irrigation and Pump Station	850,000	1,500,000
Components (tees, greens, bunkers)	1,065,000	2,130,000
Finish Shaping	225,000	400,000
Cleanup and Seeding, Trees, and Bridges	160,000	350,000
TOTAL for Golf Course	$3,282,500	$ 6,140,000
Maintenance Building and Equipment	$ 650,000	$ 800,000
Golf Shelters	50,000	800,000
Maintenance of Turf (until course opens)	250,000	450,000
Clubhouse (20,000 square feet)	3,000,000	
Two Separate Clubhouses for 36 Holes		
Private (15,000 square feet)		2,250,000
Public (8,000 square feet)		1,200,000
TOTAL	$7,232,500	$11,640,000

Figures are generated from information and master plans for a specific project site and are provided for illustration only. They should not be applied to any other project.

Source: Robert Muir Graves, Ltd.

Statement of Probable Construction Cost

Project:_____

Date:_____

Job No._____

Address:_____

I. STAKING
   A. Set Vertical and Horizontal
      Reference Points $_____
   B. Set Main Golf Course Points   _____
   C. Survey Proposed Roads and
      Building Sites   _____

II. CLEARING
   A. Buildings   _____
   B. Refuse   _____
   C. Underground Utilities   _____
   D. Weeds and Grass   _____
   E. Brush   _____
   F. Trees   _____
   G. Rocks   _____

III. ROUGH GRADING
   A. Required Cut   _____
   B. Required Fill   _____
   C. Required Topsoil Work   _____
   D. Engineered Fill   _____
   E. Flood Control   _____

IV. DRAINAGE
   A. Swales   _____
   B. Interceptor Ditches   _____
   C. Drain Pipes   _____
      1. Perforated   _____
      2. Solid   _____
   D. Vertical Drain Sumps   _____
   E. Catch Basins   _____
   F. Large Drain Lines   _____
   G. Drainage Structures   _____
   H. Flood Control   _____
   I. Culvert Crossings   _____

V. IRRIGATION WATER SUPPLY SYSTEM
   A. Supply Structure   _____
      1. Turnout/Well   _____
      2. Sump   _____
      3. Pump House   _____
   B. Pump System   _____
      1. Foundation   _____
      2. Pump(s) and Valving   _____
      3. Pressurization System   _____

VI. IRRIGATION
   A. Golf Course with Rough   _____
   B. Practice Area(s)   _____
   C. Maintenance Facilities   _____
   D. Remote Planting Areas   _____
   E. Drinking Fountains   _____

VII. UTILITIES
   A. Electrical Services $_____
      1. Clubhouse   _____
      2. Maintenance Area   _____
      3. Irrigation Water Supply
         System   _____
      4. Irrigation Controllers   _____
      5. Shelters   _____
   B. Potable Water   _____
      1. Clubhouse   _____
      2. Maintenance Area   _____
      3. Shelters/Drinking Fountains   _____
   C. Sewage System   _____
      1. Clubhouse   _____
      2. Maintenance Area   _____
      3. Shelters   _____
   D. Telephone   _____
      1. Clubhouse   _____
      2. Maintenance Area   _____
      3. Shelters   _____

VIII. GOLF COURSE COMPONENTS
   A. Tees   _____
   B. Fairways   _____
   C. Fairway Bunkers   _____
   D. Greens with Green Bunkers   _____
   E. Practice Facilities   _____
      1. Putting Green(s)   _____
      2. Chipping/Putting Green   _____
      3. Practice Bunker   _____
      4. Practice Tee   _____
      5. Practice Range   _____
      6. Target Green(s)   _____
      7. Safety Screen   _____
   F. Bridges   _____
      1. Pedestrian   _____
      2. Vehicular   _____
   G. Water Features   _____
      1. Lake(s)   _____
        a. Lining   _____
        b. Structures   _____
        c. Circulation Equipment   _____
      2. Streams   _____
   H. Golf Car Paths   _____

IX. TREE INSTALLATION
   A. Trees   _____
      1. Large   _____
      2. Medium   _____
      3. Small   _____
      4. Specimen   _____
   B. Maintenance after Planting   _____

X. TURF INSTALLATION AND DEVELOPMENT
   A. Golf Course with Rough $_____
   B. Practice Areas   _____
   C. Turf Nursery   _____
   D. Remote Areas   _____
   E. Maintenance after Installation   _____

XI. MAINTENANCE FACILITIES
   A. Building   _____
   B. Paving   _____
      1. Parking   _____
      2. Work Area   _____
   C. Service Road   _____
   D. Golf Course Maintenance
      Road   _____
   E. Equipment, Supplies,
      Hand Tools, Shop Equipment   _____
   F. Landscaping   _____

XII. SHELTERS
   A. Access Road   _____
   B. Parking   _____
      1. Golf Cars   _____
      2. Employees' Cars   _____
   C. Building   _____
   D. Landscaping   _____

XIII. CLUBHOUSE
   A. Access Road   _____
   B. Parking   _____
      1. Golfers   _____
      2. Employees   _____
   C. Building   _____
   D. Landscaping   _____
   E. Irrigation   _____
   F. Golf Car Storage   _____

XIV. MISCELLANEOUS ITEMS
   A. Land Acquisition   _____
   B. Design Fees   _____
   C. Tests/Permits   _____
   D. Prints   _____
   E. Administrative Costs of
      Construction   _____
   F. Operating Equipment   _____
      1. Golf Course   _____
      2. Practice Facilities   _____
   G. Operating and Maintenance
      Costs to Opening   _____

TOTAL $_____

Source: Robert Muir Graves, Ltd.

Master Equipment List for an 18-Hole Golf Course
Warm Season and/or Cool/Warm Season Grassing

This list will accommodate needed golf maintenance equipment for 18 months after grassing is completed.

ROLLING EQUIPMENT

Quantity	Description*	Per Unit	Cost
	Phase 1		
1	Ford Ranger Pick-up Truck, 4-wheel drive, 1/2-ton capacity	$12,000	$12,000
3	Jacobsen 2015 Utility Vehicle, 20 HP gas, 5-speed transmission, hyd. lift PTO adapter kit, univ. mounting frame (may substitute E-Z-Go equal)	7,000	21,000
1	Turfco Meter-Matic Topdresser, walk behind, 11.5-cu.-ft. capacity	4,000	4,000
1	Ford F-350 Dump Truck, 1-1/2-ton capacity	19,000	19,000
2	Gandy Drop Spreader, 42"	250	500
3	Lesco Rotary Spreader	250	750
1	Jacobsen Greens King IV, triplex seat, grooved front rollers, vertical mowing reels (large tees and approaches)	15,500	15,500
4	Jacobsen 22" Greens Mower, brush attachment, front rollers, solid and sectional (tees and collars)	3,264	13,056
5	Jacobsen 19" Greens Mower, turf groomer, front rollers, solid and sectional (greens)	4,310	21,550
1	John Deere Trap King Bunker Rake, front blade attachment	6,700	6,700
2	Jacobsen Turfcat Riding Rotary Mower, 60" deck, pneumatic caster (rough trim mower)	12,300	24,600
1	Jacobsen G-20 Tractor, 3 pt. hitch, PTO, draw bar, turf tires, bi-spool hydraulics	18,000	18,000
1	Ford Industrial Tractor, loader, backhoe, fork lift	30,000	30,000
2	Vicon Pendulum Spreader with Sand Spout, to be attached to a small utility truckster	1,500	3,000
2	Hahn 418 Truckster with Sprayer, 160-gal. tank, multiple spray tips	10,000	20,000
2	Homelite 20" Chain Saw	500	1,000
1	Homelite 1-1/2 Trash Pump	850	850
2 (cool only)	National 84" Mower, 14-hp OHC engine, 6-blade reels, front rollers, special tire option (rough trim mower)	7,000	14,000
2 (warm only)	Jacobsen Tri-King 1684G, 5-blade reels, fixed height adj., traction sulky w/wheel weights (rough trim mower)	14,000	28,000
1	8-ft. Box Blade	1,200	1,200
1	8" York Rake	1,500	1,500
2	Jacobsen String Line Trimmer	350	700
6	Flymo or Allen Rotary Mowers	700	4,200
4	Jacobsen Residential Rotary with Bagger	250	1,000
3	Jacobsen 810 or E-Z-Go GX800 Cart, 8.5-hp gas, tailgate, lights, 4 wheel, light utility	4,000	12,000
1	Jacobsen Model 40 Blower	3,000	3,000
1	Utility Trailer	3,500	3,500
2	Jacobsen Back Pack Blower	375	750
	Miscellaneous Tools and Equipment: wheelbarrows, shovels, rakes, hammers, picks, axes	3,000	3,000
	Total—Phase 1		$284,356
	Phase 2		
1	Gandy 10-ft. Drop Spreader	3,700	3,700
2	Jacobsen 810 or E-Z-Go GX800 Cart, 8.5-hp, tailgate, lights, 4 wheel, light utility	4,000	8,000
1	Jacobsen Greens King IV, triplex seat, grooved front rollers, vertical mowing reels, spiker attachment (3) (large tees and approaches)	17,000	17,000
2	Jacobsen LF 100 Arm Rest, pressure spring kit, scrapers (5), 7-blade reels, 3" grooved rollers, 2" solid (fairway mower)	24,500	49,000
1	Toro Rak-O-Vac Sweeper, tow behind, PTO power	20,000	20,000
1	Jacobsen G-20 Tractor, 3 pt. hitch, PTO, draw bar, turf tires, bi-spool hydraulics	18,000	18,000
1	Ryan Sod Cutter Jr., 18"	2,600	2,600
2	Jacobsen Greens Aerifier	7,200	14,400
2	Red Max Bunker Edger	500	1,000
2	Jacobsen String Line Trimmer	350	700
1 (cool only)	Jacobsen Model 524/100 Seeder/Aerator	3,300	3,300
1	300-gal. Fairway Sprayer, 25-gpm pump, tow behind	10,000	10,000
1	Jacobsen Turfcat Sweeper Attachment, 72"	3,000	3,000
1	Jacobsen Blower Turfcat Attachment	2,500	2,500
1	Jacobsen 590 Aerator, tow behind, 3/4" closed tines, slicing knives, weight tray, and weights	4,000	4,000
1	Jacobsen 5-Gang Ram Lift, ground driven, 6-blade mowers (rough mower)	16,500	16,500
2	5-gal. Back Pack Sprayer	250	500
1	20-gal. Manual Roller	150	150
	Contingency Parts and Supplies		4,000
	Total—Phase 2		$178,350
	TOTAL Rolling Equipment		$462,706

SHOP EQUIPMENT

Quantity	Description	Per Unit	Cost
1	Complete Set Wrenches	2,500	2,500
1	Air Compressor, cast iron	2,300	2,300
2	Grease Guns	60	120
1	Arc Welder, AC	425	425
1	Battery Charger w/Boost	250	250
1	Bench Grinder	250	250
1	Gas Torch w/o Tanks	250	250
1	One-Ton Hoist & Trolley	1,200	1,200
1	Large Bench Vise	100	100
1	Two-Ton Floor Jack	250	250
1	1/2" Pneumatic Wrench	175	175
1	Pressure Washer/Steam Cleaner	2,000	2,000
2	Foley Lapping Machines	375	750
5	3 x 10 Work Benches	100	500
1	Portable Air Tank	50	50
1	1/2" Electric Drill	150	150
1	1/4" Electric Drill	80	80
1	8" Circular Saw	110	110
1	Builders Level & Rod	500	500
1	Pipe Wrench Set	400	400
1	Portable Generator	900	900
6	Fire Extinguishers, Wall Mount	60	360
6	Fire Extinguishers, Vehicle Mount	25	150
1	Wire Fault Finder & Tracker	2,500	2,500
1	Hydraulic Testing Kit	1,000	1,000
1	Foley Spin Reel Grinder	9,000	9,000
1	Foley Automatic Bedknife Grinder	4,000	4,000
1	Drill Press	450	450
1	Paint Gun Kit	100	100
	TOTAL Shop Equipment		$30,820

OFFICE EQUIPMENT

Quantity	Description	Per Unit	Cost
3	Desk and Chairs	600	1,800
2	Chairs (hard back)	60	120
1	Adding Machine	185	185
1	Computer Table, 8 Ft.	200	200
2	Four-Drawer File Cabinets	400	800
1	Copy Machine	1,000	1,000
5	FM Hand-Held 2-Way Radios	1,000	5,000
1	FM Base Station Radio	2,000	2,000
1	Set Double Wall Lockers	800	800
4	Lunch Room Tables	100	400
25	Folding Chairs	15	375
1	Water Cooler/Fountain	350	350
1	Industrial First Aid Kit	150	150
1	Miscellaneous Supplies	500	500
	TOTAL Office Equipment		$13,680

Summary

Total Rolling Equipment	$462,706
Total Shop Equipment	30,820
Total Office Equipment	13,680
GRAND TOTAL	$507,206

*Specified manufacturers and models are suggestions. Retail prices are estimated.

Source: Nicklaus Design.

conditions, and local laws and regulations among them. Because of the range of variables, it is generally most prudent to have the golf course architect generate cost estimates for a specific site or project as past estimates for other sites are often not good indicators.

Cost estimates can be broken down into three different levels of detail: rough or "ball park" estimates, preliminary construction estimates, and detailed cost estimates. Rough estimates are usually generated without detailed information on the site or any significant design work. Numbers are usually derived from an examination of comparable projects in the area. Basic information about the location, site, golf course program, topography, and type of course assists in making rough estimates more specific to the project. Rough estimates cite either a lump sum or a cost per hole for a golf course.

Preliminary construction cost estimates are prepared after completion of the master plan for the golf course. With more detailed information available, it is easier to prepare a site-specific cost estimate. If more than one master plan is under consideration, estimates should be prepared for each to provide a basis for comparison. A preliminary construction cost estimate breaks down figures into categories based on the phase of the construction process, as shown in the accompanying feature box. The estimated costs for other components, such as maintenance facilities, the clubhouse, shelters, and maintenance of the course during grow-in, are added to the total cost for construction of the golf course, thus providing the developer with a fairly definitive estimate on which to base financial decisions.

As the project proceeds from master plan to construction plans and specifications, information becomes more detailed, and the estimator knows the size of the course's components and quantities of materials to be used. Detailed cost estimates are generated and continually updated after construction plans and specifications have been developed. Al-

though each golf course architect has his or her own format for this estimate, the format usually includes the same breakdown by project phase or operation. The figures are derived from actual calculations based on the construction documents and specifications, multiplied by cost factors to accommodate local differences in labor and material costs. The detailed estimate provides the developer with information with which to compare bids from would-be contractors. Often, a "blind copy" of the estimate is provided for contractors' use during bidding, showing the list of materials and labor required *without the costs.* These bid sheets provide actual quantities for bidders but allow the developer or owner to compare costs for specific items from different contractors.

Notes

1. The USGA (U.S. Golf Association) sets forth the rules governing the game of golf in the United States and handicapping for tournament or competitive play, while the NGF (National Golf Foundation) is a nonprofit organization devoted to the advancement of golf, through its role as the primary source of research and information on the business of golf and as a leading proponent of golf course development.

2. National Golf Foundation, *Golf Course Design and Construction* (Jupiter, Fla.: Author, 1990), p. 6.

3. Ibid.

4. U.S. Golf Association, *The Rules of Golf* (Far Hills, N.J.: Author, 1991), p. 118.

5. Ibid.

6. This section is from USGA, *Uncle Snoopy's Guided Tour of the USGA Handicap System* (Far Hills, N.J.: Author, 1992).

7. Ibid.

8. NGF, *Golf Course Design*, p. 26.

9. Ibid., p. 27.

10. USGA, *Rules of Golf*, p. 46.

11. Ibid.

12. NGF, *Golf Course Design*, p. 27.

13. Ibid., p. 30.

14. Rees L. Jones and Guy L. Rando, *Golf Course Developments* (Washington,

D.C.: ULI–the Urban Land Institute, 1974), p. 4.

15. NGF, *Golf Course Design*, p. 28.

16. Ibid.

17. Ibid., p. 30.

18. Ibid., p. 32.

19. James Beard, *Turf Management for Golf Courses* (New York: Macmillan, 1982), p. 261.

20. Geoffrey S. Cornish and Ronald E. Whitten, *The Golf Course* (New York: Rutledge Press, 1987), p. 16.

21. Point-to-Point Golf™ is a trademark of Guy L. Rando & Associates Inc.

22. Philip A. Wogan, *Golf Courses and the Environment: A White Paper by the American Society of Golf Course Architects* (Chicago: ASGCA Environmental Impact Committee, n.d.).

23. See further discussion in "Controlling Pests" and "Turf Nutrients and the Environment."

24. The kind of formal environmental analysis required is dictated by local, state, or federal laws. A checklist that identifies the potential impacts of a proposed project, an EIS is the less stringent type of analysis established by the National Environmental Policy Act (NEPA) of 1969. An EIR, in contrast, is a full report of environmental impact based on local or state regulatory requirements. A public agency might order an EIR when a project is expected to pose a substantial danger to the environment; in some cases, an EIR is required as a normal course of action in environmentally sensitive communities. An EIR not only describes the specific impacts of a project (air, water, and soil quality, noise, traffic, solar access, and so on), but also proposes appropriate measures to mitigate them. Thus, this report can also be termed an "environmental mitigation plan" or a "resource management plan." EIRs are more costly than EISs to prepare because they require more detail. Changes to a development plan generally require the EIR to be revised. The tendency is to contract with an environmental consultant to complete the EIR only after the master plan is in its final stages, but environmental consultants can often recommend important mitigation measures that should be implemented in early concept studies, saving the time and cost of revising preliminary concept and master plans. The EIR is

often part of the required documents presented for public approval and can be used for presentations in public hearings.

25. This concept was developed by Guy L. Rando & Associates Inc. with support from the Ralph Hudson Environmental Fellowship.

26. Anne R. Leslie, *Development of an IPM Program for Turfgrass* (Washington, D.C.: U.S. Environmental Protection Agency, Council on the Environment, 1989), p. 317.

27. Ibid.

28. Ibid., pp. 317–18.

29. Pennsylvania State Univ., Dept. of Agronomy, *The Effect of Nutrients and Pesticides Applied to Turf on the Quality of Runoff and Percolating Water: A Summary of Research Conducted by the Northeast Regional Turfgrass Research Project*, NE-169 (University Park, Pa.: Author, n.d.), pp.8–9.

30. Ibid., pp. 3–5.

31. "Good Management Guards against Nitrate Contamination," *Golf Course News* (October 1989), p. 3.

32. Thomas W. Tatnall, "How Green Is Your Golf Course?" *Parks and Recreation* (May 1991), p. 31.

33. James H. May, John R. Hall, David R. Chalmers, and Patricia R. Carry, "Nutrient Management for Golf Course Managers," *Ecological Turf Tips to Protect the Chesapeake Bay*, ETT No. 2 (Virginia Cooperative Extension), p. 2.

34. Xeriscape™, a response to the critical environmental issue of water conservation, is a trademark of the National Xeriscape Council.

35. National Golf Foundation, "Disabilities Act Means Changes for Golf Industry," *Golf Market Today*, September/October 1992, pp. 1–5.

36. For more details, a copy of the ADA with a handbook and other information is available from the Equal Employment Opportunity Commission, Washington, D.C.

37. *Feng shui* are principles of environmental harmony used in Chinese geomancy. The two characters, *"feng"* and *"shui,"* are literally translated as "wind" and "water." The principles of *feng shui* are based on precepts laid down thousands of years ago, particularly the *Li shu*, or *Book of Rites*, a sacred book that enshrines the basic tenets of Chinese religious belief. Concerned with order, the harmony of heaven and earth, and the ways in which humanity can best keep the balance of nature intact, the practice of geomancy today is a highly complex and sophisticated discipline based on points of the Lo P'an or geomancer's compass and a blend of common sense (solar/wind orientation, for example), logic, tradition, and even superstition. The geomancer examines the features of the surrounding landscape (or urban surrounds) and notes alignments to the Lo P'an and the site or building in consideration. It is believed that interference with the terrain (putting up a building, digging a lake, etc.) can bring about an imbalance and thus calamities. For instance, it is well known that skyscrapers cause major changes in wind patterns that could adversely affect the building or surrounds and that the impoundment of a river for flood control can have disastrous effects downstream because of the disruption of water movement. The determination of a site's *feng shui* is analyzed much as a western site analysis might be conducted to determine a site's suitability for a particular use, based on ancient principles of environmentally sensitive planning. See Derek Walters, *The Feng Shui Handbook* (London: Aquarian Press, 1991).

38. National Golf Foundation, *Planning and Developing a Private Golf Facility* (Jupiter, Fla.: Author, 1987), p. 295.

39. Ibid., p. 296.

CHAPTER FIVE

The Business of Golf

A golf course is a business, with various structures for its operation defined by ownership and control of the facilities. A number of factors determine the most appropriate operational structure for a golf course. That determination is particularly important when a golf course is developed in association with real estate, for the type of operation can significantly affect a project's economic performance. In a golf-oriented

Water crossing at Horseshoe Bay Resort and Conference Club.

GUY L. RANDO & ASSOCIATES INC.

real estate development, golf facilities are an integral amenity to aid in marketing the real estate.

Operational Structures

Public Courses

A daily-fee golf course is so named because the course is open to the general public upon payment of daily greens fees, golf car fees, and other user fees. A daily-fee course can be owned by a private business enterprise or by a public agency, such as a county or city parks department.

For the golf course developer, a daily-fee operation is the simplest and least expensive golf course operation to create or implement, as it does not require the extensive legal structuring and expensive marketing program associated with membership programs for private clubs. It offers the greatest operational flexibility, because the owner/operator has complete control over decisions affecting ownership, management, and operations. For a golf-oriented real estate development, this type of operation provides golf at the least cost to homebuyers around the course.

The daily-fee structure also has some disadvantages. Potential homebuyers in a golf-oriented residential real estate development might not perceive a facility that is open to the public as "their own." A daily-fee course might provide less sense of community when compared with private club operations. The acceptability of a daily-fee operation is related to the targeted housing market, however. Homebuyers in expensive residential communities, for example, typically place a high value on privacy and exclusivity, making a daily-fee operation, with its inherent lack of privacy, undesirable. In more moderately priced communities, however, a daily-fee operation could be viewed as a significant positive feature that adds value to the surrounding residences.

Ownership and management of the golf course are beyond the control of property buyers in the community. Homebuyers in lower-priced or resort

Legal counsel frequently participate in the negotiation and preparation of management, franchise, loan, and refinancing agreements as well as the acquisition, disposition, and operation of hotel and resort properties. Access to surrounding amenities is often critical for resort and hotel properties. In such cases, legal counsel is essential for negotiating and preparing access agreements.

communities are generally more willing to accept this lack of control, but those in higher-priced and primary-home communities usually want to control the operation of amenities in the community to be assured that they will be able to preserve the lifestyle they desire. Further, homebuyers must compete with nonresidents for tee times, which can be a significant marketing disadvantage in a market with a heavy demand for golf. A reservation system that gives priority to homeowners could ease the situation, however.

The owner/developer of the golf course does not realize revenue from the sale of club memberships and therefore must recover the cost of building the golf course solely from operational revenues (user fees), although potential revenues from a successful and cost-efficient daily-fee operation can exceed potential revenues from the sale of memberships.

Private Clubs

Many golf courses in residential communities are operated as private clubs. A person must be a club member to use the golf course and related facilities, and use of the facilities is limited to members and their guests.

The two basic types of private club membership structures—equity and nonequity—are distinguished by who controls ownership and operation of the facilities. In an equity membership structure, a nonprofit corporation, whose members each acquire an ownership interest, owns and operates the golf course and related facilities. Although the developer usually retains control of the nonprofit corporation until the project is substantially sold out, the membership structure, through the articles of incorporation and bylaws, provides for control of the corporation eventually to be turned over to the equity members.

This structure creates the strongest sense of community for a real estate development project, particularly a residential development, because the equity members eventually control the golf course, which is a highly valued part of their lifestyle. In turn, this sense of control provides a substantial marketing advantage, particularly for higher-priced residential communities. Because equity membership includes ownership interest in the club and voting privileges allowing members to participate in the management of the club, equity memberships usually have a much higher value in the marketplace than nonequity memberships, providing the developer with the highest potential for return on investment from the proceeds of the sale of memberships.

On the other hand, an equity membership program requires relatively complex legal and marketing preparation, making it the most costly membership program to implement. Purchasers must be able and willing to pay the higher price of equity memberships required to offset the developer's higher costs. Because of the high costs, this structure is generally more suited for upscale, higher-priced primary-home projects than moderately priced projects. And it is ill-suited for projects with a substantial number of transient guests, such as a resort or hotel.

The developer has the least flexibility in managing and operating the course, because equity members eventually receive permanent membership rights. The developer must decide when to offer equity memberships—at the beginning of a project or when it is converted from another type of structure—and how and when ownership will be turned over to members. The developer must be a skilled negotiator to protect the marketability of unsold real estate against possible legal opposition by existing club members and property owners as the project approaches sellout.

In a nonequity membership structure, acquisition of a membership merely bestows a right to use the facilities. Members have no ownership interest in the golf course and little, if any, control over its management and operation. Membership can be a short-term right of use, such as an annual membership subject to annual renewal by the club, or a long-term right of use, such as a lifetime membership.

A nonequity club might require membership dues only, or an initiation or membership fee *plus* membership dues. The membership dues are usually annual and provide a means of covering the continuing operating costs of the facilities. The membership or initiation fee is a one-time fee that might be nonrefundable, partly refundable, or fully refundable upon resignation or resale of the membership.

If the membership or initiation fee is fully refundable, it is commonly called an initiation deposit or membership deposit. Whether or not the membership or initiation fee is refundable affects the perceived value of a nonequity membership: a nonrefundable fee is perceived as the least valuable and thus tends to limit the amount a person is willing to pay for the membership. At some point, perhaps 30 years after the member acquires the membership, the membership or initiation fee is fully refunded and that membership slot no longer requires the fee. Few members retain a membership for such a long term, however, and the new member also pays a membership or initiation deposit. The golf course owner or operator usually repays the resigning member out of the proceeds received from resale of the membership.

Substantial proceeds can be generated from the sale of memberships in addition to use fees and other charges, and the owner/developer, not nonequity members, can modify the operational structure in response to changes in the market. Use of the facilities exclusively by members and their guests enhances both the perceived and actual value of the memberships. In a residential development project, this sense of exclusivity creates a greater sense of community among homebuyers.

The nonequity structure can be a disadvantage for marketing certain types of projects—if, for example, targeted purchasers want to control amenities. Purchasers might feel uncomfortable with the element of uncertainty about the possibility of drastic changes in the membership structure or operation of the facilities. In some residential developments, members of nonequity clubs have filed lawsuits against developers who significantly changed the club's operational structure, arguing that they acquired vested rights to continue using the club's facilities under the same terms and conditions in effect when they purchased property in the community. The developer must therefore include a disclaimer in membership documents, promotional materials, and purchase and sale agreements for both a nonequity club and the residential community, clearly stating that the owner can modify the privileges of members and the operational structure of the club.

A membership structure developed in recent years in response to legal and marketing issues relating to equity memberships is the convertible club. It starts with a nonequity membership structure with additional documentation expressly providing that the club will or could be converted to an equity membership structure later. The developer retains operational control during critical marketing. Convertible memberships have been successfully used, for example, when the developer of a residential golf course development, for marketing reasons, did not want an equity club during the project's initial phases but wanted to convert to one later.

With membership documents clearly stating that the club could be converted to an equity structure later, the risk of litigation at the time of conversion can be substantially reduced. Legal risks can be further reduced if the documents specify how the conversion will affect those who acquire nonequity memberships before conversion (for example, a description of how the equity club will operate after conversion, the amount of a nonequity member's contribution to become an equity member). A convertible membership removes the element of uncertainty regarding future operations associated with nonequity memberships, substantially reducing a major marketing obstacle.

The convertible membership structure is complicated—perhaps too complex for consumers to understand—thus increasing the costs of legal work and marketing programs. The developer is caught in a dilemma: whether to reduce legal risks by providing specific details about conversion to equity membership or to remain flexible in the face of changing market conditions by remaining silent.

Membership Programs

For a private club, the next step after determining an appropriate membership structure is to design a membership program that will provide members with the privileges or services they want. Membership programs could take one of three basic forms: tiered programs, unitary programs, and add-on programs.

A tiered program offers several categories of membership with different privileges and different fees. Membership categories typically include "golf," "tennis," "social," and the like. Some programs include various limited golf categories, which are designed to increase the use of the golf facilities during nonpeak periods. The number of members permitted in each membership category is limited, and each category requires the payment of membership fees and dues commensurate with the degree of privileges.

A tiered program is most often used when the facilities are part of a residential development project where the offer of amenities is based on satisfying potential homebuyers' demands for recreational facilities. Depending on the size of the development project, the extent of amenities offered, and the desired degree of exclusivity,

a limited number of memberships for nonresidents might be made available in each category. Limiting the total number of memberships promotes exclusivity and ensures that the facilities are less crowded, thereby enhancing the value of memberships. The image of exclusivity can also benefit the marketing program for the associated residential real estate.

Unitary membership programs offer a single type of membership that permits members to select one of several categories of dues each membership year. Membership categories are similar to those in a tiered membership program. In the unitary program, all members pay the same membership fee to become a member, but annual dues are based on the category of dues selected and its related privileges. While the number of members may be limited, the number of persons selecting any particular category of dues usually is not limited, and members are not restricted to the same category each year.

The unitary membership program is most often used in resort communi-

ties where members' use of amenities can change over time.

Add-on membership programs offer a variety of membership categories with different privileges, similar to the membership categories typical of tiered programs. As for the tiered program, members pay different membership fees and dues based on the category of membership they select. The basic difference is that the add-on program imposes no limit on the number of memberships available in any one membership category. Add-on programs are most successful in moderately priced residential developments where the number of houses is relatively large in comparison to the extent of recreational facilities offered.

Hybrid Membership Structures And Programs

Several hybrid membership structures and programs have been developed to better suit various types of real estate development projects. Two of the most significant are association clubs and resort or vacation clubs.

The Woods Resort

Location:	Hedgesville, West Virginia
Owner/Developer:	Potomac Valley Properties, Inc.
Operator:	The Woods Club, Inc.
Golf Course Architects:	Ray Johnston and Guy L. Rando

The Woods Resort is a vacation and second-home retirement community 90 miles northwest of Washington, D.C., in West Virginia. The 1,800-acre development includes an 800-acre resort with 566 houses built between 1976 and 1986. In 1987, construction began on an additional 1,000 acres that, when completed, will include another 500 single-family detached houses, 200 townhouses, and 100 luxury apartments oriented around a 27-hole golf course, driving range, and clubhouse. Besides golf, the resort offers swimming pools; tennis courts; an indoor recreation center containing racquetball, tennis, and multipurpose courts, a fitness and exercise center, a pool, and a sauna; ponds; trails connecting to an adjacent state forest; and meeting facilities.

The Woods golf course is operated by the Woods Club, Inc., a subsidiary of the development corporation. The Woods Club is a successful semiprivate, non-equity-membership, golf-oriented real estate development. Memberships are granted to homebuyers without initiation fees. (The developer does not offer lots for sale.)

The membership must be continuous to remain valid, and if it is allowed to lapse, it may not be renewed. As a result, nearly all homeowners retain their memberships and pay their dues, assuring the developer of sufficient revenue to maintain the facilities and minimal dues for homeowners.

The Woods Club offers several classes of memberships:

- Outdoor (all outdoor swimming pools, tennis courts, and so on);
- Indoor/Outdoor (outdoor facilities plus all indoor facilities in the recreation center);
- Indoor/Outdoor Weekday Only (same as above but restricted to weekdays);
- Outdoor/Golf (outdoor facilities plus the golf course);
- Indoor/Outdoor/Golf (all recreational facilities).

Purchasers of resale homes are entitled to purchase the same class of membership the seller held for 30 days. To discourage a gradual change from vacation homes to low-income primary housing, the developer does not offer memberships to permanent residents of resale homes in vacation sections of the resort.

Membership initiation fees are due upon becoming a homeowner in the resort. Annual dues cover the fixed costs of operating and maintaining the facilities. Family memberships include the husband, wife, and children under age 21. Single members are issued one additional annual guest pass, with guests restricted to use of the same facilities as the sponsoring member and required to pay guest fees. Golf memberships include priority in reserving starting times, no greens fees, and participation in the club's activities.

Lessons Learned

The developer retained the right to permit public play upon payment of a greens fee to the extent required to raise sufficient revenue to maintain and operate the facilities in "a first-class manner." While the developer's intent is to make the golf course as private as possible, it was careful to clearly state management's authority and philosophy regarding public play in membership documents. As vacationers, members play golf primarily on weekends and holidays; public greens fees generate substantial revenues from what would otherwise be unused weekday time. Members' broad acceptance of the club's operating policies is largely a result of the developer's forthright statement of operating philosophy and objectives—to protect property values and the community's well-being.

Association Clubs

Under traditional equity membership programs, the membership fee repays the developer for the cost of constructing the facilities and, in effect, represents the purchase price of those facilities for members. Buyers of property in the related real estate development are not required to join the club, because club membership is voluntary. The amount of membership fees and dues is usually relatively high, because the number of members in the club is limited. An equity membership structure is therefore not feasible for some development projects, particularly residential developments, because property buyers cannot afford the purchase price.

An alternative, the association club, enables a developer to recover the cost of amenities without expensive membership fees. A community association (sometimes called a property owners association or a homeowners association) acquires the recreational facilities from the developer subject to a mortgage. When the recreational facilities are completed, an independent accounting firm certifies the cost of constructing them. This amount is the association's purchase price for the recreational facilities, and the amount of the debt is secured by a mortgage. (As an alternative, a fixed purchase price for the recreational facilities can be established.) The mortgage is then paid off through periodic assessments of homeowners or property owners and by positive cash flow from the facility's operations. All property owners have access to the amenities; they are required to pay assessments to the association for operational expenses and debt service. The board of directors of the association operates the amenities.

Del Vera Country Club

Location:	North Fort Myers, Florida
Developer:	Del Vera Limited Partnership
Owner/Operator:	Del Vera Country Club Homeowners Association, Inc.
Golf Course Architect:	Ron Garl

Del Vera is a master-planned community governed by the Del Vera Country Club Homeowners Association. Each homeowner in this community of 1,100 to 1,300 single-family houses automatically becomes a member of the homeowners association, entitled to use the golf, tennis, and social facilities in Del Vera upon payment of applicable fees and charges. The developer established the homeowners association to promote community interest and to acquire and maintain the common property within Del Vera.

The common property within Del Vera includes the guard gate, entrance features, community walls and landscaping, community roadways and sidewalks, and recreational facilities—an 18-hole golf course with pro shop, driving range, putting green, and a 23,000-square-foot clubhouse, a swimming pool, six tennis courts, shuffleboard courts, and a minirecreational area.

The target market for this community is adults over age 55. The developer and other builders designated by the developer construct all the residences in Del Vera from a variety of models and options. The golf course and other recreational facilities were constructed in phases, and the developer will lease approximately 5,500 square feet of the clubhouse for a sales office, a branch bank, and administrative offices until the clubhouse is turned over to the homeowners association. The association is responsible for lawn care and irrigation service for all lots, and members are assessed a fee to cover costs. The association pays for cable television outlets and propane gas outlets for each residence, and members pay for connections to the outlets and use charges directly to the respective operators.

The developer maintains control over the homeowners association until the prescribed "turnover date" (the end of the fiscal year during which the total outstanding class A votes equals or exceeds 75 percent of the total number of lots to be sold or leased by the developer, or, at its discretion, the developer determines to relinquish control of the association), when the developer relinquishes control of the association to its members. At that date, the homeowners association will acquire fee simple title to the recreational facilities by purchasing them from the developer for an amount equal to the cost of construction and the actual cost of all furnishings and equipment on hand as of the day of the turnover, with no deductions made for depreciation. An independent accounting firm will confirm actual costs. Immediately before the turnover date, the board of directors will arrange for a loan secured by a mortgage on the recreational facilities. The developer will transfer the recreational facilities to the homeowners association subject to the mortgage. The developer will pay all closing costs incurred in connection with the transfer of the property, and the homeowners association will pay other closing costs, including closing costs for the mortgage.

The developer will retain ownership of the fee title to the underlying land where the recreational facilities are constructed (approximately 200 acres); the homeowners association will acquire a leasehold interest in the land upon turnover, subject to a land lease agreement for the recreational facilities. The property subject to the lease includes the site of the golf course, clubhouse, pro shop, tennis courts, minirecreational area, and lakes abutting the golf course and clubhouse. The association begins paying rent only as portions of the recreational facilities are completed and made available to the members for use. The lease requires that the association pay all costs of maintenance, taxes, and insurance on the recreational facilities.

The homeowners association has been organized as a Florida not-for-profit corporation to operate and acquire the common property and to promote the health, safety, and welfare of Del Vera and its residents. The association offers three classes of membership: class A (lot owners), class B (lot lessees), and class C (the developer). Each class is entitled to different voting privileges: class A members have one vote per lot owned, class B members are not allowed to vote, and the class C member has three votes for each lot owned. On the turnover date, class C membership terminates and is converted to class A membership. The association's board of directors has exclusive authority to manage and control the association's affairs and to establish rules and regulations governing the common property. Before the turnover date, the developer will designate all of the members of the board of directors. On the turnover date, those directors will resign, and class A members must elect nine directors, three for a three-year term, three for a two-year term, and three for a one-year term.

The homeowners association offers its members the opportunity to acquire an annual golf membership, either single or family, which permits a member's use of the golf course without paying greens fees (although members are still required to pay golf car fees). The single option entitles that member only to membership benefits, the family option both the member and spouse. The number of annual golf memberships that may be issued to residents has no limit. Annual golf members are also entitled to reserve starting times when announced by the golf pro. Members of the homeowners association, at their option, may own their own golf cars or may lease a golf car from the homeowners association on a yearly or daily basis.

The board of directors, at its discretion, can offer nonresident annual full memberships and annual golf memberships. These nonresident memberships provide only a revocable license to use the recreational facilities and are subject to renewal each year at the board's sole discretion. The association can also allow nonresidents to use the golf course upon payment of greens fees and golf car fees, but the board of directors retains the right to restrict or terminate nonresidents' use of recreational facilities at any time. A tenant at a member's home is automatically designated the beneficial user of the member's rights to use common property, provided the tenant

Each property owner, by virtue of membership in the association, has an easement to use the recreational facilities upon payment of applicable assessments, use fees, and charges. The association might make several options for annual dues available to resident members of the association. In addition, the association might issue annual memberships to nonresidents at the discretion of its board of directors. The board might also limit the number of options for annual dues.

The association collects assessments for operating and maintaining common areas (land and other facilities held in common ownership by all homebuyers or property owners) and for making payments due on the mortgage for the recreational facilities. Assessments are based on the association's annual budget, first calculated by determining the estimated annual revenues from operation of the recreational facilities minus total estimated annual operating expenses and mortgage payments. The total shortfall is then divided by the number of lots or other real estate units to determine the annual assessment per unit. Assessments are often collected monthly or quarterly to minimize members' cash outlay at any one time. The association can secure a debt against the real property through a lien for nonpayment of assessments and has the right to temporarily suspend a member's use of the facilities for nonpayment.

The association structure enables a developer to provide golf and other recreational facilities to property buyers or homebuyers at one of the lowest costs per member. Because all property owners automatically become members of the association, the number

---

registers with the homeowners association and pays any fees and charges required for use of the recreational facilities.

The board of directors each year determines the amount of the base assessment, user assessments, and annual dues. The base assessment is calculated using the following formula:

Expenses for

■ operations and maintenance (O&M) of the common property

■ O&M of the golf course

■ O&M of the clubhouse and other recreational facilities

■ mortgage payment for the recreational facilities

■ land lease payment for the recreational facilities

■ repairs and replacements

MINUS

Estimated revenues received from

■ annual membership dues

■ greens fees and golf car fees

■ trail fees

■ annual golf car lease fees

■ guest fees

■ food and beverage charges

■ other use fees and charges

■ payments from the developer for the lease of commercial space.

The excess of expenses over revenues is allocated among all the lots to be constructed in Del Vera. The mortgage for the recreational facilities is not effective until the turnover date; therefore, amortization of this amount is not included in the initial annual budgets. To determine the base assessment, however, the mortgage is assumed to be in place before the turnover date. The developer pays interest that would be incurred under the mortgage semiannually, in advance, and base assessments for the unsold or unleased lots it owns.

Source: Hillier & Wanless, P.A.

Del Vera Country Club Homeowners Association
Schedule of Assessments, Annual Dues, Charges, and Use Fees: 1991

ASSESSMENTS*
(Paid Semiannually in Advance)

Base Assessment	$96.18/month
Lawn Maintenance	$22.33/month
Cable Television	$15.00/month

ANNUAL DUES**
Annual Membership, Resident

Golf Family	$850
Golf Single	$700
Annual Membership, Nonresident	
Full Family	$1,200
Full Single	$1,050
Golf Family	$1,000
Golf Single	$850

GOLF FEES**

	In Season (Nov. 1 to April 30)		Off Season (May 1 to Oct. 31)		
	18 Holes	9 Holes	18 Holes	9 Holes	Twilight (after 1 PM)
Greens Fees (including golf car) for Residents and Guests of Members	$20	$13	$15	$10	$11
Golf Car Fees for Annual Members (per person, per 18 holes)	$7	$5	$7	$5	$7

OTHER FEES AND CHARGES

Annual Trail Fee (charged when member owns and uses his own golf car)	
Family	$450
Single	$350
Annual Golf Car Lease (includes trail fee)	$1,200
Locker Fees (annual)	$50
Renter Designation Fee (for a tenant)	$50
Houseguest Fee (weekly)	$10

*Base and user assessments prorated based on date of residential closing.
**Annual dues and golf fees based on the availability of nine holes of golf. Assessments, dues, fees, and charges are subject to change and to all applicable Florida state taxes.

of members is usually considerably larger than if membership is voluntary. The costs of operating the recreational facilities are relatively low per property owner, as total costs are spread among all property owners. The association membership structure therefore provides a viable alternative for providing golf facilities in a moderately priced residential development where purchasers ordinarily would not be able to afford the costs of traditional private club membership fees and dues.

Resort or Vacation Clubs

Resort developers have had to formulate new ways to attract clients and accommodate their demands. One approach that has been gaining popularity is the vacation club. Vacation club programs are a variation of private club membership programs and can be structured with equity or nonequity memberships.

The vacation club is a promising alternative to the traditional timeshare program, where a purchaser buys the right to stay in a particular unit for a particular period of time during the year. A vacation club program allows the purchaser of a club membership the right to use overnight accommodations and other resort amenities throughout the year, pursuant to a reservation system.

A special system for advance reservations means that each member can reserve a minimum number of days each year. Before the beginning of each year (or more frequently as the club deems appropriate), each member is allowed to reserve a certain number of days at the facility. These guaranteed days are allocated over the membership year, based on the specific season and the facilities available at the resort. For example, a resort that offers golf and skiing might guarantee 14 days during the golf season and 14 days during the ski season. A lottery is often used to resolve scheduling conflicts.

The total number of guaranteed days allocated to each member is based on the total number of memberships offered in the club, the capacity of overnight accommodations available at the club, the length of the applicable season or seasons, and the desired number of unsold days under the program.

The Melrose Club

Location: Daufuskie Island, South Carolina

Development Partners: The Melrose Company

Land Planners: Edward Pinckney Associates, Ltd.

Club Operator: Melrose Club Owners Association, Inc.

Golf Course Architect: Jack Nicklaus Design, Inc.

The Melrose Club is a private resort community located along two miles of Atlantic beach on an island less than a mile from the Hilton Head vacation resort. Its facilities include a 50-room inn and 100 beach cottages, tennis courts, beach clubs, a marina, stables and equestrian fields, a sportsman's lodge, nature trails, and an 18-hole golf course. No bridge connects Daufuskie Island to the mainland, and access to the resort is via ferry to the west side of the island, with a shuttle providing transportation across the island to Melrose. The use of automobiles is limited at the resort; in fact, the primary mode of transportation at the resort and on the island is by foot. Golf cars are available at the resort, and beach cottages have facilities to house golf cars overnight.

The Melrose Club is a resort or vacation club, with membership limited to a maximum of 1,550. The resort's population density is less than one person per acre. Each owner receives a deed to an equal, undivided interest in the land, buildings, and facilities, and nonseverable membership in the Melrose Club Owners Association. The owners, as a group, equally own the land, houses, and other facilities. In essence, owners hold a deed and title to an equal share of the facility held in common. Melrose calls this concept of ownership "undivided resort interest."

The Melrose Club is operated as a nonprofit corporation (Melrose Club Owners Association, Inc.). An elected board of governors is fully empowered to carry out the purposes of the club, including determining annual assessments, dues, fees, and any other charges. The facility is fully equipped, managed, and staffed by the developer, The Melrose Company, which arranged for initial operation of the facility by Jack Nicklaus Club Management. The board of governors retains the right to continue the contract with the same management company or to hire a different management company or staff of its choice to operate the facility.

As a member of the club, each owner has an equal right to use the club's facilities. Three categories of membership are available:

- *Founding and charter memberships:* The first 425 members of Melrose are the "founding members." All other original owners are "charter members."

- *Corporate or partnership memberships:* Founding and charter memberships may be owned by a corporation, partnership, trust, or pension plan. Such memberships are required to designate one individual as the "designated member" at the beginning of each year, with other partners or corporate employees permitted to visit Melrose under normal procedures for guests.

- *Family memberships:* Children of members under the age of 25 are welcome to use the facilities when accompanied by parents. Children from 25 to 35 may have membership rights and may substitute for their parents with advance reservations. They may also make their own reservations if space is available up to 30 days in advance.

The board of governors establishes annual dues to cover all of the annual fixed costs of operating and maintaining the facilities and services offered, plus a reserve fund for future repairs. In addition to annual dues, members pay an overnight charge of $30 per night for a room in the inn and $40 per night for a cottage, equipment rentals, food and beverage services, and some special events. Greens fees and transportation are included in the annual dues. User fees and charges for accommodations are comparable to those at Hilton Head. Members are permitted to bring guests with them at any time and may send a limited number of "designated guests."

Unlike ownership in a timeshare, no restrictions apply as to how often members can use the facilities. Members may use the facilities 365 days of the year, subject to its reservation system, with overnight accommodations regulated through advance reservations. The advance reservation system is divided into three seasons: spring (January through April), summer (May through August), and fall (September through December). Before the beginning of the year, members are provided with a schedule of events for the year and reservation forms. At that time, each member is entitled to reserve 28 days (seven days in each of two seasons and 14 days during the third season). The reservations are not required to be consecutive days. Any conflicts are resolved through a "reservation priority number" assigned each year by a random drawing. Melrose anticipates that the advance reservation system will establish reservations for approximately 75 percent of the year. Members may reserve the remaining days or weeks within 60 days of the visit. A toll-free number keeps members informed about up-to-the-minute status of available accommodations.

Source: Hillier & Wanless, P.A.

A vacation club differs from a timeshare program in a number of significant ways:

- Timeshares are usually sold as a modestly priced high-volume product. Each purchaser acquires one week of time, and 50 or 51 weeks are sold for each unit. Vacation club memberships are generally sold as a high-end low-volume product. Each membership often provides three or four weeks of guaranteed use time, and only eight to 12 memberships are sold per living unit.
- Timeshare interests are frequently for specific weeks or blocks of time; vacation club memberships usually are not.
- Timeshare programs generally have little or no unsold time. Vacation club programs normally leave 20 to 40 percent of the available days unsold so that members can use the facilities during periods in addition to their guaranteed time.
- Service at timeshare projects is generally kept to a minimum to keep annual maintenance fees as low as possible. The level of service is higher at a vacation club, made possible through members' payment of annual dues.

Vacation clubs successfully combine many of the most attractive features of a private club with those of a luxury resort to provide a desirable alternative for a vacation. One of the best-known examples of a vacation club is the Melrose Club on Daufuskie Island, South Carolina.

Asset Management

Economic success for a golf course, like any business, requires effective management. The economic climate of the 1990s requires that a golf operation be financially self-sustaining. Whatever the entity that owns or controls a golf club or golf course, the responsibilities of management include general administration, personnel management, property and equipment transactions, membership activities or facilities programs, public relations and publicity, marketing, and financial and operating reports.

Golf operations can involve one of several management structures:

- Management and operation by salaried personnel;
- Management by an operator or concessionaire, who might or might not be a golf professional;
- Management by a contracted professional.

Determining which management structure is most appropriate for a golf operation is a complex business decision. The decision should be based on which management structure is most conducive to a profitable, efficient operation relative to its type and size and on the needs of the users and/or members of the facility.

Managing a golf course requires highly specialized skills, education, and training. The PGA (Professional Golfers Association) is working with four undergraduate institutions that offer programs in golf management. A number of other institutions offer programs and/or courses in golf management as part of recreation or business programs. The PGA's Education Department conducts a number of training courses in various aspects of golf management. Its program is aimed toward persons seeking to become golf professionals and members of the PGA, and toward continuing education of its existing members. The NGF/Oglebay Golf Management School in Wheeling, West Virginia, provides an annual course. Both PGA and NGF publish a number of publications and articles about golf operation and management.

Staffing

The staff required to effectively manage a golf operation varies according to the size and scope of the operation and the staff's responsibilities. For a smaller operation—and 90 percent of all golf operations in the United States are 18 holes or smaller—responsibility for management usually falls entirely on the golf pro or pro/manager, working closely with a golf superintendent.

For larger operations, a more complex management staff involving several persons might be required. For example, the key management staff for a major year-round golf operation with extensive club operations might include a head golf pro, pro/manager, or professional manager, an assistant golf pro, a golf superintendent, a kitchen manager (chef), and a club activities director. Support staff might include golf car assistants, the golf course maintenance staff, golf shop clerks, the food and beverage staff, mechanics, and other maintenance staff.

The golf operation's functional success is directly related to the capability and service orientation of every staff member, regardless of the operation's size or complexity. Management policies and the responsibilities of every staff member must be clearly defined in writing to facilitate the selection of staff and provide a measure against which the qualifications of a potential employee can be measured.

The golf pro's responsibilities vary from one course to another. The PGA's description of the golf pro's general duties include:

- Supervising personnel in the performance of their duties;
- Enforcing club rules and regulations governing the use of the course, golf cars, and other golf facilities;
- Supervising the detailed day-to-day operation of the golf facility, including starting play by golfers, charging greens fees, and renting golf cars;
- Operating and maintaining the pro shop and practice range;
- Providing competent golf instruction for all groups and levels of players;
- Planning and promoting golf and fellowship, including play with members outside of lessons;
- Planning and coordinating tournaments and events;
- Supervising the operation of the handicap system to the extent directed by the golf committee;
- Representing the facility in area professional golf activities, including the local section of the PGA, in tournaments with members, and in state or national golf events; and
- Maintaining a close relationship and cooperation with the course superintendent.

Legal counsel sensitive to the subtleties of the financial, operational, legal, and marketing aspects of recreational development is essential when selecting and designing membership programs.

The golf superintendent is the person entrusted with the maintenance, operation, and management of the land area of the golf course. The superintendent's typical responsibilities include:

■ Supervising construction and maintenance of the course;

■ Supervising maintenance and repair of construction and maintenance equipment;

■ Assigning and directing the work of maintenance personnel and perhaps participating in recruiting, hiring, and firing them;

■ Maintaining effective employee and public relations;

■ Ordering supplies and materials;

■ Maintaining records of annual maintenance activities; and

■ Planning and preparing annual budget estimates.

Selecting management personnel involves matching capabilities of a candidate with the specific needs of a golf operation as well as matching personalities, for a golf operation is a *service*-oriented business. The PGA and NGF publish a number of resources and information about staffing personnel for golf facilities.

The selection of the golf pro and the golf superintendent should occur early during the planning stages of a project, because their input in planning and design is often invaluable. The golf pro has key roles in decision making for the golf course and clubhouse, from design programming to selecting fixtures and equipment, and might also have key responsibilities in preparing marketing strategies for a project. The golf superintendent also has key roles in decision making, from design programming to detailing

and equipping the golf course and maintenance facilities. The golf superintendent should be on board before the main components of the golf course are constructed, particularly the irrigation system. The superintendent must know where all the major drainage structures, utilities, irrigation lines, and other below-grade elements of the golf course are located to facilitate maintenance and repairs. While as-built drawings might provide this information, no substitute exists for knowledge gained in the field during construction. The superintendent might also have key responsibilities during the grow-in period. Although the superintendent can have important input in the design process, he or she should not be responsible for actual design of the course. Design is the architect's job.

Management Philosophy

In the golf business, having the right people on staff and in key positions can make the difference between success and failure. The philosophy of J.W. Marriott, Sr., is to "take care of the employee and the employee will take care of the guest." Creating a positive work environment allows a facility to attract, retain, and promote highly qualified, enthusiastic individuals—critical to a service-oriented business like golf. Proponents of motivational management often speak of the three R's of management: responsibility, recognition, and rewards. For many businesses, responsibility is outlined in manuals in the form of standard operating procedures. Such manuals should clearly state management's policies, employees' responsibilities, and operational procedures. But beyond the standard operating procedures, a structured training program for personnel can provide them with tools to handle normal and extraordinary situations. Education through training programs is an ongoing process that responds to changes in employees' responsibilities and changes that can arise as a result of business trends or management systems. Employees should be allowed to attend after-hours presentations by vendors, controllers, or marketing representatives, and their participation in professional associations and conferences should be encouraged so their knowledge remains current.

Recognition comes in many forms and at many levels, usually through salary and compensation. Traditionally, compensation came directly from golf car fees, sales of merchandise in the pro shop, income from lessons, bag storage fees, locker fees, and range revenues. The current trend, however, is toward a salary plus bonus. Recognition also comes in other forms, ranging from expressions of personal appreciation (employee picnics or banquets) to crediting special achievements or involving employees in decision-making or problem-solving sessions. Recognition might also take the form of a reward—from cash incentives for exceeding a sales goal to payment of professional association memberships, special privileges, or promotions.

Teamwork, communication, continued training, recognition, and rewards promote employees' satisfaction and morale. The investment in training and caring for personnel realizes paybacks many times over through fewer turnovers and greater loyalty, commitment, and pride. This positive attitude carries over to the day-to-day dealings with the most important person who walks into the pro shop—the golfer. Marketing might lure a golfer to the golf course the first time, but the employees are the ones who can make the golfer want to come back.

The Pro Shop

The pro shop is the nerve center of the golf operation. It functions as a:

- Control point through which golfers enter and exit;
- Meeting place for players;
- Registration station and ticket window;
- Marketplace for golfing merchandise;
- Center of communications;
- Social and service center; and
- Merchandising area.

While the size and scope of pro shops vary widely, the business goals of pro shops are universal:

- To promote golf and the pleasure of the game;
- To provide outstanding service;
- To consistently execute management's policies;
- To provide a well-organized and attractive operation (both the physical aspects of the shop itself and the personnel who serve there) that makes golfers and other customers feel comfortable;
- To provide an outlet for equipment, apparel, and supplementary items.

Generally, the golf pro and his staff are responsible for formulating a business plan to cover all aspects of the facility, including staffing, marketing, a merchandising plan, inventory control, display and sales in the pro shop, guests' satisfaction, tee reservations, and operation of the golf range.

The details of day-to-day operation of the golf shop are typically guided by a procedures manual, which usually includes outlines for opening and closing the shop, registering or checking in golfers, operating the cash register, and keeping daily records and reports. It also includes rules and regulations for employees, with clearly stated management policies, and rules and regulations for patrons, with enforcement procedures.

Tee Time Systems

Tee time systems ensure the maximum potential rounds of golf at a facility. Most golf operations use a tee time reservation system that allows golfers to secure specific tee times in advance on a first-come, first-served basis. Semi-private clubs can structure advance reservation systems to give preference to members over daily-fee players (perhaps members may reserve space 72 hours in advance, daily-fee players 48 hours). The advance reservation system is a useful tool for modulating fluctuations of peak traffic. Computerized phone-in tee time reservation systems have been particularly helpful for public or daily-fee operations experiencing problems with excessive traffic on weekend mornings, when long lines of golfers would wait for a facility to open in the morning and hope to get a starting time.

Operations experiencing slow pickups or incomplete sales of available tee times might identify windows of opportunity and market them to secure tee times without loss of potential play as a result of tee times available at competing facilities. The golf pro might analyze the trend of incomplete pickups and might offer consistently available tee times to area businesses, hotels, or groups for tournament play or other events. If, on the other hand, a facility is consistently selling out tee times, driving rates up might be justified, thus enhancing operating profits. Other alternatives include adjusting the spacing of starting times or restructuring privileges by modifying policy.

Merchandising

"Merchandising" generally refers to the retail sales operation in the pro shop. Monitoring merchandising involves analyzing sales against established budgets to determine the shop's success or failure and as an indicator of performance. The analysis might be expressed in terms of:

- Sales per hour per employee (not often used);
- Retail sales per square foot (which can be difficult to measure because of the range of functions in the pro shop); or, more typically,
- Total sales per round, broken down by soft goods (clothing) and hard goods (golf equipment).

The trend in merchandising toward maintaining profit margins and an annual positive increase in sales volume is becoming more challenging. The price point of merchandise has declined, requiring the sale of more units to realize a growth in sales per round. Therefore, remaining current on retail trends and market demands is critical.

The type of golf operation affects the size of the merchandising area and its inventory. A wide range of hard goods and soft goods with the logo of the golf club or resort is essential in today's competitive market. Memorable golf holes aid significantly in the sale of sports items.

The length of the playing season also affects the size of the merchandising area and its inventory. A 1990 survey of golf operations conducted by the PGA shows that peak season inventories at private equity facilities with golf pros had an average retail value of $87,000, compared to an average inventory for the year of $41,000. In comparison, municipally owned facilities with golf pros had an inventory during peak season of $65,000 and an average for the year of $36,000. The highest volume of sales typically as for apparel, golf clubs, and golf balls.

In the majority of private golf clubs, the golf pro owns the pro shop (the retail operation) (over 60 percent in the 1990 survey by the PGA). In this case, the golf pro is responsible for purchasing, ordering, and merchandising goods and for maintaining inventory. In daily-fee operations, the golf pro might own the merchandising operation, or the inventory might be owned by the facility's owners with merchandising handled by the golf pro and staff. When the golf pro does not own the golf shop concession, the pro might be compensated by a bonus tied to personnel management, customers' satisfaction, and meeting the budget.

Effective merchandising covers a broad spectrum that goes beyond goods on the shelves. It begins with providing a full range of services rendered in a manner that reflects a positive professional image, directly related to:

- How personnel are dressed and present themselves to the public each day;
- The shop's neatness and orderliness;
- Readiness and orderly line up of golf cars or pull carts;
- Cleanliness of the storage room and bag room;
- How members and guests are treated;
- Cleanliness of equipment left or entrusted to the care of employees by guests;
- Quality of the scoreboards, signs, and scorecards.

Pro Shop Services

Providing "full service" is the key to a successful golf business. The pro shop (the golf pro and staff) provides a variety of services other than merchandising, including rentals of golf cars and golf clubs, bag storage for golfers and their guests, club repair, instruction, handicap services, and locker room services.

Golf car rentals are an integral part of the golf operation, as electric or gas golf cars are used at the majority of regulation golf facilities. At many facilities, their use is *required* during peak playing times. If golfers do not own their golf cars, they can lease them at the pro shop. The golf pro often owns the golf car concession and assumes responsibility for maintaining the fleet, and revenues from the concession are a key component of income. A successful golf car concession requires a high level of service, at the very least the provision of clean, well-maintained golf cars, scorecards, and information about the course, and easy access to and exit from the course.

Over 80 percent of clubs surveyed by the PGA in 1990 rented golf clubs. Such rental operations are generally more extensive at resorts and daily-fee facilities. Storage for golf bags is generally provided at private clubs and daily-fee facilities with a membership program, although storage facilities are usually less extensive at daily-fee facilities. The majority of pro shops repair golf clubs—gripping, whipping, reshafting, refinishing, and adjusting clubs—and assembling custom clubs.

The majority of golf facilities offer golf instruction for individuals or groups by the golf pro and staff. Teaching facilities generally consist of the golf range, putting and chipping greens, and, in some instances, practice holes. Facilities specializing in golf instruction (associated with large resorts or formal golf schools) usually include indoor classrooms, videotape facilities, and other teaching aids.

The pro shop should also provide a handicap service, for at many golf facilities, a player cannot participate in local events without an established handicap. A player usually establishes his or her handicap by playing a minimum number of rounds at the "home" course. The service generally entails issuing a handicap card and providing a means for posting scores and maintaining related records. Some computerized systems are designed specifically for the handicap service. Providing such a service, coupled with the minimum number of rounds required, provides a method of generating income through greens fees.[1] A separate fee can be charged for the handicap service, or the cost of the service can be rolled into the greens fee.

USGA has established a "slope rating" system that enables golfers who play on courses of varying difficulty to compete with each other on the same level. A new golf facility should arrange for the course to be rated by the governing golf committee (organized by the state or region) before the course opens to establish the rating for each tee position and the slope rating for the course. The golf committee follows the prescribed procedures established by USGA for rating the course. The ratings should then be made available for golfers' use by posting the course rating and slope rating on signs and on scorecards.

Food and Beverage Facilities

Food and beverage operations have become more streamlined over the past decade, reflecting changing lifestyles and the cost of maintaining them. In the 1990 PGA survey cited earlier, about 60 percent of golf clubhouses offered a full-service dining room, over 80 percent provided a snack bar, and about 70 percent provided a bar/lounge. Because this survey represents all types of operations, it is likely that food and beverage operations at recently completed facilities are scaled back.

Full-service, formal dining rooms are generally offered in larger private facilities, which might also provide service for outside banquets and meetings. More often, family-oriented eating facilities are the norm. Clubs that host a high volume of golf tournaments or special events might provide the additional capacity to handle the food requirements for such events, perhaps casual, buffet-style lunches, picnics, or dinners following the event.

In a golf-oriented real estate development, certain factors can affect the viability of the food and beverage operation, such as accessibility to the clubhouse from outside the development and competing restaurants in the area.

Golf operations without a membership base, such as a municipal or daily-fee course, normally have a small snack bar with limited food service (a grill). For these operations, the food and beverage concession is often leased to an outside vendor.

Service on the course is often provided during special events. It could take the form of vending carts or soft drink vending machines at "halfway houses" or other rest areas. Providing convenient services for golfers, such as roving beverage carts, can be very profitable, and the aroma of hot dogs

cooking on a grill near the ninth green can be a good draw.

Cleanliness of the food and beverage facilities is a primary concern. Personnel must know the proper temperatures and techniques for holding and preparing food, as illness from improperly handled food is a high probability. Local and state regulations govern the proper storage of food and the storage and handling of chemicals in food preparation areas. Certificates are required of all employees who work in these areas, and management's policies should reinforce careful adherence to established guidelines.

The chef or manager of food and beverage facilities generally sets standards for portion control and presentation of food. Cost-effective inventory control is essential for eliminating waste from spoilage and from tying up cash in excessive inventory.

Although achieving a profit in a food and beverage operation can be difficult, creative marketing and merchandising and cost-effective controls can yield positive results.

Marketing Golf

A golf operation is a profit center. If the market does not supply sufficient rounds of golf to sustain a profitable operation, then management might need to seek out other sources of business by promoting the golf operation. The basic keys of a promotional marketing program include advertising, publicity, and public relations.

Planning the promotional marketing program for a golf facility can occur with the project's inception and the hiring of a name golf course architect or the design of a signature hole to create a marketable image for the golf course. The design of the course strongly influences a facility's perceived image, identity, value, and marketability.

Marketing a golf facility should be geared to specific objectives for the operation. Depending on those objectives, the marketing program could be designed to:

■ Build up play when the facility opens;
■ Fill in soft periods, such as shoulder and off-seasons;

■ Develop repeat business; or
■ Capitalize on the facility's competitive advantage over other facilities in the market.

Repeat business is a key to successful golf operations, whether public or private. Providing the highest standards of professional service, value, and satisfaction brings back customers.

Marketing Tools

A key marketing tool for the sales program of a golf facility is a top-quality (but not necessarily expensive) brochure and rate card. It might simply provide information about how to reach the facility. Graphics and text should reflect the emotional values of the golfing experience the facility offers.

The brochure could serve as a calling card that can be left for distribution to potential patrons or buyers in a hotel or travel agency, for example. It could also be used for potential customers to look over after visiting another course. Brochures can be distributed through a direct-mail campaign. Business cards, scorecards, bag tags, and ball markers are effective marketing tools that can be used in conjunction with the brochure and rate card. Methods of distributing brochures vary according to the targeted market and the marketing program, but potential places for distribution include area hotels and transit centers, the local chamber of commerce or visitors center, convention bureaus, travel agencies and group tour organizers, major businesses, and golf and sporting goods stores.

The golf facility's logo is a particularly useful graphic tool for establishing the project's image. Typically, the logo is used on all signs and other graphic materials, including letterhead, business cards, brochures, and scorecards. A strong graphic design coupled with its repeated use on marketing materials aids in establishing identity and recognition for the project. Often, the logo is used as a merchandising tool as well, particularly for large destination resorts where the sale of merchandise imprinted with the resort's logo is an integral part of the marketing program. Logos can be imprinted or em-

Shinyo #7, the signature hole.

- *Electronic media:* Radio and television coverage. Because of its expense, this type of advertising is usually limited to coordination with special events.
- *Direct mail:* Coordinated campaigns are used to reach targeted audiences, which might include individual residences, markets, businesses, or travel and real estate companies.
- *Sales call:* Brochures and other print materials are key tools of advertising a facility to potential customers and generating referral business from hotels, travel agencies, convention planners, visitors bureaus, and so on.
- *Outdoor advertising:* Identification signs, directional signs, billboards, and bench and temporary signs.

Publicity

Free advertising results from media coverage of special events or news. The facility's management can use several strategies to obtain free exposure or publicity:

- Develop press releases on upcoming major events and the results of major events;
- Submit articles to trade publications;
- Invite representatives of the print media as guests to see what the facility has to offer;
- Host free clinics, contests, or meetings of area business organizations;
- Participate in awards programs that acknowledge excellence in different categories, such as merchandising, grounds maintenance, and operation of golf shops, requiring only a small investment of time to file an application.

Promoting the course should be coordinated with the golf course architect's promotional program.

Public Relations

Public relations is often the most powerful method of generating and keeping business at a golf course, for the backbone of any marketing effort is the personnel who manage the facility's day-to-day operations. The manner in which staff members greet guests, service their needs, and assist in solving any problems that arise affects a

broidered on everything from tees, bag tags, balls, and ball markers to towels, shirts, and hats. It is a powerful means of gaining exposure and free advertising.

Advertising

Advertising can be an expensive means of gaining exposure, and selecting opportune times and appropriate publications to get the message to the public is a critical factor in cost-effective advertising. Generally, advertising should be used in conjunction with rate adjustments to generate business during the shoulder season and off-season. If a golf course is part of a real estate development, advertising is often coordinated with real estate sales and marketing. Advertising should be directed to specific target markets and appeal to the emotional reasons for going to a golf course; its sole purpose is to deliver more rounds to the golf course and to sell real estate products faster.

Several methods of advertising can be used, depending on the market:

- *Print media:* Local newspapers, general- and special-interest magazines, travel guides.

patron's desire to return, again and again. Word-of-mouth testimonials from satisfied customers are for the most part the least costly and most effective marketing tool available, for "first-class service and programming are the biggest business-drawing and advertising factors, next to the character and condition of the course itself."[2]

While publicity is often a useful vehicle for generating additional business, the testimonials of satisfied patrons can generate additional business through referrals. Editorial coverage by local and regional newspapers, newsletters, or magazines add to the credibility and visibility of a golf facility. An in-house newsletter is a useful vehicle for generating good feelings and a sense of community pride between management and membership by providing a forum for communications and recognition of accomplishments by staff and members. Press releases about special events, guests' accomplishments (tournament results), and staff members' accomplishments (professional awards) are useful for enhancing public relations.

The golf pro's involvement in community and golf associations helps public relations and marketing a golf facility. Arrangements can be made to host local, state, and regional amateur golf events during off seasons and slow days of the week. The pro's active involvement with schools and local civic groups can generate business for the off season and slow days.

The need for and desirability of acquiring the services of a professional public relations firm should be explored in the context of a particular development. A club with no significant national tournament will not need such services, while a facility that is home to a PGA event could. When golf is part of a large project like a resort complex or new community, public relations and marketing go hand-in-hand.

Creative Marketing

In very difficult markets, it might be better to join forces with the competition than to struggle alone, thereby establishing a stronger customer base and greater repeat business and translating into more rounds of golf. Working together, two or more facilities can collectively promote the sport of golf and golfing facilities in a mutually beneficial manner that is more productive than a single campaign. Collective advertising and promotions can feed rounds of golf from one facility to another. The alliance of facilities can provide golfers with more variety, encouraging more play.

This type of arrangement is not particularly revolutionary. Many private clubs have reciprocal membership agreements with other clubs. In some cases, such reciprocal agreements engender higher membership fees, because golfers in essence buy the privilege of playing golf at other clubs, making the membership more valuable. A group of resort courses might join a collective marketing effort to tap a highly competitive market, offering golfers the opportunity to play several different courses as part of a vacation package. Similarly, a collective of daily-fee courses might offer a "bounce-back coupon," which allows golfers to play another course at a reduced fee during the week as space is available. Competition is not necessarily an enemy.

Marketing Golf-Oriented Real Estate

Residential developments oriented toward the lifestyle surrounding a golf course have an almost universal appeal in the marketplace. Residential

---

Orlando World Center

Location: Orlando, Florida

Owner: Marriott Hotel Properties Limited Partnership

Operator: Marriott Golf (division of Marriott Corporation)

Golf Course Architect: Joe Lee

Marriott's Orlando World Center is located near Walt Disney World in central Florida. The 200-acre resort and convention center includes a 1,500-room hotel and conference center with 150,000 square feet of exhibit space and several conference rooms, five restaurants, and a golf clubhouse. An additional 200 timeshare units are oriented around the 18-hole, 6,300-yard golf course. The Orlando World Center also includes an extensive swimming pool complex, 12 lighted tennis courts, and fitness/exercise facilities. The golf clubhouse includes a 2,500-square-foot restaurant, a 1,500-square-foot pro shop, locker rooms, and a golf car facility.

Orlando World Center is a highly successful resort with a simple and effective management structure. The director of golf and the director of marketing confer on the best methods for blending golf into the resort's overall marketing plan, keeping in mind budgeting and management constraints developed under the direction of the resort's general manager. Marriott Golf provides consulting services and philosophical guidance for the golf operation, establishing a high level of operating standards.

The resort is oriented toward convention and group business. The golf course is just a few paces from the front door and serves as a strong selling point. The marketing

Management structure.

program's focus is international in keeping with the demand associated with Disney World. While golf is a secondary attraction for transient resort guests, it is a strong factor in attracting meeting planners. The golf operation nevertheless benefits from the golf rounds and revenue generated by the resort's substantial clientele. The golf marketing programs are focused on local daily-fee play and on increasing activity from the guests at hand. Minimal effort is made to market the facility as "a golf resort."

An additional 175 timeshare units are under development. Timeshare owners have a 60-day window in which to reserve their stay. A specially tailored package plan for weekly unlimited play is aimed at timeshare owners. Tee time is otherwise the same as for other resort guests, which is 90 days in advance.

Source: Tony Austin, director of golf, Orlando World Center.

products might range from single-family estates to high-rise condominiums and rental apartments. The ambience of a golf course community attracts golfers and nongolfers alike.

The golf course has tremendous potential as a major marketing tool for real estate sales, and the real estate sales program should take full advantage of that potential. Marketing golf-oriented real estate involves merchandising the distinctly attractive combination of *location* and *lifestyle.* Buying golf-oriented real estate is just as much, if not more, an emotional purchase of the prestige, recognition, services, and amenities associated with golf-oriented projects as it is a purchase of needed shelter. Marketing consultants advise that individuals prefer to think of *joining* a club or community rather than *buying* a membership or real estate product.

Sales and Marketing

A developer of golf-oriented real estate can target the sales program directly to consumers (buyers of sites or houses, just like a residential development), or they can target builders to stimulate speculative building of selected sites through purchase or a joint venture or contract fee arrangement. For either scenario, it is generally advisable that the developer maintain complete control over the real estate sales and merchandising programs. Thus, the developer can supervise sales for the entire project, coordinate marketing for the golf course and the real estate, and maintain control over merchandising the real estate to prevent the introduction of poorly selling products that might create a negative image for the project.

Under a master marketing/sales program, the developer can charge each builder a marketing/sales fee based on percentage of the gross sale price, payable upon closing. Under this arrangement, the developer advances costs, and builders pay only for performance. The primary thrust of such a coordinated marketing plan must be "community" and "lifestyle" first, with individual housing taking a secondary position. With a master marketing/sales program, builders can achieve a higher level of professionalism and greater market penetration and economies of scale.

Marriott's Desert Springs Resort

Location: Palm Desert, California
Operator: Marriott Corporation
Golf Course Architect: Ted Robinson

Marriott's Desert Springs Resort is located in the resort community of Palm Desert, centrally positioned in the Coachella Valley 120 miles east of Los Angeles. Developed as an oasis in the California desert, the 400-acre resort includes an 895-room luxury hotel, 51,000 square feet of meeting and exhibit space, two 18-hole golf courses, an 18-hole putting course, 20 tennis courts, three swimming pools, a 27,000-square-foot spa, and several restaurants—all set among 35 acres of freshwater lakes and streams. Phased construction of 236 timeshare villas is part of the resort's real estate development master plan, with completion anticipated in 1994.

Desert Springs Resort is marketed as a showcase of luxury and activity. Management is strongly committed to providing superb service and hospitality, luxury accommodations, and unsurpassed recreational experiences for guests. During the winter season, Desert Springs targets an international market; during the summer, it shifts the emphasis to a regional market. It also targets large corporations that can bring groups to the hotel for conventions and business meetings.

Management of the resort operations and golf operations is coordinated. The director of golf and the resident manager coordinate decisions about golf. The marketing program for resort and golf operations, for example, offers a four-day/three-night or seven-day/six-night single- or double-occupancy accommodations at the resort hotel with unlimited golf, free breakfast, and welcoming gifts. Another package provides double-occupancy accommodations at the resort hotel with unlimited golf, unlimited tennis, and entrance to the spa. The golf courses are open to the public, but hotel guests and villa guests are given a 30-day window for booking tee times, while non-hotel guests are given only a three-day window.

The timeshare units are marketed under Marriott's vacation ownership plan, which makes timeshare ownership more flexible. Owners can trade a vacation week (Friday

Management structure.

Marriott's Desert Springs Resort in Palm Desert, California.

It is the developer's responsibility to ensure that the real estate products created in the community satisfy the needs and desires of the marketplace for design and price. At a minimum, covenants should be created to regulate design through architectural review and the developer's approval. The developer should encourage complementary product lines by builders to ensure maximum absorption of housing rather than head-to-head competition between builders.

Staffing

Staffing for a community real estate sales office usually includes a sales manager, a secretary/receptionist, and a sufficient number of sales associates to serve prospective buyers. It is generally preferable to have a developer-owned and -operated on-site sales operation staffed with personnel who are dedicated to sale of the community. The staff must be trained and supervised in the intricacies of selling golf-oriented real estate. A full-time staff should be available on-site to handle new traffic, follow up with undecided buyers, and develop prospects.

Selecting personnel is critical. On-site sales of golf communities require a special personality and demeanor. Personnel must be willing to staff the sales office and make the same presentation over and over again with enthusiasm. They must be highly motivated and have a strong ability to close a sale on a limited group of products instead of relying on a multiple listing book to select another house to show.

Staff must receive professional training so they have full knowledge of the product and the marketing presentation. Sales personnel must be of appropriate age, social status, and lifestyle so they can identify with prospective clients and establish credibility and rapport. Sales associates must first sell themselves, then the community and lifestyle, and finally the product. Staff should dress appropriately to reflect the golfing lifestyle.

Marketing Presentation

The marketing presentation should be organized to assist the staff in merchandising the community and lifestyle. A typical marketing presentation might include the following steps:

---

to Friday) within the season they own for vacations in other locations all over the world. A "floating time reservation system" allows owners to request reservations in advance by mail on the basis of first received, first reserved. Four options are available for ownership:

1. Occupancy

This option allows three choices:

- *Regular occupancy,* entitling owners to use a two-bedroom, two-bath villa for seven nights within the season they own;

- *Lockout option,* allowing owners to use the master suite for a seven-night interval of their choice and the guest suite for a separate seven-night interval within the season owned. (Each two-bedroom villa is designed so that the master suite [one bedroom, bath, kitchen, and dining and living rooms with a sleeper sofa in the living room] can be used independently of the guest suite [an efficiency unit with two double beds and a bath].)

- *Split-week option,* allowing owners to divide the entire two-bedroom villa for the seven-night vacation into two segments: a three-night period (Friday through Sunday) and again for a four-night period (Monday through Thursday).

2. Exchange

An owner may trade for time at another Marriott-owned resort, another season at the home resort, or one of 800 resorts worldwide. Comparable accommodations are determined by the villa's sleeping capacity and the season owned. Only full weeks may be exchanged.

3. HGA Points

Each deeded week of ownership may be traded for "points" in the Marriott Honored Guest Awards (HGA) program. HGA points are credited to an account, which may be redeemed in the form of travel certificates honored by Marriott hotels, selected airline partners, and car rental agencies.

One of the golf courses at Marriott's Desert Springs Resort.

COURTESY: MARRIOTT'S DESERT SPRINGS

4. Rental

Owners may choose to rent the week(s) they own through their own rental broker, or they may list their week for rent through the Marriott Resorts Hospitality Corporation. MRHC does not guarantee rental of the villa, but it does notify owners two weeks in advance if it cannot rent the villa. If the villa is not rented, owners still have the option of a "Flexchange" deposit, which accommodates last-minute travel plans from seven to 59 days before the desired travel date.

The 1,650-square-foot timeshare villas are completely furnished. The villas are reached via an entry road dedicated to the complex, and the complex has its own clubhouse, swimming pools, exercise room, and convenience store, as well as access to the hotel and resort. The two-story villas front on the golf course.

Source: Tim Skogen, director of golf.

- *Greeting.* Initial impressions are critical. The secretary/receptionist is often the first representative a visitor sees. The greeting should always be pleasant and welcoming.
- *Warm-up and gathering information.* Sales associates must establish their credibility and rapport with the visitor, known as the "warm-up." Upon establishing rapport, sales associates must learn information about visitors to determine their needs and then tailor the presentation accordingly. Friendly inquiries about the visitor's name, where he or she lives, and how he or she learned about the community provide sales associates with an idea of the visitor's qualifications.
- *Presentation.* The presentation should be an interactive process between the sales associate and the visitor, with the visitor allowed to do at least half the talking. Appeals to all five senses should be used to create the strongest possible impressions. Graphic displays should support the sales associate's efforts to sell location and lifestyle. A tour of the property, if appropriate, should include all amenities and housing products.
- *Reduction to writing.* The sales associate next calculates purchase figures for the visitor, with the financial burden presented as a net monthly "investment" (after tax advantages). Visitors are provided with brochures or packages to allow them to reflect on their visit in a more leisurely and informal setting.
- *Closing.* While closing a sale on the first visit is not typical, the sales associate should always try. At the minimum, the associate should make a specific appointment for a follow-up, with follow-up phone calls considered a required part of any sales effort.

Cooperative Brokerage Programs

A cooperative brokerage program is a means of providing access to prospects who cannot otherwise be reached effectively through advertising. Such a cooperative program costs nothing until a sale is made; therefore, it provides a means of expanding the market without risking advertising dollars.

Cooperative brokerage allows a developer to gain referrals from outside brokers or real estate agents without relinquishing control over the marketing and sales program. Implementing a cooperative brokerage program must be professional, thorough, and direct. Typically, such a program is initiated through direct mail to outside brokers, inviting them to attend sales presentations and promotions by on-site sales staff. The on-site sales staff can also promote and enhance cooperative brokerage programs through active and visible participation in local real estate activities. The goal is to generate visits to the site by individual brokers for registration in a cooperative brokerage program.

On-site sales associates give brokers or agents visiting the site a full tour and formal presentation about the community's features, lifestyle, products, financing techniques, and so on, as if they were prospective buyers. The presentation also details the broker referral program and arrangements for commissions. Brokers are provided with a complete package, including a written description of specific procedures and terms of the cooperative brokerage program, and are effectively registered in the program upon completion of the presentation.

A broker can refer a prospect to the on-site sales staff by phone to set up a specific appointment with the on-site staff. Generally, the broker is not required to attend the sales presentation with the client but may do so if the client desires. The on-site sales staff makes the sales presentation on behalf of the referring broker; the advance arrangements and registration protect the broker's commission.

Sales Center

Because the golf course serves as a major marketing tool, an on-site sales office should be located nearby to convey the project's image and lifestyle. Thus, key sales staff must be involved in planning and design. The strategies and timing involved in real estate sales can directly affect the project's design and construction phasing. For instance, the sales office might be located in a model unit or temporary structure, particularly if the real estate sales program precedes the construction of the golf course and related facilities. The sales office could then later be moved or relocated to the clubhouse, a model unit, or a sales center near the golf course.

The design team must create an environment that reflects the project's image from the moment the real estate sales staff is scheduled to begin its efforts. Whether the sales effort is kicked off from a temporary trailer parked on the construction site or an office in a remote location, the sales center must convey a positive image of the project. Ideally, the sales center is a separate building overlooking a lake on the golf course.

Important elements of site design directly affect the sales efforts:

- All signs should clearly reflect the project's image and quality on and off the site, including an identification sign, sales and advertising signs, and directional signs.
- The streetscape should project a strong organization of circulation systems and orientation, including furnishings (sidewalks, lighting, benches, trash receptacles, and so on), landscaping, and views of the golf course.
- The layout and design of the sales center should include a reception area, a display and presentation area, an office for the sales staff, and support spaces like rest rooms, lounges, and storage.

The location and layout of the sales center should provide the sales staff with maximum management and control over traffic and flow through the project. The overall environment should capitalize on the development's every positive aspect, and marketing and competitive advantage. Every reason that could cause a prospect not to buy or not to close with the sales staff should be removed.

Merchandising

To properly present the community and real estate, an integral part of the sales process includes the use of on-site displays and graphics that will attract and educate prospective purchasers. These displays and graphic elements must be properly sequenced to build the buyer's acceptance, excitement, and interest. In essence, they act as cue cards for the sales presentation or a self-tour during peak traffic. The sales display area should create an exciting and appealing presentation about the location, environment, community, amenities, real estate products, lifestyle, and developer/ builder team. Ideally, such a presentation would include a welcome board, storyboards to convey information, the master plan and/or site plans, floor plans, and building elevation drawings.

Because many people find it difficult to visualize a project from drawings, a three-dimensional scale model of the project, including the golf course, can be an important marketing tool. Scale models of houses, retail shops, hotels, and other elements of the project are also significant marketing tools, particularly when sales precede actual construction.

Brochures and Collateral Materials

The package provided prospective purchasers to take with them allows them to review materials in a less-controlled environment. The package must be carefully developed to reinforce the project's image and desirability. Graphics should impart credibility, prestige, and a sense of substance with photos of the site appropriate to target markets. Graphics and text should stress the attractive lifestyle, the community's distinctiveness and superior location, and the livability of houses. The package sets the stage for conversion of the prospect to a purchaser.

A typical package for a residential development oriented toward golf might include:

- *A master brochure/"holder-folder"* that includes a location map on the back cover with highlights of all conveniences and features. This master brochure serves as a folder for other inserts.
- *Village/neighborhood inserts* detailing the identity of individual neigh-

borhoods, their lifestyle, amenities, and site plan.
- *Golf course inserts* promoting the lifestyle, image, and quality of the course, with information about what the facilities offer, how to join or reach the facilities, membership packages, rates, special programs and events, and so on. (If the golf course is owned or operated by someone other than the developer, the presentations must be carefully coordinated so that the materials appear to be part of the presentation.)
- *Product inserts* that include floor plans (at a minimum 1/4" scale) to accentuate roominess, elevations, and features and options. Generally, the prospect should be given only one or two plans to avoid confusion. Materials from a number of builders should be coordinated to have the appearance of being part of the presentation.
- *A purchase analysis* to present an estimate for a specific buyer of effective cost of ownership for a specific house with options and features selected. It illustrates initial investment (not downpayment) and effective monthly investment after tax benefits. A price list is not advisable, because it displays absolute numbers that can frighten away a prospect.
- *Promotional items* that might include carefully selected reprints of editorials, feature stories, and other testimonials about the project, principals, and team from local, regional, national, or international sources. They might also include items of general interest about the area's quality of life.

Model Homes

Model homes are a popular method of merchandising residential projects. Whether the developer is the primary builder or a number of builders are involved, model homes should be professionally merchandised. Both the exterior streetscape and interior design of a model home are as important in many ways as its architectural design. Properly decorated models should highlight special features and lifestyles, show rooms that are spacious and livable, and impart a feeling of comfort. A poorly decorated model

home can make a good product substantially less salable. Model homes must be merchandised to potential markets with a clear view of buyers' lifestyles, incomes, ages, and tastes. While furnishings and accessories can be innovative and imaginative, they must be directed specifically to potential purchasers with regard to their budget, sophistication, and lifestyle.

Special consideration must be given to convenience and comfort of circulation in the display of model homes. If access to the models is by automobile, the parking area and sidewalks should allow comfortable and easy exit from the auto and approach to the models. Doing so generally includes providing a level, paved surface for the parking area and sidewalks sufficiently wide to allow two people to walk comfortably side by side. If several model units are offered, the circulation system should be designed to minimize walking distance. Landscaping should be used to direct views toward the golf course, provide shade or shelter from wind, heighten the emotional appeal of the model, and assist in orientation and direction. On the interior, passage doors, hinges, and hardware are usually not installed to facilitate free access and to enlarge the perceived size of the unit. Doors to linen closets are also usually not installed, often replaced with Plexiglas barriers to provide visual access while protecting the display. The placement of furniture must preserve sight lines and allow appropriate traffic patterns. Exterior living spaces, such as decks and patios, should also be fully furnished and landscaped to reflect the golf lifestyle. Model units should be located on the golf course or with a view of it. Special attention should be given to enhancing and framing desirable views from the model, as well as from the golf course to the models.

Notes

1. Martin T. Kavanaugh II, *Marketing the Public Golf Course* (Palm Beach Gardens, Fla.: Professional Golfers Association of America, 1990), p. 16.

2. Herb Graffis, *Golfdom Magazine*, 1941, cited in Kavanaugh, *Marketing the Public Golf Course*, p. 13.

Looking Back And Looking Ahead

The Past Is Prologue
by Desmond Muirhead

Golf course communities should not be cold or rigid enterprises but filled with the passions of life and living. Their design should stir men's blood. We who design these communities must be more than engineers. We must call on emotions and know-how, and we must insist on generating a fundamental human warmth as well as technical correctness.

Wakagi #14.

Golf courses by their very nature are intensely romantic creations, following a loose set of principles. I can think of no golf course that is considered "great" that is confined to single fairways surrounded by houses. Nor do the most celebrated golf course communities depend on single fairways alone. Experience tells us that the strictest program combined with the most direct technical methodology seldom produces the best architecture in terms of buildings or golf. Perversely, greatness stubbornly breaks the mold and bends the rules, and a truly great or original golf course affects land values for miles around, regardless of frontage on the fairway.

Golf courses like Pebble Beach or Cypress Point are more famous than the landmarks they occupy. While they accept some houses, these courses have made few concessions to the idea of a golf course community, yet the land around both courses is now priceless.

In a much more modest way, land values at some of our own golf course communities have increased. The early designs of 25 years ago were the first of the genre to combine the then new ideas of condominiums and planned unit developments. The first three we designed were Bay Meadows in Jacksonville, Florida, Mission Hills in Palm Springs, California, and Boca West in Boca Raton, Florida. The sites when I first saw them were flat and empty fields or sandy wastelands miles from nowhere.

Real estate analysts told us that all the projects were too far out of town and highly speculative ventures. But I knew that real estate analysts could only follow trends and were unable to predict the powerful stimulus of new ideas. Each of these projects was in its own way a break-through; each became the central hub for numerous other golf course communities as well as hotels, offices, and shopping centers. The residents of Bay Meadows have seen the surrounding countryside converted into a massive industrial and commercial edge city covering thousands of acres. Clearly, our golf course communities must have identity and thus create a sense of place.

How Did We Get Where We Are?

Three great international booms have occurred in the history of building golf courses—in the 1860s, the 1920s, and the 1980s. The most recent saw years of impetuous spending worldwide by the deregulated savings and loan (S&L) institutions in this country and by the Japanese elsewhere. Some good projects were built, but the S&Ls produced hordes

of large ugly houses on single fairways, and most of these projects are now bankrupt or in dire financial straits. The Japanese government, uncomfortable because of the adverse balance of payments among its trading partners, told its citizens that it was patriotic to spend freely on luxury items abroad, including golf. The Japanese spent huge sums gambling on a nonexistent market overseas, incorrectly assuming it would be like home. Much of their investment consequently was lost on impossibly expensive golf ventures. With Japan in a recession, similar investments are restricted by the banks. None of this money is likely to be so readily available again.

With the end of the present boom in the United States and in most of the rest of the world, belt tightening has become common. We should never forget that over 4,000 golf courses in this country were closed during the Great Depression of the 1930s. Little doubt remains that investors in golf course communities of the future will require a very thorough, realistically conservative analysis of the possible returns and a viable exit strategy before they get involved. Realistic financial analysis will be healthy for the entire golf industry, and this book should be valuable for that purpose.

Any serious discussion of the future of golf course communities must start with the golf course itself and must answer a question: Why do we need golf courses at all? Some years ago, two ingredients would put a neophyte community firmly on the map—a shopping center or a golf course. It is almost impossible to build a shopping center of any size until the adjoining community provides a market, but it is nearly always possible to build a golf course if the developer does his homework. Today golf courses must not only raise the value of the land around them, but must also pay their way after they are launched. The days of very high membership fees are gone, and steep monthly dues are increasingly unpopular. A realistic attitude to the various problems requires the reduction of the cost of constructing a golf

course and its subsequent maintenance.

The alternative could be for the private courses attached to golf communities to move gradually toward the Japanese ideal of 1,000 corporate memberships for each course, with about 6,000 potential players, each of whom is lucky to play once a month. These numbers probably are not reasonable for the United States or Britain, although numbers of members per course will undoubtedly increase in both countries. Much higher membership numbers are already occurring in some more densely populated areas of the world.

Cutting the costs of golf courses might not be as difficult as it seems. Extravagant clubhouses, loose design, overly wide fairways, elaborate waterfalls, extensive bulkheads, planting of large or mature trees, unnecessarily heavy grading, and other elements can often be cut in half with careful budgeting. Selecting the site for its golfing and housing qualities can significantly reduce the cost of the course. The ideal site is in a valley where the land rolls every 200 to 250 yards with grades of less than 10 percent, good sites for greens, a change in elevation of about 70 feet, well-drained sandy soil that dries quickly after rain, tall existing trees of a species suitable for golf, and lakes already there. If all or most of these requirements are present, the cost of the course can be much reduced. By being ruthlessly realistic with the figures, the developer can always balance the budget without a total collapse in the quality of design.

Maintenance for Golf Courses

Annual maintenance costs must be cut sharply, and just to hold the line will need some drastic revisions. We have unfortunately become used to the nail-clipper-perfect turf and synthetic traps and mounds of modern golf courses. Our urge in this country is to clarify, simplify, organize, sanitize, glamorize, and glorify, and that is exactly what we have done to golf courses, resulting in skyrocketing maintenance costs and monthly dues.

A little history might help here. My home course in England had one maintenance man and no irrigation system. It cost almost nothing to build, but it had an excellent site. The greens fee was a quarter. In the early days of St. Andrews in Scotland, there was no greens fee; later it was a dollar. In the 1950s, St. Andrews had a maintenance staff of 13 for four courses. Few people complained. Noted golf writer Ron Whitten grew up on a course in Kansas with a maintenance crew of six, and he remembers it with great affection. Pine Valley in Clementon, New Jersey, one of the world's finest courses, once had a maintenance crew of fewer than 10 and a superior sense of authority and integrity. Today 36 people maintain 18 holes at Pine Valley. The original majesty of this fascinating and beautiful course has been much reduced by the morbid chastity of the island fairways and the elaborately manicured roughs.

This new style of maintenance at Pine Valley is contrary to the original spirit of the game of golf, and this particular brand of golf course kitsch is a disparagement of the memory of its architects and builders. Unfortunately, the quest for perfect turf is affecting other courses anxious to emulate the leading golf clubs. Abetted by escalating pressure from homeowners with perfect lawns and touring pros who could lose $50,000 on an imperfect lie, we now have fairways that are better than greens on the older courses. The proliferating schools for golf superintendents have put additional pressure on their graduates to produce perfect turf—and the costs of maintenance keep going up. Somehow golf needs a simpler, more reasonable attitude toward maintenance.

Many effective ways can reduce maintenance costs—using slowly growing or low-maintenance grasses, reducing the number and complexity of traps and other hazards, making all grades subject to a nine-gang hydraulic-lift mower, or using special grasses, far less water, and a more efficient system for irrigation. But what we really need to change is the philosophy of maintenance.

John MacLaren, the Scotsman who built the bellwether of city parks, Golden Gate in San Francisco, and maintained it for 60 years, knew he could not afford a Versailles. So he allowed the park to go semiwild with relaxed, informal edges. He used drifts of four trees—Monterey pine, Monterey cypress, Tasmanian blue gum, and Sydney golden wattle—which made naturally elegant groups however they were planted. He made a counterpoint to the tree groups with rough-cut lawns that swooped and rolled across the landscape to create a thousand vistas. Golden Gate has an easy, rugged naturalness, with the whole greater than its parts. It is not a pallid imitation of nature, but a celebration of the essence of nature. Our golf courses will have to reduce their emphasis on perfect turf and edges and take a leaf out of John MacLaren's book. We must try to strike a balance between the naturalness of Golden Gate Park of 50 years ago and the demands of the modern golfer.

Ecology and Golf

Ecology, that much-misused term, is firmly entrenched in the game of golf. We tend to forget that ecology is dynamic, even though coastlines recede, sandhills shift, and lakes and marshes fill in. Golf courses are also dynamic and need not be negative influences on the environment. In many places, golf courses, like efficient farming, have become part of the working landscape. Unfortunately, a kind of morbid, negative ecology seems to be here to stay.

In Japan, technicians for the prefectural governments test the groundwater from the golf courses regularly for the concentration of nitrates and other harmful chemicals. The architects, owners, and maintenance crews are kept honest by this simple, recommended method. Tournament golf takes in so much money and gives so little back to ecological causes. This situation will have to change, and golf sorely needs

stronger leadership to make the changes. A commissioner with far-reaching powers over both amateur and professional golf, like the one for baseball, and a national public relations and advertising campaign, are surely necessary. No strong leadership exists at the moment, and the environment has become a serious stumbling block. It need not be if golf's ecological problems and solutions are properly publicized. If we do not solve this issue head on, the number of golf courses and golf course communities built will decline.

Safety in Golf

Safety standards have little validity. They are arbitrarily changed by individuals and organizations whose power is more apparent then real. Like any game, golf entails certain risks for the player. Safety standards in sports are eroded by increasingly strong players and increasingly improved equipment, and architects are expected to change the design of golf courses accordingly. Golf courses in general have grown by over 1,000 yards in length and an average of 30 yards in width since the turn of the century. If present trends continue, fairways will be as wide as they are long and costs will become prohibitive. Some sort of limits must be observed to regulate equipment and to put some sort of cap on safety requirements. The industry itself should emphasize that safety standards are impossible and should then close ranks on legal decisions by providing qualified witnesses endorsing this fact.

Golf Course Communities

The type of course to build poses another problem. Driving ranges, par-3 courses, and executive courses are the most profitable to build but are the shortest and have the least desirable frontage. Courses for the PGA tour complete with spectator mounds that are used once a year are potentially expensive white elephants, and homeowners in general do not like annual tournaments because of the

need for added security. Something in between is needed.

The future of golf courses is invested with their value for sales promotion. Originality, personality, and identity are increasingly required for successful sales. Clubhouses generally should be smaller and neater, more human and less pretentious. The new generation is less status conscious than its parents. We enclose too much space and so lose intimacy in the clubhouses—and incidentally increase the costs of air conditioning. Locker rooms must be celebrated as airy palaces with bars, not sequestered as latter-day dungeons.

Roads should be designed as though they have a purpose. They should lead somewhere and have a destination. They should not just be a connection of meandering S-curves from some landscape architect's drawing. Housing around golf courses needs some serious thinking. We must return a new form of clustering to avoid the limp linear expression and the numbing repetition of so much frontage housing today.

Individual units need small changes in color, features, and detail so that they feel different. A sense of place should be developed for each village as well as for the whole community. Each village should have a different color and texture for its roofs and walls, and be separated in communities of like interests. Changes of pace and orientation points, such as clusters of trees, should give each village and the entire community a solid identity. A personality and a sense of place should emerge.

A recent trend toward large resorts with several golf courses points toward new towns with complete facilities. The trend toward working at home—30 million U.S. citizens now work out of their homes—will create an ever-greater tendency toward recreational suburban satellite communities. Lippo Village in Jakarta, Indonesia, for example, is one such recreational town, where the golf course is also used as a park and a point of identification for the entire community instead of a few wealthy inhabitants.

The future will undoubtedly dictate three-story and higher-density developments, such as Park Newport in Newport Beach, California, which has 1,300 units on 36 acres, and more Desert Islands, whose distinct residential village areas are separated by golf courses. Such schemes have more coherence than simple single-fairway developments, and the incremental value is often larger. (They do require more development capital, however.)

It takes a person of exceptional ability—and often exceptional ruthlessness—just to stop a golf course community from going bankrupt, let alone make it beautiful and economically and psychosociologically successful. Economic stability is the one essential in any golf course real estate venture. The general manager is the key to its success or failure, as the superintendent can be for the golf course. We need a pool of tough, talented young architects who can work with these developers. It would help a return to village-like clustered units and the inevitable reduction of prices by increasing density.

The problem of social situations is a thorny one: How well do the residents enjoy the golf course and the community? How well do they like living there? The answers might surprise you. Senior citizens might like a short yet challenging course; every-one might like the trees that are left to provide a shady walk between tee and green. The design of the first 250 units at Mission Hills encourages people to meet and socialize with their neighbors. The newer houses, however, provide little sense of community or neighborhood, and the sale and resale prices of these units have been dramatically lower than those for the early units. In the future, we must concentrate on social as well as physical and financial solutions.

All designers and architects must have a personal philosophy. Golf course communities should be happy, colorful places where people can lead happy, colorful lives. Rich color is easy— red roofs, blue lakes, ocher mountains, bright green greens—but social richness needs more work. We should strive for something more than technical correctness and projects that are merely clean and glossy. We should create comfortable houses and exciting environments for human beings.

The Need for Good Clients

The course on all short lists of the greatest, Pine Valley in Clementon, New Jersey, is generally accredited to George Crump and Harry Colt. Harry Colt was the ranking golf course architect in the world at the time, and the course itself is instantly recognizable as a Colt golf course. Yet Crump, who was the owner and totally untrained as an architect, is usually given the premier position.

People of quality and character place their signatures on anything they design. Their background, education, culture, intelligence, range of humanity, temperament, humor, grace, tolerance, sense of proportion, and graphic touch are all combined in the final work of art: Harry Colt is written all over Pine Valley. Yet the unreasonable assumption that Crump was the architect with a little advice from Colt has persisted over the last 70 years. What people have failed to realize is that Crump, who obviously had a great deal to do with the building and design of the course, was a *great client*. He absorbed Colt's ideas and helped give them expression.

This is our biggest problem with golf course communities. First-rate planners, architects, and golf architects abound in this country, but very few good clients are out there and that is where the challenge lies. It is the authors' hope that this book will find some good clients for many of our best designers, and make its writing, design, and editing worthwhile.

Looking Back
And Looking
Ahead

The Future Is Now

by Guy L. Rando

All the statistics from the golf industry generally point to a rosy future in which the supply will never exceed the demand for more golf courses. The continued demand is further assured in an age when the costs of creating new golf courses continue to rise while sources of financing decline. Ray Johnston, the successful developer of the largest vacation

Deer at Horseshoe Bay Resort and Conference Club.

GUY L. RANDO & ASSOCIATES INC.

resort community in West Virginia, notes that the lack of competing recreational properties, the demographics of a rapidly growing golf market, and a continuing shortage of places to play, whether caused by regulation or unavailability of construction financing, all bode well for builders of golf courses and golfing communities for the rest of the 20th century. However rosy this picture might be, neither the golf course nor real estate development industries can afford to rest easily.

Economic Potential

In 1981, some 21,000 golf courses existed throughout the world,[1] and thousands more have been added since then. The United States contains over 14,000 golf courses, translating into millions of acres dedicated to this single use of land. Added to that figure are the millions of acres of associated real estate development, particularly in the United States. Over half the new golf courses opened in 1989 were real-estate- or resort-related courses. During the faltering economy of the early 1990s, the number of real-estate-related golf courses dropped significantly, accounting for about one-third of the new courses opened. The demand for new golf courses continues to be strong in some parts of the United States, but the demand is not being met by golf courses that are part of speculative real estate development. The major factor contributing to this trend has been the fundamental problem between lending and real estate during a recessionary economy,[2] when land values stagnate.

According to the National Golf Foundation, those involved in financing golf courses are choosing projects with "larger, more risk dispersed partnerships with equity of 30 to 60 percent on the part of the developers and collateral packages that include assets far beyond the course acreage itself."[3] As a result of the tight economy, disciplined research of both golf and real estate market conditions, realistic financial projections, and flawless land planning and golf

course design have become necessities for developers seeking financing for golf-oriented real estate projects. The resulting discipline has its positive side, having forced the issue of long-term quality of life over short-term profits into the forefront.

Historically, municipal projects often took up the slack in development during economic downturns and recessions. The development of public daily-fee golf courses tends to surge during tight economies, as developers broaden and maximize their market bases to ensure adequate revenues to sustain the operation. The public perception of golf as an activity that benefits only a limited population, however, has forced many municipalities to stop subsidizing public golf courses, particularly in tight economic times. Municipally owned golf courses must now be operated as business enterprises and profit centers. Golf courses must prove themselves self-sustaining to gain public acceptance in the case of municipally owned facilities and earn the confidence of lenders and investors for privately owned enterprises. Golf organizations like USGA and NGF have taken the leadership through funding research and providing critical sources of information. A number of organizations regularly sponsor conferences to disseminate information and encourage dialogue about golf courses and real estate development. The future, it is hoped, will see continued, intensified outreach beyond conversations within the industry to involve the general public and public policy makers.

The alliance of golf and real estate development has tremendous potential value not only in terms of profitable business ventures, but also in terms of effecting positive solutions to universal concerns about the environment and the quality of life on this planet. "It is said that there are three types of people in the world: those that make things happen; those who watch things happen; and those who don't know what hit them."[4] Neither the golf industry nor the real estate development industry can afford to do anything less than

take an active role in making things happen. If golf course development and golf-oriented real estate development are to enjoy a healthy future, the industries must recognize the true costs and potential value of golf courses and take an active role to keep the options open and to ensure that the potential will still be available for us in the future.

Environment and Quality of Life

Our culture persistently runs from crisis to crisis, throwing short-term, politically expedient solutions at mounting problems with little thought to what could be done to prevent the crisis in the first place, much less to the long-term consequences of band-aid solutions—with the notable exception of environmental issues. Preventing degradation of the environment is one of a few issues where consensus has been reached because of the direct and tangible effect on the well-being of virtually every individual on this planet. The golf industry has taken on the role of leader and has made great strides in responsibility for the environment. In some areas of the United States, however, according to golf course architect Robert Trent Jones II, "A strong environmental movement has targeted golf courses as a menacing threat to the environment. In many cases, the arguments these well-organized groups advance are highly emotional, with little factual basis, for they see the game as an elitist pastime." Their arguments are not entirely unfounded, and if we are to change this perception, we must acknowledge and address these concerns.

In fact, developers of golf courses and real estate are generally on the same side of the environmental fence. So, if we hold environmental values in common, what is the disagreement? Often, the real issue is the tendency of people to resist change borne out of fear of unknown consequences in the future. It is safer to keep the status quo. Developing land is a change that affects people at every level and thus can threaten their security and well-being.

Opponents are blamed for driving the cost of new golf courses sky-high, both in time and upfront dollars to navigate the permitting process. Determining whether an opposition lobby is potentially present has become a required factor in the feasibility of golf course projects in many areas of the United States. Both golf course developers and real estate developers bear the image as bad guys, and both have tried many times to bring the facts to light—not easy when it must be done from a defensive rather than offensive position. The strength of the opposition, under the guise of environmental protection, is evidenced by the flood of well-intentioned but often misguided regulations enacted by public policy makers. Rule by regulation provides a politically expedient way of dealing with symptoms but does little to get to the root of the problem. It also discourages innovative and creative problem solving by removing the incentive to solve problems.

The negative public perception will persist unless the golf and real estate development industries take a joint, active role in education at every level. We must raise ourselves out of the defensive position into the offensive. It is not enough to complain about the inequities of the opposition: we must identify, acknowledge, and address rational and justifiable arguments and seek solutions to the problems. Education and the dissemination of information provide the basis for rational problem solving, and the commitment and investment of each individual involved in golf and real estate development to education provide the most powerful means of effecting change in public perception and public policy. Golf courses and real estate development should be part of the environmental solution, not the problem.

The primary issues that we collectively must address focus on management of the earth's resources under the increasing demands of human population. The development of the built environment that houses hu-

Horseshoe Bay Resort and Conference Club.

GUY L. RANDO & ASSOCIATES INC.

man activities must be balanced against the needs of the system that sustains life: the environment. In an age of specialization, we must find a way to bring together the minds and talents of many. Through cooperation and the free exchange of information and ideas, we have the freedom to find innovative and creative solutions.

The forming of cooperative alliances between apparently opposing interests can provide a powerful vehicle for education and the dissemination of information. Recently, the USGA and the Audubon Society of New York formed one such cooperative alliance, the Audubon Cooperative Sanctuary Program for Golf Courses. This effort provides a means for exchanging information toward the common goal of increasing environmental awareness and enhancing wildlife habitat through specific resource management programs. The program facilitates dissemination of technical information and encourages the active participation of golfers, golf course superintendents, golf officials, and the general public in conservation programs.

Real estate can be developed parcel by parcel, piece by piece, with little or no concern for the overall impact on land use patterns and quality of life. It certainly is easier than to assemble a large tract of land and/or

many landowners, plan and design an entire lifestyle that encourages individuals, government, and business to work together, install the infrastructure, mitigate the impacts, nurture it through several years, and subsidize it until it has a self-sustaining population. The building of communities requires great foresight, skill, commitment, and resources and the formation of cooperative alliances between government, financial institutions, and private enterprise.

Golf courses have the potential to play a significant role in mitigating the impacts of human demand for shelter, livelihood, and recreation. Other open spaces can be integrated with the golf course. Golf courses can be used for multiple duties: permanently dedicating and managing common open spaces, managing and treating stormwater runoff from adjacent development, treating and recycling sewage effluent, siting water conservation programs, reclaiming spoiled sites (landfills, quarries, mines) for profitable recreational use, and protecting and enhancing wildlife habitats. We can also significantly improve accessibility to golf courses for nongolfers.

Increasing Accessibility

Broadening accessibility to golf courses is one means of gaining

167

wider public acceptance for golf courses by nongolfers. Safety is the primary reason for excluding nongolfers on and immediately around the course, particularly during active play. Although a satisfactory way has not yet been found to integrate golfers, nature walkers, and joggers, the problem can be solved. For example, a new course designed as an ecologic sanctuary with significantly wider buffer areas between fairways and between fairways and adjacent land uses opens the opportunity to design controlled physical access to the ecologic sanctuary and out-of-play areas of the course. And the potential for such innovative design solutions can be one key to gaining greater public acceptance of golf courses.

The recent enactment of the Americans with Disabilities Act has added a new set of regulations regarding employment and accessibility of golf clubhouses as well as the golf course and other related facilities. The golf industry is just beginning to determine the implications of this new law on golf and how to comply with the intent of the law appropriately and cost-effectively. Some foreseeable steps are necessary:

- Development of a methodology and guidelines for auditing the course and facilities for accessibility;
- Identification of problems with accessibility and development of alternative solutions;
- Development of standards for analysis, development, and implementation of plans for compliance, from the design of equipment, golf courses, and facilities to the development of new options and rules for the game;
- Education and training of management and operations personnel regarding accommodations for diversity and employment of the disabled;
- Education and training of management and staff regarding accommodations for disabled golfers, including specific education and training for golf pros regarding teaching techniques for various types of disabilities.

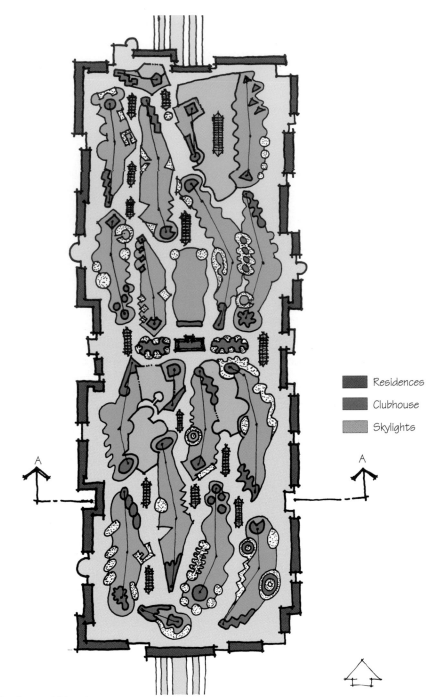

Residences
Clubhouse
Skylights

A   A

Rooftop golf for the 21st century in Japan. Plan.
Source: Guy L. Rando & Associates Inc.

The golf industry will likely respond to requirements of the ADA in a positive manner, in keeping with its efforts to dispel the label of "elitist."

Ethics in Land Planning and Development

Among the predicted changes is a trend toward shorter golf courses, fueled by economics, the high cost of land, and the need to provide wider margins of safety. Golf course architect William Amick notes, "The average middle- to high-handicap golfer likes easier (shorter) courses, because they can shoot better scores and because it is easier to walk a shorter total distance." "On the other hand," observes John Wong of The SWA Group, "environmental constraints, preservation requirements, and conservation needs could create much larger golf course zones.

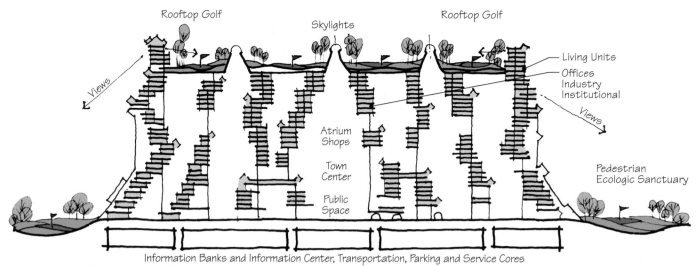

Rooftop Golf   Skylights   Rooftop Golf

Views

Living Units
Offices
Industry
Institutional

Atrium
Shops

Town
Center

Public
Space

Views

Pedestrian
Ecologic Sanctuary

Information Banks and Information Center, Transportation, Parking and Service Cores

Rooftop golf in Japan. Section A-A.
Source: Guy L. Rando & Associates Inc.

Undevelopable, sensitive lands woven throughout the golf course can begin to change the physical look, feel, and playability of golf courses." Increasing land values of the future could create high-density demand for golf-course-oriented developments. Values of frontage could escalate, resulting in a change in the nature of the golf course and views from the course. As a result, landscape design will take an increasingly important role as a means of buffering the built environment. In addition, frontage values on nongolf open spaces, such as ecologic sanctuaries, will increase, resulting in a change in land planning and development patterns.

This change in land planning and development patterns could well occur on an international scale. While the current trend in Europe and Asia is to build "core" golf courses to enhance the "purity of the golfing experience," many believe that international golf course development will shift toward the U.S. model of integrating development with the golf course. Rick Pariani of The SWA Group notes that international proj-

ects in Japan, Taiwan, and Mexico (like the United States) are scrutinized for their ecologic aspects, and projects that do not mitigate or eliminate any environmental conflicts cannot obtain permitting. Surface and groundwater resources and their natural habitats must be protected in perpetuity for a golf course development to have any chance for approval.

I hope to see the universal application of the concept of Golf Courses as Ecologic Sanctuaries™ to the common good of people of all nations. Many developing countries seek golf courses as a means of attracting tourist dollars to build their economies. They are beginning to look more closely, however, at environmental impacts as well as impacts on the local culture. In Indonesia, for instance, the tolerance for golf courses has significantly diminished, largely because the golf courses that were built to serve almost exclusively as playgrounds for a few elite tourists and foreigners have displaced many locals. The development of the golf courses provided few, if any, benefits to the socioeconomic, cultural, or environmental welfare of the local

population. The failure to consider the larger issues beyond the financial success of the golf course itself has only enhanced the image of bad guy. Golf courses and golf-oriented real estate development, whether in the United States or abroad, can no longer be considered isolated entities, and the burden of responsibility to effect change falls on those involved in land development today and in the future. We would all do well to remember that what we build today will affect the quality of life for many generations to come.

Notes

1. Geoffry Cornish and Ronald Whitten, *The Golf Course*, rev. ed. (New York: Rutledge Press, 1987).

2. David Gould, "Course Construction Slowdown Seen Despite Record '91 Activity," *Golf Market Today*, March/April 1992, pp. 1–5.

3. David Gould, "Financing Trend: Definite Signs of Flight to Quality," *Golf Market Today*, March/April 1992, pp. 1–2.

4. David Osborne and Ted Gaebler. *Reinventing Government* (Reading, Mass.: Addison-Wesley, 1992), p. 229.

Determining a Real Estate Project's Feasibility

The first stages of the development process consist primarily of developing an idea and assessing its feasibility. Market and economic studies are key to an accurate assessment of the project's viability, and they are significant factors in ascertaining and managing risk. A number of different types of market and economic studies are used in real estate development.

The variety of names for the various market studies and the inconsistent use of the terms "market analysis," "marketability analysis," and "financial feasibility analysis" can lead to confusion, even among veterans in the business. Each study has a distinctive purpose in determining feasibility, but they are linked in that one provides information required to perform another one. The market and marketability analyses provide estimates of a proposed project's potential revenues in relation to the market, and those potential revenue figures are used later in the financial feasibility analysis to substantiate estimates of stabilized net operating income (NOI) and to set the appropriate premium for risk in the discount rate. The financial feasibility analysis provides the developer, financial partners or investors, and lenders with an estimate of the risks and rewards of the proposed venture. That is, market and marketability analyses provide "top-line" figures, while financial feasibility analysis provides "bottom-line" figures. The developer should have a clear idea of the objectives for each study and the allotment of time and funding available for each study before actually conducting the study. Certainly, a description of the purpose and scope of a study should be set out in detail when contracting planners and market consultants or analysts to avoid any confusion.

Types of Market and Economic Studies

Type of Study	Purpose
Alternative Concept Plan	Preliminary design study in which the proposed development program is located on a site to test physical feasibility of the development program and to determine the optimal use of the site through marketability and financial feasibility analysis of each alternative. Ideas are refined, and the developer tentatively settles on a preliminary concept plan or master plan that reflects what is believed to be the "highest and best use" for the site at this stage.
Appraisal	Determines the value of a site (improved or unimproved) using standard methodologies of valuation.
Cost/Benefit Analysis	Usually undertaken when the public has an investment or equity interest in the project to determine the net value of a project to the *public.*
Land Use Study	An inventory of existing land uses and land use patterns within a defined geographic area.
Market Study	Determines the demand for and supply of a particular type of real estate based on information about the character of the community within a specified market area.
Marketability Study	Determines the specific features, sizes, functions, prices, and other factors required to capture a market share.
Financial Feasibility Analysis	Determines the potential financial return a proposed project can attain.
Site Analysis	An inventory of existing physical site conditions and characteristics and an analysis of physical conditions and characteristics to determine constraints and suitability of the site for the proposed land uses.

Source: Guy L. Rando & Associates Inc.

The cost of market and economic studies is a major concern for the developer. Various types of studies and the level of detail required are associated with particular stages of the development process. In conducting or contracting for market and economic studies, the developer seeks maximum return with a minimum commitment of time and money, particularly in the early stages of the process when ideas are still being tested for feasibility. Generally, the farther one advances into the development process, the more detailed the study and the higher the cost. Ideally, the studies performed at each preceding stage should provide the developer with enough information to determine whether any further time or money should be committed to the project to advance it to the next stage. Thus, market and economic studies are important means of risk control. Market studies should also provide information to guide the refinement of design to increase the project's chances of profitability and success.

The following discussion provides an overview of activities that occur during the first three stages and the public approval process of development, discussing the types of market and economic studies in terms of objectives and level of detail typically required to manage risk at each stage of the process. When possible, examples lend greater clarity to the discussion. The reader should note, however, that the figures noted in the examples were generated for specific projects at a particular time and should not be unilaterally applied to other projects, even if they appear similar.

Use of Market Studies in the Development Process

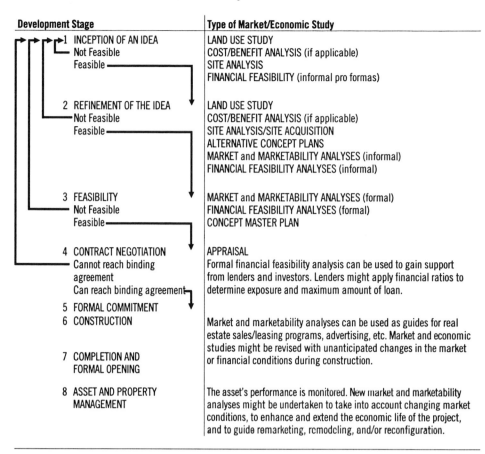

Development Stage	Type of Market/Economic Study
1 INCEPTION OF AN IDEA — Not Feasible — Feasible	LAND USE STUDY COST/BENEFIT ANALYSIS (if applicable) SITE ANALYSIS FINANCIAL FEASIBILITY (informal pro formas)
2 REFINEMENT OF THE IDEA — Not Feasible — Feasible	LAND USE STUDY COST/BENEFIT ANALYSIS (if applicable) SITE ANALYSIS/SITE ACQUISITION ALTERNATIVE CONCEPT PLANS MARKET and MARKETABILITY ANALYSES (informal) FINANCIAL FEASIBILITY ANALYSES (informal)
3 FEASIBILITY — Not Feasible — Feasible	MARKET and MARKETABILITY ANALYSES (formal) FINANCIAL FEASIBILITY ANALYSES (formal) CONCEPT MASTER PLAN
4 CONTRACT NEGOTIATION — Cannot reach binding agreement — Can reach binding agreement	APPRAISAL Formal financial feasibility analysis can be used to gain support from lenders and investors. Lenders might apply financial ratios to determine exposure and maximum amount of loan.
5 FORMAL COMMITMENT 6 CONSTRUCTION	Market and marketability analyses can be used as guides for real estate sales/leasing programs, advertising, etc. Market and economic studies might be revised with unanticipated changes in the market or financial conditions during construction.
7 COMPLETION AND FORMAL OPENING	
8 ASSET AND PROPERTY MANAGEMENT	The asset's performance is monitored. New market and marketability analyses might be undertaken to take into account changing market conditions, to enhance and extend the economic life of the project, and to guide remarketing, remodeling, and/or reconfiguration.

Source: Adapted from Mike E. Miles et al., *Real Estatee Development Principles and Process* (Washington, D.C.: ULI–the Urban Land Institute, 1991), p.5.

Inception of an Idea

The first stage of the development process is often characterized as brainstorming—an intensive search for as many creative ideas as possible. It is often the most difficult stage; it is certainly the most creative and least methodical stage of the process.

A developer might generate ideas based on experience, knowledge, or observations of the market. The information used to generate ideas can be as broadly based as macroeconomic trends or international events to something as minutely detailed as market preference for a certain color of kitchen appliances. Even information that is completely unrelated to real estate can spark an idea. The pattern of a colorful quilt might inspire an unusual idea for a cluster of houses, or the smell of sea spray might inspire an interior color scheme. Every individual processes information in his or her own way—information that is the universal basis for ideas.

Market research and analysis at this stage are informal. The main objective of market research at this stage is to consider market opportunities and to assist the developer in defining the target market. At a minimum, informal market analysis provides credible information about customers who have purchased similar real estate products in the past. Basic data about potential consumers and competitors provide key information that the developer will require to identify market segments, which might be defined by geographic area or socioeconomic distinctions.

The following example shows how market research information is used to provide an informal analysis of the supply and demand for a hypothetical residential project (typical for Stage One of the development process). In itself, this quick analysis is inadequate for identifying a specific market segment and capture rate, as it does not allow for fluctuations in demand from one year to the next and other varying factors. A more detailed or formal market analysis is required to determine whether a proposed project can meet more rigorous analyses for feasibility in Stages Two and Three of the development process.

Projected Population (based on current data for the defined market area, adjusted over next 10 years)	500,000
Estimated Housing Required (500,000 ÷ 3) (assuming average of 3 people per household)	166,667
Plus 5 Percent Vacancy (assumed average for market)	8,333
Total Estimated Housing Required in 10 Years	175,000
Units Presently Constructed (115,000)	
Units Permitted but Not Constructed (10,000)	
Minus Total Existing Stock	125,000
Additional Housing Required in 10 years	50,000
Required per Year for next 10 years (50,000 ÷ 10)	5,000
Estimated Present Population (in defined market area)	350,000
Estimated Present Housing Required (350,000 ÷ 3)	116,667
Plus 5 Percent Vacancy	5,833
Estimated Total Present Housing Required	122,500
Minus Existing Units/Units under Construction	125,000
Existing Supply (oversupply)	2,500
Estimated Time to Deplete Existing and Planned Stock (2,500 ÷ 5,000)	6 months

Many developers rely on national and regional forecasts as a basis for making rough local projections. Census data, trade journals and newsletters, and familiarity with the local market all contribute to the information base developers can use to generate ideas in this stage of the process.

The primary objective of this first stage is to turn the creative spirit loose and generate ideas. Once the ideas are proposed, the process of judging their feasibility begins, starting with quick financial feasibility tests to determine which ideas warrant further attention. In this stage, data for quick pro forma analyses of a project's potential economic perfor-

mance are usually limited to the developer's knowledge or available information about comparable projects in the market. These feasibility tests are usually very broad and general, as the majority of the ideas never make it beyond this point and it is difficult to justify the time and cost of more than a quick study of each idea. At this stage, the developer compares a rough estimate of value with a rough estimate of cost. These numbers are often no more than a quick mental calculation or pro forma calculation. For example, the developer might determine that a market exists for quarter-acre, single-family residential lots and that a site is available that looks promising for such development. The developer multiplies the number of lots the site might accommodate by an estimate of income generated by lot sales minus the cost of land, estimated cost of improvements, and other development costs.

The project's estimated life, finance rates, and many other factors critical for determining feasibility in later stages of the process are usually not entered into calculations in this early stage.

In terms of risk management, if the estimated cost exceeds the estimated value, the idea is tossed out and the developer goes back to the drawing board. The developer must also evaluate the idea in terms of qualitative criteria, such as the current and projected state of the economy, whether the capability exists to carry out the idea, whether the idea is in keeping with the developer's personal ethics or the firm's business image, or whether support from lenders, investors, or the public sector is likely. For those ideas that do pass muster, the developer must then decide whether to spend the time and money to carry the idea to Stage Two.

Refinement of the Idea

At this stage, the developer's idea evolves into a design for a project attached to a specific parcel of land. This stage has several objectives:

1. To find a site;
2. To determine its suitability;

Quick Pro Forma

REVENUES	
150 acres × 4 lots per acre × $40,000 per lot =	$24,000,000
COSTS	
Land	$6,000,000
Development, Excluding Financing (150 acres × $30,000 per acre)	4,500,000
Marketing (5 percent of sales)	1,200,000
Administration (5 percent of development costs)	225,000
SUBTOTAL	$11,925,000
Financing (average balance of $2,981,250 per year for 4 years at 12 percent interest[1])	1,431,000
TOTAL COSTS	$13,356,000
PROFIT (revenues minus costs)	$10,644,000

[1]Assuming the amount of the loan covers 100 percent of the development costs over a sales period of four years. The average balance shown is one-fourth of the subtotal ($11,925,000). A more accurate estimate, however, would start with land costs, peak at the end of construction (say two years), and decline to zero over the sales period.
Source: Guy L. Rando & Associates Inc.

3. To define the development program;
4. To explore alternative design concepts, expanding on the development program; and
5. To perform informal market, marketability, and financial feasibility analyses to provide a basis for decisions involving the best use of the site.

Typical market and economic studies during this stage are aimed primarily at providing the developer with a better understanding of the local market and the potential of a particular site or sites.

Before embarking on this stage, the developer clarifies objectives and assembles the development team. The developer must determine what expertise is required and how much time and money will be expended to accomplish the objectives. The roles of the team members and the tasks they are to accomplish must be defined. Team members can be selected from in-house staff, newly hired staff, or outside consultants.

Site Acquisition Studies

If a site has not already been selected, then the first task is to find a site that can accommodate the developer's idea. Site acquisition studies are undertaken early during the second stage to evaluate alternative sites in terms of physical, market, legal, economic, and political criteria.

A developer rarely commits funds to purchase a site at this stage of the process. Instead, an option agreement, to secure the right to purchase selected property over a specified period of time, is negotiated after the completion of site acquisition studies. In very large or complex projects like mixed-use developments, or on difficult sites with challenging physical constraints, an option might not be exercised until the developer is assured that the site can physically accommodate the proposed development. In this case, the option is negotiated only after alternative concept plans have been prepared and analyzed. Option agreements might include contingencies specifying that the program is subject to the developer's obtaining financing or subject to the buyer's acceptance of soils, title, marketing, site planning, and economic feasibility studies.

A site acquisition study includes site and market analyses in sufficient detail to assist the developer in determining whether to exercise an option agreement on a property. In some cases, the broker for or owner of a property might already have performed market and economic studies to demonstrate the site's potential to prospective buyers, but such studies can be biased. Land use studies providing important, broad-based data are usually available from local or state planning agencies. Developers can augment these studies with their own to verify the site's suitability for the potential development. Or developers can conduct their own site acquisition studies or negotiate with the owner/broker to bear some or all of the cost for the studies.

On many occasions during planning and design, certain factors might indicate advantages in acquiring additional land around the project site or the need to acquire additional land to accommodate the desired development. In this case, abbreviated site acquisition studies can be undertaken during the later stages of development.

Site acquisition studies should provide important information that is useful for negotiating the purchase price for a site. The cost of land in itself can be a significant factor in the project's feasibility, particularly where land prices are high.

Site Analysis

The site's capacity to physically support the proposed development program must be determined, and if it cannot, then another site must be found.

Broad-based land use studies, environmental resource management plans, soil surveys, aerial surveys, zoning and tax maps, and other inventories of resources conducted by public agencies could provide sufficient information for initial determination of a site's suitability. But beyond a site's physical suitability and its availability, developers must also consider the logistical problems of acquiring the land and legal, political, and market factors: whether acquisition involves a single parcel or assembly of several parcels, zoning or subdivision regulations, water rights, mining rights, easements and rights-of-way, proximity to utilities and needed services, capacity of existing roads, and community sentiment about development. The objective is to obtain sufficiently detailed information to determine whether negotiation of an option agreement is justified.

Site information is recorded in both written and graphic forms. Four basic types of maps are used to record information about the site: a site map, a boundary survey map, a utilities map, and a topographic survey map. The site map shows the location of the site in the context of surrounding neighborhoods and major roads. The boundary survey map shows the bearings, distances, curves, and angles of all the project's property boundaries as well as locations of streets, utilities, easements, and benchmarks from which boundaries are measured. The boundary survey provides a legal description of the site, a precise calculation of the total area of the site, and areas of floodplains, easements, and subparcels, necessary for determining allowable development densities, net developable area, and sales price. The utilities map shows the locations of all above- and below-grade utilities and their associated easements and rights-of-way, and the locations, sizes, and capacities of storm drains, sanitary sewers, and water mains. The topographic survey map shows the contours of the land at regular intervals, usually every one or two feet. It also records existing buildings, roads, walls, fences, rock outcroppings, water courses and water bodies, property boundaries, floodplain boundaries, and existing vegetation. The topographic survey map is used as a base map for recording site information from design studies. The topographic survey, boundary survey, and utilities maps should all be drawn to the same scale.

Information gathered from the site analysis is synthesized into a diagram summarizing the site's opportunities and constraints and delineating areas that are severely, moderately, or minimally constrained for the proposed development.

Informal Market and Marketability Analyses

Informal market and marketability analyses during Stage Two provide the developer with information required to refine the development program and to project a position for a specific project and site. At this point, market research and analysis focus on segmenting the market in relation to existing and proposed supply. The developer examines features of competing projects more closely, obtains a more detailed picture of market demand, and formulates a strategy for capturing the market. Thus, the development program moves from a broad idea to a detailed development program and market strategy.

These informal analyses also provide information required to prepare a comparative analysis of alternative concept plans generated by the design

173

team. The developer might perform research and informal analyses at this stage to keep costs to a minimum, using input from members of the design team and the development team and, for very large or complex projects, by a market analyst (see "Formal Market and Marketability Analyses" later).

The goal of this stage is to refine the idea into a believable strategy for capturing the market, which includes having a convincing definition of the proposed project's competitive characteristics (as opposed to its competition for the targeted market).

Alternative Concept Plan Studies

Design is particularly intensive during this stage, when the design team must respond to input from other members of the development team regarding every facet of the proposed development. Often, many alternative solutions—alternative concept plan studies—are generated as new input, problems, or ideas arise. The developer might revise the development program and reposition the project several times in the process, requiring a new design solution with each change. Or the design team might expand upon a developer's program, finding an innovative idea that prompts the developer to reposition the project.

Public Approval

The public sector might be involved informally at this stage to gauge acceptability of alternative concepts with regulatory agencies, particularly if a project involves innovative concepts or sensitive site conditions, or if the community is sensitive about development and/or environmental issues. At this stage, the developer examines regulations for specific sites to determine whether the proposed development is allowed "by right," according to applicable zoning for the property, or whether special hearings or reviews will be required to secure a special exception or other zoning change. When a potential site or sites have been identified and preliminary design concepts developed, the developer (or design consultant designated

by the developer) might test alternative concepts in informal meetings with staff of public agencies and/or citizen groups. After the developer settles on a preliminary concept master plan, the development team prepares a description of the project outlining its objectives, land uses, general densities, public facilities, and design strategies. The developer then meets with public staff to review the preliminary concept, define initial issues, and determine the appropriate approval procedures. The public staff might decide to test the concept with other agency staff.

Financial Feasibility

The informal pro forma analyses conducted in Stage One are continuously revised during Stage Two, with the development team estimating costs, comparing costs with value, and projecting revenue and expenses to test and compare alternatives for potential risks and rewards. These pro formas can be used to guide further refinement of the idea. Financial feasibility analyses during Stage Two are always done with an eye toward the formal financial feasibility analysis of Stage Three, which is used to convince others to support the project.

In addition to the pro forma analyses, the determination of financial feasibility moves another step forward into estimating cash flows during development. The developer must determine whether he or she can finance the project through start-up, the amount of start-up capital needed, and sources of start-up capital. This calculation depends on the selection and design of a specific site to determine cost of the land and estimates for site improvements (including construction and related soft costs). Estimated cash flow projections incorporate operating revenues and expenses over a defined period of time, and revenues minus expenses yields estimated NOI. Estimated projections of cash flow also assign the asset's reversionary value at the conclusion of analysis, and estimated cash flow is used in the financial feasibility analysis of Stage Three to assess the risk and time value of money by

applying a discount rate (the discounted cash flow).

Discounted cash flow (DCF) is a financial analysis tool commonly used to make business and investment decisions. It provides the developer with a means of addressing the trade-off between risk and reward, allowing decisions to be made based on whether to reduce risk by spending more and thus reducing the potential return or vice versa. DCF analysis allows an investor to reduce various factors about an investment to a single dollar figure at a particular time.

Risk Management

Stage Two ends with the developer's tentatively settling on a development program and design that combines the program with a site. Market and marketability analyses are critical for risk management at this point. They must be of sufficient detail and credibility to provide the developer with a means to assess feasibility objectively in terms of estimated cash flows over the period of development and to decide whether the project can be financed through start-up. The developer should have confidence that the potential returns justify the risks to proceed to the next stage. Developers must rely on intuition to determine whether the expenditures required to carry the project through to the next stage are justified. If the developer lacks confidence at this stage, the idea should be revised or scrapped.

Feasibility

The third stage of the development process is a rigorous test of feasibility. Every aspect of the market must be considered, including physical, legal, political, sociocultural, economic, and financial factors that could affect the proposed project. At this stage, the developer can request an objective consultant to prepare formal market and/or marketability analyses of the proposed project. The preliminary concept plan can be refined, sometimes many times over, based on input from market and marketability analyses during this third stage. The design document resulting from this refinement in the third stage is the master plan; it reflects the developer's "highest and best use" for the site, given the proposed development program. It is the primary design document, formally presented for public approval. The master plan and the formal market and marketability analyses provide the base information for preparation of the financial feasibility analysis. Together, these studies help the developer to determine feasibility and whether to commit time and money to proceed to the fourth stage of the development process.

Risk Management

If the developer perceives untenable risk at any time during this stage of the process, the project should be stopped or refined. Contractual agreements with consultants should contain provisions for such events should the developer find it necessary to place a stop order on work in progress.

Formal Market and Marketability Analyses

The main purpose of formal market analyses is to identify and describe in detail the target market. A thorough understanding of consumers comes through systematic and objective research. Informal market analyses provide quick snapshots, while formal market analyses provide detailed portraits of the community and customer base where the project is proposed. Information from market research is translated into a form that can be used for objective analysis of a specific project's market and marketability.

Formal market research and methods of analysis vary, depending on the type and scope of the project. For example, market analysis for a residential project differs from that for a commercial or office project.

Lenders and investors might require the use of objective outside market analysts for these formal studies. The credibility and reputation of the market analyst can be a factor in finding financing and start-up capital for a proposed project, particularly for projects that are perceived to be more complex and risky. The many methods of market research have their own advantages and weaknesses, and a good, professional market analyst should review different methodologies with the developer and delineate a specific strategy for the market research and analysis. With clear objectives and strategy in place, efforts can focus on achieving maximum detail at a cost-effective level. One advantage of working with a professional market analyst is the ready access to information data bases they maintain. But whether outside analysts are used or not, formal market and marketability analyses must always be systematic and objective.

Formal market analysis is based on information gathered through strategic market research. It involves gathering demographic data and information about existing and projected competition within a defined geographic area around the proposed project. Information is available through a number of resources, including the U.S. Bureau of the Census, public agencies, commerce groups, private business entities that specialize in market research and analysis, and competitive projects. Data are available from national, regional, and local sources. The data might be broadly or narrowly defined; the level of detail required to make an acceptably accurate market analysis depends on the scope of the proposed project. For example, a major resort project might draw upon a much broader market area than a small residential development of primary homes. Much critical information is available from unpublished sources. The market analyst and development team members might provide critical observations of specific factors that provide a needed advantage in a competitive market. Market research must be as specific to the project as possible for greater accuracy.

The first task of market analysis is to define the market area. Formal analysis usually begins with the metropolitan area where the project is to be located and then focuses on the submarket where the project will compete. Employment centers or major transit corridors often define the broad market area, and the primary market area is usually within a certain distance or travel time from the project site. A secondary market area should also be defined to include possible spillover markets or submarkets that are not as sensitive to geographic location.

An analysis of supply and demand uses statistical techniques to refine estimates about the market. For a residential project, an analysis of demand includes consideration of the number, size, and character of households (families with children, couples without children, singles, for example), age distribution, characteristics of employment growth in various types of businesses and industries, population growth in the submarket, trends in migration, social characteristics, education, and income distribution. The analysis provides an estimate of the number of units (by specific types of products) that will be needed over the next few years, based on projections of population. The supply side of the analysis includes an inventory of the existing housing stock, units currently under construction, and units that could be constructed in the future (perhaps units in proposed projects that have received permits but are not yet built). Again, specific characteristics of the submarket or targeted market should be considered.

Public Approval

The public is a partner in every real estate development project. Even if the public is not a direct equity partner in the project itself, the public ultimately receives the benefits and bears the consequences of any development. The public sector has a dual role on the development team: both regulator of private development and provider of needed facilities and services. Real estate development is highly regulated at all levels by local, state, federal, and even international legislation, regulations, and public policy, and the developer must be aware of everything from zoning, permits, and impact fees to laws on taxes, labor, property, public infrastructure, financial markets, and trade. Considerable negotiation might be necessary between the developer and the public sector in projects requiring major public improvements, such as roads and sanitary sewer, water, and community services. The developer might be required to bear the costs of funding these capital improvements through exactions and fees, or the developer might negotiate "payment" through dedication of land, construction of the improvements, proffers, contributions, or direct payment of the fees. Experienced developers recognize and treat the public sector as a partner or an equal through every step of the development process. Overlooking or antagonizing the public ultimately costs the developer both time and dollars. In communities that are highly sensitive about environmental issues, treating the public sector as an equal partner and establishing a cooperative working relationship with it are abso-

lutely mandatory for golf-oriented real estate developments.

The developer must work closely with local government officials to ensure that plans conform with public plans (comprehensive plans, economic growth/management plans, special overlay zoning districts, capital improvement plans, for example), requirements for zoning and subdivisions, and other policies and regulations. In some jurisdictions, state and federal regulations might also affect development. The process of public approval varies from one jurisdiction to the next, and the developer should be familiar with the process in the project's locality early during the project.

If public approval is attained, the developer must then decide whether to proceed to Stage Four of the development process (contract negotiation). During that stage, it might be necessary to refine the design to conform with requirements of conditional approval. In that case, the market

analysis, marketability analysis, and financial feasibility analysis used to gain support from financial partners, investors, lenders, and the public sector must be adjusted to the specifics of the revised design, and they must decide whether the market can support the project and the likelihood of its achieving financial objectives. Appraisals, required by lenders for underwriting loans, determine the expected market value of the project. It is common to have more than one appraisal, particularly if the project is large and complex or involves innovative features. Often, investors conduct their own appraisals to determine whether the estimated value justifies their financial participation. Design work is finalized during this stage, construction drawings and other construction documents prepared, and any necessary permits secured.

Project Financing

Financial feasibility analyses provide key information that developers can use to obtain loans; therefore, it is important to understand the basics of the financial ratios lenders use to determine their exposure in a real estate loan. Lenders use NOI to calculate critical financial ratios, and questionable figures for NOI can cause a lender to be more conservative about requirements for the loan. The two most common financial ratios used in real estate loans are the debt service coverage (DSC) ratio and the loan-to-value (LTV) ratio.

$$\text{DSC Ratio} = \frac{\text{NOI}}{\text{Debt Service}}$$

Debt service is the product of the maximum loan constant (MLC) multiplied by the amount of the loan:

$$\text{Debt Service} = \text{MLC} \times \text{Loan Amount}$$

The MLC is the amount that must be paid each period (perhaps monthly) so that the entire principal plus interest is repaid by the end of the loan's term. As the interest rate increases, the MLC increases; as the term of the loan increases, the MLC decreases.

Thus, the DSC ratio is calculated as follows:

Public Approval Process

Stage 1: Inception of an Idea	Developer becomes familiar with federal, state, and local regulatory standards, processes, and requirements and determines procedures for securing applicable zoning, building, and occupancy permits.
Stage 2: Refinement of the Idea	Developer examines regulations for specific sites to determine whether the proposed development is allowed "by right," according to applicable zoning for the property, or whether special hearings or reviews will be required to secure a special exception or other zoning change. When a potential site or sites have been identified and preliminary design concepts developed, the developer (or design consultant designated by the developer) might test alternative concepts in informal meetings with staff of public agencies and/or citizen groups. After the developer settles on a preliminary concept master plan, the development team prepares a description of the project outlining its objectives, land uses, general densities, public facilities, and design strategies. The developer then meets with public staff to review the preliminary concept, define initial issues, and determine the appropriate approval procedures. The public staff might decide to test the concept with other agency staff.
Stage 3: Feasibility	Development team prepares reports, drawings, and plans required for the approval process.
	Application for public approval is routed through appropriate public agencies. Developer meets with public agencies to resolve any questions or problems. Public staff initiates the public hearing process.
	Development team prepares final plans for submission (adjusted to respond to the public agency's concerns). Public staff prepares final reports and recommendations.
	Developer presents plans before the public and public agencies in public hearing(s).
	Public agencies can prepare modifications or conditions needed to gain approval.

Source: Guy L. Rando & Associates Inc.; and Mike E. Miles et al., *Real Estate Development Principles and Process* (Washington, D.C.: ULI—the Urban Land Institute, 1991), p. 5.

$$\text{DSC Ratio} = \frac{\text{NOI}}{\text{MLC} \times \text{Loan Amount}}$$

The lender can determine the maximum loan amount by manipulating the DSC ratio as follows:

$$\text{Maximum Loan} = \frac{\text{NOI}}{\text{DSC Ratio} \times \text{MLC}}$$

A larger loan is the result of higher NOI, a lower DSC ratio, or a lower MLC (a longer-term loan and/or lower interest rate).

Lenders use the LTV ratio to determine their position if they must foreclose on a loan. The LTV ratio is the loan amount divided by the appraised value:

$$\text{LTV Ratio} = \frac{\text{Loan Amount}}{\text{Appraised Value}}$$

The higher the risk perceived by the lender, the lower the allowable LTV ratio. Very conservative lenders might also limit the appraised value.

The DSC ratio measures the likelihood that the property can service its own debt. A ratio of 1.0 indicates that the expected NOI will equal the debt service; a ratio less than 1.0 indicates that a shortfall will occur, even if all expectations are met. Usually, lenders require the DSC ratio to be greater than 1.0 unless the borrower has sufficient resources to cover any shortfall. If lenders perceive more risk, they increase the required DSC ratio. A conservative lender might require a DSC ratio of 1.05 or 1.10 on a low-risk loan for a borrower with very good credit, but a DSC ratio of 1.5 or higher can be required for a purely speculative project or a very unusual project that causes a perception of high risk.[1] The DSC ratio a lender requires is an important consideration in determining a project's feasibility, because it determines the maximum amount of the loan.

Note

1. Mike E. Miles et al., *Real Estate Development Principles and Process* (Washington, D.C.: ULI–the Urban Land Institute, 1991).

Glossary

Base. The generally flatter area of a bunker at the toe of the face, farthest from the green or fairway.

Birdie. A score of one less than par on a hole.

Bunker. A hazard consisting of a prepared area of ground from which turf or soil has been removed and replaced with sand or a similar material. Does not include grass-covered ground bordering or within the bunker.

Caddie. An employee of the club who assists golfers, especially by carrying their clubs.

Cape. The long grass (sometimes of a different variety) immediately surrounding the sand in a bunker.

Championship course. Usually used to describe a course on which championship tournaments are held. Often reserved for courses that, according to the NGF, by virtue of their design and maintenance are capable of providing an exacting challenge and excellent playing conditions for superior golfers in regional, state, or national competition. Never used to describe the caliber of a course.

Chip shot. A low running shot normally played from near the edge of the putting green toward the hole.

Collar. A narrow area of turf adjacent to the putting green that is mowed at a height between those of the fairway and the putting green (sometimes called an "apron").

Course length. A measurement of horizontal distance expressed in yards from the middle of the tee area to the center of the putting green, following the line of play planned by the architect.

Dogleg hole. A hole that changes direction along the intended centerline of play, normally in the landing area, turning either right or left.

Drive the green. The ability to drive the ball in one shot from the tee to the green.

Driver. A golf club with a long shaft and wooden head with a nearly straight face used to drive the ball from the tee.

Eagle. A score of two strokes less than par on a hole.

Elbow point. See *Landing area.*

Executive course. No official definition, but generally considered to be a golf course that is shorter than what is accepted to be a regulation course, with a total par usually between 55 to 67 for an 18-hole course, a course length of approximately 3,000 to 4,500 yards, consisting of par-3 and par-4 holes, with a par-5 hole if possible within the constraints of the site.

Face. The sloped area of a bunker normally visible to players.

Fairway. The area of the course between the tee and green that is maintained to reward a well-hit shot, usually an area of closely mown turf. Often surrounded by the "rough," where the turf is maintained at a greater height than the fairway and might include shrubs, trees, and other plants.

Flagstick. A movable, straight marker with or without bunting or other material attached, centered in the hole to show its position.

Golf car. A two-seat, two-bag gas or electrically powered vehicle (often incorrectly called a "golf cart").

Golf cart. A hand-pulled, two-wheel carrier for a single bag.

Golf corridor. The land area where a golf course will be located.

Golf course. The whole area within which play is permitted, comprised of holes played in a specific sequence.

Green. The area of ground especially prepared for putting, into which the hole is cut. Originally, the term "green" was used to describe the whole course; hence, a "three-green" tournament was one played over three courses (Campbell 1991, p. 330). See *Putting green.*

Green-up. See *Grow-in.*

Grow-in. The period of time after a course is seeded but before it is ready to play on.

Handicap. An advantage given or disadvantage imposed on a golfer in the form of strokes to enable players of varying abilities to play against each other on theoretically equal terms. Usually based on the average scores of a player compared to a course standard (Campbell 1991, p. 330).

Hazard. An obstacle on a golf course that makes play more challenging.

Hole. A general term describing the entire area between and including the tee and the green, but also the specific target in the ground that is 4.25 inches in diameter and at least four inches deep.

Hook. A shot that deviates sharply from a straight course in the direction opposite to the dominant hand of the player (to the left).

Iron. Any of a series of numbered golf clubs having metal heads.

Landing area. Includes all of the points along the centerline of intended play where a well-hit ball should land. These points are also called "elbow points," because at these points the intended centerline of play can be turned on an angle to form a dogleg.

Lie. Situation where the ball rests after completion of a stroke (Campbell 1991, p. 331).

Lip. An abutment of sod raised three to four inches above the sand level in the bunker and facing the putting green that prevents a player from putting out of the bunker (Beard 1982, p. 615).

NGF. National Golf Foundation. A primary source of research and information on the U.S. golf market, with a membership over 6,000, including associations, equipment manufacturers, publications, architects, owners, and operators.

Par. The estimated score standard for each hole of a golf course, based on the length of the hole and the number of strokes a scratch golfer would be expected to make for a given hole, in errorless play without flukes and under ordinary weather conditions, allowing two strokes on the putting green.

Par-3 course. A course consisting of all par-3 holes, thus having a total par of 54, usually ranging from 2,000 to 2,400 yards.

PGA. Professional Golfers Association (of America). The largest sports association in the United States, with a total membership of over 20,000.

Putt. A stroke made on a putting green to cause the ball to roll into or near the hole.

Putter. A golf club used for putting.

Putting green. Ground especially prepared for putting, into which the hole is cut.

Regulation course. Under generally accepted guidelines, a course consisting of 18 holes with a total par of 72, consisting of ten par-4 holes, four par-3 holes, and four par-5 holes, and a length ranging from 6,000 yards to 6,700 yards measured from the middle tees, and provision of front and back tees, resulting in a course length of approximately 5,200 to 7,200 yards.

Rough. An area where the turf is maintained at a greater height than the fairway. Might include shrubs, trees, and other plants.

Round. A completed game of golf.

Sand trap. A bunker.

Scratch golfer. A golfer who has no handicap.

Shank. To hit a golf ball with the extreme heel of the club so that the ball goes off in an unintended direction.

Shoulder season. In a seasonal market, the transitional period between "in season" and "off season."

Signature hole. A hole of unusual or exceptionally dramatic or challenging design so that it creates a lasting and memorable impression and identity for a golf course; or a hole of particular stylistic or thematic design that is associated with or peculiar to an individual golf course architect.

Slice. The flight of a ball that deviates sharply from a straight course in the direction of the dominant hand of the golfer propelling it (to the right).

Soft goods. Nondurable items sold in the pro shop, such as clothing.

Tee. A small mound or a peg where the golf ball is placed before the beginning of play on a hole.

Tee marker. A movable marker used to define the front and side limits of the teeing ground.

Teeing ground. The rectangular starting place for a hole to be played, two club lengths in depth, with front and side outside limits defined by tee markers.

Through the green. The whole area of a course except for the teeing ground, putting green, and hazards. Close to what is commonly referred to as "fairway," but through the green includes both fairway and rough.

USGA. United States Golf Association, the body that sets forth the rules governing the game of golf in the United States and handicapping for tournaments or competitive play.

Water hazard. Any sea, lake, pond, river, ditch, surface drainage ditch, open water course (whether or not containing water), or anything of a similar nature intended to make the play of golf more challenging.

Wedge. An iron golf club with a broad, low-angled face for maximum loft.

Wood. A golf club with a thick wooden head.

Bibliography

Adams, Les. "Endophytes in Turf: Small Fungus, Big Advantage." *Turf South*, September 1991, pp. 18–19.

Beard, James B. *Turf Management for Golf Courses.* New York: Macmillan, 1982.

Campbell, Malcolm. *The Random House International Encyclopedia of Golf: The Definitive Guide to the Game.* New York: Random House, 1991.

Cliffer, Harold J. *Planning the Golf Clubhouse.* Chicago: National Golf Foundation, 1956.

Cornish, Geoffrey S., and Ronald E. Whitten. *The Golf Course.* New York: Rutledge Press, 1987.

Cox, Greg. "New Restrictions: Effect of New EPA Announcement Hard to Judge." *Turf South*, February 1990, pp. 10–11.

Daar, Sheila. *Least Toxic Pest Management for Lawns.* Berkeley, Calif.: Bio-Integral Resource Center, 1986.

Dawson, Bill. "High Hopes for Cattails." *Civil Engineering Magazine*, May 1989, pp. 48–50.

Doak, Tom. *The Anatomy of a Golf Course.* New York: Lyons & Burford, 1992.

Dyke, Peter. "Trees Competing with Turf for Attention." *Chicagoland Golf*, Fall 1991, pp. 12–13.

———. "Water: Nature's Renewable Resource." *Chicagoland Golf*, May 1992, pp. 10–11.

Federal Interagency Committee for Wetland Delineation. *Federal Manual for Identifying and Delineating Jurisdictional Wetlands.* Cooperative technical publication. Washington, D.C.: U.S. Army Corps of Engineers, U.S. Environmental Protection Agency, U.S. Fish and Wildlife Ser-vice, and U.S.D.A. Soil Conservation Service, 1989.

"Good Management Guards against Nitrate Contamination: Cornell University Study Lists Recommendations for Golf Course Superintendents." *Golf Course News*, October 1989, p. 3.

Grant, Zachary. "Integrated Pest Management Update: The Sherman Hollow Story." *Golf Course Management*, November 1987, pp. 6–82.

Hatt, Kathleen. "Bats, Birds, and Birdies: They Can Coexist." *Turf South*, May 1992, pp. 10–12.

Jones, Robert Trent, Jr. "A Challenging Environmental Issue: Use of Wetlands in Golf Course Design." *Golf Course Management*, July 1989, pp. 7–16.

Karnok, Keith J. "The Use of Plant Hormones as Nonnutritional Turf-grass Growth Enhancers." *Golf Course Management*, July 1989, pp. 28–38.

Kavanaugh, Martin T., II. *Marketing the Public Golf Course.* Palm Beach Gardens, Fla.: Professional Golfers Association of America, 1990.

Kerns, Waldon, John Luna, Jim May, Diane Relf, Eric Thunberg, and Mike Weaver. *Groundwater Quality and the Use of Lawn and Garden Chemicals by Homeowners.* Va.: Virginia Cooperative Extension Service, 1988.

Kriner, Richard E. *Results of a National Survey of Pesticide Usage on Golf Courses in the U.S.* Final report. Washington, D.C.: American Association of Retired Persons/U.S. Environmental Protection Agency, April 1985.

Leslie, Anne. "Address to the Clarke County Golf Course Committee," Clarke County, Virginia, March 30, 1989. Typewritten.

———. *Development of an IPM Program for Turfgrass.* Washington, D.C.: U.S. Environmental Protection Agency, Council of the Environment. 1989.

MacKenzie, A. *Golf Architecture.* Reprint. London: Ailsa, 1987.

Marble, Anne D. *A Guide to Wetland Functional Design.* McLean, Va.: U.S. Dept. of Transportation, Federal Highway Administration, 1990.

May, James H., John R. Hall III, David R. Chalmers, and Patricia R. Carry. "Nutrient Management for Golf Course Managers." *Ecological Turf Tips.* EET No. 2. Va.: Virginia Cooperative Extension, n.d.

National Golf Foundation. *Golf Course Design and Construction.* Jupiter, Fla.: Author, 1990.

———. *Planning and Developing a Private Golf Facility.* Jupiter, Fla.: Author, 1990.

Peiser, Richard B., with Dean Schwanke. *Professional Real Estate Development.* Washington, D.C.: Dearborn Financial Publishing & ULI–the Urban Land Institute, 1992.

Pennsylvania State Univ., Dept. of Agronomy. "The Effect of Nutrients and Pesticides Applied to Turf on the Quality of Runoff and Percolating Water: A Summary of Research Conducted by the Northeast Regional Turfgrass Research Project." NE-169. Typewritten. University Park, Penna.: Author, n.d.

Phillips, Patrick L. *Developing with Recreational Amenities: Golf, Tennis, Skiing, and Marinas.* Washington, D.C.: ULI–the Urban Land Institute, 1986.

Putz, Bob, and Tom Kelch. *Ecological Assessment of the Altona Piedmont Marsh Complex.* Shepherdstown, W.Va.: Conservation Fund, Spring and Ground Water Resources Institute, 1989.

Rottier, Barbara, Karen Roy, Richard Jarvis, David Fleury, Brian Grisi, and Daniel Spada. *Evaluation of Pesticide Impacts on Golf Course Wetlands and Riparian Habitats.* Raybrook, N.Y.: Adirondack Park Agency, 1988.

"Runoff Concentration Estimation." Draft. Ray Brook, N.Y.: Adirondack Park Agency, 1985.

Stirk, David. *Golf: The History of an Obsession.* Oxford: Phaidon Press, 1987.

Talbot, Michael. "Ecological Lawn Care." *Mother Earth News*, May/ June 1990, pp. 60–66.

Tatnall, Thomas W. "How 'Green' Is Your Golf Course?" *Tennis & Golf*, May 1991, pp. 30–32.

U.S. Golf Association. *Golf Rules in Pictures.* New York: Putnam, Perigee Books, 1988.

———. *USGA Golf Handicap System with USGA Course Rating System[R] and Golf Committee Manual.* Far Hills, N.J.: Author, 1984.

U.S. Golf Association and the Royal and Ancient Golf Club of St. Andrews, Scotland. *Rules of Golf.* Far Hills, N.J.: Author, 1991.

Ward-Thomas, Pat, Herbert Warren Wind, Charles Price, and Peter Thomson. *The World Atlas of Golf: The Great Courses and How They Are Played.* New York: Gallery Books, 1976.

Wogan, Philip A. *Golf Courses and the Environment: A White Paper.* Chicago: American Society of Golf Course Architects, Environmental Impact Committee, n.d.